Conquistador!

Conquistador!

The True Life Adventures of Bernal Diaz and His Part in the Spanish Conquest of the Americas in the Early Sixteenth Century

VOLUME 1

Bernal Diaz

Conquistador! The True Life Adventures of Bernal Diaz and His Part in the Spanish Conquest of the Americas in the Early Sixteenth Century
Volume 1
by Bernal Diaz

Leonaur is an imprint of Oakpast Ltd

ISBN: 978-0-85706-292-5 (hardcover)
ISBN: 978-0-85706-291-8 (softcover)

http://www.leonaur.com

Publisher's Notes

Contents

Translator's Preface

The history of the conquest of New Spain is a subject in which great interest is felt at the present day, and the English public will hail these memoirs, which contain the only true and complete account of that important transaction.

The author of this original and charming production, to which he justly gives the title of was himself one of the conquistadores; one who not only witnessed the transactions which he relates, but who also performed a glorious part in them; a soldier who, for impartiality and veracity, perhaps never had his equal. His account is acknowledged to be the only one on which we can place reliance, and it has been the source from which the most eloquent of the Spanish writers on the same subject, as well as those of other countries, have borrowed their best materials. Some historians have even transcribed whole pages, but have not had sufficient honesty to acknowledge it.

The author, while living, was never rewarded for the great services he had rendered his country, and it is remarkable that, after his death, his very memoirs were pillaged by court historians, to raise a literary monument to themselves.

Most of the other writers on the conquest, particularly the Spanish, have filled their works with exaggerations, to create astonishment and false interest; pages are filled with so termed philosophical remarks, which but ill supply the place of the intelligent reader's own reflections. Bernal Diaz differs widely from those writers, for he only states what he knows to be true. The British public, fond above all others of original productions, will peruse with interest and delight a work which has so long been the secret fountain from which all other accounts of the conquest, with the exception of those which are least faithful, have taken life.

In respect of its originality, it may vie with any work of modern times, not excepting *Don Quixote*. The author seems to have been born to show forth truth in all its beauty, and he raises it to a divinity in his mind. Can anything be more expressive of an honest conscience than what he says in his own preface: "You have only to read my history, and you see it is true."

The reader may form a general idea of this work from the following critique, which Dr. Robertson, the historian, passes upon it:

> Bernal Diaz's account bears all the marks of authenticity, and is accompanied with such pleasant *naïveté*, with such interesting details, with such amusing vanity, and yet so pardonable in an old soldier, who had been, as he boasts, in a hundred and nineteen battles, as renders his book one of the most singular that is to be found in any language.

One circumstance, and that very justly, he is most anxious to impress on your mind, namely, that all the merit of the conquest is not due to Cortes alone; for which reason he generally uses the expression "Cortes and all of us."

This is an allowable feeling in our old soldier, and it must be remembered that the greater part of the men who joined Cortes were of good families, who, as usual on such expeditions, equipped themselves at their own expense, and went out as adventurers of their own free choice.

With respect to our author's style of writing, it is chiefly characterized by plainness and simplicity, and yet there are numerous passages which are written with great force and eloquence, and which, as the Spanish editor says, "could not have been more forcibly expressed, nor with greater elegance." Some readers may at first feel inclined to censure our author for going into minute particulars in describing the fitting out of the expedition under Cortes; for instance, his describing the qualities and colours of the horses; but all this, it will be seen, was of the utmost importance to his history, and of the horses he was bound to take special notice, for they performed a conspicuous part in the conquest. The honest old soldier even devotes a couple of his last chapters to the whole of his companions in arms, in which he mentions them all by name, describes their persons, their bravery, and the manner in which they died.

To conclude these few remarks on this work, I must observe, that it not only surpasses Cortes' despatches in completeness, but also in truth and *naïveté.* He represents the whole to you with a simplicity truly sublime; at times he astonishes with a power of expressing his sentiments peculiar to himself, and with a pathos that goes to the very heart.

Bernal Diaz was of a respectable family, and born in Medina del Campo, a small town in the province of Leon. He was what in Spain is termed an hidalgo—though by this little more was signified than a descent from Christian forefathers, without any mixture of Jewish or Moorish blood. With respect to the precise year of his birth he has left us in the dark, but, according to his own account, he first left Castile, for the New World, in the year 1514; and as, on his first arrival in Mexico, in the year 1519, he still calls himself a young man, we may safely conclude that he was born between 1495 and 1500. In the year 1568 he completed his work, at which time there were only six of the conquistadores alive, and he must then have been about seventy years of age, but there is every reason for supposing that he reached the advanced age of eighty-six. Endowed with singular nobleness of mind, he had the happiness to enjoy an unblemished reputation.

The excellent Torquemada, in speaking of him in his voluminous work entitled *Monarchia Indiana,* says, "I saw and knew this same Bernal Diaz in the city of Guatimala; he was then a very aged man, and one who bore the best of reputations." Quoting him in another passage, he has, "Thus says Bernal Diaz del Castillo, a soldier on whose authority and honesty we can place reliance." He was a man devoted to his religion, and it must be particularly borne in mind that the Catholic faith was never stronger than at that time; yet we find him the least superstitious of all the Spanish historians on the conquest, and, in the 34th chapter, he has shown a mind superior to the times in which he lived.

If we contemplate the period in which the conquest of New Spain took place, we can easily imagine that Cortes considered it imperative on him to plant his religion among the Indians by the power of the sword, if he could not by kind remonstrances; and we are often reminded of Joshua in the Old Testament. The Spaniards themselves certainly entertained that idea; for in the edition of Cortes' despatches published at Mexico in 1770, his sword is termed, *Gladius Domini et Gideonis*: yet the Spaniards were not the cruel monsters they have generally been described during those times. As far as the conquest of New Spain is concerned, they were more humane than otherwise; and if at times they used severity, we find that it was caused by the horrible and revolting abominations which were practised by the natives. We can scarcely imagine kinder-hearted beings than the first priests and monks who went out to New Spain; they were men who spent their lives under every species of hardship to promote the happiness of the Indians. Who can picture to his mind a more amiable and noble disposition than that of father Olmedo? He was one of the finest characters, Dr. Robertson says, that ever went out as priest with an invading army!

We may have become exceedingly partial to a work which has now been constantly before our eyes for the last two years, yet we can scarcely imagine that any one could take up a volume, whether a novel or a history, which he would peruse with more delight than these memoirs.

With regard to the translation, which is from the old edition printed at Madrid in 1632, we have acted up to the author's desire, and have neither added nor taken anything away, and have attempted to follow the original as closely as possible. To the original there is not a single note, and particular care has been taken not to overburden the translation with them. In the spelling of the names of the Indian chiefs, the townships, and of the provinces, we have mostly followed Torquemada, who is considered more correct on this point, for he lived fifty years in New Spain, was perfect master of the Mexican language, and made the history of that country his peculiar study.

Author's Preface

I, Bernal Diaz del Castillo, *regidor* of the town of Santiago, in Guatimala, author of this very true and faithful history, have now finished it, in order that it may be published to the world. It treats of the discovery and total conquest of New Spain; and how the great city of Mexico and several other towns were taken, up to the time when peace was concluded with the whole country; also of the founding of many Spanish cities and towns, by which we, as we were in duty bound, extended the dominion of our sovereign.

In this history will be found many curious facts worthy of notice. It likewise points out the errors and blunders contained in a work written by Francisco de Gomara, who not only commits many errors himself in what he writes about New Spain, but he has also been the means of leading those two famous historians astray who followed his account, namely, Dr. Illescas and the bishop Paulo Jovio. What I have written in this book I declare and affirm to be strictly true. I myself was present at every battle and hostile encounter. Indeed, these are not old tales or romances of the seventh century; for, if I may so say, it happened but yesterday what is contained in my history. I relate how, where, and in what manner these things took place; as an accredited eyewitness of this I may mention our very spirited and valorous captain Don Hernando Cortes, marquis del Valle Oaxaca, who wrote an account of these occurrences from Mexico to his imperial majesty Don Carlos the Fifth, of glorious memory; and likewise the corresponding account of the viceroy Don Antonio de Mendoza. But, besides this, you have only to read my history and you see it is true.

I have now completed it this 26th day of February, 1568, from my day-book and memory, in this very loyal city of Guatimala, the seat of the royal court of audience. I also think of mentioning some other circumstances which are for the most part unknown to the public. I must beg of the printers not to take away from, nor add one single syllable to, the following narrative, etc.

CHAPTER 1

My Departure From Castile

In the year 1514 I departed from Castile in the suite of Pedro Arias de Avila, who had just then been appointed governor of Terra Firma. At sea we had sometimes bad and sometimes good weather, until we arrived at Nombre Dios, where the plague was raging: of this we lost many of our men, and most of us got terrible sores on our legs, and were otherwise ill. Soon after our arrival, dissensions arose between the governor and a certain wealthy cavalier, named Vasco Nuñez de Balboa, who had brought this province to subjection, and was married to one of the daughters of Avila. As, however, suspicion had been excited against him, owing to a plan he had formed of making a voyage to the South Sea at his own expense, for which he required a considerable body of troops, his own father-in-law deposed him and afterwards sentenced him to decapitation.

While we were spectators of all this, and saw, moreover, how other soldiers rebelled against their superior officers, we learnt that the island of Cuba had just been conquered, and that a nobleman of Quellar, named Diego Velasquez, was appointed governor there. Upon this news some of us met together, cavaliers and soldiers, all persons of quality who had come with Pedro Arias de Avila, and asked his permission to proceed to the island of Cuba: this he readily granted, not having sufficient employment for so great a number of men as he had brought with him from Spain. Neither was there any further conquest to be made in these parts; all was in profound peace, so thoroughly had his son-in-law Balboa subdued the country, besides which it was but small in extent and thinly populated. As soon, therefore, as we had obtained leave, we embarked in a good vessel and took our departure. Our voyage was most prosperous, so that we speedily arrived at Cuba. The first thing we did was to pay our respects to the governor, who received us with great kindness, and made us a promise of the first Indians that might be discharged. Three years, however, passed away since our first arrival in Terra Firma and stay at Cuba, still living in the expectation of the Indians which had been promised us, but in vain. During the whole of this time we had accomplished nothing worthy of notice: we therefore, the 110 who had come from Terra Firma, with some others of Cuba, who were also without any Indians, met together to concert measures with a rich cavalier named Francisco Hernandez de Cordoba, who, besides being a person of wealth, possessed great numbers of Indians on the island. This gentleman we chose for our captain; he was to lead us out on voyages for the discovery of new countries, where we might find sufficient employment.

We purchased three vessels, two of which were of considerable burden; the third was given us by the governor, Diego Velasquez, on condition namely, that we should first invade the Guanajas islands, which lie between Cuba and the Honduras, and bring him thence three cargoes of Indians, whom he wanted for slaves; this he would consider as payment for the vessel. We were, however, fully aware that it was an act of injustice which Diego Velasquez thus required at our hands, and gave him for answer: that neither God nor the king had commanded us to turn a free people into slaves. When he learnt our determination, he confessed that our project for the discovery of new countries was more praiseworthy, and he furnished us with provisions for our voyage.

We had now three vessels and a sufficient supply of *cassave* bread, as it is there made from the *juca* root. We also purchased some pigs, which cost us three *pesòs* a piece; for at that time there were neither cows nor sheep on the island of Cuba: to this I must also add a scanty supply of other provisions; while every soldier took with him some glass beads for barter. We had three pilots; of whom the principal one, who had the chief command of our vessels, was called Anton de Alaminos, a native of Palos; the two others were, Camacho de Triana, and Juan Alvarez el Manquillo of Huelva. In the same way we hired sailors, and furnished ourselves with ropes, anchors, water-casks, and other necessaries for our voyage, all at our own expense and personal risk.

After we had met together, in all 110, we departed for a harbour on the north coast of Cuba, called by the natives Ajaruco. The distance from this place to the town of San Christoval, then recently built, was twenty-four miles; for the Havannah had then only been two years in our possession. In order that our squadron might not want for anything really useful, we engaged a priest at the town of San Christoval. His name was Alonso Gonzalez, and by fair words and promises we persuaded him to join us. We also appointed, in the name of his majesty, a treasurer, called Bernardino Miguez, a native of Saint Domingo de la Calzada. This was done in order that if it pleased God we should discover any new countries, where either gold, silver, or pearls were to be found, there might be amongst us a qualified person to take charge of the fifths for the Emperor.[1] After everything had been thus properly ordered and we had heard mass said, we commended ourselves to God, our Lord Jesus Christ, and the virgin Mary his blessed mother, and set out on our voyage, as I shall further relate.

1. During the first conquests of the Spaniards in New Spain, one half of the profits arising from the gold mines was paid to the crown; but the ill effects of this exorbitant demand soon began to show themselves, and it was reduced to one third, and then to a fifth, called the *real quinto*, which continued for a length of time, until it was further reduced. I must take this opportunity of observing, that the Spanish "*peso*" is equal to about 4s. 6d. of our money.

CHAPTER 2

The Discovery of Yucatan

We sailed in the year 1517 from the harbour of Jaruco and left the Havannah. This harbour lies on the north coast of Cuba, and is so called by the natives. After twelve days' sail we had passed the coast of Saint Antonius, which in Cuba is called the country of the Guanatavies, a wild tribe of Indians. We now made for the wide ocean, steering continually towards the west, totally ignorant of the shoals and currents or of the winds which predominate in this latitude. Certainly most hazardous on our part, and indeed we were very soon visited by a terrible storm, which continued two days and two nights, in which the whole of us had nigh perished.

After the storm had abated and we had changed our course, we came in sight of land on the twenty-first day after our departure from Cuba, which filled every heart with joy and thanks towards God. This country had never been discovered before, nor had any one ever heard of it. From our ships we could perceive a considerable sized town, which lay about six miles from the sea shore. On account of its magnitude, and because it was larger than any town in Cuba, we gave it the name of Grand Cairo.

We resolved that our smallest vessel should near the shore as much as possible, to learn the nature of the spot and look out for a good anchorage. One morning, the 5th of March, we perceived five large canoes full of men coming towards us as swift as their paddles and sails could bring them from the town just mentioned. These canoes were hollowed out of the trunks of large trees, after the manner of our kneading troughs. Many of them were big enough to hold from forty to fifty Indians.

As these Indians approached us in their canoes, we made signs of peace and friendship, beckoning at the same time to them with our hands and cloaks to come up to us that we might speak with them; for at that time there was nobody amongst us who understood the language of Yucatan or Mexico. They now came along side of us without evincing the least fear, and more than thirty of them climbed on board of our principal ship. We gave them bacon and *cassave* bread to eat, and presented each with a necklace of green glass beads. After they had for some time minutely examined the ship, the chief, who was a *cazique*, gave us to understand, by signs, that he wished to get down again into his canoe and return home, but that he would come the next day with many more canoes in order to take us on shore. These Indians wore a kind of cloak made of cotton, and a small sort of apron which hung from their hips half-way down to the knee, which they termed a *maltates*. We found them more intelligent than the Indians of Cuba, where only the women wear a similar species of apron made of cotton, which hangs down over their thighs, and is called by them a *nagua*.

But to continue my narrative. Very early the morning following, our *cazique* again called upon us: this time he brought with him twelve large canoes and a number of rowers. He made known to our captain, by signs, that we were good friends and might come to his town: he would give us plenty to eat with everything we wanted, and could go on shore in his twelve canoes. I shall never forget how he said, in his language, *con escotoch*, *con escotoch*, which means, come with me to my houses yonder. We therefore called the spot Punta de Cotoche, under which name it stands on the sea charts.

In consideration of all these friendly invitations from the *cazique* to accompany him to his village, our captain held a short consultation with us, when we came to the resolution to lower our boats, take the smallest of our vessels with us, and so proceed together with the twelve canoes all at once on shore, as the coast was crowded with Indians from the above-mentioned village. This was accordingly done, and we all arrived there at the same time. The *cazique* seeing us now landed, but that we made no signs of going to his village, again gave our captain to understand, by signs, that we should follow him to his habitation, making at the same time so many demonstrations of friendship, that a second consultation was held as to whether we should accompany him or not. This was carried in the affirmative, but we took every precaution to be upon our guard, marching in close order with our arms ready for action. We took fifteen crossbows with a like number of matchlocks, and followed the *cazique*, who was accompanied by a great number of Indians.

As we were thus marching along, and had arrived in the vicinity of several rocky mountains, the *cazique* all at once raised his voice, calling aloud to his warriors, who it seemed were lying wait in ambush, to fall upon us and destroy us all. The *cazique* had no sooner given the signal, than out rushed with terrible fury great numbers of armed warriors, greeting us with such a shower of arrows, that fifteen of our men were immediately wounded. These Indians were clad in a kind of cuirass made of cotton, and armed with lances, shields, bows, and slings; with each a tuft of feathers stuck on his head. As soon as they had let fly their arrows, they rushed forward and attacked us man to man, setting furiously to with their lances, which they held in both hands. When, however, they began to feel the sharp edge of our swords, and saw what destruction our crossbows and matchlocks made among them, they speedily began to give way. Fifteen of their number lay dead on the field.

At some distance from the spot where they had so furiously attacked us was a small place in which stood three houses built of stone and lime. These were temples in which were found many idols made of clay which were of a pretty good size; some had the countenances of devils, others those of females: some again had even more horrible shapes, and appeared to represent Indians committing horrible offences. In these temples we also found small wooden boxes containing other of their gods with hellish faces, several small shells, some ornaments, three crowns, and other trinkets, some in the shape of fish, others in the shape of ducks, all worked out of an inferior kind of gold. Seeing all this, the gold, and the good architectural style of the temples, we felt overjoyed at the discovery of this country; for Peru was not discovered till sixteen years after. While we were fighting with the Indians, the priest Gonzalez ordered the gold and small idols to be removed to our ships by two Indians whom we had brought with us from Cuba. During the skirmish we took two of the natives prisoners, who subsequently allowed themselves to be baptised and became Christians. One was named Melchior and the other Julian; both were tattooed about the eyes. The combat with the natives now being at an end, we resolved to re-embark, and prosecute our voyage of discovery further along the coast towards the west. Having dressed the wounds of our men we again set sail.

CHAPTER 3

The Coast of Campeachy

Continuing the course we had previously determined upon, more westward along the coast, we discovered many promontories, bays, reefs, and shallows. We all considered this country to be an island, because our pilot, Anton de Alaminos, persisted in it. During daytime we proceeded with all caution, but lay to at nights. After sailing in this way for fourteen days, we perceived another village which appeared to us of considerable magnitude. Here was a bay with an inner harbour, and it appeared to us that there might also be some river or small stream where we could take in fresh water, which latter had become very scarce, as our supply in the casks, which were none of the best, was fast diminishing; for, as the expedition was fitted out solely by persons in poor circumstances, we had not been able to purchase good ones. It happened to be Sunday Lazari when we landed, and we therefore named this place in honour of this day, although we were well aware that the Indians called it the land of Campeachy.

In order that the whole of us might land at the same time, we determined to go on shore in our smallest vessel and three boats, all of us well armed, to be ready in case we should meet with a similar rencontre as at the cape of Cotoche. The sea in these bays and roads is very shallow, so that our vessels were forced to anchor at more than three miles distance from the shore. Thus precautious we landed near the village, but were still a good way from the place were we intended to fill our casks. From this spot the natives also had their water; for we now found that there was no rivulet in the neighbourhood.

When we had brought our casks on shore, filled them with water, and were about to embark again, about fifty Indians from the village came up to us. They all wore stately mantels made of cotton, appeared friendly disposed, and to be *caziques*. They asked us, by signs, what our business was there? We told them to take in water, and that we were about to re-embark. They further pointed with their hands to the rising of the sun, and asked us whether we came from that quarter, at the same time pronouncing the word *castilan, castilan*; but at that moment we did not pay any particular attention to the word *castilan*. In the course of this interview, however, they gave us to understand that we might go with them to their village.

We held a consultation amongst ourselves as to whether we should accept the invitation, and at length unanimously agreed to follow them, but to use the utmost circumspection. They took us to some large edifices, which were strongly put together, of stone and lime, and had otherwise a good appearance. These were temples, the walls of which were covered with figures representing snakes and all manner of gods. Round about a species of altar we perceived several fresh spots of blood. On some of the idols there were figures like crosses, with other paintings representing groups of Indians. All this astonished us greatly as we had neither seen nor heard, of such things before. It appeared to us that the inhabitants had just been sacrificing some Indians to their gods, to obtain from them the power to overcome us.

There were great numbers of Indians with their wives who received us with pleasing smiles, and otherwise made every show of friendship; but their numbers gradually increasing we began to entertain fears that it would end in the same hostile manner as at Cape Cotoche. While we were thus looking on, a number of Indians approached us clad in tattered cloaks, each carrying a bundle of dried reeds, which they arranged in order on the ground. Among them we also perceived two troops of men armed with bows, lances, shields, slings, and stones, having their cotton cuirasses on. At the head of these, and at some distance from us stood the chiefs. At this moment ten Indians came running out of another temple, all dressed in long white robes, while the thick hair of their heads was so entangled and clotted with blood that it would have been an impossibility to have combed or put it in order without cutting it off. These personages were priests, and in New Spain are commonly termed *papas*.[1] I repeat it, that in New Spain they are termed *papas*, and I will therefore in future call them by that name. These *papas* brought with them a kind of incense, which looked like resin, and is termed by them copal. They had pans made of clay filled with glowing embers, and with

1. Bernal Diaz is thus particular in laying stress on this remarkable circumstance, because the pope of Rome, in Spanish, is termed *pápa*.

these they perfumed us. They also gave us to understand, by signs, that we should leave their country before the bundles of reeds, which had been brought and were going to be set fire to, should be consumed, otherwise they would attack and kill us every man.

Upon this they ordered the bundles to be lighted, and as soon as they began to burn, all were silent, nor did they utter another syllable. Those, on the contrary, who had ranged themselves in order of battle, began to play on their pipes, blow their twisted shells, and beat their drums. When we saw what their real intentions were, and how confident they appeared, it of course reminded us that our wounds which we had received at Cape Cotoche were not yet healed; that two of our men had died of the consequences, whom we had been obliged to throw overboard. As the number of Indians continued to increase, we became alarmed, and resolved to retreat to the shore in the best order we could. In this way we marched along the coast until we arrived at that spot where our boats and the small vessels lay with the water-casks. Not far distant from this place stood a rock in the midst of the sea; for, on account of the vast numbers of Indians, we durst not venture to re-embark where we had at first landed, as they would no doubt have fallen upon us while we were getting into our boats.

After we had thus managed to get our water safe on board and re-embark at the small harbour which the bay here forms, we continued our course for six days and six nights without interruption, the weather being very fine. But now the wind suddenly veered round to the north and brought stormy weather, as is always the case with a north wind on this coast. The storm lasted twenty-four hours, and indeed we had nearly all of us met with a watery grave, so boisterous was the sea. In order to save ourselves from total destruction we cast anchor near the shore. The safety of our ship now depended upon two ropes, and had they given way we should have been cast on shore. Oh, in what a perilous situation we were then placed! had we been torn away from our anchors we must have been wrecked off the coast! But it was the will of Providence that our old ropes and cables should preserve us. When the storm had abated we continued our course along the coast and kept in as much as possible, that we might take in water when required. For, as I have before stated, our casks were old and leaky; nor was the best economy used with the water, for we thought by going on shore we should be certain either to meet with some spring or obtain it by digging wells.

Thus coasting along we espied a village from our ships, and about three miles further on there was a kind of inner harbour, at the head of which it appeared to us there might be some river or brook; we therefore resolved to land here.

The water, as I have above mentioned, being uncommonly shallow along this coast, we were compelled to anchor our two larger vessels at about three miles distance from the shore, fearing they might otherwise run aground. We then proceeded with our smallest vessel and all our boats in order to land at the above-mentioned inner harbour. We were, however, quite upon our guard, and carried along with us, besides the water-casks, our arms, crossbows, and muskets.

It was about midday when we landed. The distance from here to the village, which was called Potonchan, might be three miles. Here we found some wells, maize plantations, and stone buildings. Our water-casks were soon filled, but we could not succeed to get them into our boats on account of an attack made upon us by great numbers of the inhabitants. I will, however, break off here and relate the battle we fought, in the next chapter.

Chapter 4

We are Attacked

While we were busy taking in water, near the above-mentioned houses and maize plantations, great numbers of Indians were making towards us from the village of Potonchan, as it is termed by the natives. They had all their cotton cuirasses on, which reached to their knees, and were armed with bows, lances, shields, and swords. The latter were shaped like our broadswords, and are wielded with both hands. They also had slings and stones, their bunches of feathers on, and their whole bodies painted with white, brown, and black colours. They approached us in profound silence, as if they came with the most peaceable intentions, and inquired of us by signs if we came from the rising of the sun, thereby pronouncing the very same words which the inhabitants of St. Lazaro had used: namely, *castilan, castilan*. We told them, likewise by signs, that we indeed came from the rising of the sun. We certainly did not understand what they meant; nevertheless it was something for us to reflect on, while it at the same time gave rise to a variety of conjectures, since the natives of St. Lazaro had used the identical words.

It was about the hour of Ave Maria, when the Indians approached us in this manner. A few country houses were scattered round about the neighbourhood. We took the precaution to post watches in different quarters, and upon the whole kept a sharp look out, as the manner in which the natives were assembling seemed to forebode very little good. When we had closed our ranks and taken every necessary precaution, our ears were assailed by the cries and yells of large bodies of Indians who were advancing from different quarters. As they were all armed for battle we could no longer doubt that some evil design was lurking behind; we therefore held a consultation with our captain as to the course we should adopt. Many were of opinion that the best we could do would be to re-embark ourselves in all haste; but, as is always the case in critical moments, one advised this and another that, and so this proposal was overruled as unadvisable, for the vast numbers of Indians would certainly fall upon us while we were getting into our boats and we should all stand in danger of being killed. Others again, among which number I also was, were of opinion that the enemy should be attacked that very night; for, according to the old saying, he who strikes the first blow remains master of the field; but we might make up our minds that each of us singly would have to encounter thirty Indians at least.

Day now began to dawn, and we emboldened each other to meet the coming severe conflict by putting our trust in God and commending our cause to him, while every one was determined to defend himself to the utmost. As soon as daylight had fully broken forth, we perceived more troops of armed natives moving towards the coast with flying colours. They had on their feather-knots, and were provided with drums, bows, lances, shields, and joined themselves to the others who had arrived in the night. They divided themselves into different bodies, surrounded us on all sides, and commenced pouring forth such showers of arrows, lances, and stones, that more than eighty of our men were wounded at the first onset. They next rushed furiously forward and attacked us man to man: some with their lances, others with their swords and arrows, and all this with such terrible fury that we were compelled also to show them earnest. We dealt many a good thrust and blow amongst them, keeping up at the same time an incessant fire with our muskets and crossbows; for while some loaded others fired. At last, by dint of heavy blows and thrusts we forced them to give way; but they did not retreat further than was necessary, in order that they might still continue to hem us in in all safety; constantly crying out in their language, *al calachoni, al calachoni*; which signifies, kill the chief! And sure enough our captain was wounded in no less than twelve different places by their arrows. I myself had three; one of which was in my left side and very dangerous, the arrow having pierced to the very bone. Others of our men were wounded by the enemy's lances, and two were carried off alive; of whom, one was called Alonzo Bote, the other was an old Portuguese.

Perceiving how closely we were hemmed in on all sides by the enemy, who not only kept constantly pouring in fresh troops but were copiously supplied on the field of battle with meat, drink, and quantities of arrows, we soon concluded that all our courageous fighting would not advance us a step. The whole of us were wounded, many shot through the neck, and more than fifty of our men were killed. In this critical situation we determined to cut our way manfully through the enemy's ranks and make for the boats, which fortunately lay on the coast near at hand. We therefore firmly closed our ranks and broke through the enemy. At that moment you should have heard the whizzing of their arrows, the horrible yell they set up, and how the Indians provoked each other to the combat, at the same time making desperate thrusts with their lances. But a still more serious misfortune awaited us; for as we made a simultaneous rush to our boats, they soon sunk or capsized, so that we were forced to cling to them as well as we could; and in this manner by swimming we strove to make the best of our way to the small vessel, which was now in all haste coming up to our assistance. Many of our men were even wounded while climbing into the vessel, but more particularly those who clung to its side; for the Indians pursued us in their canoes and attacked us without intermission. With the greatest exertions and help of God we thus got out of the hands of this people.

After we had gained our vessels we found that fifty-seven of our men were missing, besides the two whom the Indians had carried off alive, and five whom we had thrown overboard, who had died in consequence of their wounds and extreme thirst. The battle lasted a little longer than half an hour. The spot where it took place was certainly called Potonchan. Our seamen, however, gave it the name of Bahea de mala Pelea, (the bay of the disastrous engagement,) as it stands on the maps. As soon as we found ourselves in safety we returned thanks to Almighty God for the preservation of our lives. Our wounded, however, had still great sufferings to undergo, as we had nothing but salt water to wash their wounds with, which caused them to swell very much. Some of our men swore most bitterly against our chief pilot Alaminos, and the conduct he had pursued; he having steadfastly maintained that this was an island and not a continent. I must, however, break off here, and relate what further happened to us, in the next chapter.

Chapter 5

To Havannah

After we had got into our vessels, as above related, and returned thanks to God for our preservation, we commenced dressing our wounds. None of us had escaped without two, three, or four wounds. Our captain had as many as twelve, and there was only one single soldier who came off whole. We therefore determined to return to Cuba; but as most of the sailors who had accompanied us on shore were also wounded, we had not sufficient hands to work the sails, we were therefore forced to set fire to our smallest vessel and leave it to the mercy of the waves, after taking out all the ropes, sails, and anchors, and distributing the sailors, who were not wounded equally among the two other vessels. We had, however, to struggle with another far greater evil. This was our great want of fresh water; for although we had filled our barrels and casks near Potonchan, we did not succeed to bring them off, owing to the furious attack of the natives and the hurry we were in to get on board: thus we had been compelled to leave them behind and return without a single drop of water. We suffered most intensely from thirst, and the only way we could in some measure refresh our parched tongues was to hold the edges of our axes between our lips. Oh, what a fearful undertaking it is to venture out on the discovery of new countries, and place one's life in danger, as we were obliged to do! Those alone can form any idea of it who have gone through the hard school of experience.

We now kept as close into the shore as possible, to look out for some stream or creek where we might meet with fresh water. After thus continuing our course for three days we espied an inlet or mouth of some river as we thought, and sent a few hands on shore in the hopes of meeting with water. These were fifteen sailors who had remained on board during the battle at Potonchan, and three soldiers who had been only slightly wounded. They carried along with them pickaxes and three small casks. But the water in the inlet was salt, and wherever they dug wells it was equally bad. They nevertheless filled the casks with it, but it was so bitter and salty as to be unfit for use. Two soldiers who drank of it became ill of the consequences. The water here swarmed with lizards; we therefore gave this place the name of Lizard Bay, under which name it stands on the sea charts.

But, to continue my history, I must not forget to mention that while our boats were on shore in search of water, there suddenly arose such a violent tempest from the north-east, that our ships were nigh being cast on shore. For, as we were forced to lay to, the wind blowing hard from the north and north-east, our position was extremely dangerous, from a scarcity of ropes.

When the men who had gone on shore with our boats perceived the danger we were in, they hastened to our assistance, and cast out additional anchors and cables. In this way we lay for two days and two nights. After the expiration of that time we again heaved our anchors and steered in the direction of Cuba. Our pilot Alaminos here held a consultation with the two others, when they concluded that the best plan would be to get, if possible, into the latitude of Florida, which, according to their charts and furthest measurement, could not be more than 210 miles distant; for they assured us if we could get into the latitude of Florida, we should have a better and speedier sail to the Havannah. It turned out exactly as they had said; for Alaminos had been in these parts before, having accompanied Juan de Leon when he discovered Florida, about ten or twelve years previously. After four days' sail we crossed this gulf and came in sight of Florida.

Chapter 6

In Search of Water

As soon as we had arrived off the coast of Florida we determined that twenty of our men, who had almost recovered from their wounds, should go on shore. Among the number was myself and the pilot, Alaminos. We each took a mattock and a small cask, being, moreover, well armed with crossbows and muskets. Our captain, who was dangerously wounded and very much weakened by the extreme thirst he suffered, begged of us, in the name of God, to bring him some sweet water, as he was almost dying of thirst. Indeed, the water, as I have before said, which we then had was quite salty and not drinkable. We landed in a creek, and our pilot again recognized this coast, which he had visited ten or twelve years previously with Ponce de Leon, when he discovered these countries. They had here fought a battle with the natives, and lost many of their men.

We therefore took every precaution lest the natives should also fall upon us unawares. We posted two sentinels at a spot where the stream had a considerable breadth. We then dug deep wells where we thought fresh water was likely to be found. The sea was just ebbing, and it pleased God that we should find sweet water there.

With joyful hearts we then took our fill of the refreshing beverage, and washed the bandages of our wounded. A good hour's time was spent in this, and as we were on the point of re-embarking with the casks of water, quite overjoyed at our success, one of the men whom we had placed sentinel on the coast came running towards us in all haste, crying aloud, "To arms! to arms! numbers of Indians are approaching, both by land and sea." And indeed the Indians came up to us almost at the same time with the sentinel.

They had immense sized bows with sharp arrows, lances, and spears—among these some were shaped like swords—while their large powerful bodies were covered with skins of wild beasts. They made straightways to us, let fly their arrows, and wounded six of our men at the first onset. I was also slightly wounded in my right arm. We, however, received our enemies with such well-directed blows and musket-shots that they very soon quitted us who had been digging the wells, and turned towards the creek to assist their companions who in their canoes were attacking those left behind in the boat. The latter had been forced to fight man to man, and had already lost the boat, which the Indians were towing off behind their canoes. Four of the sailors had been wounded, and the pilot, Alaminos, himself severely so in the throat. We, however, courageously faced our enemy, went up to our middles in the water, and soon compelled them, by dint of our swords, to jump out of the boat again. Twenty-two of the enemy lay dead on the shore; three others, who were slightly wounded, we took on board with us, but they died soon after.

After this skirmish was ended, we questioned the soldier who had stood sentinel as to what had become of his companion, Berrio. He related that his comrade had left him with an axe in his hand, in order to go and cut down a palm-tree, and that this was near the inlet where the Indians first made their appearance. He had also heard him cry out in Spanish, upon which he himself had immediately hastened to give us the information. His companion, no doubt, had been murdered by the Indians. Singular that this man should have lost his life here, he being the only one who escaped without a wound at the battle of Potonchan. We made every search for him, and followed the track of the Indians who had just attacked us; this indeed led us to a palm-tree which had been recently cut, around which were numerous foot-marks. We could, however, discover no marks of blood; and concluded, therefore, that the Indians had carried off the man alive. After we had fruitlessly searched for him in every quarter for upwards of an hour, and repeatedly called out aloud to him, without receiving any answer, we returned to our boat, and brought the water on board. The joy of our men was as great as if we had brought them new life; and one of the soldiers, from excessive thirst, leaped from the vessel into the boat, seized one of the small casks, and poured such an abundance of water into his body, that he instantaneously swelled out and expired.

Having brought the water on board our vessels, hauled in our boats, we hoisted our sails and stood direct for the Havannah. The day and following night the weather was most beautiful as we passed the Martyr Islands and sand-banks of the same name. We had only four fathoms water, where the sea was deepest; our principal ship consequently struck against the rocks and became very leaky, so that all hands were engaged at the pumps, without then being able to get the water under, while we every moment feared the vessel would go down. I never shall forget the answer which some sailors from the Levant, who were among the crew, made when we cried out to them:

"Come on, my boys, help us to pump out the water, or we shall all be lost! you see how our wounds and hard labour have debilitated us."

"That's your own look out," said they; "we get no pay, suffer both from hunger and thirst, and have, in the bargain, to share your fatigues and wounds."

Nothing now remained but to drive them to the pumps by main force; and in this way we had alternately to work the sails and the pumps, however distasteful to us, until the Lord Jesus brought us into the port of Carena, where now the town of Havannah stands, the latter being previously called Puerto de Carenas, and not the Havannah.

As soon as we had set foot on shore we returned thanks to the Almighty for our safe return, and got the water out of our principal ship, in which a Portuguese diver, who happened to be on board another vessel, greatly assisted us. We also immediately wrote to the governor, Diego Velasquez, giving him an account of the countries we discovered with large townships and houses built of stone, whose inhabitants were clad in cotton, and wore *maltates*; likewise of the gold and the regular maize-plantations of the country. Our captain journeyed overland to Santispiritus, where he had his Indian commendary: he died, however, ten days after his arrival there, from his wounds. The rest of our men became dispersed through the island, and three more of our men died of their wounds at the Havannah.

Our vessels were taken to Santiago de Cuba, where the governor resided. Here the two Indians were brought on shore whom we had taken with us from the Punta de Cotoche, as above related, called Melchorillo and Julianillo. When, however, we brought forth the box with the crowns, the golden ducks, the fish, and the idols, more noise was made about them than they really merited, so that they became the common topics of conversation throughout the islands of St. Domingo and Cuba; indeed the fame thereof even reached Spain. There it was said that none of the countries which had hitherto been discovered were as rich as this, and in none had there been found houses built of stone. The earthen gods, it was said, were the remains of the ancient heathen times; others again went so far as to affirm that they were descendants of the Jews whom Titus and Vespasian had driven from Jerusalem, who had been shipwrecked off this coast. Peru, indeed, was not then known, and in so far the countries we had discovered were justly considered of the greatest importance. Diego Velasquez closely questioned the two Indians as to whether there were any gold mines in their country. They answered in the affirmative; and when they were shown some of the gold-dust found in the island of Cuba, they said there was abundance of it in their country. In this they told an untruth, as it is very well known there are neither goldmines on the Punta de Cotoche nor even in whole Yucatan. They were likewise shown the beds in which the seeds of that plant are sown from whose root the *cassave* bread is made, and in Cuba called *yuca*: they assured us that the same plant grew in their country, and was called by them tale. As the *cassave*-root at Cuba is called *yuca*, and the ground in which it is planted by the Indians tale, so from these two words arose the name of the country, Yucatan; for the Spaniards who were standing around the governor at the time he was speaking to the two Indians said, "You see, sir, they call their country Yucatan." And from this circumstance the country retained the name of Yucatan, although the natives call it otherwise.

In this beautiful voyage of discovery we had spent our all, and returned to Cuba covered with wounds, and as poor as beggars; yet we had reason to congratulate ourselves that it had not been equally disastrous to us all as to many of our companions who had lost their lives. Our captain, as I have already mentioned, died soon after his return; and all of us suffered for a considerable time after from our wounds. Our whole loss amounted to seventy men, which was all we had gained by this voyage of discovery.

Concerning all this the governor Diego Velasquez wrote to those gentlemen in Spain who at that time managed the affairs of India, and boasted of the discoveries *he* had made, and of the vast expense it had put *him* to. This actually obtained credit, and the bishop of Burgos, Don Juan Rodriguez de Fonseca, who also bore the title of archbishop of Rosano, and was president of Indian affairs, wrote in that strain to his majesty, in Flanders, vastly extolling the merit of Diego Velasquez, at the same time not as much as even mentioning the names of any of us who had really discovered the country.

I will, however, break off here, and relate in the following chapter what further fatigues I and three more of my companions in arms had to undergo.

Chapter 7
Trinidad

I have already above related that I with some other soldiers who had not quite recovered from our wounds remained behind in the Havannah. As soon as the latter began to heal a little we three made up our minds to go in company with a certain Pedro d'Avila, an inhabitant of the Havannah, to the town of Trinidad. This man was going to make a voyage in a canoe along the south coast, and had taken a lading of cotton shirts, which he intended to dispose of in Trinidad. As I have above stated, these canoes are hollowed out of the trunks of trees, after the manner of our bakers' troughs: in this country they are used for coasting; and we had to pay Pedro d'Avila ten doubloons for the voyage.

As we were coasting along, sometimes rowing, sometimes sailing, we arrived after the eleventh day in sight of an Indian village, subject to the Spaniards, and called Cannareon; there arose at night-time such a terrible gale of wind, that, although we rowed with all our strength, we could not keep the sea any longer. Notwithstanding every exertion of Pedro d'Avila, of some Indians from the Havannah, and several other good rowers we had with us, nothing at last remained but to run the canoe aground between the steep rocks. The canoe was dashed to pieces, the whole lading of Pedro d'Avila went to the bottom, and we made the best of our way on shore, naked as the day we were born, our bodies cut and bruised all over by clambering over the rocks, for we had stripped ourselves of our clothes in order to be the better able to swim, and also, if possible, to save the canoe. As we had only escaped with our lives among these rocks, none other choice was left us than to continue our road over them to Trinidad, which lay along the coast through a barren country full of rugged rocks, where our feet soon became blistered and wounded; as to think of getting anything to eat was quite out of the question; while we had continually to struggle with a terrific gale of wind and the sea breaking over the rocks. Although we had not neglected to cover our bodies as much as possible with leaves and herbs, we nevertheless got sore boils between our legs, which bled very much. At last we could proceed no further; for the sharp stones had covered our feet with wounds: we managed, however, with considerable trouble to reach a more elevated spot. None of us having his sword left, we contrived by means of sharp stones to loosen the bark of some trees and bind it as well as we could under the soles of our feet, with the tendrils of climbers, which grew among the wood. And in this way, after suffering great fatigues we reached a sandy district on the coast, whence in a couple of days we arrived in the Indian village Yeguarama, at that time the property of Bartholomeus de las Casas,[1] who was a priest. I knew him afterwards when he belonged to the order of the Dominicans, and became bishop of Chiopia. Here the Indians gave us to eat, and on the following day we arrived at another village, called Chipiona, which was the joint property of Alonso de Avila, and of Sandoval, but this was not the captain of the same name who gained such vast renown in New Spain. From this place we at last came to Trinidad, where I had an acquaintance, by name Antonio de Medina, who provided me with a suit of clothes as they were worn in that town; my comrades were similarly provided by other of the inhabitants. Quite worn out by fatigue and miserably poor, I set off for Santiago de Cuba, where the governor Diego Velasquez resided. He was just then busily engaged fitting out another squadron, and was highly delighted at seeing me again when I called upon him, for we were related to each other: and as one word led to another, he asked me if my wounds were sufficiently healed to make another trip to Yucatan? I could not help smiling at this and said, "who gave the country that name? For the natives do not call it so."

"So Melchior, whom you brought with you, calls it," resumed he.

"Call it rather, (said I,) the land where they killed one half of our men and wounded the other."

"Well, (said he,) if you have undergone many fatigues, you have only shared the same fate with all others who have ventured out on the discovery of new countries. But, on the other hand, you will not fail to be highly honoured and rewarded by his majesty the king, to whom I will transmit a faithful account of all this. Therefore, my friend, you may in all safety join yourself to the squadron I am now fitting out, and I will take care that you shall have an honourable post."

What further happened I will next relate.

1. This is the celebrated Las Casas, the protector of the rights of the Indians.

Chapter 8
Yucatan

It was in the year of our Lord 1518, after Diego Velasquez had learnt the good account we gave of the newly-discovered country, called Yucatan, that he determined to send thither another expedition. For this purpose he selected four vessels, among which were the two in which we warriors had accompanied Cordoba on our recent voyage to Yucatan, purchased at our own expense. At the time this squadron was fitting out there were staying at Santiago de Cuba, Juan de Grijalva, Pedro de Alvarado, Francisco de Montejo, and Alonso de Avila; who had commendaries of Indians in these islands, and had come to transact business with the governor. As these were all men of courage and energy, Velasquez soon made arrangements with them to take part in this expedition, on the following terms: that Juan de Grijalva, who was related to him, should have the chief command of the whole expedition as captain-general, while Pedro de Alvarado, Francisco de Montejo, and Alonso de Avila, should be appointed to the command of the three other ships. They had also to furnish the vessels with provisions of *cassave* bread and pickled meat; Diego Velasquez had, on the other hand, to procure the four vessels, furnish the necessary crossbows, muskets, goods for barter, and other matters of less importance. Our account that the houses in the newly-discovered country were built of stone and lime, had spread a vast idea of its riches, added to which the Indian Melchorejo had given to understand by signs that it abounded in gold mines. All this created a great desire among the inhabitants and soldiers throughout the island, who possessed no commendaries of Indians, to go in quest of such a rich country; consequently, in a very short time, we mustered 220. Each person, moreover, furnished himself with additional provisions, arms, and other matters which might be useful.

Thus I again took my departure for that country, under the same commanders I subsequently once more visited it. The instructions which our commanders received from Diego Velasquez, were to this effect, that they should barter for as much gold and silver as they could get, and if they deemed it advisable settle colonies, but left this entirely to their own judgment. A person of the name of Penolosa accompanied us in the capacity of comptroller; for priest we had a certain Juan Diaz. We had also the same three pilots who accompanied us on our former voyage; and a fourth, whose name I do not remember. Each had charge of one of the vessels; but the first in command, as chief pilot, was Anton de Alaminos.

But before I proceed with my narrative, I must here remark, that it is not for want of deference on my part, that I barely give the names of the noblemen who were our commanding officers, without adding their titles and describing their several escutcheons, but shall simply call them thus, Pedro de Alvarado, Francisco de Montejo, and Alonso de Avila. I therefore now take this opportunity of saying, that Pedro de Alvarado was a bold cavalier, who, subsequent to the conquest of New Spain, became governor and chief justice of the provinces of Guatimala, Honduras, and Chaopo, and *comptoir* of Santiago. In like manner Francisco de Montejo, a man of great courage, subsequently was governor and chief justice of Yucatan. I shall merely call them by their proper names, up to that time when his majesty conferred on them honorary titles and sovereign authority.

But to return to my subject, our four vessels lay in the harbour of Matanza on the north coast, not far from the old Havannah, which at that time was not built where it now stands. In this harbour, or at least in its neighbourhood, most of the inhabitants had their stores of *cassave* bread and pickled meat. Here consequently our vessels were provided with everything they further required. This place moreover had been appointed the rendezvous for all the officers and men.

But, before I continue my narrative, I will explain how this harbour obtained the name of Matanza,[1] though it may seem rather out of place here; yet, as so many persons have asked me how it originated, there is some excuse.

Some time ago, when Cuba was not quite subdued, it happened that a vessel, bound from the island of St. Domingo to the Luccas, during a heavy storm, was wrecked off the coast. This took place near the river and harbour of Matanza; there were thirty Spaniards

1. Puerto de Matanza, the harbour of the massacre.

and two Spanish ladies on board. In order to convey them across the river, numbers of Indians had collected together from the Havannah and other districts. They appeared most friendly inclined, and offered to carry the shipwrecked across in their canoes and take them to their habitations, where they would give them to eat. The Spaniards accepted this offer; when the Indians, however, had arrived in the midst of the stream, they upset their canoes and drowned them all, save three of the men and one of the females. The men were allotted to the other Indians, but the female, a very beautiful woman, was given to the most powerful of the *caziques*, the person who had concocted this piece of treachery. From this circumstance it was that the harbour got the name of Matanza.

I was personally acquainted with the female whose misfortune I have just related. After the total conquest of Cuba, she left the *cazique* in whose power she then was, and married a citizen of Trinidad, by name Pedro Sanchez Farsan.

I was also acquainted with the three Spaniards whose lives had been spared. One was Gonzalo Mexia, an old man, and native of Xeres; the other, Juan de Santiste-ban, from Madrigal; and the third was Cascorro, a sailor and fisherman, of Huelva. The *cazique* in whose power he was, had given him his daughter in marriage, and bored holes through his ears and nose, after the Indian fashion.

Having thus detained the reader for a while with these old stories, it is time I return to the thread of my narrative.

On the 5th of April, 1518, all of us having met together, the officers and soldiers, the pilots made acquainted with the signals, and the hour of departure fixed, we attended mass with fervent devotion, and weighed anchor. After ten days' sail, we passed the cape of Guaniguanico, called by the sailors San Anton. Eight days after, we came in sight of the island of Cozumel; it happened to be the feast of the Holy Cross. This time our ships were carried further off by the currents than the time before under Cordoba; the consequence was that we now landed on the south coast of the island. We here espied a village, and found a good anchorage near it, perfectly free from all rocks. Our commander-in-chief, therefore, went on shore here with a good body of soldiers. The inhabitants, who had never witnessed such a sight before, immediately took to flight when they saw our vessels approaching, so that not a single one of them had remained in the village. At length we discovered two Indians among the recently cut maize plants, who had not been able to get off quick enough. We brought them into the presence of our captain, who spoke to them with the help of Julianillo and Melchorejo, whom we had captured at the Punta de Cotoche, and who understood their language. The distance between their countries was only four hours' sail, which accounts for the inhabitants of Cozumel speaking the same language. Our commander was very kind to them, gave each some green glass beads, and sent them away to bring the *calachoni* of the district, (so the *caziques* are termed here;) they, however, never returned. While we were still waiting for them, an Indian woman came towards us, comely in appearance, and who spoke the language of Jamaica. She told us that the Indians had fled, out of fear, to the mountains. As I myself and many others among us understood her language, which is the same as that of the island of Cuba, we were quite astonished at the circumstance, and inquired of her how she had got here.

She told us that, two years ago, she had left Jamaica with ten Indians, in a large canoe, in order to go fishing among the islands in this neighbourhood, but had been driven on shore by the currents, when the inhabitants killed her husband with most of her companions, and sacrificed them to their gods.

It struck our commander, as soon as he had learnt this, that the woman might be employed as a negotiator. He therefore desired her to go and fetch the inhabitants and *cazique* of the district, and gave her two days to return in. We durst not send Melchorejo and Julianillo with her, lest they should run away and return to their own country.

The day following, the Indian woman returned, but informed us that, notwithstanding all her representations, she could neither persuade the Indians nor their wives to accompany her. We called this place Santa Cruz, because we had discovered it four or five days before the feast of the Holy Cross. In this neighbourhood there was plenty of honey, manioc, patates, and large herds of musk swine, which have their navels on their backs.[2] This island contains three poor villages, of which the one I am now speaking of is the largest; the two smaller ones were both situated on a promontory at about six miles distance from each other. Our commander Grijalva, perceiving that it was mere loss of time to make any further stay here, gave orders for re-embarking. The Indian woman of Jamaica went along with us, and we continued our voyage.

2. The *sus tajassu*, *pecary*, or Mexican musk hog; but what our old soldier, with other writers, mistook for a navel, is an open gland on the lower part of the back, which discharges a fetid ichorous liquor.

Chapter 9

How We Landed at Champoton

From this point we sailed in the same direction we had taken under Cordoba, and arrived after eight days' sail off the coast of Champoton, the place where the Indians had so ill used us, as has been related in the proper place. The sea being very shallow in these parts we dropt our anchor at about three miles distance from the shore, and immediately landed in all our boats with half of our men, as near to the village as possible. The inhabitants and other Indians in the neighbourhood gathered themselves together as they had the time before, when they killed fifty-six of our men and wounded all the rest of us. From their bearing and proud demeanour we could easily perceive that they had not forgotten their victory. They were all well armed according to their fashion, with bows, lances, shields, and broadswords, which they wield with both hands. Added to all this they had slings, cotton cuirasses, drums and trumpets, while most of them had their faces painted black and white. They had arranged themselves along the sea shore in order to fall upon us as soon as we landed. But, as our previous loss had taught us prudence, we took with us this time some falconets, and otherwise well armed ourselves with crossbows and matchlocks.

When we were near enough they let fly such a shower of arrows and lances that the half of our men were speedily wounded. As soon, however, as we got on shore, we quickly gave them an evil return with our matchlocks and sabres. Nothing daunted by this they each selected their man, whom they particularly aimed at with their arrows, but we had taken the precaution to put on cotton cuirasses. They continued to combat with us for some time, until the arrival of another of our long boats, when we drove them back to the wells near the village. In this conflict we lost Juan de Quitera and many other soldiers. Our commander, Juan de Grijalva, got three arrow wounds and lost two of his teeth, and above sixty of our men were wounded. Immediately upon our putting the enemy to flight, we entered the village, dressed our wounds, and buried the dead. Not a single person had remained behind in the village, and even those whom we had driven back to the wells had merely staid there a sufficient time to carry off their property. In this skirmish we made three prisoners, one of whom was a person of rank. Our commander set them at liberty, desiring them to go and call the *cazique* of the district. He also presented them with green glass beads and small bells to distribute among the inhabitants, in order to gain their friendship. We treated the three prisoners upon the whole with every kindness, and gave them glass corals to encourage them and gain their good faith. They left us indeed, but took good care not to return; we thought it possible, however, that Julianillo and Melchorejo had misrepresented our commission to them. We staid four days in this place, and I shall never forget it on account of the immense sized locusts which we saw here. It was a stony spot on which the battle took place, and these creatures, while it lasted, kept continually flying in our faces; and as at the same moment we were greeted by a shower of arrows from the enemy, we also mistook these locusts for arrows. But, as soon as we had discovered our mistake, we deceived ourselves in another more direful way, for we now mistook arrows for locusts, and discontinued to shield ourselves against them. In this way we mistook locusts and arrows to our great sorrow, were severely wounded in consequence, and otherwise found ourselves in a very awkward predicament.

Chapter 10
Terminos Bay

On our further voyage we came to an opening on the coast, which to us appeared to be the mouth of some broad and large river. It was, however, not a river as we had supposed, but a good harbour, which reached so far inland, and had such a considerable breadth, that it appeared like a sea; and our pilot Anton de Alaminos confidently asserted that this was an island whose two promontories reached nigh to the continent. We, therefore, termed this opening the Boca de Terminos, under which name it may be found on the sea charts. Our commander and the other officers went on shore here with the greater part of our men, among which number I also was.

We remained three whole days in this place in order thoroughly to explore the opening and sail through it in all directions. We discovered, however, that it was no island, but a deep indented bay, formed by the continent, affording us a most commodious harbour. As we also found temples here built of stone and lime, full of idols made of wood or clay, with other figures, sometimes representing women, sometimes serpents, also horns of various kinds of wild animals, we concluded that an Indian village must be near at hand: we considered, moreover, that this would be a most excellent spot to found a colony. We had, however, deceived ourselves in one thing, the district being quite uninhabited.

The temples most probably belonged to merchants and hunters, who on their journeys most likely ran into this harbour and there made their sacrifices. Fallow deer and rabbits abounded in this neighbourhood, and with one greyhound only we killed ten of the former and great numbers of the latter. Our dog took such a liking to this spot that it ran away while we were busy re-embarking, nor did we see it again until we visited this place subsequently with Cortes, when it appeared in excellent condition, quite plump and sleeky.

Having thoroughly explored Terminos harbour, and sounded it throughout, we pursued our course along the coast to the River Tabasco, which at present, after the name of its discoverer, is called the River Grijalva.

CHAPTER 11
The Tabasco River

As we thus by day sailed along the coast of the continent, for at night we lay to on account of the shallows and rocks, we perceived on the third morning a very broad mouth of some river. We approached the shore as near as possible, thinking we should find a good harbour here. As we came closer to the mouth we saw that the waves broke over its shallows: we consequently lowered our boats to make soundings, and found that our two larger vessels could not come in here. It was therefore immediately resolved that they should anchor further out at sea, but that the two remaining vessels which did not draw so much water, with all our boats well manned, should proceed up the river. We could perceive in the canoes along the shore numbers of Indians with bows and arrows, and in other respects armed exactly like those of Champoton. We concluded from their numbers that a village could not be far off; we also found as we proceeded further up the river along the banks, basket *kiddles* put out, from two of which we took the fish and placed them in a boat a-stern of our principal ship.

This river was previously called after the *cazique* of the district, the Tabasco; as we, however, discovered it during this expedition, we gave it the name of the Grijalva River, in honour of our chief commander, under which name it stands on the sea charts.

We might still have been about two miles from the village when we distinctly heard the crackling noise of the felling of trees; for the Indians were constructing barricades and making other preparations of war against us, of the issue of which they entertained no doubts, as they had been duly advertised of the occurrence at Potonchan. As soon as we learnt this, we disembarked our men on a projecting point of land, about two miles from the village, where some palm trees were growing. As soon as they perceived this, about fifty canoes with Indians completely armed after their fashion made towards us, while many other canoes, manned in the same way, lay dispersed about the haven, at a greater distance, not daring to approach us so near as the first.

Seeing how ready they were for action, we were just upon the point of firing off our great guns, and giving them a volley of musket-shots, when it entered our minds, through a merciful Providence, that we ought first to try if we could not gain their friendship. We therefore by means of Julianillo and Melchorejo, (who were natives of the Punta de Cotoche, and certainly understood the language spoken here,) told the chiefs they had nothing to fear from us: we were desirous of discoursing with them and had things to disclose, which, as soon as they had learnt, would make our arrival pleasing to them: they should come to us and we would gladly give them of the things we had brought.

Upon this invitation four of the canoes approached us, containing thirty Indians, or thereabouts. We showed them necklaces of blue glass beads, small mirrors, and green imitation corals. At the sight of the latter they appeared quite delighted; for they thought them to be *chalchihuis* stones, which are highly esteemed in their country.

Our captain then told them, by means of our interpreters, that we came from a distant country, and were the subjects of a great emperor, whose name was Don Carlos, who had numerous sovereigns and *caziques* among his vassals: they should likewise acknowledge this emperor as their lord and master, for then it would go well with them;—he further desired them to give us fowls in exchange for our glass beads.

Two of the Indians, one of whom was the chief and the other a papa—this is a kind of priest, who performs the ceremonies in presence of their idols—answered and said, "they would bring the provisions we required and commence a trade of barter with us.—For the rest they had already a master, and could not help feeling astonished that we, who had but just arrived and knew nothing of them, should that instant wish to impose a master on them. We had better consider a bit before we commenced war with them, as we had with those at Potonchan. That already all the warriors of the country had been ordered out against us, and two armies, each composed of 8000 men were ready for action. They certainly had learnt that a few days ago we had killed and wounded 200 men; but they were more powerful than the inhabitants of that country, which was the reason why they first wished to know what our intentions were. Our declaration would be communicated to the *caziques* of the numerous districts, who had united themselves for war or for peace."

Upon this they embraced our commander, in token of peace, who presented them with necklaces of glass beads, and desired them to return as quickly as possible with an answer; adding that if they did not return we would enter their town by main force, though we had no evil intentions whatever.

These delegates communicated with the *caziques* and *papas*—the latter having also a voice in their councils,—and they declared that our offer of peace was acceptable to them. Provisions were ordered to be sent us, and all present agreed that they themselves with the neighbouring tribes should each contribute their quota in order to make us a present in gold to insure our good friendship, and obviate a recurrence of what had taken place at Potonchan. From what I subsequently learnt and witnessed I found that it was customary with the inhabitants of these countries to make each other presents whenever they were in treaty about peace.

All I have been relating took place on the promontory where the palm trees stood. About thirty Indians soon arrived, laden with broiled fish, fowls, fruit, and maize-bread. They also brought pans filled with red-hot embers, on which they strewed incense, and perfumed us all. After this ceremony was ended they spread some mats on the ground, over which they laid a piece of cotton cloth; on this they put some trifling ornaments in gold in the shape of ducks and lizards, with three necklaces made of gold, which had been melted into the shape of round balls. All these things, however, were of an inferior kind of gold, not worth 200 *pesos*. They next presented us with some mantles and waistcoats, as they themselves wore, and begged of us to accept them in good kind; saying they had no more gold to give us, but that further on towards the setting of the sun there was a country where it was found in great abundance; hereby often repeating the word Culba, Culba, and Mexico, Mexico. We however did not understand what they meant. Although the presents they had brought us were of little value, we nevertheless rejoiced exceedingly on account of the certainty we had gained that there was gold in this country. Having handed over the presents to us with due formality they told us we might now continue our voyage. Our captain thanked them; presenting each at the same time with some green beads. We now determined to re-embark, for the vessels were in great danger on account of the north wind, which in our present situation was quite contrary. We had, moreover, to go in quest of the country, which, according to the assurances of the Indians, abounded in gold.

Chapter 12
Aguajaluco

Having again re-embarked we continued our course along the coast, and perceived on the second day a town close to the sea shore, called Aguajaluco. We could discern numbers of Indians hurrying to and fro with huge shields made out of large tortoise-shells, which glittered so beautifully in the sun, that some of our men believed they were made of an inferior species of gold. The inhabitants appeared to be walking up and down the shore in great consternation, which induced us to call the village La Rambla, under which name it stands on the sea charts.

As we proceeded further along the coast we came to a bay, into which the River Tonola empties itself: it was this same river we entered on our subsequent voyage. We gave it the name of Sant Antonio, which it still retains on the maps. We next passed the mouth of the great River Guacasualco, and would gladly have run into the bay which it forms if contrary winds had not prevented us. We now came in sight of the great Snow Mountains—Sierras Nevadas. These are covered the whole year round with snow. There were also other mountains, nearer the coast, to which we gave the name of Holy Martin, because a soldier of the name of San Martino, a native of the Havannah, first descried them. One of the commanders, Pedro de Alvarado, whose vessel was the fastest sailer of the whole, being a great way ahead of the others, ran his ship up a river called by the natives Papalohuna: this we termed the Alvarado, after the name of the discoverer. Some Indian fishermen of the village Tlacotalpa gave him fish: we could perceive this, though at a great distance from him. Alvarado was followed by two more of our ships; we were therefore obliged to wait until they returned. This digression without the general's leave occasioned ill blood; and Grijalva forbade Alvarado in future to sail in advance of the squadron, fearing he might meet with some accident or other before the rest could possibly come up to his assistance. From this time the four vessels kept close together. We soon after arrived at the mouth of another river, which we termed the Bandera's Stream, (Flag Stream,) from the circumstance that the banks of the river were crowded with Indians bearing small flags of white cloth attached to their lances. They called out and invited us to come on shore: but I will relate in the next chapter what further took place here.

Chapter 13

We Gain 1500 Pesos

By this time the existence of the great city of Mexico must be known throughout the major part of the Spanish provinces and the greater part of Christendom: how, like Venice, it was built in the water; and of the mighty monarch who resided there, king of many provinces and lord of all these countries, which in extent were more than quadruple that of Spain. The name of this monarch was Motecusuma: his power was so great that he would gladly have extended it to places where it was impossible, and he wished to know things which he never could learn. He had, however, heard of our first visit under the command of Cordoba, and of our battle at Cotoche and Champoton, also of the second engagement we had had at the last-mentioned spot. He was moreover aware that we had been but a handful of men in comparison with the multitude of the inhabitants; and lastly, it had been made known to him that we gladly exchanged our goods for gold. All this information had, from time to time, been sent him by means of painted figures or signs, drawn, as is the custom with this people, on a thick kind of cloth manufactured from the *maguey*,[1] very much resembling our linen. Being also informed that we were continuing our course along the coast, he issued orders to the governors of the several districts that at every place where we landed they should exchange their gold for our glass beads, but particularly for the green ones, which so much resembled their *chalchihuis* stones; and further he commanded them to gain every information with respect to our intentions. What made him dwell more particularly upon the latter was the ancient

1. The author sometimes also calls this *nequen*, of which the garments of the poorer classes were manufactured. The *maguey* is the well-known *agava* Americana, the sap of which formed the national drink of the Indians, and the Mexicans were accustomed to write most of their hieroglyphics on the cloth manufactured from the leaves.

tradition in the country, which spoke of a people that would come from the rising of the sun who would at some future period get the dominion of the country.

For whatever purpose it may have been I will leave, but certain it is that the powerful Motecusuma had ordered sentinels to be posted along the banks of the river above mentioned. These sentinels had all small flags attached to the points of their lances, and called out aloud, inviting us to come to them. While we were contemplating from our vessels this, to us, so novel a sight, our commander-in-chief with the other officers and soldiers came to the determination to inquire their meaning. We therefore lowered two of our boats and manned them with twenty soldiers, well armed with crossbows and muskets. The command of this was given to Francisco de Montejo. I was likewise among the number. Our instructions were to send immediate information to the commander-in-chief if anything of a hostile nature should take place and in general to let him know how matters stood. It pleased God that the weather should be calm, which is seldom the case on these coasts. We all got safe on shore, and were met by three *caziques*, one of whom was a governor under Motecusuma. These were attended by great numbers of Indians, carrying fowls, maize-bread, pines, *sapotas*, and other provisions; they spread some mats in the shade of the trees, on which they invited us to sit down. All this was done by signs, as Julianillo did not understand their language. Next they brought pans made of clay, filled with glowing embers, on which they strewed a species of resin, smelling very much like our incense, with which they perfumed us.

Francisco de Montejo sent information of all this to our commander-in-chief, who immediately resolved to run the whole squadron into the bay, and proceed on shore with all our men.

When the *caziques* and the governor saw our general on shore, who, they had been given to understand, was our chief officer, they paid him in their way the greatest possible respect, and perfumed him most vehemently. We thanked them kindly, and in return made many protestations of friendship, also presenting each with white and green glass beads, desiring them at the same time to bring us gold in exchange for our commodities. Motecusuma's governor strongly advised the Indians to comply with our request; the consequence of which was that the inhabitants of the surrounding districts soon brought us every trinket they possessed in the shape of gold, and commenced a trade of barter with us. During the six days we stayed in this spot we obtained upwards of 1500 *pesos'* worth of gold trinkets, of various workmanship, but of inferior quality. The historians Francisco Lopez de Gomara and Gonzalo Hernandez de Oviedo have also mentioned this circumstance in their works. They err, however, when they say it took place in the Tabasco or Grijalva River; for it is a well-authenticated fact that there is no gold found in the provinces which border on the River Grijalva, and, upon the whole, very few ornaments of gold. I will not, however, detain my reader with their account, but rather inform him that we took possession of this country for his imperial majesty the Emperor, in the name of Diego Velasquez, the governor of Cuba. This being done, our general told the Indians that he was now desirous of re-embarking, and presented them with some Spanish shirts. We took one of the Indians with us, who subsequently learnt our language and was converted to Christianity, when he took the name of Francisco. I met with him afterwards at Santa Fé, where he had settled himself after the conquest of Mexico. Our commander, finding that the inhabitants brought no more gold, and considering that we had already been here six days, and that our present anchorage was rather dangerous on account of the contrary winds, gave orders for re-embarking. Pursuing our voyage, we came to an island which was quite covered with white sand, lying above nine miles from the main land. We gave it the name of Isla Blanca, as it stands on the sea charts. Not far from this lay another island, nearly five miles from the main land, which offered us a very commodious landing-place.

Our general, therefore, ordered the boats to be lowered, and landed, with the greater portion of our men, in order to explore the island. We found two houses, which were strongly built of stone and lime; both were ascended by a flight of steps, and surmounted by a species of altar, on which stood several abominable idols, to whom, the previous evening, five Indians had been sacrificed. Their dead bodies still lay there, ripped open, with the arms and legs chopped off, while everything near was besmeared with blood. We contemplated this sight in utter astonishment, and gave this island the name of Isla de Sacrificios. Quitting this place, we landed on the neighbouring continent, where we constructed ourselves huts on one of the large downs, with some sails and the branches of trees. Numbers of Indians soon made their appearance, bringing with them small pieces of gold for barter, in the same way as at the Bandera stream, according to the commands of Motecusuma, as we subsequently learnt. The inhabitants, however, approached us in great fear, and what they brought with them was a mere trifle. Our captain, therefore, soon weighed anchor again. The next place we landed at was in view of another island, which lay about two miles from the continent. This at present is considered the best harbour of the country. What happened to us in this place I will relate in the next chapter.

Chapter 14
San Juan De Culua

Having disembarked on a part of the coast where it was very sandy, we were annoyed by such multitudes of *muschetoes* that we were forced to construct ourselves huts on the great downs and in the tops of trees: this, being done, we carefully examined the harbour in our boats, and were fully satisfied that it contained a good anchorage, it being moreover sheltered against the north wind by the island, to which our general now proceeded with thirty men all well armed. Here we found a temple on which stood the great and abominable-looking god Tetzcatlipuca, surrounded by four Indians, dressed in wide black cloaks, and with flying hair, in the same way as our canons or Dominicans wear it. These were priests, who had that very day sacrificed two boys, whose bodies they had ripped up, and then offered their bleeding hearts to the horrible idol. They were going to perfume us in the same way they had done their gods; and though it smelt like our incense, we would not suffer them, so shocked were we at the sight of the two boys whom they had recently murdered, and disgusted with their abominations. Our captain questioned the Indian Francisco whom we had brought with us from the Bandera stream as to what was meant by all this, for he seemed rather an intelligent person; having, at that time, as I have already stated, no interpreter, our captain put these questions to him by means of signs. Francisco returned for answer that this sacrifice had been ordered by the people of Culua; but, as it was difficult for him to pronounce this latter word, he kept continually saying *olua, olua.* From the circumstance of our commander himself being present, and that his Christian name was Juan, and it happening to be the feast of St. John, we gave this small island the name of San Juan de Ulua. This harbour was ever after much frequented. Great numbers of ships have been refitted there, and all merchandise for Mexico and

New Spain are here shipped or unladen. During the time we were encamped on these downs, numbers of Indians from the surrounding districts, brought us their gold trinkets in exchange for our goods; but there was so little of it, and that so very inferior in quality, that we scarcely troubled ourselves about it. We remained, nevertheless, seven days in the huts we had constructed, though we were constantly annoyed by swarms of *muschetoes*, which rendered our stay most uncomfortable. As we had now been so long at sea, and had fully convinced ourselves that it was no island, but a continent, we had discovered, containing considerable towns; as our *cassave*-bread was become quite mouldy and unfit for eating; considering, moreover, that our numbers were too small to think of making any settlement here, particularly as we had lost ten of our men in consequence of their wounds, besides having four others dangerously ill,—we determined to forward Diego Velasquez an account of the state of affairs, and desire him to send us succours; indeed Grijalva had a great mind to have founded a colony even with the few men we had to spare. Our captain had throughout shown a magnanimous spirit, and proved himself a brave soldier, let the historian Gomara say anything to the contrary he likes. Pedro de Alvarado was selected to go on this mission to Cuba, with the ship San Sebastian, which had become rather leaky: this vessel could be refitted there, and return with succours and provisions. He also took with him all the gold we had bartered for, the cotton stuffs presented us by the Indians, and our sick. Our principal officers, moreover, each sent Diego Velasquez a written account, according to their several views, of all we had seen. We will now leave Pedro de Alvarado to his own good fortune on his voyage to Cuba, and relate what happened to the vessel which Diego Velasquez sent in quest of us.

CHAPTER 15

Diego Velasquez Searches for Us

From the very moment in which Juan de Grijalva had quitted Cuba for the wide ocean, Diego Velasquez became downcast and thoughtful; he was constantly harassed by the idea that some misfortune would befall us. In the height of his impatience he at last sent out a small vessel, with seven men, in quest of us. The command of this was given to a certain Christobal de Oli, a man of great courage and energy. His instructions were to follow the same course in which Cordoba had sailed, until he should have met with us. It appears, however, that Christobal de Oli, while riding at anchor near the coast, was overtaken by a violent storm, and found himself compelled, in order to save his vessel from being cast ashore, to cut the cables; at least he had no anchor left on his return to Santiago de Cuba, nor had he been able to bring the governor any information respecting us.

Diego Velasquez now despaired more than ever. The arrival of Pedro de Alvarado with the gold and other things, fortunately set his anxiety at rest, who, moreover, detailed to him the discoveries we had made. His joy was excessive when he saw the gold, and how it was worked into various shapes; from which very circumstance it appeared to him and others who happened to be present on business, of much greater value than it really was; nor were his majesty's officials, who had to take the fifth part, less astonished at the riches of the countries we had discovered. Pedro de Alvarado, who knew how to humour Diego Velasquez, afterwards related that the governor had continually embraced him,—that festivities and tournaments were celebrated for eight successive days. If the fame of the riches of these countries had been rumoured abroad before, it was now, on account of the gold we had sent, the more so; it soon spread through all the islands, and the whole of Spain.

I shall have occasion to speak of this hereafter, and will also leave Diego Velasquez to his festivities, and return to our vessels at San Juan de Ulua.

Chapter 16

Along the Tusta and Tuspa Mountains

After Pedro de Alvarado had set sail for Cuba, our general and other officers held a consultation with the pilots, when it was determined that we should continue our course along the coast, and push our discoveries as far as possible. As we sailed along, we first came in view of the Tusta, and, two days after, of the more elevated mountains of Tuspa, both of which take their names from two towns lying close to the foot of these mountains. On the whole, we saw numbers of towns lying from six to nine miles inland, now the province of Panuco. At last we arrived at a large stream, to which we gave the name of Canoe River, and dropped anchor at its mouth.

While our vessels were lying at anchor here, and our men had become less careful than usual, sixteen large canoes full of Indians, all equipped for battle, with bows, arrows, and lances, came down the stream and made straight for our smallest vessel, commanded by Alonso de Avila, which lay nearest the shore. They greeted our men with a shower of arrows, wounding two of the soldiers, and then lay hold of the vessel as if they meant to carry her off, after they had cut one of the cables. We now hastened to the assistance of Alonso, who was still bravely repelling his assailants, and had capsized three of their canoes. We were well armed with crossbows and muskets, and very soon wounded at least above a third of our enemies, who speedily retreated to where they had come from, not exactly in the best of spirits. Upon this we weighed anchor and continued our course along the coast until we arrived at a wide projecting cape, which, on account of the strong currents, we found so difficult to double that we considered our further course now impeded. The chief pilot, Alaminos, here told our commander that it was no longer advisable to sail on at a venture, for which he gave us many plausible reasons. This matter being duly considered in council, it was unanimously agreed that we should return to Cuba.

To this step we were, moreover, induced by the approach of winter, scarcity of provisions, and the bad condition of one of our vessels which had become very leaky. To this may also be added the disagreement between our commanders; for Juan de Grijalva persisted in his opinion that they should make an attempt to leave a colony behind, while Francisco de Montejo and Alonso de Avila, on the contrary, maintained that any such attempt would be fruitless, considering the multitude of warriors which inhabited these countries: to all this may be added that our men were heartily sick of the sea. We therefore turned our vessels about, hoisted all the sails, and arrived in a few days, being greatly assisted by the currents, in the wide waters of the Guacasualco River. We could not make any stay here on account of the boisterous state of the weather, and therefore continued our course along the coast until we arrived at the mouth of the River Tonala, to which we gave the name of St. Antonio. We ran up this river and careened the leaky vessel, which had struck there several times against the rocks.

While we were busily engaged at this work, numbers of Indians came up to us from the harbour of Tonala, which lay about four miles from this place, bringing with them maize-bread, fish, and fruits, which they readily gave us. Our commander was particularly kind to them, and presented each with white and green glass beads, giving them at the same time to understand by signs that they should bring us gold in exchange for our goods. They soon complied with our wishes, but their gold was of a very inferior quality, for which they received imitation corals. As soon as the inhabitants of Guacasualco and the neighbouring districts had learnt that we offered our goods for barter, they brought us all their golden ornaments, and took in exchange green glass beads, on which they set a high value. Besides ornaments of gold, every Indian had with him a copper axe, which was very highly polished, with the handle curiously carved, as if to serve equally for an ornament as for the field of battle. At first we thought that these axes were made of an inferior kind of gold; we therefore commenced taking them in exchange, and, in the space of two days, had collected more than 600, with which we were no less rejoiced as long as we were ignorant of their real value, than the Indians with our glass beads. One of our sailors, who had by stealth bought seven of these axes and was secretly congratulating himself on this piece of good fortune, was betrayed to our commander-in-chief, who, ordering the man in his presence, commanded him to deliver up his treasure. Still of opinion that these axes were of gold, the poor fellow, though forced, reluctantly parted with them. This brings to my mind what befell one of our men, named Bartolome Prado: this fellow had managed to get inside of a temple, called by the Indians a cue,[1] which stood upon an elevated spot, and had found in it numerous idols, and some copal, which is the incense of the Indians; also knives made of hard flint, with which they cut their meat offerings, and otherwise make use of in their sacrifices. Besides these things, he found two small wooden boxes, filled with golden trinkets which are worn about the head and neck; also small idols, and other ornaments somewhat resembling our pearls. The idols he brought to his commander, but took care to keep the gold himself. It seems, however, that some one had been watching him all the time, who reported what he had seen to our captain. We all felt concerned at this, and spoke a good word for him, as he was a kind-hearted being: we begged hard of our commander that he might be allowed to retain his treasure, minus the fifth part claimed for the emperor, which being granted, the man had nigh upon eighty *pesos* left for himself. In this place I must also acquaint my readers how I sowed some orange seeds close to one of these temples. On account of the numbers of *muschetoes* which swarm along this river, I had, being tired, laid myself down to rest on the summit of a high temple: in gratitude for the quiet slumber I enjoyed there, I sowed, at the foot of this building, eight orange seeds which I had brought with me from Cuba. These seeds grew very fast, and when grown to small plants, were most probably watered and preserved from the ants by the *papas*, as soon as they perceived the new plant. I have merely related this in order to acquaint my reader that these were the first orange seeds that were planted in New Spain. Subsequent to the conquest of Mexico and friendly subjection of the Indian tribes on the Guacasualco, this province, being excellently situated, was considered of greater importance than any other, no less on account of its mines than for its beautiful harbour. The country, moreover, abounded in gold, and

1. According to Humboldt, the word cue was imported by the Spanish into New Spain from Cuba. The great temple of Mexico was called by the Indians *teocalli*; a word which Torquemada (*Monarchia Indiana*) thus explains: *"Que es come decir, templo, u casas de Dios;"* i.e. "As much as to say, a temple, or house of God."

contained fine pastures for sheep, which was the reason why the most illustrious of the conquistadores[2] of Mexico settled themselves there; among which number was myself,—and I did not forget to look for my orange trees, which, indeed, I transplanted, and they afterwards flourished uncommonly.

I am well aware that it will be said, such old tales as these are quite out of character here; I will not, therefore, say another syllable on the subject, but merely acquaint the reader that the inhabitants of these districts were all very much pleased with us, and embraced us at our departure. We set sail for Cuba, and arrived there in the space of forty days, during which time the weather was sometimes favourable and sometimes boisterous. We were most friendly received by the governor Diego Velasquez, who was highly delighted with the additional gold we brought him. Altogether it was well worth 4000 *pesos*; so that with the 16,000 brought over by Alvarado, the whole amounted to 20,000 *pesos*. Some make this sum greater, some less; but one thing is certain, the crown officials only took the fifths of the last-mentioned sum. When they were about to take this also of the Indian axes, which we had mistaken for gold, they grew excessively angry on finding them to be merely of a fine species of copper; nor did this circumstance fail to produce the usual laughter at the expense of our trade of barter. Diego Velasquez, however, appeared perfectly satisfied, though not so with his relative Grijalva. This was wrong on his part, for it originated solely in the misrepresentations of Alonso de Avila, a man of a bad disposition, who did all he could, backed by Montejo, to lower Grijalva in his eyes. All this—rumour spread—was done in order to fit out another armament, and select a new commander.

2. So those Spaniards, who made the first conquests in New Spain, termed themselves, by way of preference, which name they ever after retained as an honorary title. Even to this day in Spain it is considered very distinguishing to be descended from one of the Conquistadores, and some of the first families there date all their greatness from one of these bold adventurers.

Chapter 17

An Official Goes to Spain

My readers may perhaps think, that what I am now about to relate does not exactly belong to this history; but in the course of it they will readily perceive that I have been obliged to notice many circumstances before I could introduce them to the captain, Hernando Cortes. They ought also to bear in mind, that it often happens that two or three things take place at the same moment; in which case there only remains for the historian to treat of one circumstance after the other, and begin with that which lies nearest at hand. In this place the following comes first under our consideration.

After the arrival of Pedro de Alvarado with the gold which we had made in the newly-discovered country, Diego Velasquez began to fear that some one at court, who might have received private information of all this, would anticipate him, in forwarding his imperial majesty the first news of our important discovery, and so rob him of the reward. He, therefore, despatched one of his chaplains, named Benito Martinez, a thorough man of business, to Spain, with letters and a few of the valuable things, to Don Juan Rodriguez Fonseca, bishop of Burgos, and archbishop of Rosano. He wrote at the same time to the licentiate Louis Zapata, and the secretary Lope Conchillos, who at that time had the conduct of all Indian affairs under the archbishop.

Diego Velasquez was quite devoted to these gentlemen, and had presented them with considerable Indian villages in Cuba, with the inhabitants of which they worked their gold mines. But he took particular care to provide well for the archbishop, troubling himself very little about his majesty, who was at that time in Flanders.

He sent moreover to these, his patrons, a great portion of the gold trinkets which Alvarado had brought with him; for everything that was determined in the imperial council of India depended upon these gentlemen. Diego Velasquez therefore sought, by means of his chaplain, to obtain unlimited permission to fit out armaments at any time he might think proper to make voyages of discovery, and to found colonies in the new countries as well as in those that might subsequently be discovered: in the accounts he transmitted to Spain, he spoke of the many thousands of gold-*pesos* which he had already spent in like undertakings; thereby giving such a favourable direction to the negotiations of his chaplain, Benito Martinez, that his expectations were more than fulfilled, who even obtained for him the additional title of *adelantado* of Cuba. This latter appointment, however, did not arrive until the new expedition under Cortes had left. I will not make any further remarks on these matters at present, but rather say a few words respecting Francisco Lopez de Gomara's *History of the Conquest of New Spain and Mexico*. His history fell into my hands while I was writing my own, and I soon foresaw that I should have to contradict him in many instances. My intention is to give a faithful account, and that in due order, of every circumstance; this will greatly differ from his narrative, which is quite at variance with truth.

Chapter 18

Francisco Lopez de Gomara's Errors

While busily engaged writing this narrative, the eloquent History of the Conquest of Mexico and New Spain, by Gomara, fell into my hands; and when I perceived the elegance of his style, and considered the rudeness of my own, I laid down my pen, ashamed at the very thoughts of its being read by men of distinction. With my spirits thus damped, I once more undertook to go through his history; it was then I, for the first time, discovered how mistaken this author was with respect to the occurrences which had really taken place in New Spain. He is equally bad whenever he writes about the magnitude of the towns and number of the inhabitants; in which, whenever it suits him, he does not, for instance, hesitate a moment to put 8000 for eight. In the same way he mentions the extensive buildings we were stated to have commenced, though, in fact, we were only 400 in number when we first went out to war, and had sufficient work to defend ourselves and prevent the victory from going over to our enemies. Though the Indians may have been timid, we were, nevertheless, guiltless of such wholesale slaughter and other barbarities as Gomara would lay to our doors. On the contrary, such was our situation, and I hereby seal my words with an oath when I state, that we daily offered up our prayers to God and the Holy Virgin to preserve us from destruction.

Alaric was certainly a most courageous monarch, and Attila a soldier whose excessive pride would not allow him to shrink back from anything; yet they never slaughtered such multitudes of human beings on the Catalonian plains as we do in the book of Gomara!

In the same way he mentions what numbers of towns and temples we either burnt or destroyed. I am speaking of the Indian temples, called by the inhabitants cues. This latter circumstance would certainly be most pleasing to his readers; but he never gave it a thought, when he was writing, that the conquistadores themselves, and those better informed, would detect his errors and falsehoods. Even in his other works, whenever he speaks about New Spain, he immediately commits blunders. In one place he praises a commander far above his merits, for which very reason he in another most unjustly diminishes that of a second. In another place again, he gives many a one a command who was not even in the army during the conquest: he gives, for instance, the chief command at the battle fought near the town afterwards called Almeria, to Pedro d'Irico, when, in fact, it was Juan de Escalante who commanded on that occasion, and was killed with seven of his men. Again he says, that Juan Velasquez de Leon founded the colony of Guacasualco, although it was Gonzalo de Sandoval, of Avila. There is as much truth in his account when he says that Cortes ordered the Indian Quezal Popoca, one of Motecusuma's chiefs, to be burnt, together with the village in which it was stated he had hid himself. Equal reliance may be placed in his description of our entry into the town and fortress of Anga Panga, where everything happened exactly contrary to what he has stated. In his narrative of our proceedings on the downs, when we had appointed Cortes captain-general and chief justice, he has allowed himself to be deceived by false information, while he has totally misrepresented our taking of the town Chamula, in the province of Chiapa. A still greater blunder he commits when he states that Cortes issued his orders secretly for the destruction of the eleven vessels which had brought us to New Spain, for it is perfectly well known that the ships were run on shore by our unanimous consent, and in presence of us all, in order that the sailors might also be armed and accompany us on our march.

In like manner he lowers the merits of Juan de Grijalva, although he had proved himself such a worthy officer; while he passes by Hernandez de Cordoba in silence, though he was the first who discovered Yucatan: of Francisco de Garay he says, that he had accompanied us on the previous expedition under Grijalva, though he first visited New Spain during this last expedition. In the account he gives of the arrival of Narvaez, and the victory we gained over him, he is certainly more faithful, and has been well informed of all the circumstances; but, with respect to the battles with the Tlascallans, up to the time when peace was concluded with them, he has again diverged from the truth. Concerning the battle we fought in the city of Mexico itself, in which we were worsted and beaten back with the loss of 860 of our troops, of whom a great portion was sacrificed to the idols,—I repeat, where above 860 of our men were killed, for out of 1300 soldiers who had marched into the town to the relief of Pedro de Alvarado, which made out the united forces of Narvaez and Cortes, only 440 escaped, and even these were all wounded,—of this great and important deed of arms he speaks as if it were a mere nothing. He says as little of the subsequent conquest we made of the great city of Mexico, or the manner in which we accomplished it, and omits to mention the number of our killed and wounded; as if this undertaking had merely been a jolly marriage-procession. But why should I continue to enumerate all these particularities one by one, it is a mere waste of ink and paper! I can only say that it is a great pity if Gomara pursues the same course in all his works; for in the beautiful style in which he writes, he ought to make truth perceptible, and distinguish himself therein. But enough of Gomara; I have sufficiently proved, to the sorrow of his readers, how far he has gone beside the truth. I will now return to my history, and strive to act up to the advice of wise men, who say that honesty and truth are the true ornaments to history. Indeed, my rude style of writing would be insupportable without truth, and therefore I was determined to put my trust in it, and continue my narrative in the way I had begun, that it might go to the press, and publish to the world the conquest of New Spain, as it really took place. In this way his imperial majesty will also learn the great services which we, the true conquistadores, have rendered to the crown; how small our numbers were when we first arrived in this country, under the command of our highly-favoured and faithful captain, Hernando Cortes; what dangers we had to brave; and, lastly, how we conquered this kingdom, which forms a great part of the New World, and for which reason his majesty, our most Christian king and master, has so often ordered that we should be rewarded. However, I will not say anything further on this head, though much might be said. In resuming my pen I will, like a careful pilot who throws out the lead when he is in danger of shallows, search after truth, where the historian Gomara flies away from it. I will not, however, detain my readers by entering into minute particulars, but always keep the whole in view, in order that the costs of gathering the leasings may not amount to more than the value of the full vintage. If other historians should further swell out my narrative, and bestow on Cortes, our commander, and on the brave conquistadores in this great and holy expedition, their just measure of praise, I can at least say that I have witnessed for the truth. These, indeed, are not stories about strange countries, or dreams, or contradictory statements; everything I relate, if I may so say, happened but yesterday, and the whole of New Spain can test these representations, and judge how far those are correct who have written on the same subject. I will relate that of which I myself was an eyewitness, facts which I know to be true, and will pay no attention to the contradictory statements of those who merely write from hearsay, for truth is a sacred thing. I will therefore say no more on this head, though I could, if I liked, say a good deal; and merely add, that there are good grounds for believing that when Gomara was writing his history, he had been deceived by false information: with him, every circumstance is made to turn to the glory and honour of Cortes, while no mention is made of the other brave officers and soldiers; but, the partiality of this author is sufficiently seen from the circumstance of his having dedicated his work to the present Marquis del Valle, son of Cortes, and not to his majesty the king. But, alas! these untruths and errors are not peculiar to Francisco Lopez de Gomara, but have also been the means of leading many other writers and historians who had followed his work into like error, as for instance, Doctor Illescas and Paulo Jovio, who have exactly copied Gomara's account, without adding or taking away a single word. For all their blunders they are indebted to Gomara.

Chapter 19

Hernando Cortes and the Secret Cabals

Immediately after the return of Juan de Grijalva from our last voyage of discovery, in the year 1518, Diego Velasquez issued orders for the fitting-out of a more considerable armament than the foregoing. For this purpose he had ten vessels lying in the harbour of Santiago de Cuba, at his disposal. Among these were the four vessels in which we had just returned with Grijalva, which had been immediately refitted and careened. The six others had been collected from the different ports of the island. The vessels were provided with sufficient provisions, consisting in *cassave*-bread, tobacco, and smoked bacon, to last us on our voyage to the Havannah, where they were to be fully equipped, for at that time there was neither beef nor mutton to be had in Cuba. In the meantime, however, Diego Velasquez could not make up his mind to whom he should entrust the command. Some cavaliers certainly mentioned Vasco Porcallo, a captain of great renown, and related to the Earl of Feria, who, it was said, would shortly arrive to take the command. This man, however, did not suit Diego Velasquez; he feared his daring spirit, and was apprehensive that once having the armament under his command he would declare himself independent of him. Others again spoke of Augustin Bermudez, Antonio Velasquez Borrego, and Bernardino Velasquez, who were all three relatives of Velasquez. We soldiers, however, would not hear of any other than Juan de Grijalva, who, besides being a brave officer, bore an unblemished character; a man moreover who fully understood the art of commanding. While such like rumours were afloat, the affair was secretly settled, by two confidants of Diego Velasquez, Andreas de Duero, secretary to the governor, and Almador de Lares, the royal treasurer, with Hernando Cortes. Cortes was a cavalier of rank, a native of Medellin, and son of Martin Cortes de Monroy, and of Catalina Pizarro Altamirano, both descendants of two ancient noble families of Estremadura, though then in rather straitened circumstances. Cortes had an Indian commendary in Cuba, and had been recently married to Doña Catalina Suarez Pacheco, daughter of the late Diego Suarez Pacheco of Avila, and of Maria de Mercaida of Biscay; and sister to Juan Suarez Pacheco, who, subsequent to the conquest of New Spain, took up his abode in Mexico, where he had a commendary. This marriage proved very expensive to Cortes, and had even occasioned his imprisonment. Diego Velasquez favoured the family of Cortes's wife, who had been averse to the match: but I must leave this for others to expatiate upon, and rather confine myself to the principal subject in this place, which is, to acquaint my reader that the above-mentioned confidants of Diego Velasquez did all in their power to obtain the appointment of commander-in-chief for Cortes; who, on the other hand, had promised to share equally with them all the profits arising from the gold, silver, and jewels, which pending this expedition should fall to his share, which might turn out very considerable, since the real design of Diego Velasquez, in fitting-out this expedition, was not to make settlements, but that a trade of barter should be carried on with the natives. Duero and the royal treasurer, therefore, employed all their cunning with the governor. They took every opportunity of placing Cortes in the most favourable light—extolling his great courage, in a word, declared him to be the most proper person whom he could entrust with the command. In him he might place implicit confidence, the more so since he himself had been present as a witness at Cortes's marriage, and given the bride away, and was thus spiritually related to him. Their endeavours were indeed crowned with success, by Diego Velasquez conferring the appointment of captain-general of the expedition on that gentleman. The secretary Duero did not fail on this occasion, as the saying is, to write out the commission with the best of ink, to word it agreeably to Cortes's wishes, and finish it in all haste. When the appointment became known to the public, some approved of it and others not.

On the Sunday following, as Diego Velasquez was on his way to church, accompanied by the principal personages in the town, as was due to him in his capacity of governor, it happened that he did Cortes the honour of placing him on his right side; on the road they were met by a jester, nick-named the fool Servantes: this fellow kept in front of the governor, cutting all manner of ridiculous figures and playing all sorts of pranks. "Well-a-day, friend Diego, (commenced this jack-pudding,) what manner of a captain-general have you appointed? He of Medellin and Estremadura! A captain who wants to try his fortune in no small way. I am afraid he will cut his sticks with your whole squadron; for he is a terrible fellow when he once begins, this you may read in his countenance." As he was chattering on in this strain for some time and growing more severe in his observations, Andreas de Duero, who was walking by the side of Cortes, hit him a good blow on the head, crying out at the same time, "begone you drunken fool! I am sure these scandalous pleasantries never emanated in your brain." The buffoon, however, took no notice of this, but commenced a-new. "Long live my friend Diego and the bold captain Cortes! Upon my life, master Diego, I must really go myself with Cortes to those rich countries, in order that you may not repent of the bargain you have made!" Nobody doubted for a moment that it was Velasquez, the governor's relative, who had feed the jester with a few *pesos* to utter these complaints, all emanating from a bad feeling. Everything this fool had predicted, however, took place to the very letter, and only proves that fools often speak the truth. It is nevertheless certain that the appointment of Hernando Cortes was pleasing in the eyes of God, a blessing to our holy religion, and of the first importance to his majesty, as will be clearly proved in the sequel.

Chapter 20

Cortes' Plans

After Hernando Cortes had thus been appointed captain, he immediately set about to collect all manner of arms and ammunition, consisting of matchlocks, crossbows, powder, and the like; in the same way he took care to provide a large stock of goods for barter, and other necessaries requisite for our expedition. He was now also most particular in adorning his outward person, more than ordinarily: he stuck a bunch of feathers in his cap, to which he fastened a golden medal, which gave him a very stately appearance. Notwithstanding all this he was at that time greatly pinched for money to purchase the things he required, being, in addition, head and ears in debt: for, though his commendary was a lucrative one, and his gold mines very productive, he required it all for his own person and the dress of his young wife. For the rest his countenance was most winning, his conversation agreeable, while he was beloved by every one. He had been twice *alcalde* of Santiago de Boroco, where he resided, which is esteemed a great honour in these parts. When, therefore, his friends among the merchants, Jaime Tria and a certain Pedro de Xeres, heard of his appointment, they lent him 4000 gold *pesos* and other merchandise, upon the income arising from his commendary. With this money he bought a state robe with golden trains, ensigns bearing the arms of our sovereign the king, on each side of which was the figure of a cross, beneath this a Latin inscription, the meaning of which was: "Brothers, let us in true faith follow the cross, and the victory is ours!" He then made known by sound of drum and trumpet, in the name of his majesty and Diego Velasquez the governor, that all those who felt inclined to accompany him to the conquest and colonization of the newly-discovered countries, should have a share in the gold, silver, and jewels they might gain;

also that, when any one settled himself there, he should be presented with an Indian commendary, the distribution of which his majesty had confided to Diego Velasquez.

Although this proclamation was made previous to the return of the chaplain Benito Martinez, whom Diego had despatched to Spain to procure for him such authority and other powers, yet it made a deep impression among the inhabitants of the island. Cortes, also, at the same time wrote to all his friends, inviting them to join the expedition. Many there were who sold all they were possessed of, to buy themselves arms and a horse; others purchased stores of *cassave*-bread and salted bacon to provision the ships, and otherwise equipped themselves as well as they could. Our numbers had increased to 300 soldiers when we left Santiago de Cuba: we were even joined by some of the principal personages of Diego Velasquez's household; among the number was Diego de Ordas, his steward. To this he had certainly been advised by his master, to see that nothing was done opposed to his interests, as he did not altogether trust Cortes. There was also Francisco de Morla, Escobar, Herredia, Juan Ruano, Pedro Escudero, and Martin Ramos de Pares of Biscay, with many other friends and acquaintances of Velasquez. Myself I speak of last. Though I have merely enumerated these warriors as they came to my memory; without wishing, however, to give one any preference above the other. I intend hereafter to give the names of them all in the proper place.

While Cortes was thus making every exertion to expedite the equipment of the vessels, the malice and envy of the relatives of Velasquez was not silent, who felt themselves most grievously neglected that the command should have been entrusted to Cortes. Velasquez had only shortly beforehand shown his hatred to Cortes on account of his marriage, and even persecuted him; they were therefore the more spiteful, and in every way strove to lower him in the eyes of the governor, hoping thereby to deprive him of the command. Cortes, who was fully acquainted with this, took care to be always at Velasquez's side. He took every opportunity of showing his attachment to him, and spoke of nothing but of the glory of this undertaking, and of the vast riches it could not fail, in a short time, to bring his patron Velasquez. Even Andreas de Duero urged Cortes by all means to hasten the embarkation, as the relatives of Velasquez had already succeeded in altering his sentiments with regard to Cortes. The latter therefore desired his wife to send him on board the provisions and other presents which women under such circumstances are accustomed to give their husbands. He made known to the masters and pilots of the different vessels the day and hour of departure, and ordered all the men to be on board by a certain day.

Everything being now ready for his departure, and all the men on board, Cortes called upon the governor to take leave of him, and was accompanied on this occasion by his best friends and companions in arms, Andreas de Duero, the royal treasurer, Almador de Lares, and the principal inhabitants of the town. Velasquez and Cortes vowed eternal friendship, and did not part until they had several times embraced each other.

The next morning early we attended mass, after which we marched to our vessels accompanied by the governor and a number of cavaliers in honourable escort.

The weather being very fine, we arrived, after a few days' sail, safely in the harbour of Trinidad, and landed there.

From what has already been said, and will further be seen in the following chapter, the reader may easily imagine the various difficulties Cortes had to struggle with; though, when my narrative is confronted with that of Gomara, it will be found how greatly they differ. Gomara, for instance, will have that Andreas de Duero was a merchant, though, as private secretary to the governor, he had considerable weight in the island; and of Diego de Ordas, he says, that he accompanied the expedition under Grijalva, though he never went out until this time with Cortes. But I will leave Gomara and his miserable history, and relate our doings in the town of Trinidad.

CHAPTER 21

Cortes' Occupies Trinidad

On the first notice of our arrival at Trinidad, the inhabitants came out to welcome us and our commander Cortes. Among the great body of cavaliers in this place, every one strove hardest to have Cortes for his guest. Cortes immediately planted his standard in front of his dwelling, and made the public acquainted with the particulars of the expedition in the same way as he had done at Santiago, and further collected whatever he could in the shape of firearms with other necessaries. Here we were also joined by the Alvarados, namely, Pedro, who has often been mentioned in this history, his brothers Gonzalo, Jorge, Gomez, and his natural brother the elder Juan Alvarado. Further we were here joined by Alonso de Avila of Avila, who had a command in the last expedition, under Grijalva; Juan de Escalante, Pedro Sanchez Farsan of Sevilla; Gonzalo Mexia, subsequently treasurer at Mexico; Vaena, Juanes de Fuentarabia, and Christobal de Oli, who had a command at the taking of Mexico, and in all the battles fought in New Spain. Further, Ortiz, the musician, and Gaspar Sanchez, nephew to the treasurer of Cuba; Diego de Pinedo, Alonzo Rodriguez, who possessed some lucrative gold mines, and Bartolome Garcia. To which may be added many other cavaliers whose names at present I cannot remember, all personages of influence and respectability. From this place Cortes also wrote letters to Santispiritus, fifty-four miles from Trinidad, and made our expedition known to the public there. He knew so well how to mix up his sentences with inviting expressions and great promises, that many of the first personages of that town were thereby induced to join us. These were Hernando Puertocarrero, cousin to the earl of Medellin, and Gonzalo de Sandoval, who had been eight months *alguacil*-major and governor, and was afterwards a commander in New Spain; also Juan Velasquez de Leon, a relation of

Diego Velasquez; Rodrigo Rangel, Gonzalo Lopez de Ximena, with his brother Juan Lopez, and Juan Sedeño. This latter gentleman was an inhabitant of Santispiritus, and had joined Cortes because of the two other Sedeños who were among us. These gentlemen, who were all men of consequence, had arrived at the same time in Trinidad, when Cortes, accompanied by the whole of us, went out to meet them. Cannons were fired, and other rejoicings took place on this occasion, while professions of esteem and friendship were past from one party to the other. All these men possessed land in the neighbourhood of this town, where they ordered *cassave*-bread to be made, and bacon to be cured, and otherwise collected all the provisions they possibly could for our vessels. Here also we hired soldiers, and purchased some horses, which latter, at that time, were very scarce, and only to be had at exorbitant prices. Alonso Hernandez de Puertocarrero, whom I had previously known, had not sufficient money to purchase himself a horse; Cortes, therefore, bought one for him, and paid for it with the golden borders of the velvet robe he had procured at Santiago. About this time there also arrived in the port of Trinidad a vessel belonging to a certain Juan Sedeño, of the Havannah, laden with *cassave*-bread and salted meat, which was destined for the mines of Santiago. This Sedeño, who had called upon our commander to pay his respects, was soon persuaded, by the eloquence and address of Cortes, to sell him his ship with the lading and all, and himself to join the expedition. We had now eleven ships in all, and everything, thanks to Providence, was going on well, when letters arrived from Diego Velasquez with peremptory orders that Cortes was to be deprived of the command. But I will detail this matter in the following chapter.

Chapter 22

Diego Velasquez and Cortes

I must now carry my narrative back a few days, in order to relate what happened at Santiago de Cuba after our departure. We had scarcely set sail when Diego Velasquez's friends left him not a moment's peace, harassing him until they had totally revolutionised his sentiments with regard to Cortes. They now plainly told him that he might consider Cortes as lost to his interests from his having so secretly sneaked away from the harbour. Neither had he made any secret of his determination to have the chief command of the armament, whether Diego might wish it or not; for which reason he had embarked his men at night-time, that if any attempt were made to deprive him of the squadron, he would resist it by main force. He, the governor, had been deceived by his private secretary Duero, and De Lares the royal treasurer, who had both made some previous agreement with Cortes to procure him the command. But in particular the relatives of Velasquez were constantly urging him to cancel the recent appointment of Cortes, in which they were backed by a certain old man, named Juan Millan, commonly termed the astrologer, who was considered by many not to be exactly in his proper senses. This old man repeatedly told the governor that Cortes would now revenge himself for his having, some time ago, thrown him into prison: *"Sly and artful as he is, he will be the means of ruining you, if you are not upon your guard."*

These hints were not thrown away upon Velasquez; they brought about a revolution in his mind, which ended in his despatching two trustworthy persons out of his establishment, with private instructions to his brother-in-law Francisco de Verdugo, then *alcalde* major of Trinidad, by which he was peremptorily commanded, under all circumstances, to deprive Cortes of the squadron, whose appointment of captain had been withdrawn, and given to Vasco Porcallo. At the same time he wrote letters to Diego de Ordas, Francisco de Morla, and to his relations and friends, desiring them, at all events, to leave the squadron.

As soon as Cortes got information of this, he had a secret interview with Ordas and all those officers and inhabitants of Trinidad, who, he thought, might feel inclined to obey the orders of Velasquez. To these he spoke so feelingly, and in such kind terms, accompanied by such great promises, that they were all soon gained over to his side. Diego de Ordas even undertook to advise the *alcalde* major Francisco de Verdugo not to put these commands immediately into execution, and to keep them secret; telling him, at the same time, he had seen nothing in Cortes which gave the slightest reasons for suspecting him of anything wrong; on the contrary, he had, on every occasion, given proofs of his adherence to the governor. He assured him, moreover, that it would be an impossibility to deprive Cortes of the command of the squadron, in which he had so many friends among the cavaliers, and Diego Velasquez so many enemies, who would not easily forgive him that he had neglected to bestow on them more profitable commendaries. Besides the number of friends Cortes had among the officers, he could rely upon most of the soldiers, and thus it would be useless to attempt anything against him. The whole town would become mixed up in the quarrel, which would be plundered by our men, and even worse consequences might follow. By these arguments, Ordas prevented all violent measures; and one of the above-mentioned officials, whom Diego had sent with despatches to his nephew, named Pedro Laso, even joined our expedition. The other, Cortes sent back with a letter to the governor, in which he made use of every kind sentiment, and expressed his utter astonishment at the resolution he had taken, particularly as he had no other design than to serve God, his majesty the king, and the governor. He earnestly advised him not to listen any further to his cousin Velasquez, nor to allow the kind feeling he entertained for him to be poisoned by such an old fool as Juan Millan. Cortes, at the same time, wrote to his other friends, and in particular to his two confederates, the private secretary and royal treasurer.

The next step he took was to command his men to put their arms into good repair. Every smith in the town was set to work to fix points to our lances, and the gunners were ordered to search every magazine for arrows. He at last even persuaded the very smiths to join the armament.

We remained altogether twelve days at Trinidad, and thence sailed for the Havannah. From the foregoing statement, the reader will readily perceive how differently all this has been related by Gomara, who even makes Velasquez confer the chief command on Ordas; the latter, he says, invited Cortes to dine with him on board his vessel, had him seized while at dinner, and taken off prisoner to Santiago. I could cite many similar errors from Gomara's history, and thereby convince the reader that it is better to believe an eyewitness than an author who writes about things he never saw. However, enough of Gomara; let us return to our subject.

Chapter 23

Cortes embarks for Havannah

Cortes, finding that he had nothing further to do at Trinidad, acquainted his officers and men with the hour of departure, leaving it to each one's choice either to proceed to the Havannah by sea, or march thither overland, under the command of Pedro de Alvarado, who would be joined by some men from one of the colonies, on his road. Alvarado was a kind-hearted man, who knew best how to deal with soldiers; wherefore I myself, with fifty other military men, gladly joined him; our numbers were, moreover, increased by all our horse. Cortes also sent a vessel, under the command of Juan de Escalante, which was to shape its course around the north coast to the Havannah. Cortes then embarked, and proceeded, with the whole squadron, for the same port. The transport ships must, however, have missed the vessel of our commander-in-chief in the night, as they all arrived safe at the Havannah without it. The troops under Pedro de Alvarado also arrived in good time, and the vessel under the command of Escalante, which had sailed around the north coast.

Cortes alone remained behind; nor could any one account for his delay, or what could possibly have detained him. Five days passed away without our obtaining the least tidings of him, and we already began to fear that he had been shipwrecked off the Jardines,[1] which lie from thirty to thirty-six miles from the Havannah, near the Pinos isles, where the sea is very shallow: we therefore determined to send out our three smaller vessels in quest of her; but what with the fitting-out of these vessels, added to the manifold opinions and advices, two more days elapsed, and Cortes still remained behind. All manner of artifices were now had recourse to, as to whom the com-

1. Jardines, or the Caribbee islands, lying along the south coast of Cuba, better known as the Windward and Leeward islands.

mand should be given, until some certainty was gained respecting the fate of Cortes, in which Diego de Ordas, in his capacity of steward over the household of Velasquez, and secret observer of our movements, was most active.

The following misfortune had befallen Cortes. When his vessel, which was of considerable tonnage, had arrived off the Pinos isles on the shallows of the Jardines, there was not sufficient depth of water to carry her, and she consequently got aground. The ship had now to be unladen, which was an easy matter, on account of the nearness of the shore. As soon as she was set afloat again and brought into deeper water she was reloaded and pursued her voyage to the Havannah. The joy among the officers and soldiers was very great as soon as she became visible in the horizon, to those excepted who had prized themselves with the command, to whose machinations, however, there was now an end. We accompanied Cortes to the house of Pedro Barba, Velasquez's lieutenant at Trinidad, where quarters had been got ready for his reception. He immediately hoisted his standard in front of his dwelling, and by public proclamation invited the inhabitants to join the expedition.

It was here that Francisco de Montejo first joined us, of whom I shall often have to speak in the course of this history: subsequent to the conquest of Mexico he became *adelantado* and governor of Yucatan and the Honduras. Here we were also joined by Diego de Soto of Toro, namely, who afterwards was Cortes's steward in Mexico; further, Angula and Garci Caro, Sebastian Rodriguez, Pacheco, Gutierras, Royas (this is not he commonly called the wealthy); also by a young fellow of the name of Santaclara; the two brothers, Martinez del Frexenal and Juan de Najara—not the deaf one of the tennis-court at Mexico: all of whom were men of rank and quality. There were also other soldiers who joined us, whose names I have forgotten.

When Cortes, therefore, beheld all these cavaliers together, his heart leaped with joy, and he sent off another ship for a further supply of provisions to the promontory of Guaniguanico, where Velasquez had landed property. Here was a village where *cassave*-bread was made, and quantities of swine's flesh cured. He gave the command of this vessel to Diego de Ordas, who, as Velasquez's steward, ordered matters on his master's property as he liked. Cortes wished to keep him out of the way, having learnt that Ordas had not spoken in very favourable terms of him during the dispute as to whom the command should be given, when he was detained off the Pinos isles.

Ordas's instructions were to remain in the harbour of Guaniguanico, after he had taken in his lading, until the arrival there of the vessel which was to sail around the north coast, with which he was then to proceed to the island of Cozumel, provided he received no further instructions by Indian canoes.

Francisco de Montejo and other cavaliers of the Havannah likewise furnished quantities of *cassave*-bread and cured bacon; there being no other kind of provisions to be had. In the meantime Cortes ordered all our heavy guns, consisting in ten copper cannons and a few falconets, to be brought on shore and given in charge of an artilleryman, named Mesa, a certain Arbenga who traded to the Levant, and Juan Catalan, to prove them, and otherwise put them into good repair; also to furnish for each the right-sized balls and proper quantity of powder. He also gave them an assistant, named Bartolome de Usagre, and furnished them with vinegar and wine to polish the copper pieces. In the same way all our crossbows were inspected, and their strength ascertained by shooting at the target. Cotton being very plentiful here we constructed ourselves cuirasses with it, which form the most efficient protection against Indian arrows, pikes, and slings. Here it was also that Cortes put his establishment on a much superior footing, and had himself served as a person of the first quality. He took for his butler a certain Guzman, who was subsequently killed by the Indians; he must not, however, be confounded with Christobal de Guzman, who afterwards became his steward, and was the man whom took the king Quauhtemoctzin prisoner, during the battle in the suburbs of Mexico. Rodrigo Rangel he appointed his chamberlain, and Juan de Caceres his house-steward, who after the conquest of Mexico was considered a man of great wealth. Having ordered all these things, he commanded us to hold ourselves in readiness for embarking, and to distribute the horses among the vessels, for which the necessary quantity of maize and hay had been provided.

For memory's sake I will here likewise describe the horses and mares which we took with us on our expedition. Cortes had a dark chestnut stallion, which died afterwards at St. Juan de Ulua. Pedro de Alvarado and Hernando Lopez d'Avila had jointly an excellent brown mare, which had been broken-in for the field of battle as well as for tournaments. After our arrival in New Spain, Alvarado bought Lopez's share, or perhaps took forcible possession of it. Alonso Hernandez Puertocarrero had a grey-coloured mare, which Cortes had purchased for him with the golden borders of his state-robe, it was capitally trained for the field of battle. Juan Velasquez de Leon's mare was of the same colour, a noble and powerful animal, full of fire and eager for battle: we commonly termed it the "short tail."

Christobal de Oli had a dark brown fine-spirited horse. Francisco de Montejo and Alonso de Avila had between them a sorrel-coloured horse, but of little use in battle. Francisco de Morla had likewise a dark chestnut stallion, one full of fire and wonderfully swift. The light-coloured horse of Juan de Escalante was not worth much. The grey-coloured mare of Diego de Ordas, which would never foal, was neither very swift. Gonzalo Dominiguez had a small dark-brown nag, a very swift and noble animal. Also the brown-coloured horse of Pedro Gonzalez de Truxillo was a swift animal. Moron, who was a native of Vaimo, had a small horse which was pretty well trained. Vaena, of Trinidad, had a darkish-coloured horse, though a bad leaper. The light-coloured chestnut Galloway of De Lares was, on the other hand, a splendid animal and a capital runner.

Ortiz, the musician, and a certain Bartolome Garcia, who had applied himself to the art of mining, had between them a very good dark-coloured horse, which they named the *arriero* (mule-driver,) and was one of the best animals of the whole corps. Juan Sedeño, of the Havannah, had a fine chestnut mare, which foaled on board. This Sedeño was considered to be the most wealthy man amongst us; for he had a ship of his own, a horse, a few negroes to attend upon him, and his own lading of *cassave* and cured bacon. Just about this time horses and negroes were only to be purchased for very high prices, which accounts for the small number of the former we had with us on this expedition.

However, I will stop here, and relate in the next chapter what happened as we were just about to embark.

CHAPTER 24

Diego Velasquez Seeks to Take Cortes Prisoner

In order that my history may be perfectly intelligible to my readers, I must sometimes recur to prior events. In this place I have to return to Diego Velasquez, who, when he learnt that his brother-in-law, Francisco Verdugo, sub-governor of Trinidad, had not only confirmed Cortes in his appointment over the squadron, but even, conjointly with Diego de Ordas, lent him every possible assistance, fell into such a rage that he roared like a wild beast. He accused his private secretary Andreas de Duero, and the royal treasurer Almador de Lares, of a conspiracy to cheat him, adding, that Cortes had run off with the whole squadron. Nor did Velasquez stop here, but despatched one of his officials with imperative commands to Pedro Barba, sub-governor of the Havannah, at the same time writing to all his relatives in that town, to De Ordas and to Juan Velasquez de Leon, who were his special confidants, requiring them to swear, by the friendship they bore him, not, under any pretence whatsoever, to allow the squadron to depart, but to send Cortes prisoner to Santiago. As soon as Garnica, the bearer of these despatches, arrived, it was immediately guessed for what purpose he came. Cortes was even apprized of it by means of the very bearer himself: for one of the brethren of Charity, who was much in company with Velasquez, and greatly in favour with him, had forwarded by this same Garnica a letter to a brother of the same order, named Bartolome de Olmedo, who had joined our expedition. By means of this letter, Cortes was apprized of the whole posture of affairs by those interested with him, Andreas de Duero and the royal treasurer. Ordas, as we have above seen, having been sent off in quest of provisions, Cortes had now only to fear opposition from Juan Velasquez de Leon; but even him he had half gained over to his side, not being on the best of terms with his relative the governor, who had only presented him with a very poor commendary. Thus it was that the design of Velasquez was frustrated by those very persons to whom he had written. Indeed, from that very moment, these personages only united themselves the closer to Cortes, particularly the sub-governor Pedro Barba, the Alvarados, Puertocarrero, Montejo, Christobal de Oli, Juan de Escalante, Andreas de Monjaraz, and his brother Gregorio, who, with all of us, were ready to stake our lives for Cortes. Had the orders of Velasquez been kept secret in Trinidad, they were now the more so in this place; and Pedro de Barba despatched Garnica to Diego Velasquez with the information that he durst not venture to take Cortes into custody, as he was too powerful and too much beloved by the soldiers; fearing, if he should make the attempt, that the town would be plundered, and the whole of the inhabitants forcibly dragged away. For the rest, he could assure Diego Velasquez that Cortes was quite devoted to him, and did nothing that could be said to militate against his interests. Cortes himself also wrote a letter couched in those smooth terms he so very well knew how to employ, assuring Velasquez of the unabated friendship he entertained for him, and that he was going to set sail the very next day.

Chapter 25

Cortes Sets Sail for Cozumel

Cortes deferred the review of his troops until we should have arrived at the island of Cozumel, and gave orders for the embarking of our horses. Pedro de Alvarado, in the San Sebastian, which was a very fast sailer, was ordered to shape his course along the north coast, and his pilot received strict orders to steer direct for the cape of St. Antonio, where all the other vessels would meet and set sail for Cozumel: like instructions were forwarded to Diego de Ordas. Mass having been said, the nine remaining vessels set sail, in a southerly direction, on the 10th of February, 1519. There were sixty soldiers on board the San Sebastian, under Alvarado, among which number I was myself. Camacho, our pilot, took no notice of the orders he had received from Cortes, but shaped his course direct for Cozumel, so that we arrived two days earlier there than the rest. We landed our men in the same harbour I before mentioned in our expedition under Grijalva. Cortes had been detained on his passage by the breaking of the rudder of Francisco de Morla's vessel, which had to be replaced from what they had at hand.

Our vessel, as I have stated above, arrived two days earlier at Cozumel than the rest, and the whole of the men proceeded on shore. We did not meet with a single Indian in the village of Cozumel, as all the inhabitants had fled away. Alvarado, therefore, ordered us to another village at about four miles distance from the latter. Here the inhabitants had likewise fled to the woods, without, however, being able to carry off all their property, so that we found numbers of fowls and other things; of the former, Alvarado would not permit us to take more than forty. Out of a temple near at hand we took several cotton mats, and a few small boxes containing a species of diadem, small idols, corals, with all manner of trinkets made of an inferior sort of gold. We also took two Indians and a female prisoners, after which we returned to the village near which we had landed.

In the meantime Cortes had arrived with the remaining vessels. He had scarcely stepped on shore when he ordered our pilot Camacho to be put in irons, for having followed a contrary course to what he had been ordered. But his displeasure was still greater when he learnt that the village was quite deserted, and that Alvarado had taken away, besides the fowls, the religious implements and other matters, though of little value, being half copper. Having shown no lenity to Camacho, he now also gave Alvarado an earnest reproof, telling him that it was not the way to gain the love of the inhabitants by beginning to rob them of their property. He then ordered the two Indians and the female whom we had taken prisoners to be brought into his presence, and put several questions to them. Melchorillo, whom we had captured at the promontory of Cotoche, (Julianillo had since died,) and taken with us, perfectly understood the language of this country, and interpreted on the occasion. Cortes sent the three Indians to the *cazique* and the inhabitants, desiring them to state that they had nothing to fear from us, and to return to their village. He also restored to them the religious implements, with the golden trinkets, and gave them glass beads in exchange for the fowls, which we had eaten: besides this, he presented each of them with a Spanish shirt. They faithfully executed Cortes's commission; for the very next day the *cazique* returned with the whole of the inhabitants, and so confidently did they converse with us as if they had known us all their lives: indeed, Cortes had given peremptory orders that they should in no wise be molested. It was here also that Cortes began strict discipline, and set to work with unremitting assiduity, to which Providence lent his blessing; for everything in which he concerned himself went well, particularly with regard to making peace with the tribes or inhabitants of these countries. This the reader will find fully confirmed in the course of my history.

CHAPTER 26

Cortes Reviews His Troops

On the third day after our arrival at Cozumel, Cortes reviewed the whole of his troops. Without counting the pilots and marines, our number amounted to 508 men. There were 109 sailors, and sixteen horses, which were trained equally for tournaments or for war. Our squadron consisted of eleven vessels of different tonnage; among these, one was a kind of brigantine, the property of a certain Gines Nortes. The number of crossbow men was thirty-three, and of musketeers thirteen: add to this our heavy guns and four falconets, a great quantity of powder and balls. As to the precise number of crossbow men I cannot exactly swear, though it matters not whether there were a few more or less.

After this review, Cortes ordered the artillerymen Mesa, Bartolome de Usagre, Arbenga, and a certain Catalonier whose name I forget, to keep all our firearms bright and in good order, to see that each cannon had its right-sized ball, to prepare the cartridges, and distribute the powder properly. The chief care of our gun department he confided to a certain Francisco de Oroze, who had proved himself a brave soldier in the Italian wars. Juan Benitez and Pedro de Guzman had to inspect the crossbows, and see that they were supplied with two or three nuts and as many cords. They had also to superintend the exercise of shooting at the target, and the breaking-in of our horses, particularly to accustom them to the noise of our firearms. I have now said sufficient of our armament: indeed, Cortes was most particular with the merest trifles in these matters.

Chapter 27
Spanish Prisoners

As Cortes paid attention to every circumstance, he ordered myself and Martin Camos of Biscay into his presence, and asked us what our opinion was of the word *castilan, castilan,* which the Indians of Campeachy had so often repeated when we landed there, under the command of Hernandez de Cordoba.

We again informed him of every circumstance that had there taken place. He said, he had often turned this matter over in his mind, and could not help thinking but that the inhabitants must have some Spaniards among them, and he thought it would not be amiss to question the *caziques* of Cozumel upon this head. This Cortes accordingly did, and desired Melchorejo, who by this time had gained some little knowledge of the Spanish, and perfectly understood the language of Cozumel, to question the chiefs about it. Their several accounts perfectly corresponded; and they satisfactorily proved that there were several Spaniards in the country, whom they had seen themselves; that they served the *caziques,* who lived two days' march inland, as slaves, and that it was only a few days ago some Indian merchants had spoken with them.

We all felt overjoyed at this news. Cortes told these chiefs that he would send the Spaniards letters, which they call *amales* in their language, in which he would desire them to come to us. The *cazique* and other Indians who undertook to forward these letters were most kindly treated by Cortes, who gave them all kinds of presents, and promised them more on their return. Upon which the *cazique* remarked to Cortes, that it would be necessary to send a ransom to the chiefs whom the Spaniards served as slaves before they would let them go. Various kinds of glass beads were therefore given to the messengers for this purpose, and Cortes sent two of the smaller vessels, armed with twenty crossbow men and a few musketeers, under command of Diego de Ordas, to the coast of Cotoche, with orders to remain there for eight successive days with the larger of the two vessels, and to send him information from time to time by the other vessel, while the messengers brought letters to and fro; for the distance to the promontory of Cotoche from this place was only nine miles, the whole appearing, moreover, to form but one country. The following were the contents of the letter which Cortes wrote to the Spaniards:

> *Dear Sirs and Brothers,*
> Here, on the island of Cozumel, I received information that you are detained prisoners by a *cazique*. I beg of you to come here to me on the island of Cozumel. To this end I have sent out an armed ship, and ransom-money, should it be required by the Indians. I have ordered the vessel to remain stationary off the promontory of Cotoche for eight days, to wait for you. Come as speedily as possible; you may depend upon being honourably treated by me. I am here with eleven vessels armed with 500 soldiers, and intend, with the aid of the Almighty and your assistance, to proceed to a place called Tabasco, or Potonchon; etc.

With this letter the two Indian merchants embarked on board our vessel, which passed this narrow gulf in three hours, when the messengers with the ransom-money were put on shore.

After the lapse of a couple of days they actually handed over the letter to one of the Spaniards in question, who, as we afterwards learnt, was called Geronimo de Aguilar, and I shall therefore in future distinguish him by that name. When he had read the letter and received the ransom-money we had forwarded, he was exceedingly rejoiced, and took the latter to the *cazique* his master to beg for his liberation. The moment he had obtained this he went in quest of his comrade, Gonzalo Guerrero, and made him acquainted with all the circumstances; when Guerrero made the following reply:

> *Brother Aguilar,*
> I have united myself here to one of the females of this country, by whom I have three children; and am, during wartime, as good as *cazique* or chief. Go! and may God be with you: for myself, I could not appear again among my countrymen. My face has already been disfigured, according to the Indian custom, and my ears have been pierced: what would my country-

men say if they saw me in this attire? Only look at my three children, what lovely little creatures they are; pray give me some of your glass beads for them, which I shall say my brethren sent them from my country.

Gonzalo's Indian wife followed in the same strain, and was quite displeased with Aguilar's errand. "Only look at that slave there, (said she,) he is come here to take away my husband from me! Mind your own affairs, and do not trouble yourself about us."

Aguilar, however, afterwards made another attempt to induce Gonzalo to leave, telling him to consider that he was a Christian, and that he ought not to risk the salvation of his soul for the sake of an Indian woman. Moreover, he might take her and the children with him if he could not make up his mind to separate himself from them. Aguilar, however, might say what he liked, it was all to no purpose; he could not persuade Gonzalo to accompany his heretofore companion in good and ill fortune. This Guerrero was most probably a sailor, and a native of Palos.[1] He remained among the Indians, while Geronimo de Aguilar alone took his departure with the Indian messengers, and marched towards the coast where our ship was to have waited for them: but she had left; for De Ordas, after staying there the eight days, and another in addition, finding that no one appeared, again set sail for Cozumel. Aguilar was quite downcast when he found the ship was gone, and he again returned to his Indian master.

Ordas, however, did not meet with the best of reception when he returned without the ransom-money or any information respecting the Spaniards, and even without the Indian messengers. Cortes said to him, with great vehemence, he expected he would have fulfilled his commission better than to return without the Spaniards, and even without bringing him any information respecting them, although well aware they were staying in that country. Cortes had, moreover, just that moment been greatly put out by another circumstance. A soldier, called Berrio, had accused some sailors of Gibraleon of having stolen from him a couple of sides of bacon, which they would not return. They positively denied that they had committed the robbery, and even took an oath to that effect; however, after a good search, the bacon was found among their clothes. There were seven

1. Palos, a small town of Spain, lying on the River Tinto. This port produced the best Spanish sailors during the early voyages of discovery, and here also the expedition under Columbus was fitted out.

sailors who had been concerned in the robbery, and Cortes, notwithstanding their officers interceded in their behalf, ordered them to be severely whipped.

The island of Cozumel, it seems, was a place to which the Indians made pilgrimages; for the neighbouring tribes of the promontory of Cotoche and other districts of Yucatan, came thither in great numbers to sacrifice to some abominable idols, which stood in a temple there. One morning we perceived that the place where these horrible images stood was crowded with Indians and their wives. They burnt a species of resin, which very much resembled our incense, and as such a sight was so novel to us we paid particular attention to all that went forward. Upon this an old man, who had on a wide cloak and was a priest, mounted to the very top of the temple, and began preaching something to the Indians. We were all very curious to know what the purport of this sermon was, and Cortes desired Melchorejo to interpret it to him. Finding that all he had been saying tended to ungodliness, Cortes ordered the *caziques*, with the principal men among them and the priest, into his presence, giving them to understand, as well as he could by means of our interpreter, that if they were desirous of becoming our brethren they must give up sacrificing to these idols, which were no gods but evil beings, by which they were led into error and their souls sent to hell. He then presented them with the image of the Virgin Mary and a cross, which he desired them to put up instead. These would prove a blessing to them at all times, make their seeds grow and preserve their souls from eternal perdition. This and many other things respecting our holy religion, Cortes explained to them in a very excellent manner. The *caziques* and priests answered, that their forefathers had prayed to their idols before them, because they were good gods, and that they were determined to follow their example. Adding, that we should experience what power they possessed; as soon as we had left them, we should certainly all of us go to the bottom of the sea.

Cortes, however, took very little heed of their threats, but commanded the idols to be pulled down, and broken to pieces; which was accordingly done without any further ceremony. He then ordered a quantity of lime to be collected, which is here in abundance, and with the assistance of the Indian masons a very pretty altar was constructed, on which we placed the image of the holy Virgin. At the same time two of our carpenters, Alonso Yañez and Alvaro Lopez made a cross of new wood which lay at hand, this was set up in a kind of chapel, which we built behind the altar. After all this was completed, father Juan Diaz said mass in front of the new altar, the *caziques* and priests looking on with the greatest attention.

Before I close this chapter, I have to remark that the *caziques* on the island of Cozumel, like those on the land of Potonchan, are likewise termed *calachionies*.

Chapter 28
Cortes Divides the Squadron

The following were the officers which commanded the several vessels. Cortes himself commanded, in the principal vessel, over the whole squadron. To the San Sebastian, which was a very capital sailer, he appointed Alvarado and his brother. The other vessels were severally commanded by Alonso Hernandez Puertocarrero, Francisco de Montejo, Christobal de Oli, Diego de Ordas, Juan Velasquez de Leon, Juan de Escalante, Francisco de Morla, and Escobar the page. The smallest vessel, a kind of brigantine, was commanded by its owner, Gines Nortes.

Every vessel had its own pilot, who received his instructions, and also the signals with the lanterns from Alaminos.

As soon as Cortes had ordered these matters he took leave of the *caziques* and priests, commended them most emphatically to the image of the holy Virgin and to the cross, desiring them to pray before it, not to damage either but continually to decorate them with green boughs. He assured them that thereby they would derive great benefit. They promised to comply with all his wishes, presented him with four more fowls and two jars of honey, and then took leave of us under the most friendly embraces. It was some day in the month of March, in the year 1519, when we again set sail; we were pursuing our course with the most favourable of winds, when on the very first day at ten o'clock in the morning, signals of distress were made on board one of our vessels, both by flags and the firing of guns. As soon as Cortes saw and heard this, he looked over the poop of his vessel, and found that the ship commanded by Juan de Escalante was making straight again for the island of Cozumel. What is the matter there? What does all this mean? cried out Cortes to the vessel nearest him. A soldier, named Zaragoza replied, that the vessel of Juan de Escalante, laden with *cassave*-bread, was sinking fast. God forbid! cried Cortes, that any misfortune should befall us here, and desired our chief pilot, Alaminos, to make signals for all the vessels to return to the island Cozumel. So we again put into the harbour we had just left: we unloaded the *cassave*-bread; and found, to our great joy, that the image of the holy Virgin and cross were in the best condition, and that incense had been placed before them. It was not long before the *caziques* and priests again made their appearance, and asked what had caused us to return so speedily. Cortes told them that one of our vessels was leaky and had to be repaired, begging of them to assist us with their canoes in unloading our *cassave*-bread. This they most readily complied with, and it took us four more days to repair the vessel.

Chapter 29

Geronimo de Aguilar

When the Spaniard, who was in the power of the Indians got certain information that we had again returned to the island Cozumel, he rejoiced exceedingly and thanked God with all his heart.

He immediately hired a canoe, with six capital rowers, for himself and the Indians who had brought him the glass beads. The former being richly remunerated with these, so valuable in their estimation: they performed their work so well, that the channel between the island and mainland, a distance of about twelve miles, was soon crossed. After they had arrived off the island and stepped on shore, some soldiers who were returning from the chase of musk swine, informed Cortes that a large canoe had just arrived from the promontory of Cotoche. Cortes immediately despatched Andreas de Tapia with a few men to learn what news they had brought. As Tapia with his men approached the shore, the Indians, who had arrived with Geronimo, evinced great fear and ran back to their canoe in order to put off to sea again. Aguilar, however, told him in their language they need have no fear; for we were their brothers. Andreas de Tapia, who took Aguilar also for an Indian, for he had every appearance of one, sent to inform Cortes that the seven Indians who had arrived were inhabitants of Cozumel. It was not until they had come up to them and heard the Spaniard pronounce the words—God, holy Virgin, Sevilla, in broken Spanish, and ran up to Tapia to embrace him, that they recognized this strange-looking fellow. One of Tapia's men immediately ran off to inform Cortes that a Spaniard had arrived in the canoe, for which news he expected a handsome reward.

We all greatly rejoiced at this information, and it was not long before Tapia himself arrived with the strange-looking Spaniard. As they passed by us many of our men still kept inquiring of Tapia which among them was the Spaniard? although he was walking at his very side, so much did his countenance resemble that of an Indian. His complexion was naturally of a brownish cast, added to which his hair had been shorn like that of an Indian slave: he carried a paddle across his shoulder, had one of his legs covered with an old tattered stocking; the other, which was not much better, being tied around his waist. An old ragged cloak hung over his shoulders, his *maltatas* was in a much worse condition. His prayer book, which was very much torn, he had folded in the corner of his cloak.

When Cortes beheld the man in this attire, he, as all the rest of us had done, asked Tapia where the Spaniard was? When Geronimo heard this, he cowered down after the Indian fashion, and said: "I am he." Upon this Cortes gave him a shirt, a coat, a pair of trousers, a cap and shoes, from our stores. He then desired him to give us an account of the adventures of his life, and explain how he had got into this country.

He said, though still in broken Spanish, that his name was Geronimo d'Aguilar, and was a native of Ecija. About eight years ago he had been shipwrecked with fifteen men and two women, on a voyage between Darien and the island of St. Domingo, which they had undertaken on account of a lawsuit between a certain Enciso and a certain Valdivia. They had 10,000 *pesos* on board, and papers relating to the lawsuit. The ship struck against a rock, and they had not been able to get her off again. The whole of the crew then got into the boat, in the hopes of making the island of Cuba or Jamaica, but were driven on shore by the strong currents, where the *calachionies* had taken them prisoners and distributed them among themselves. The most of his unfortunate companions had been sacrificed to their gods, and some had died of grief, of which also both the women pined away; being soon worn out by the hard labour of grinding, to which they had been forced by the Indians. He himself had also been doomed as a sacrifice to their idols, but made his escape during the night, and fled to the *cazique*, with whom he had last been staying, whose name, however, I cannot now remember. Of all his companions, he himself and a certain Gonzalo Guerrero, were only living. He had tried his best to induce him to leave, but in vain.

When Cortes heard this, he returned thanks to the Almighty, and told the Spaniard that he hoped, with the blessing of God, he would never find reason to regret the determination he had taken. He then put some questions to him about the country and its inhabitants. Aguilar said he was not able to give him much information about either, as he had been treated like a slave, having been merely employed to fetch wood, water, and to work in the maize-plantations. It was only upon one occasion he was sent on some business to a distance of about twelve miles from his village, but, owing to a heavy burden he had to carry and the weak state of his body, he had not even been able to reach that distance; for the rest, he had been given to understand that the country was very thickly populated. With regard to his companion Alonso Guerrero, he had married an Indian woman, and was become the father of three children. He had in every respect adopted the Indian customs,—his cheeks were tattooed, his ears pierced, and his lips turned down. He was a sailor by profession, native of Palos, and was considered by the Indians to be a man of great strength. It might have been about a year ago that a squadron, consisting of three vessels, had touched at the promontory of Cotoche, (probably the expedition under Hernandez de Cordoba,) when Guerrero advised the inhabitants to commence hostilities, who, in common with the *caziques* of a large district, commanded on that occasion. Cortes here remarked, that he very much wished to get the man into his power, for his staying among the Indians would do us no good.

The *caziques* of Cozumel showed Aguilar every possible friendship when they heard him speak in their language. Aguilar advised them always to do honour to the image of the holy Virgin and cross we had set up, as they would prove a blessing to them. It was also upon his advice they begged of Cortes to give them letters of recommendation to other Spaniards who might run into this harbour, in order that they might not be molested by them. Cortes readily complied with this request; and, after mutual protestations of friendship had passed between us, we weighed anchor, and set sail for the River Grijalva.

For the rest, I can assure the reader that what I have related of Aguilar is all the man told us himself, although the historian Gomara gives a very different account; which, however, should not excite our surprise, as he merely thereby intended to divert his readers with some strange story.

CHAPTER 30

We Sail for the River Grijalva

On the 4th of March, 1519, the day after we had had the good fortune to obtain such an excellent and trustworthy interpreter, Cortes gave orders for re-embarking. This took place in the same way as before, and similar instructions were issued with regard to the night signals with the lanterns. For some time we had the most favourable weather imaginable; when, towards evening, it suddenly changed, the wind blowing most violently against us, so that all our vessels were in danger of being cast on shore. Towards midnight, it pleased God the wind should abate, and, when daylight broke forth, our vessels again joined each other; one only was missing, that namely of Velasquez de Leon, which occasioned a good deal of anxiety, for we concluded she had been wrecked off some of the shallows. We did not discover her loss until midday; and as night was now fast approaching, and the vessel still nowhere to be seen, Cortes told our principal pilot Alaminos that we ought not to continue our course without gaining some certain knowledge as to her fate: signals were, therefore, made for all the vessels to drop anchor, to give the missing ship time to come up with us, on the supposition it had been driven into some harbour and there retained by contrary winds. Alaminos, still finding she did not make her appearance, said to Cortes:

"You may be sure, sir, that she has run into some harbour or inlet along this coast, where she is now wind-bound; for her pilot Manquillo has twice before visited these seas, once with Hernandez de Cordoba, the second time under Grijalva, and is acquainted with this bay."

Upon this it was resolved that the whole squadron should return to the bay which Alaminos was speaking of, in search of the vessel: to our great joy we indeed found her riding there at anchor, and we all remained here for one day. During this time, Alaminos, with one of our principal officers named Francisco de Lugo, went on shore in two boats; they found the country inhabited, and saw several regular maize-plantations: they likewise met with places where salt was manufactured, and saw four cues, or large temples, with numerous figures, mostly in the shape of women, and of considerable height; whence this promontory was called la Punta de las Mujeres, (the promontory of women.) Aguilar observed that this was the spot where he was once a slave among the Indians; here his master had found him sunk beneath the weight of the heavy burden which he had forced him to carry: neither was the township far off where Alonso Guerrero had settled himself. Every inhabitant possessed gold, but in small quantities; he would show us the way, if we were desirous of going there. To which Cortes said, laughingly, he had not gone out for the sake of such trifles, but to serve God and his king. In the meantime he despatched Escobar, one of our commanders, with a fast-sailing vessel of small tonnage, to the Terminos bay, there to examine the country and search for a secure spot to found a colony; also to inform us whether game really was so abundant there as had been represented. All this was done according to the advice of our chief pilot, to save the trouble of running in there with the whole fleet on our passing by. Escobar, when he had explored the harbour, was merely to leave some sign on both sides of the entrance, either by felling trees or by leaving something in writing, from which we should know that he had entered safely, or that, having fully explored the harbour, he was tacking about until we fell in with him again.

With these instructions Escobar set sail, and ran into Terminos bay, where he executed the commands he had received: he likewise found the greyhound which had run away from us when we landed there with Grijalva. It was quite glossy and fat, and immediately knew the ship again as it entered the bay, wagging its tail, and jumping up against our men as it followed them on board. Escobar now quitted the bay, and intended laying-to until the rest of our vessels should come up, but was driven a considerable way out to sea by a strong south wind. We must now return to our squadron, which we left at the Punta de las Mujeres. Having left this spot next morning with a stiffish breeze blowing from the land, we arrived at the entrance of Terminos bay, without, however, seeing anything of Escobar. Cortes ordered a boat to be lowered, armed with ten crossbow-men, to run into the bay, or search whether Escobar had left any sign or written paper as desired. Some trees were found cut down, and near them a small paper, on which was written, that both the bay and country round about were charming, that the spot abounded with game, and that they had found the dog. Our principal pilot here remarked to Cortes that it would be most advisable for us to continue our course, for the south wind had no doubt obliged Escobar to hold out to sea, though he could not be far off, as he must have sailed in a slanting direction. Cortes, however, still apprehended some accident must have befallen him: nevertheless, he ordered the sails to be set, and we very soon came up with Escobar, who related all he had seen, and explained what had prevented him from waiting for us. In this way we arrived in the waters off Potonchan, and Cortes ordered Alaminos to run into the inlet where Cordoba and Grijalva had met with such disastrous treatment. Alaminos, however, declared that it was a dangerous station for the vessels, as the waters were very shallow off the coast, and we should be forced to anchor six miles from the land. Cortes's intention was to punish the inhabitants severely, and many of us who had been present at those engagements begged of him to run in that we might revenge ourselves upon them. But Alaminos and the other pilots said we should lose more than three days by running in, and, if the weather became unfavourable, we might be detained there above eight: the wind, moreover, being now most favourable to reach the Tabasco River, which was our chief object, and where we might arrive in a couple of days. We accordingly put out to sea, and reached the Tabasco after three days' sail.

Chapter 31

Battle in the River Grijalva

On the 12th of March, 1519, we arrived with our whole squadron in the mouth of the Tabasco. As we had experienced, under the expedition with Grijalva, that no vessels of any considerable burden could enter the mouth of the river, our larger ones anchored out at sea, while the smaller ones only, followed by our boats, carrying the whole of our men, sailed up the river, in order to disembark at the promontory where the palm trees grew, about four miles from the town of Tabasco; the same spot where Grijalva had landed.

We perceived numbers of Indians, all under arms, lurking between the almond trees along the shore. This circumstance greatly astonished those among us who were here before with Grijalva. Besides this, more than 12,000 men, all armed after their fashion, had assembled at the town itself in order to attack us. This town was very powerful at that time, many others being subject to it. These warlike preparations were occasioned by the following circumstances: The inhabitants of Potonchan, of Lazaro, and other neighbouring tribes, had accused the Tabascans of cowardice, for having given Grijalva their gold trinkets mentioned above: they reproached them the more because their population was more extensive, and their warriors much more numerous than those of the tribes just mentioned, who had courageously attacked and killed fifty-six of our men. It was owing to these reproaches that they now likewise took up arms against us. Cortes observing these preparations, desired our interpreter Aguilar, who perfectly understood the language of Tabasco, to ask some Indians who were passing by in a large canoe, what the meaning was of all this noise? we had not come to do them any harm; on the contrary, we were disposed to treat them as our brethren, and share our victuals with them: they should be careful how they went to war with us, for they would certainly have to repent it. This and many other things were told them by Aguilar, to incline them to peace, but the more he said the more insolent they became, threatening to destroy us all should we dare to set foot on their territory or in their town, which they had fortified by means of heavy trees felled for the purpose, and a strong stone wall. Aguilar, however, made another attempt to bring about peace, and obtain us permission to take in fresh water, barter for provisions, and incline them to listen to the disclosures we came to make in the name of our God. They, however, persisted we should not pass beyond the palm trees; if we did, they would kill us all.

When Cortes found that all attempts to make peace were fruitless, he ordered the small vessels and boats to prepare for battle. Three pieces of cannon were put on board of each of the former, the crossbow-men and musketeers being equally distributed among them. We remembered, during the expedition under Grijalva, that a narrow road ran from the palm trees along some quagmires and wells to the town. Cortes here posted three sentinels to watch whether the Indians went home at night, if so, to send him immediate notice. Information was soon brought in the affirmative. The rest of the day was now spent in reconnoitring the territory, and fitting out the vessels. The next morning early, after we had attended mass and well armed ourselves, Cortes despatched Alonso de Avila with one hundred men, among whom were ten crossbow-men, along the narrow road above mentioned, leading to the town, which, as soon as he should hear the firing of cannon, he was to attack on one side, while we did the same from the other; Cortes himself, with the rest of our officers and men, moving up the river in the small vessels and our boats.

When the Indians, who were standing under arms along the coast between the palm trees, saw us approaching, they leaped into their canoes and stationed themselves where we were going to land, in order to prevent us. The shore was covered with warriors armed with all kinds of weapons, while a terrible noise assailed our ears from their twisted shells, drums, and fifes. Cortes ordered us to halt for a few moments and not to fire as yet. As he was very particular in doing everything in proper form, he desired the royal secretary, who was with us, and Diego de Godoy, once more to request the inhabitants to allow us to come peaceably on shore to take in fresh water. Aguilar acted as interpreter. They were also to give them some notion, if possible, of the Lord God, and his imperial majesty, and explain to them, that if they attacked us, and we in defending ourselves killed any of their men, the guilt would be upon their heads, not ours. The Indians, however, continued their defiances, threatening to destroy us all if we came on shore. Indeed the battle now soon began, for immediately after they commenced pouring forth showers of arrows, the drummers to give signals for the other troops to fall upon us in a body, and in an instant they rushed bravely forward. They completely surrounded us with their canoes, and shot off their arrows so quickly, that many of us were soon wounded, we being moreover compelled for a length of time to fight up to our waists, and sometimes even higher in the water. The place where we were attempting to land was disadvantageous in another way, for the ground was composed of mud and clay, in which it was impossible to move very fast, particularly as at the same time we had to defend ourselves against the enemy's arrows and the thrusts of their lances. Cortes himself, while fighting in this way was obliged to leave one of his shoes sticking in the mud in order to get on firm land. We had all, indeed, hard work to do before we could gain the dry ground; but having once obtained this we fell so furiously upon our enemies, under the cry of our patron St. Jacob! that they began to retreat, but immediately again drew themselves up in order of battle behind the wood and the trees they had cut down. Here they made an obstinate resistance, until we likewise drove them from this place, having forced some passages leading to the town, which latter we entered fighting our way in. The battle now continued in the streets, until our progress was impeded by another barricade of fallen trees, defended by a fresh set of men. Here the conflict was continued with renewed obstinacy, the Indians incessantly crying out: *ala lala, al calachoni, al calachoni!* meaning in their language, kill the commander-in-chief. While we were thus busily engaged, Alonso de Avila appeared with his men, who had marched along from the palm-trees. He had been detained by the morass and pools of water which lay in his road. This delay now proved an advantage to us, as we had also lost time in striving to make peace with the enemy by means of our two parliamentaries, and the difficulty we had had to fight our way on shore. With our united troops we now beat the Indians from this strong post; though, like brave warriors, they set vigorously upon us with their arrows and lances, which latter had been hardened in the fire; nor did they turn their backs, until we had forced our way into a large courtyard, adjoining which were several spacious apartments and halls. Here also stood three temples, but the Indians had carried off all the religious implements with them.

The enemy being now put to flight, Cortes ordered his men to halt, that we might take formal possession of the country, in the name of his majesty. He performed this ceremony by drawing his sword, and giving therewith two deep cuts into a large *ceiba* tree, which stood in the courtyard, crying out at the same time, that he would defend the possession of this country with sword and shield against any one who should dare dispute it. The whole of us who were present gave our assent to these proceedings, swearing we would support him in its defence; all of which was formally registered by the royal treasurer. The adherents of Diego Velasquez alone were not pleased because the name of the latter had not at all been mentioned therein.

In this engagement fourteen of our men were wounded, I myself was of the number, being wounded by an arrow in the thigh, though not severely. The Indians lost, altogether, eighteen men. We passed the night in this spot, having taken the precaution to post sentinels in different places, so necessary did we deem it to be upon our guard here.

Chapter 32

Exploration of the Interior

The next day Cortes despatched Alvarado with one hundred men, among whom were fifteen crossbow-men and musketeers, to march six miles inland, in order to explore the country. He was to take along with him Melchorejo, of the Punta de Cotoche, but he could nowhere be found. He had most probably gone off in a canoe the night before with the inhabitants of Tabasco. We conjectured this at least, because the day previous he had left all his Spanish clothes behind him hanging in a tree. Cortes was greatly vexed at his escape, as he might betray many things to the inhabitants that would do us no good.

I will, however, leave the fugitive to his own fate, and continue my narrative. Cortes also sent out a second of our chief officers, named Francisco de Lugo, with another hundred men; among whom were twelve crossbow-men and musketeers, with similar instructions as to Alvarado, but to take another direction and return to headquarters towards evening.

Francisco de Lugo may have reached the distance of about four miles when he fell in with vast numbers of Indians, commanded by their several chiefs. They were armed as usual, immediately advanced towards our men, whom they surrounded on all sides, and began pouring forth a shower of arrows. The Indians, indeed, were in too great numbers for our small detachment. They first threw in their lances and the stones from their slings, then fell upon our men with sharp swords, which they wield with both hands. Though De Lugo and his men defended themselves bravely, they were unable to drive back such overwhelming numbers. They therefore began to retreat in the best order possible to our headquarters, having first despatched an Indian of Cuba, who was a swift runner, to inform Cortes of their situation and beg of him to send a reinforcement. During all this time De Lugo and his troops, particularly the crossbow-men and musketeers bravely withstood the whole body of the enemy.

In the meantime Alvarado had marched about four miles in the direction he was commanded to take, when he came to an inlet which he was unable to pass. Here the good Lord fortunately gave him the thought to return in a direction which led to the spot where De Lugo was fighting with the Indians. The firing of the muskets, the noise of the drums and trumpets, with the yelling of the Indians, soon convinced Alvarado that the latter had again commenced hostilities; he therefore marched in a direct line to the place whence the noise came, and found De Lugo in the heat of an engagement with the enemy, of whom five were already killed. Both detachments now fell with their united forces upon the Indians, who were speedily dispersed, yet they were unable to put them totally to the rout; on the contrary, they would certainly have followed us to our headquarters, if Cortes had not come up with the rest of our troops, when, after some sharp firing and heavy blows, they were obliged to fall back. Cortes, on receiving information of De Lugo's dangerous position, had immediately repaired to his assistance with the whole of his men, and came up with the two commanders at about two miles from our headquarters. In this engagement we did not escape without some loss, for two of De Lugo's detachment were killed and eight wounded; Alvarado had only three of the latter. Having arrived at our headquarters, we dressed the wounds of our men, buried the dead, and posted sentinels in proper places, that we might not be fallen upon unawares. In this battle, the enemy lost fifteen men killed, and three were taken prisoners, of whom one appeared to be a chief. Our interpreter Aguilar asked them what madness could have induced them to attack us? One of the Indians returned for answer, that Melchorejo, whom we brought with us from the Punta de Cotoche, had come over to their camp the night previous, advising them to fall upon us, and continue to do so night and day, for, in the end, they would, no doubt, be able to conquer our small numbers: so that Cortes's apprehensions with respect to the flight of this fellow were verified.

We now despatched one of our prisoners to the *caziques* with green glass beads, and offers of peace: this personage, however, never returned to bring any answer. We also learnt from our two other prisoners, who were closely questioned by Aguilar, that the day previous all the *caziques* of the neighbouring districts had been under arms to fall upon us, and that the next day they would return to storm our headquarters. All this was likewise done by the advice of Melchorejo.

Chapter 33
Battling the Indians

Cortes being now certain that the Indians would renew the attack, immediately ordered all our horses to be brought on shore, and every one, our wounded not excepted, to hold himself in readiness. When our horses, which had been such a length of time at sea, now stepped on firm ground again, they appeared very awkward and full of fear; however, the day following, they had regained their usual liveliness and agility. There were also six or seven of our men, all young and otherwise strong fellows, who were attacked with such severe pains in the groins that they could not walk without support. No one could guess the cause of this; it was only said they had lived too freely at Cuba, and that the pain was occasioned by the heat, and the weight of their arms; Cortes, therefore, ordered them again on board. The cavaliers, who were to fight on horseback, were commanded to hang bells around their horses' necks, and Cortes impressed on their minds not to rush at the Indians with their lances before they had been dispersed, and then even to aim at their faces only. The following men were selected to fight on horseback: Christobal de Oli, Pedro de Alvarado, Alonso Hernandez Puertocarrero, and Juan de Escalante. Francisco de Montejo and Alonso de Avila were to use the horses of Ortiz the musician, and of a certain Bartolome Garcia, though neither were worth much. Further, there were Velasquez de Leon, Francisco de Morla, and one of the Lares, (for there was another excellent horseman among us of that name,) and Gonzalo Dominiguez, both superior horsemen; lastly, there were Moron de Bayamo and Pedro de Truxillo. Then comes Cortes, who placed himself at their head. Mesa had charge of the artillery, while the rest of our men were commanded by Diego de Ordas, who, though he knew nothing of the cavalry service, excelled as a crossbow-man and musketeer. The morning following, which was the day of annunciation to the holy Virgin, we attended mass very early, and arranged ourselves under our ensign Antonio de Villareal. We now put ourselves in motion, and marched towards some extensive bean fields, where Francisco de Lugo and Pedro de Alvarado had fought the previous battle. There was a village in this neighbourhood called Cintla, belonging to the Tabascans, which lay about four miles from our headquarters. Cortes, on account of the bogs which our horse could not pass, was obliged to take a circuitous route. Our other troops, however, under Diego de Ordas, came up with the Indians near Cintla, where they had arranged themselves on the plain: if they felt equal ardour for the combat as we did, they could now satisfy themselves,—for this was a battle in every sense of the word which we here fought, fearful in the extreme, as will be seen.

Chapter 34

Attacked by the Caziques of Tabasco

The Indians were already moving forward in search of us, when we came up with them: every one had a large bunch of feathers on his head, a cotton cuirass on, and their faces were daubed with white, black, and red colours. Besides having drums and trumpets, they were armed with huge bows and arrows, shields, lances, and large broadswords; they had also bodies of slingers, and others armed with poles hardened in the fire. The Indians were in such vast numbers that they completely filled the bean fields, and immediately fell upon us on all sides at once, like furious dogs. Their attack was so impetuous, so numerous were the arrows, stones, and lances with which they greeted us, that above seventy of our men were wounded in no time, and one named Saldaña, was struck by an arrow in the ear, and instantly dropt down dead. With like fury they rushed at us with their pikes, at the same time pouring forth showers of arrows, and continually wounding our men. However, we fully repaid them with our crossbows, muskets, and heavy cannon, cutting right and left among them with our swords. By this means we forced them to give ground a little, but only that they might shower forth their arrows at a greater distance, where they thought themselves more secure from our arms. Even then our artilleryman Mesa made terrible havoc among them, standing as they did crowded together and within reach of the cannon, so that he could fire among them to his heart's content. Notwithstanding the destruction we made among their ranks, we could not put them to flight. I now remarked to our commander Diego de Ordas that we should rush forward upon the Indians and close with them. My motive for advising this was, because I saw that they merely retreated from fear of our swords, but still continued to annoy us at a distance with arrows, lances, and large stones. De Ordas, however, considered this not expedient, as the enemy's numbers were so vast that every single man of us would have had to encounter 300 of the enemy at once.

My advice, however, was at length followed up, and we fell so heavily upon them that they retreated as far as the wells. All this time Cortes still remained behind with the cavalry, though we so greatly longed for that reinforcement: we began to fear that some misfortune might also have befallen him. I shall never forget the piping and yelling which the Indians set up at every shot we fired, and how they sought to hide their loss from us by tossing up earth and straw into the air, making a terrible noise with their drums and trumpets, and their war-whoop *ala lala.*[1]

In one of these moments Cortes came galloping up with the horse. Our enemies being still busily engaged with us, did not immediately observe this, so that our cavalry easily dashed in among them from behind. The nature of the ground was quite favourable for its manoeuvres; and as it consisted of strong active fellows, most of the horses being, moreover, powerful and fiery animals, our small body of cavalry in every way made the best use of their weapons. When we, who were already hotly engaged with the enemy, espied our cavalry, we fought with renewed energy, while the latter, by attacking them in the rear at the same time, now obliged them to face about. The Indians, who had never seen any horses before, could not think otherwise than that horse and rider were one body. Quite astounded at this to them so novel a sight, they quitted the plain and retreated to a rising ground.

Cortes now related why he had not come sooner. First, he had been delayed by the morass; then again he was obliged to fight his way through other bodies of the enemy whom he had met, in which five men and eight horses were wounded.

Having somewhat rested from our fatigue under the trees which stood on the field of battle, we praised God and the holy Virgin, and thanked them with uplifted hands for the complete victory they had granted us: and, as it was the feast of the annunciation to the holy Virgin, the town which was subsequently built here in memory of this great victory, was named Santa Maria de la Vitoria. This was the first battle we fought under Cortes in New Spain.

---

1. *Ala lala.* What a striking similarity there is between this cry and the Turkish *Alla il Allah*, of which, as Byron says, in one of his notes to the 'Bride of Abydos,' the Turks are very profuse in battle!

After this pious solemnity we bandaged the wounds of our men with linen, which was all we had for that purpose. Those of our horses we dressed with melted fat, which we cut from the dead bodies of the Indians. We likewise took this opportunity of counting the number of killed left by the enemy on the field of battle. We found above eight hundred, numbers still showing signs of life. Our swords had done the most carnage among them, though many were killed by our cannon. Wherever the cavalry made its appearance the enemy had most work to do. The fighting lasted about an hour; and our enemies maintained their ground so well, that they did not quit the field of battle until our horse broke in among them. There were two *caziques* among the five prisoners we made.

As we were quite fatigued and hungry we returned to our quarters, buried the two soldiers, one of whom had been shot in the neck and the other in the ear, posted strong watches, then ate our supper and retired to rest.

Francisco Lopez de Gomara, in his account of this battle, says, that previous to the arrival of Cortes with the cavalry, the holy apostle St. Jacob or St. Peter in person had galloped up on a gray-coloured horse to our assistance. I can only say, that for the exertion of our arms and this victory, we stand indebted to our Lord Jesus Christ; and that in this battle every individual man among us was set upon by such numbers of the enemy, that if each of them had merely thrown a handful of earth upon us we should have been buried beneath it. Certain it is, therefore, that God showed his mercy to us here, and it may, indeed, have been one of the two glorious apostles St. Jacob or St. Peter who thus came to our assistance. Perhaps on account of my sins I was not considered worthy of the good fortune to behold them; for I could only see Francisco de Morla on his brown horse galloping up with Cortes, and even at this very moment, while I am writing this, I can fancy I see all passing before my eyes just as I have related it; although I, an unworthy sinner, was not considered worthy of beholding one of the glorious apostles face to face: yet again I never heard any of the four hundred soldiers, nor ever Cortes himself, nor any of the many cavaliers, mention this wonder, or confirm its truth. We should certainly have built a church, and have called the town Santiago, or San Pedro de la Vitoria, and not Santa Maria de la Vitoria. If, therefore, what Gomara relates is true, then we must indeed have been bad Christians not to have paid greater respect to the assistance which God sent us in the person of his holy apostles, and for having omitted to thank him daily for it in his own church. Nevertheless, I should feel delighted if this historian has spoken the truth, although I must confess that I never heard this wonder mentioned before reading his book, nor have I ever heard any of the conquistadores speak of it who were present at the battle.

Chapter 35

Cortes Assembles the Caziques

I have above related that in this battle we took five prisoners, among whom were two chiefs. Aguilar, who understood their language, often discoursed with them, and from some remarks which they made, concluded that we might employ them as delegates to their countrymen. Having communicated his thoughts to Cortes, he proposed they should be set at liberty, and despatched with a message to the *caziques* and other inhabitants of the district. To this Cortes assented, ordering both the prisoners to be presented with blue glass beads, while Aguilar told them many things which he knew would please the inhabitants and prove advantageous to us. He assured them, that after this battle, which had been entirely of their own seeking, they had nothing further to fear from us, and commissioned them now to assemble all the *caziques* of the district, for we were very desirous of communicating with them. Everything Aguilar said was done with the view of inclining the Indians to make peace with us. The prisoners most willingly complied with our wishes, which they communicated to the *caziques* and principal personages among the inhabitants, telling them how we longed to become their friends. This message was in so far successful, that they resolved to send us fifteen of their Indian slaves with fowls, baked fish, and maize-bread. These slaves had their faces blackened, and were completely covered with ragged cloaks. When these personages appeared in the presence of Cortes he received them very friendly: Aguilar, on the contrary, asked them in an angry tone, why they had come with such painted faces—appearing rather to seek war than peace? If they were desirous of making peace, continued he, persons of rank should be deputed to us, not slaves. This they were to communicate to those who had sent them. We, however, treated these black faces very kindly, presenting them moreover with blue beads in token of peace, and in order to gain the good wishes of the inhabitants. And sure enough the very next day above thirty of the principal Indians, well dressed, appeared in our quarters, bringing with them, fowls, fruits, and maize-bread, and begged permission of Cortes to burn and bury the bodies of their fallen countrymen, in order that they might not create a pestilence in the air, or become a prey to the lions and tigers. This being granted, they brought along with them a great number of Indians to burn the bodies, and bury them according to their custom. Cortes himself went to watch their proceedings, when they assured him they had lost above 800 killed, without counting the wounded; adding, that at present they durst not enter into any treaty with us, as the day following all the chiefs and principal personages of the district would assemble to take our offers of peace into consideration.

Cortes, who profited by every circumstance, said smilingly to us: "It appears to me, gentlemen, that the Indians stand in great awe of our horses, and imagine that these and our guns alone fight the battle. A thought has just struck me which will further confirm them in this notion. You must bring here the mare of Juan Sedeño which foaled on board a short time ago, and fasten her here where I am now standing. Then bring also the stallion of the musician Ortiz, which is a very fiery animal, and will quickly scent the mare. As soon as you find this to be the case, lead both the horses to separate places, that the *caziques* may neither see the horses, nor hear them neigh, until I shall be in conversation with them." All this was accordingly done. He likewise ordered our largest cannon to be heavily loaded with gunpowder and ball.

A little after midday, forty *caziques* arrived in great state and richly clothed according to their fashion. They saluted Cortes and all of us, perfumed us with their incense, begged forgiveness for what had happened, and promised to be friendly for the future. Cortes answered by our interpreter Aguilar, reminding them, with a very serious look, how often he had wished them to make peace with us, and how, owing to their obstinacy, we were almost upon the point of destroying them with the whole of the inhabitants of this district. We were vassals of the mighty king and lord the emperor Charles, he further added, who had sent us to this country with orders to favour and assist those who should submit to his imperial sway, which we would assuredly do if they were amicably inclined towards us. If, however, they were not so, the *tepustles* (so the Indians called our cannon) would be fired off, which were already embittered against them in some measure on account of the attack they had made upon us. Cortes, at this moment, gave the signal for firing our largest cannon. The report was like a sudden clap of thunder, the ball whizzing along the hills, which could be distinctly heard as it was midday and not a breath of air stirring. The *caziques* who had never seen this before appeared in dismay, and believed all Cortes had said; who, however, desired Aguilar to comfort and assure them he had given orders that no harm should be done them. At this moment the stallion was brought and fastened at a short distance from the spot where Cortes and the *caziques* were holding the conference: as the mare was likewise near at hand, the stallion immediately began to neigh, stamp the ground and rear itself, while its eyes were continually fixed on the Indians who stood in front of Cortes's tent, as the mare was placed behind it. The *caziques*, however, thought the animal was making all these movements against them and appeared greatly agitated. When Cortes found what effect this scene had made upon the Indians, he rose from his seat, and walking to the horse, took hold of the bridle, and desired his servant to lead it away. Aguilar, however, was to make the Indians believe that he had ordered the horse not to do them any injury.

While all this was going on above thirty Indian porters (whom they term *tamemes*) arrived with fowls, baked fish, and various fruits: these porters, on account of their loads, had perhaps not been able to follow the *caziques* fast enough. A lively discourse was now kept up between Cortes and the *caziques*, who in the end left us perfectly contented, with the assurance that the following day they would return with a present.

Chapter 36

The Caziques and Calachonis Bring Gifts

On the following morning, it was one of the last days in March, 1519, a number of *caziques*, with the principal personages of the Tabasco district and surrounding neighbourhood arrived. They paid us profound reverence, and brought a present, consisting in four diadems, some lizards, ear-rings, four ducks, figures like dogs, others with Indian faces, two sandals with golden soles, and various other trifling trinkets of gold,[1] whose value I have forgotten. There were also cloaks as the Indians wear them, which are very commodious. The present altogether was of little value, (most likely the province altogether possessed few riches,) and was certainly not to be compared to the twenty females with which they presented us, among whom one was a very fine woman, who subsequently became a convert to Christianity, and was named Doña Marina. Cortes was vastly pleased with this present, and held, by means of Aguilar, a long discourse with the *caziques*, telling them among other things, that their present was very acceptable; but he had something further to beg, namely, that they should again return to their dwellings with their wives and children. He should not consider the peace really concluded unless within the space of two days all the inhabitants had

1. This passage is very important, as it shows to what degree of civilization the inhabitants of this district had arrived, and that they were at least skilful in the working of gold. The Spanish words are: *"Quatro diademas, unas lagartijas, y dos como perillos, y orejeras, y cinco anades, y dos figuras de caras de Indios, y dos Suelas de Oro, como de sus Cotoras."* The *caras de Indios* (faces of Indians) were most probably shaped like masks, for similar ones, made of clay, are found to this day in the vale of Mexico. *"Suelas de Oro, como de sus Cotoras,"* we have ventured to translate "Sandals with golden soles," particularly as Bernal Diaz, in a subsequent chapter, expressly remarks that Motecusuma wore a kind of half-boot with soles of gold.

returned to the village. The *caziques* upon this issued the necessary orders, and in a couple of days all the families had returned. They showed the same readiness to comply with Cortes's wishes when he desired them to do away with their idols and human sacrifices. He likewise, as well as he could, gave them some idea of our holy Christian faith, and how we only adored one God. We also showed them a very pious figure, representing the mother of God holding her blessed Son in her arms, and explained to them how we paid reverence to this figure, and by it to the mother of God who was in heaven. Hereupon the *caziques* answered, that they were much pleased with this great *tecleciguata*, and that they should much like to keep it in their village. In their language, *tecleciguata* means a woman of distinction. Cortes promised them they should have it, and for this purpose ordered a pretty altar to be built. In the same way our carpenters, Alonso Yañez and Alvaro Lopez, were desired to construct a very high cross.

Cortes also further asked the *caziques*, why they had thus for the third time commenced war with us, though we had always sought to be at peace with them? They answered, that they were sorry enough for it, and we had forgiven them; for the rest it was at the instigation of their brother, the *cazique* of Champoton, who had previously accused them of cowardice for not having attacked us when we arrived off the coast with four ships under another commander, meaning most probably Grijalva. The same advice was also given them by our Indian interpreter, who had run away from us in the night-time, telling them not to leave us any peace day or night, as we were but few in number. Cortes desired that he should be delivered up to us, but they declared they did not know what had become of him, as on the unfortunate termination of the battle he had immediately took to flight. This, however, was an untruth, as we were well aware how dearly the poor devil had paid for his advice, as shortly after the battle he was seized and sacrificed to their gods.

On being questioned as to where they got their gold and the trinkets, they answered from the country towards the setting of the sun, and pronounced the words Culhua and Mexico. As at that time we did not comprehend the meaning of these words, we paid little attention to them. We, however, questioned our other interpreter Francisco, who remained with us from our former expedition under Grijalva, but he knew very little of the Tabasco language, being only acquainted with the Culhuan, that is to say the Mexican. He told Cortes, partly by signs, that Culhua lay at a great distance before us, at the same time continually mentioning the word Mexico, Mexico. We were then still ignorant what he wished to convey to us.

The day following the cross and altar were erected, and the figure of the holy Virgin being placed thereon: we all fell down upon our knees before it, while father Bartolome de Olmedo read mass. The *caziques* and chief Indians were present. On this occasion also the village of Tabasco was in all solemnity named Santa Maria de la Vitoria; and father Olmedo, with the assistance of Aguilar, said many excellent things to the twenty females who were presented to us, concerning our holy religion; that they should abandon their belief in idols, and no longer bring them sacrifices, for they were not gods but evil spirits; they had up to this moment lived in gross error, and should now adore Christ, our Lord. After this address the women were baptized, and she of whom I have already spoken was named Doña Marina. This was a lady of distinction, the daughter of a powerful *cazique* and a princess who had subjects of her own, which, indeed, you might see from her appearance. The circumstances which occasioned her being brought into our power I will relate hereafter. The names of the other Indian females who were baptized I cannot now bring to mind; but these were the first who were converted to Christianity in New Spain, and were distributed among Cortes's chief officers. Doña Marina, who was the prettiest, the most active and lively of the number, was given to Puertocarrero, who was a stout cavalier and cousin to the earl of Medellin. When he subsequently left for Spain, Cortes took Marina unto himself, and had a son by her, who was named Don Martin Cortes, and became *Comptoir* of Santiago.

We remained five days in this spot, partly to cure our wounds, partly for the sake of those who suffered from pain in the groins, but who soon recovered here. Cortes employed these days in useful conversation with the *caziques*, and talked to them about the emperor, our master, of his numerous lordly vassals, and the advantage they would gain by having subjected themselves to him; as, for the future, in all their difficulties they would only have to apply to him, and wherever he might be he would come to their assistance.

The *caziques* thanked him for this offer; they solemnly declared themselves to be vassals of our great emperor, and these were the first among the inhabitants of New Spain who subjected themselves to his majesty. As the day following was Palm Sunday, Cortes desired them to come early in the morning to pray before the holy mother of God and the cross. He also sent for six Indian carpenters to assist ours in making a cross on a high *ceiba* tree,[2] near the village of Cintla, where the Lord had granted us the great victory. This cross was made in a manner so as to be very durable, for the bark of the tree, which always grows to again, was so cut as to form that figure. Lastly, Cortes desired the Indians to bring out all their canoes in order to assist us in re-embarking, for we were desirous of setting sail on that holy day, as, according to our pilots, our present station was not secure from the north winds.

Early the next morning the *caziques* and the principal personages, all with their wives and children, made their appearance in the courtyard, where we had erected the altar and cross, and collected the palm branches for our procession. Upon this Cortes, with the officers and all our men, rose and made a solemn procession. Both our priests, the father Bartolome de Olmedo, belonging to the order of the charitable brethren, and Juan Dias, were dressed in their full canonicals, and read mass. We prayed before the cross and kissed it, the *caziques* and Indians all the while looking on. After the ceremony was finished the principal Indians brought ten fowls, baked fish, and all kinds of greens, which we enjoyed very much. We now took our leave, and Cortes repeatedly recommended them to take care of the image of the holy Virgin and the cross, and to hold the chapel in due reverence, in order that salvation and blessings might come upon them.

We all embarked in the evening, and on Monday morning we set sail with a good wind. We always kept close to the shore, and steered in the direction of San Juan de Ulua. As we coasted along, the weather being most favourable, we who had been here with Grijalva, and were well acquainted with these parts, pointed out to Cortes La Rambla, which the Indians call Aguajaluco; further on, the coast of Tonala or San Antonio, the great River Guacasualco, the elevated snow mountains (Sierras Nevadas), and those of San Martin. We also showed him the split rock forming two points, which stretch out into the sea, and somewhat resemble the figure of a chair. We then showed him the River Alvarado; further on the River Banderas, where we made the 16000 *pesos*; the Isla Blanca and Isla Verde, also the Isla di Sacrificios, where, under Grijalva, we found the idols with the Indians who had been recently sacrificed.

In this way we pretty quickly arrived at San Juan de Ulua, which we

2. The *bombax ceiba* of Linnaeus, and one of the tallest trees growing in America. The fruit produces a very fine cotton, resembling silk, used for stuffing bolsters and chair seats.

reached on Holy Thursday about noon. I shall never forget how Alonso Hernandez Puertocarrero just about this time remarked to Cortes:

"Methinks we are now certainly arrived in that country, of which those gentlemen who have been here twice before, sung:[3]

"Cata Francia, montesinos!
"Cata Paris, la Ciudad,
"Cata las aguas de Duero,
"Do van a dar en la mar!

"I tell you, only look at this rich country, and keep strict command over us."

Cortes, who well knew what he meant, said in return:

"If God will only grant us that good fortune in arms which he gave to Roland, the Paladin, then with your assistance and that of the other gentlemen cavaliers, we shall succeed in everything else."

This happened just at the moment when Cortes was entering the River Alvarado, which circumstance is also mentioned by Gomara.

---

3. *Cata Francia, Montesinos*, &c. This is the first *strophe* of an old Spanish romance, in which Montesinos the father desires his son to revenge him of his mortal enemy Tomillas: "Montesinos cast a glance On your lands, the soil of France; See how the Duro's sportive motion Carries its waters to the ocean!"

Chapter 37

Doña Marina

Previous to going into any details here respecting the powerful Motecusuma, his immense kingdom of Mexico, and its inhabitants, I must relate what I know of Doña Marina. She was born a ruler over a people and country,—for her parents had the dominion of a township called Painala, to which several other townships were subject, lying about twenty-four miles from the town of Guacasualco. Her father died when she was very young, and her mother married another young *cazique*. By him she had a son, of whom it appears they were both very fond, and to whom, after their death, they designed to leave their territories.

In order, however, that the daughter of the first marriage might not stand in his way, she was conveyed secretly during night-time to an Indian family in Xicalango, they spreading the rumour she had died, which gained further belief from the circumstance that a daughter of one of her female slaves happened to die at the time. The Indians of Xicalango did not keep the young girl themselves, but gave her to the inhabitants of Tabasco, by whom she was presented to Cortes. I knew her mother and half-brother myself, the latter having already reached manhood, and governed the township jointly with his mother. When they were subsequently both converted to Christianity, the latter was named Martha and her son Lazaro.

I was well acquainted with the whole of this circumstance; for in the year 1523, when Mexico and several other provinces had been subdued, and Christobal de Oli had rebelled in the Higueras, Cortes came to Guacasualco, and on that occasion visited Marina's birth-place. Most of the inhabitants of Guacasualco accompanied Cortes on this expedition; I myself was also among the number. As Doña Marina, in all the wars of New Spain, Tlascalla, and at the siege of Mexico, had rendered the greatest services in capacity of an interpretress, Cortes carried her everywhere with him. During this journey it also was that he married her to a cavalier of the township of Orizava, named Juan Xaramillo.

Among others, there was present as a witness a certain Aranda of Tabasco, through whom this circumstance became immediately known. These are the true particulars of the whole case, not, however, as related by Gomara. For the rest, Marina had the most extensive influence in New Spain, and did with the Indians what she pleased.

While Cortes was staying in Guacasualco, he ordered all the *caziques* of the province to assemble, and advised them to adopt our holy religion. On this occasion the mother and brother of Doña Marina also made their appearance with the other *caziques*. They recognized each other immediately; the former, however, appeared to be in the greatest anxiety, thinking that they had merely been called there to be killed. Doña Marina, however, desired them to dry away their tears, and comforted them by saying they were unconscious of what they were doing when they had sent her away to the inhabitants of Xicalango, and that she freely forgave the past. By this means God certainly directed everything for her best, turned her away from the errors of heathenism, and converted her to Christianity.

Thus destined, she likewise bore a son unto her master Cortes, and then married a cavalier named Juan Xaramillo. All this I consider of much greater importance than if she had been presented with the sole dominion of the whole of New Spain. She likewise gave presents to her relatives on their return home. What I have related is the strict truth, and can swear to it. Gomara's account respecting this is wholly erroneous, and he adds many other circumstances which I shall leave without comment.

This, however, is certain, that the whole affair reminds one of the history of Joseph and his brethren in Egypt, when they came into his power. After this diversion into matters which subsequently took place, I must relate how we first managed to understand Doña Marina. She was conversant with the language of Guacasualco, which is the Mexican, and with that of Tabasco. Aguilar, however, merely understood the latter, which is spoken throughout the whole of Yucatan. Doña Marina had, therefore, first to make herself understood to Aguilar, who then translated what she said into Spanish. This woman was a valuable instrument to us in the conquest of New Spain. It was, through her only, under the protection of the Almighty, that many things[1] were accomplished by us: without her we never should have understood the Mexican language, and, upon the whole, have been unable to surmount many difficulties.

Let this suffice respecting Doña Marina; I will now relate how we arrived in San Juan de Ulua.

---

1. On this woman the captain Cadahalso, in his *'Cartas Marruecas,'* passes the following encomium: *"Primera muger, que no ha prejudicado en uno exercito;"* i.e. "The first woman who ever accompanied an army without being a prejudice to it."

Chapter 38
San Juan de Ulua

On Holy Thursday, in the year of our Lord 1519, we arrived with our whole squadron in the harbour of San Juan de Ulua. As Alaminos well remembered this spot from the expedition under Grijalva, he brought our ships to anchor in a place where they were sheltered from the north wind. We had scarcely lain here half an hour when we espied two large canoes, which are called here pirogues, filled with a number of Indians, making straight for Cortes's vessel, which, from the large flag hanging from the mast-head, they recognized as our commander's ship. They climbed on board without any ceremony, and inquired for the *tlatoan*, which, in their language, means master. Doña Marina understood their question, and pointed to Cortes; they, therefore, turned to him, paying him great reverence after the Indian fashion, and bid him welcome. Their master, they said, who was a servant of the great Motecusuma, had sent them in order to ascertain who we were and what we came to seek in his country. We had only to inform them of what we wanted for our ships, and they would see that it was provided.

Cortes thanked them for their kindness, through Aguilar and Doña Marina, presented them with some blue glass beads, and ordered some meat and drink to be placed before them. After they had taken some refreshment, he told them we were merely come here to make their acquaintance, and open a trade with them: we had not the remotest intention of doing them an injury, nor need they apprehend anything from our arrival. The ambassadors now returned, well contented, to their homes. The following morning, Good Friday, we disembarked our horses and cannon near some sand-hills which here run along the whole coast. Our artilleryman Mesa placed the cannon on a very advantageous spot, and we erected an altar where mass was immediately performed: for Cortes and the other chief officers huts were constructed of green boughs; the rest of us likewise constructed huts, and slept three together: the horses also were well provided for. The whole of Good Friday was spent in this work; and on the Saturday many Indians arrived, who had been sent by a man of distinction, named Quitlalpitoc, governor under Motecusuma: this personage was afterwards christened Ovandillo. They had axes with them, and cut off an additional quantity of branches to make a better finish to Cortes's hut, which they then overhung with large pieces of cloth, to keep out the heat, which was already very great. They also brought along with them fowls, maize-bread, and plums, which were then nice and ripe; also, if I rightly recollect, they had with them some gold trinkets. All these things they handed over to Cortes, adding, that the governor himself would come the next day and bring with him a further supply of provisions. Cortes joyfully accepted of these presents, and ordered various kinds of toys we had brought for barter to be given them, with which they were uncommonly delighted. On Easter day, the governor indeed appeared in person, as had been assured us. His name was Teuthlille, and he was one of the farmer generals of the Mexican empire. He was accompanied by another person of distinction, called Quitlalpitoc. We subsequently learnt that both these personages were appointed governors over the provinces Cotastlan, Tustepec, Guazpaltepec, and Tlatateteclo, and other townships recently subdued. They were followed by a great number of Indians, carrying the presents, consisting of fowls and greens. Teuthlille having ordered the others to stand back a little, walked up to Cortes, and made him three most reverential bows, after the Indian fashion, which he repeated on turning to us who stood nearest. Cortes bid both welcome, then embraced them, and desired them to wait a little, as he would afterwards give them a more circumstantial answer. In the meantime he ordered the altar to be fitted up as prettily as possible. Francisco Bartolome and father Juan Diaz performed mass. Both the governors and the principal personages of their suite were present during the ceremony, after which Cortes sat down to dinner with them.

After the table had been cleared, Cortes, with the assistance of Aguilar and Doña Marina, entered into conversation with the Mexican officials and the *caziques*, telling them we were Christians, and subjects of the greatest monarch of the world, whose name was emperor Charles, and that he had many great personages among his vassals and servants. We had come by his command to their country, of which and its powerful monarch who now reigned over it, his majesty had heard long ago. As far as regarded himself, he was desirous of becoming his friend, and had to disclose many things to him, in the name of his emperor, which he would listen to with delight. In order that a good understanding might be established between him and his subjects, they should acquaint him with the place where their monarch resided, that he might pay his respects to him, and make the necessary disclosures. To which Teuthlille answered in a rather imperious tone, "Since you are but just arrived, it would be more fitting that you, previous to your desiring an interview with my monarch, should accept this present, which we have brought you in his name, and disclose your wishes to me." He then brought forth, out of a species of box, a quantity of gold trinkets, of beautiful and skilful workmanship, besides more than twenty packages of stuffs very prettily worked of white cotton and feathers. These they presented to Cortes, with various other costly things, which, owing to the number of years which have since elapsed, I cannot now remember, besides provisions, consisting in quantities of fowls, fruits, and dried fish. Cortes accepted all this with a joyful countenance, presenting these gentlemen in return with glass beads resembling brilliants, and other things we brought from Spain. He begged of them to desire the inhabitants of the different districts to commence trading with us, as we possessed various articles which we were desirous of exchanging for gold; this they promised to do.

Cortes then ordered an arm-chair to be brought, beautifully painted and adorned with inlaid work, some pieces of precious stones, wrapt in cotton cloth, perfumed with musk, a necklace of imitation pearls, a scarlet cap, with a medal, on which was represented the holy St. George on horseback, with lance in hand, killing the dragon. Cortes addressed Teuthlille, and said, that he presented this chair to his monarch Motecusuma, that he might sit in it when he should pay him a visit, and the string of pearls to wind around his head on the same occasion; all of which were presents from the emperor our master, who had sent these things to his monarch in token of friendship and as a proof of the esteem in which he held him: he ought now to inform us where and when he could personally wait upon him. Teuthlille accepted the presents, and said, in return, that his master Motecusuma, as he was also a great monarch, would on his side be equally delighted to learn something about our great emperor: he would hasten to lay the presents before him, and return with his answer.

Teuthlille had with him very clever painters, for there were such in Mexico, and he ordered them to sketch the likeness and whole person of Cortes, with the dress he wore; also all the other chief officers, the soldiers, our vessels, horses, Doña Marina, and Aguilar; even our two dogs, the cannon, the balls; in short, everything they could fix their eyes on belonging to us: these paintings they took along with them to show to their monarch. In order, however, to convey to him a still greater idea of our power, Cortes ordered our cannon to be heavily laden with powder, so as to produce a very loud report, commanding also Alvarado and the other cavaliers to mount their horses, to hang bells around the necks of the latter, and to gallop up in full speed in presence of Motecusuma's ambassadors. Cortes also mounted his horse, and said to the others, "It would be capital if we could gallop across these sand-hills at full speed; but, as we should so easily stick in the sand, it will be better for us to ride two and two along the sea-shore at low water." He then gave the command of the horse to Alvarado, whose brown mare was a spirited animal, and very swift. All this was done in presence of the Mexican ambassadors; but, that they might likewise see the cannon fired, Cortes, under the pretence of having something further to communicate, took them and several other principal personages to a spot where they might have a good view of it. The weather was perfectly calm; and when the cannon was fired, the stone balls flew with a tremendous crash along the sand-hills, re-echoing for a length of time. The Indians were terribly startled, and ordered their painters to represent this likewise, to them so novel a sight, that they might show it to Motecusuma.

One of our men had on a *casque*, which was partly gilt; Teuthlille, who was much more enlightened than any of his companions, remarked, when his eye fell upon it, that it bore a great resemblance to a helmet which belonged to their most ancient forefathers, and now adorned the head of their warrior-god Huitzilopochtli. Motecusuma, he further added, would certainly be uncommonly pleased if he could likewise see this *casque*. Cortes, on hearing this, ordered the *casque* to be presented to him, thereby expressing the wish, that he should like to satisfy himself that the gold of this country was similar to what we find in our rivers. If they would send him the *casque* full of gold dust, he would send it to our great emperor. Upon this Teuthlille took leave of Cortes and all of us, promising to return speedily, while Cortes, under the most tender of embraces, made him every profession of friendship.

After this personage had taken his departure, we learnt that he was not merely a distinguished statesman, but also the most nimble pedestrian at Motecusuma's court. He did, indeed, use the utmost expedition to bring his monarch information, and hand over to him the paintings and presents. The great Motecusuma was vastly astonished at everything he heard and saw, and yet he was pleased. But, when at last he espied the *casque*, and compared it with that of the idol Huitzilopochtli, he no longer doubted for an instant that we belonged to that people, whom his forefathers had prophesied would, one time or other, come and subdue the country.

Concerning these things Gomara has adduced much of which he had been ill informed; I will not, however, detain myself by contradicting him, but continue my narrative.

Chapter 39
Teuthlille's Report

After the departure of Teuthlille with the presents which Cortes sent to his monarch, Motecusuma; the other governor, Quitlalpitoc, remained behind in our camp. He took up his quarters in a kind of hut, at a distance from ours, and ordered Indians to bake maize-bread, procure the fowls, fruits, and fish, which the province had to furnish, for the table of Cortes and his officers. We other soldiers, if we wished to get our bellies full were compelled to catch shell and other fish ourselves. In the meantime numbers of Indians arrived from the above-mentioned provinces, over which the two officials sent by Motecusuma were governors, bringing with them some gold trinkets of small value, and fowls, which they gave us in exchange for our goods, consisting in glass pearls and such like; with which we were all provided, having experienced the value of these during the expedition under Grijalva.

Six or seven days may have thus been spent, when Teuthlille returned in the morning with more than a hundred Indian porters, all heavily laden, accompanied by a great Mexican *cazique*, who both in countenance, stature, and deportment, greatly resembled Cortes, and on that account only had been selected by his monarch to accompany the deputation; for, as was related, when Teuthlille brought forth the picture representing Cortes, all the grandees who were present with their monarch Motecusuma, immediately observed that he resembled a person of distinction named Quintalbor. This was the same person who now accompanied Teuthlille, we therefore called one the Cortes of this place, and the other the Cortes of that place. We must now, however, learn what the ambassadors did when they came into the presence of Cortes. First of all they touched the ground at his feet with the hand, they then perfumed him and all the Spaniards who were present, with pans made of clay. Cortes gave them a most cordial reception, and desired them to sit down at his side. The *cazique* Quintalbor was commissioned to discuss matters jointly with Teuthlille. Both, therefore, told Cortes he was most welcome in their country; and after a good deal of talking on both sides, they produced the presents and spread them out on a mat, over which they had first thrown some cotton cloths. The first was a round plate, about the size of a wagon wheel, representing the sun, the whole of the finest gold, and of the most beautiful workmanship; a most extraordinary work of art, which, according to the account of those who weighed it, was worth above 20,000 gold *pesos*. The second was a round plate, even larger than the former, of massive silver, representing the moon, with rays and other figures on it, being of great value. The third was the *casque*, completely filled with pure grains of gold, as they are found in the mines, worth about 3000 *pesos*, which was more to us than if it had been ten times the value, as we now knew for certain there were rich gold mines in the country. Among other things there were also thirty golden ducks, exactly resembling the living bird, and of splendid workmanship; further figures resembling lions, tigers, dogs and apes; likewise ten chains with lockets, all of gold, and of the most costly workmanship; a bow with the string and twelve arrows, and two staffs five palms in length, like those used by the justices, all cast of the purest gold; further, they brought small cases containing the most beautiful green feathers, blended with gold and silver, and fans similarly worked; every species of game likewise cast in gold. In short such a number of objects, which from the many years since elapsed I cannot now altogether

---

1. These remarkable presents have all been enumerated by Torquemada, (*Monarchia Indiana*, i, iv, c. 17;) and we cannot do better than give his minute description of them here: "The ambassador of Motecusuma ordered mats to be spread on the ground before Cortes, and over them some cotton cloths, on which he arranged the presents, consisting of large quantities of cotton shirts and other cotton stuffs, beautifully manufactured, and interwoven with feathers of the most splendid colours; bucklers made of the purest white staffs, decorated with feathers, gold, silver, and pearls, surpassing everything in beauty and skilfulness of workmanship that was ever seen. There was also a helmet, tastefully carved out of wood, filled with grains of gold; a *casque*, made of thin plates of gold, decorated with tassels and stones, resembling the *smaragdus*; numerous large bunches of feathers of diversified colours, fastened in silver and gold; fans for keeping off flies, made of the rarest feathers; a thousand lockets of gold and silver, of the most curious and beautiful workmanship; bracelets and military decorations of gold and silver, splendidly embossed with green and bright yellow feathers; leather made of deer skin, curried and coloured in the best possible manner; shoes and

remember.[1] There were alone above thirty packages of cotton stuffs, variously manufactured and interworked with variegated feathers. When the great *cazique* Quintalbor and Teuthlille handed over these presents to Cortes, they begged of him to accept of them in the same friendly disposition with which their monarch sent them, and to distribute them among his *teules*. Upon this they began to unfold what their monarch had in particular commissioned them to say, which was as follows: "He, Motecusuma, was delighted with the arrival of such courageous men in his states, as we, according to the accounts he had received and judging from the occurrence at Tabasco, certainly must be. He wished very much to see our great emperor, who was such a powerful monarch, of whom, although residing at such a vast distance, he had already gained some knowledge, and he would send him a present of some valuable stones. He was likewise ready to furnish us with everything we might require during our stay. But as for Cortes calling upon him, we had better give up all thoughts of that, as it was not necessary, and would be accompanied with great difficulties."

Cortes thanked them most sincerely for their kindness, gave to each a couple of shirts made of Holland, blue beads, and other trifles, begging of them to return to their great monarch Motecusuma, and tell him that our emperor and master would take it very unkind, after we had come from such distant countries and crossed such vast seas, merely with the intention of paying our respects to Motecusuma, if

---

sandals of the same leather, sewn with thin gold wire, and the soles made of splendid white and blue stone. There were other kinds of shoes, most tastefully manufactured of cotton; mirrors of *marcasite*, globular shaped, of the size of a fist, and most ingeniously set in gold, the small frame itself being very valuable, and worthy of the acceptance of any crowned head; coverings and curtains to beds, manufactured of various coloured cotton, more glossy and of finer texture than silk; a number of other gold and silver trinkets; a necklace of gold, decorated with upwards of a hundred emeralds, rubies, and various other ornaments of gold; a second necklace, consisting of numbers of large pearls and emeralds, all of the most exquisite workmanship; numerous other gold trinkets in the shape of frogs and animals; jewels in the form of medals, the shrines being even more valuable than the precious stones they contained; a quantity of large and small grains of gold. The most valuable of these presents, however, were two round plates, one of gold, on which was a sun with rays and the zodiac; this weighed above one hundred marks: the other was of silver, which in a similar manner represented the moon, weighing above fifty marks: both were massive, and of the thickness of the Spanish coin of four silver *reals*, and as large as a wagon wheel. Those who saw these splendid presents said that, without considering the beautiful workmanship, the value of the gold and silver alone amounted to 25,000 *castellanos de oro*; so that the whole together may well be estimated at 50,000 ducats."

we returned without fulfilling this object. He wished, therefore, to proceed to his residence and himself to receive his commands. The ambassadors answered, that they would mention all this to their monarch, but that any waiting upon him would be superfluous. Cortes upon this gave them out of our poverty a cup, of Florentine workmanship, gilt and surrounded with a quantity of relieved foliage, besides those shirts made of Holland, and other things; all these were to be presented to Motecusuma, and he desired them to take his answer to him. Both the delegates then departed, while Quitlalpitoc remained alone behind in our camp, commissioned, it appeared, by the two other officials of Motecusuma, to provide provisions for us out of the neighbouring districts.

Chapter 40

In Search of Another Harbour

After the Mexican ambassadors had again taken their departure, Cortes ordered two vessels to sail further on and explore the coast. The command of these was given to Francisco de Montejo, with orders to follow the same course taken by Grijalva. He was to sail on for the space of ten days, and search for a good harbour and convenient spot to form a settlement; for in the sandy region we were now staying it was impossible to live, on account of the gnats; the inhabited districts, moreover, being too far distant. Alaminos and el Manquillo who were already acquainted with these waters, piloted the vessels. Montejo departed and arrived in the waters of Rio Grande, near Panuco, as far as we had gone with Grijalva, but on account of the heavy currents there he could proceed no further; he, therefore, returned to San Juan de Ulua, bringing us no other news than that they had seen at a distance of about thirty-six miles further on a town, which to all appearance was fortified. This place was called Quiahuitzlan, having a harbour, which, according to the opinion of Alaminos, was secure from the north wind. Ten or twelve days were spent by Montejo in this expedition out and home. Quitlalpitoc, who had remained to furnish us with provisions, soon ceased to do so altogether, which, of course, created a great scarcity of food: our *cassave*-bread had likewise become quite mouldy and swarmed with worms, so that we had nothing to eat if we did not procure ourselves shellfish. In the commencement the Indians had certainly brought us gold and fowls for our goods, but now they no longer came in such great numbers as at first, and those who did come appeared quite shy and reserved. We, therefore, anxiously awaited the return of the two ambassadors from Mexico.

After some days had elapsed Teuthlille indeed returned with a great number of Indians. They observed the same courteous behaviour as on the previous occasion, perfuming Cortes and all of us, and then brought forth their presents, consisting in ten packages of mantles, richly worked in feathers; further, four *chalchihuitls*, a species of green stone of uncommon value, which are held in higher estimation with them than the *smaragdus*[1] with us; lastly, there were also all kinds of gold trinkets, which I heard valued at 3000 *pesos*. The great *cazique* Quintalbor had fallen ill on the journey, and consequently remained behind. Teuthlille and Quitlalpitoc, therefore, alone fulfilled Motecusuma's commission, and assured us that he had most graciously accepted of our present. Regarding the four *chalchihuitls* they observed, that those were intended as a present to our emperor, as each of them was worth, more than a load of gold. For the rest it was unnecessary to send any more messengers to Mexico, neither was there any further mention to be made of a personal interview between their monarch and Cortes.

Although, it was very unpleasant to the latter that his visit to Motecusuma should thus be declined in dry words, yet he thanked them most kindly; and added to some of us who were present: "Really this Motecusuma must be a great and rich gentleman; nevertheless, if God be willing, we shall one day visit him in his palace!" "We only wish, (returned we soldiers,) that we were once nicely engaged with him."

All this took place just about the hour of Ave Maria; the bell, therefore, announced that we should assemble ourselves around the cross, which we had erected on an elevated sand-hill. While we were all on our knees before it, and repeating the Ave Maria, Teuthlille and Quitlalpitoc inquired why we thus humbled ourselves so greatly before that pole.

Cortes immediately turned to Bartolome de Olmedo, and remarked to him: "This is a good opportunity, father, to give these people some notion of our holy religion through our interpreters." This father Olmedo accordingly did in a manner which would have done

---

1. *Chalchihuitls*; Bernal Diaz calls these *chalchuites*. This stone is of a light green colour, at first held in great estimation by the Spaniards, but Torquemada, a contemporary of our author, remarks, (*Monarchia*, Ind. i, p. 462,) it is a stone on which the Indians set a high value, but not so the Spaniards. He calls it a kind of *smaragdus*, "the polishing of which the Indians say was taught them by the god Quetzalcohuatl." Bustamente (*Historia de la Conquista de Mexico escrita, por* Fr. Bernardino Sahagun, Mexico, 1829,) calls it, *"Piedra jaspe, mui verde, o sea esmeralda ordinaria,"* i.e. "A jasper of a very green colour, or a common *smaragdus*." This stone represented among the Mexicans everything that was excellent in its kind, for which reason they put such a stone in the mouth of the distinguished chiefs who died.

honour to the greatest of theologians. He first of all explained that we were Christians, and then expatiated on the whole substance of our belief; he then proved that their idols were useless things, evil spirits, which fled away from the presence of the cross. On such a cross, he continued, the Lord of heaven and earth suffered death, we believed in him only, and prayed to him as the only true God, Jesus Christ, who suffered death for the salvation of the human race; who rose again on the third day, and ascended into heaven, that he would again appear to hold judgment over the living and the dead. Upon this followed everything that was edifying, which the Indians comprehended well, and which they assured us they would relate to their monarch.

Cortes then explained to them, that among the many reasons which had induced our great emperor to send us here, one was that they should abandon for ever the religion of their cursed idols, abolish human sacrifices, and abstain from kidnapping. He, therefore, must beg of them to erect crosses like this in their towns and on their temples, and also the figure of the holy Virgin, with her most excellent Son, then God would bestow great blessings on them. In short, there were many expressions replete with excellent feeling, which I am unable wholly to report, and therefore will rather leave in my pen.

Our men now commenced to barter with the Indians, who had arrived with Teuthlille for what they had brought, and obtained various kinds of things, all of inferior gold, which we gave to our sailors for catching us fish; this was the only means we had of stilling our hunger. Cortes was well aware of this, and secretly enjoyed the idea; however, the creatures of Diego Velasquez drew his attention to it, and thought he ought not to permit such a species of traffic. We shall further see what happened on this account.

Chapter 41

Bartering for Gold

This bartering for gold being continued with the Indians, the adherents of Diego Velasquez remonstrated with Cortes, and asked him how he could suffer such a thing? Diego Velasquez, they added, had not sent him hither, that the soldiers should put most of the gold in their pockets. It ought to be made known, that henceforth no one but Cortes himself should barter for gold, and that every one should render an account of the gold in his possession, in order that the emperor's fifths might be deducted therefrom. It was, moreover, necessary to appoint a treasurer. Cortes confessed they were in the right, and allowed them to choose a treasurer themselves. But, not until their choice had fallen on one Gonzalo Mexia, did he show what his real intentions were; then he said to them with a heavy frown on his brow: "Only consider, gentlemen, how hard our comrades have to fare, since provisions totally fail! In order that they might not hunger, I have up to this moment overlooked this system of bartering, and indeed it produces but a mere trifle. I hope, with the assistance of God, that our affairs will take a better turn by and bye. Everything has its two sides to be looked at, and as we have now, in compliance with your wishes, ordered that no more bartering for gold shall be allowed in future, we have to see whence we are henceforth to obtain provisions."

Gomara is in the wrong, when he relates, that Cortes issued that order, on this occasion, to make Motecusuma believe we cared little about gold. This monarch knew very well how the matter stood on this point, from the time of our arrival under Grijalva in the Bandera stream; he might also easily guess what we were after, when we begged of him to send us the *casque* full of golden grains, and our daily bartering for that metal. The Mexicans, indeed, are not the kind of folks to be thus imposed upon.

However this may be, one fine morning the Indians, who had resided near us in the huts and were accustomed to furnish us with provisions and bring gold for barter, had all secretly left with Quitlalpitoc. This, we subsequently learnt, was done by the commands of Motecusuma, who had forbidden all intercourse with Cortes, which he had been induced to do from his attachment to his idol-gods. These were named Tetzcatlipuca and Huitzilopochtli, the former being the god of hell and the latter the god of war, to whom Motecusuma daily sacrificed some young children, that they might disclose to him what he should do with us. His intention was to take us prisoners if we would not re-embark, and employ some to educate children, while others were to be sacrificed. For his idol-gods, as we afterwards discovered, advised him not to listen to Cortes, and to take no notice of what we had sent him word concerning the cross and the figure of the blessed Virgin. This was also the reason why his men had gone away so secretly.

Affairs having assumed such a posture, we now daily expected that hostilities would break out, and were particularly on our guard. It was during one of these days that I was standing sentinel on the sand-hills with another soldier, when we espied five Indians approaching along the shore. Not to alarm our camp with such a trifle we allowed them to come up. They all appeared very good humoured, made their obeisance to us after their fashion, and begged of us, by signs, to conduct them to our camp. Upon which I said to my companion, I will take them there, while you remain where you are, for at that time my legs were not so infirm as they are now, in my old age. When I presented them to Cortes, they paid him the profoundest respect, and continually repeated the word, *lopelucio, lopelucio*, which in the Totonaque language means Lord, great God. In dress and language this people differed entirely from the Mexicans, whom Motecusuma had sent to our camp. They had large holes bored in their under-lips, in which they wore pieces of blue speckled stone, or thin plates of gold; the holes in their ears were still larger in size, and adorned with similar ornaments. Neither Aguilar nor Doña Marina understood their language; but the latter inquired of them whether there was any *naëyavatos*, or interpreter, among them? Upon which two of them answered that they understood the Mexican language, and now the discourse immediately commenced. They bid us welcome, and stated that their ruler had sent them hither to inquire who we were, and that he would be delighted to be of any use to such powerful men as we were. They would have waited upon us earlier if they had not shunned the people of Culhua, namely, the Mexicans (meaning as much as villains,) who had been with us. Most probably these people had heard of our battles at Tabasco and Potonchan; they at least knew that the Mexicans had secretly departed from us three days ago. Cortes learnt from them many things which were of the greatest importance to him, particularly respecting the enemies and opponents of Motecusuma: Cortes, therefore, was most friendly to these people, gave them various kinds of presents, and desired them to return to their ruler and acquaint him that he would visit him shortly in person. From this moment we called these Indians by no other name than *lopelucios*. However, it was impossible for us to remain on these sand-hills, on account of the long-legged and small gnats, which they call *chechenes*, and are the worst of all: we could get no sleep for them. Moreover, we had no kind of provisions left; our *cassave*-bread was quite mouldy and uneatable, on account of the worms, with which it swarmed: it was, therefore, no wonder that several of our men, who had Indian possessions in the island of Cuba, should wish to return home, which was in particular the case with all the friends and creatures of Velasquez. Cortes, observing this disposition, gave orders for our departure to Quiahuitzlan, which had been seen by Montejo and Alaminos, and where the vessels would be secure from the north winds, being sheltered by the rock above mentioned.

While preparations were making for our departure, the whole of Diego Velasquez's adherents united to remonstrate with Cortes. They asked him how he was to commence the march without provisions; it was, indeed, quite impossible to proceed further on by sea. Already thirty-five of our men had died either of the wounds they received at Tabasco, of sickness, or of hunger. The country we were now in was extensive, the population numerous, and the inhabitants would, no doubt, attack us in a few days. It was, therefore, most advisable to return to Cuba, and render an account to Diego Velasquez of the gold we had bartered for, of which we possessed a good deal: to this might be added the presents sent by Motecusuma, the golden sun, silver moon, the *casque* full of gold dust, and all the other precious things, which I have above mentioned. To which Cortes answered, "that he did not consider it advisable to return without having even seen the country. Up to this moment we had no reason to complain of ill luck; on the contrary, God had everywhere lent us his support. If we had lost any of our men, such things were to be expected in warlike undertakings. We should first explore the country more thoroughly; and with regard to provisions, there was sufficient maize in the country, with which we must make a shift for the present."

By these arguments Cortes succeeded in quieting the partisans of Diego Velasquez; yet it was of short duration, for they held secret meetings, and commenced setting all manner of intrigues on foot to bring about our return to Cuba: how far they succeeded we shall presently see.

Chapter 42

Hernando Cortes—Captain-General

I have already remarked how the relatives and friends of Diego Velasquez united to stop our further progress, and bring about our return to Cuba. Cortes, on his part, however, was no less active, and managed with his friends to get himself appointed our captain-general. In this the following personages acted the chief part: Alonso Hernandez Puertocarrero, Pedro de Alvarado, with his four brothers Jorge, Gonzalo, Gomez, and Juan; further, Christobal de Oli, Alonso de Avila, Juan de Escalante, Francisco de Lugo, myself, and many other cavaliers and officers.

Francisco de Montejo soon perceived what our intentions were, and kept a sharp look-out upon everything that was going on. I was drawn into this affair in the following manner: at midnight, Puertocarrero, Escalante, and De Lugo, to whom I stood somewhat related, both of us, moreover, being born at the same place, called upon me in my quarters, and said, "Bernal Diaz del Castillo, take your arms and follow us: we are to accompany Cortes, who is going to make the rounds." When we had arrived at some distance from my hut, they again commenced, "We have something to tell you, sir, but you must keep it a secret, for it is of great importance, and those of Diego Velasquez's partisans who mess with you must know nothing about it. We are of opinion that Cortes does not act rightly towards us. At Cuba he made known that he was going out to found a colony, and now we hear that he was not empowered to do so, but was merely sent out to barter for gold, and then to return to Cuba with all we should make. If this takes place, we are altogether ruined men, and Diego Velasquez will himself comfortably pocket the gold, and keep it, as he has on previous occasions. Do but reflect, sir, that this is the third expedition of the kind which you have accompanied, that you have spent your whole in them, and undergone so many fatigues, risked your life, and suffered from wounds, all for nothing. This we cannot allow. We cavaliers are sufficient in number, your friends one and all, and we must insist that Cortes founds a colony here, in the name of his majesty; we must also find means to acquaint our sovereign immediately with this. Promise that you also will be one of us. We have united to elect Cortes our captain-general. It would, indeed, be rendering God and our king a great service."

To all this I answered that I considered it equally inadvisable to return to Cuba, and that I was quite ready to give my consent towards electing Cortes captain-general and chief justice, until his imperial majesty should have communicated his wishes to us on that point. As this plan went round from one to another, the partisans of Diego Velasquez, who were much more numerous than we, soon got wind of it, and boldly asked Cortes what intrigues had been set on foot to form a colony here? and why he should shirk from rendering the account which was due to him by whom he had been appointed head of the expedition? Diego Velasquez would certainly be ill pleased with such proceedings: we could not do otherwise than re-embark: all his intrigues with the men were useless: to found a colony, we were in want both of provisions, men, and everything else to ensure success. Cortes, without showing the least irritability, answered, that he was quite of their opinion, and had not the remotest intention to act contrary to the instructions and wishes of Diego Velasquez, and immediately issued orders that every one who had come with him should repair on board by the next day.

As soon as we others, who had confederated, heard this, we declared to Cortes that he was doing wrong in thus wishing to deceive us. At Cuba he had publicly announced that he was going out to found a colony, and now it appeared it was merely for the sake of trafficking. We begged of him, for the sake of God and our king, not to break his word, but to found a colony, as was required of us, to promote the interests of his majesty and the service of God. It would be impossible for us to return here at any future time, as the inhabitants would certainly not permit us to land: but, if a colony was once founded, soldiers from every island in these parts would come flocking hither in order to assist us. Diego Velasquez had deceived us when he falsely announced that he was empowered by his majesty to found colonies: we were, therefore, determined to found one, and left it to the choice of the others if they wished to return to Cuba. Cortes at first refused to comply, and only submitted after much begging and entreating; as the saying goes, *what you desire Is my wish.*

He, however, made the condition that we should nominate him chief justice and captain-general, and, what was worse, that a fifth part of the gold should fall to his share which remained after deducting the fifths for his majesty: concerning all which and everything else, the royal secretary Godoy was to draw up a formal deed. Upon this we resolved that a town should be built, and called Villa Rica de la Vera Cruz, as we arrived off this coast on Holy Thursday, and stepped on land on Good Friday. The addition of Villa Rica (rich town) was owing to what Puertocarrero had some time previous said to Cortes, "He might look upon these rich countries,—he would know how to govern them;" meaning to say thereby, that he wished Cortes to be appointed captain-general.

After the ceremony of laying the first stone of the town was ended, we nominated the *alcalde*s and *regidors*. The chief *alcalde*s were Alonso Puertocarrero and Francisco de Montejo: Cortes purposely appointed the latter because he was not on the best terms with him. To give all the names of the *regidors* would be superfluous, and it must suffice to mention their names as they appear in the course of this narrative. We also erected a pillory inside the town, and a gallows outside. Pedro de Alvarado was appointed city-major; Christobal de Oli, colonel; Juan de Escalante, *alguacil*-major; treasurer, Gonzalo Mexi Mexia; book-keeper, Alonso de Avila; standard-bearer, a certain Corrar, as Villareal, who first filled this post, had got into disgrace with Cortes about an Indian female of Cuba, and was obliged to relinquish it. Achoa of Biscay and Alonso Romero were nominated *alguacil*s of the camp.

The reader will wonder that I have not yet mentioned the name of one of our principal men, Gonzalo de Sandoval, though he was such a renowned officer, being second to Cortes only, and particularly distinguished by our emperor himself. There is no other reason than that Sandoval was still very young, and that we did not make so much of him and other brave officers then as we did subsequently, when we saw all his real qualities developed in a manner that drew forth unbounded praise from Cortes and every soldier: indeed he was considered equal to Cortes himself.—Gomara has likewise related a good deal respecting these matters, of which he has been ill informed. I could not leave this unnoticed, however beautiful his style of writing may be, in which his strength really lies.

Chapter 43

Diego Velasquez and Cortes' Power

The partisans of Diego Velasquez, finding we had elected Cortes captain-general, and appointed the other officers just mentioned, were terribly annoyed and vexed. They armed themselves in small troops, and threw out the most insolent language against Cortes and those among us who had chosen him captain-general. All this they considered should not have been done without the consent of the whole of the officers and soldiers. Diego Velasquez had merely empowered Cortes to barter with the natives. In short, their dissatisfaction rose to such a pitch, that our party was afraid matters would be carried much farther, and end in hostilities. Cortes now secretly desired Juan de Escalante to intimate that we should demand the instructions to be produced which he had received from Velasquez. This was accordingly done, and Cortes pulled them out from under his waistcoat, handing them over to the royal secretary to be read aloud. And sure enough the words were, *After you have bartered for as many precious things as possible, you shall return home.* This document was signed by Velasquez, and countersigned by his private secretary Andreas de Duero. Upon this we desired of Cortes that these instructions should be entered into the appointment we had given him, and announced by a public crier, as had been done at Cuba, in order that his majesty might convince himself of the true state of things, and that everything was done to further his sovereign interest only. This step was most agreeable to our purpose, as the bishop of Burgos, Don Juan Rodriguez de Fonseca, was wrongly informed respecting these proceedings, and only laboured to ruin us, as we subsequently learnt. The partisans of Diego Velasquez, however, were not to be silenced by this; and as the election had been made without their knowledge, they considered it illegal, and maintained that they were not called upon to obey his commands, but were determined to return to Cuba. Cortes answered, that he would not compel them to remain, but would discharge any one who might wish it, even if he himself should, in the end, remain alone behind. By this some were silenced. Juan Velasquez de Leon, (who was closely related to Velasquez,) Diego de Ordas, Escobar, (whom we commonly termed the page,) Pedro de Escudero, and others of Velasquez's party, still continued refractory, and things at last came to such a pass, that, in the end, they formally refused to obey Cortes. In such a state of affairs it was necessary to adopt some stronger measure, which was carried into execution with our consent. We seized the persons of the above-mentioned refractory officers, bound them in chains, and kept watch over them as if they had been prisoners.

Respecting these circumstances Gomara has again been misinformed, and not a word is to be credited of anything he says on the subject.

Chapter 44

Pedro De Alvarado Goes Into the Interior

It was now resolved that Pedro de Alvarado should make an excursion into the interior to explore the country, gain further knowledge of some townships which we knew by name, and procure maize and other provisions, of which we were in the greatest want. For this purpose 100 men were selected, among whom were fifteen crossbow-men and six musketeers; above half, moreover, were adherents of Velasquez: the rest of us, on whom Cortes could fully depend, remained with him, in order that no conspiracy might be set on foot against him.

Alvarado, during this expedition, visited some small townships which were subject to a greater one, called, in the Aculhua language, Costatlan.[1] This language is that of Mexico and Motecusuma; and when we speak of persons of Aculhua, we must always understand subjects of his empire. Alvarado nowhere met with any inhabitants, but found sufficient proofs in the temples that boys and full-grown people had very recently been sacrificed; for the altars and walls were covered with drops of fresh blood. The flint knives with which the unfortunate victim's breast is cut open to tear the heart away, and the large stones on which they are sacrificed, still lay in their proper places. Most of the bodies thus seen by our men were without arms or legs, which, according to the accounts of the Indians, had been devoured. Our men were perfectly horror-struck at such barbarities: however, I will not waste another word on the subject, for we found the same thing over again in every district we visited in this country. Alvarado

1. Costatlan, Bernal Diaz also adds here, *"Y este nombre de Culua es en aquella tierra, como si dixessen los Romanos hallados."* As this passage is rather obscure, we thought it best to insert it here. The literal translation is: "And this appellation of Culua, in this country, means as much as when one would say, 'the merry Romans.'" In the 31st chapter he makes a similar remark.

found these districts well stocked with provisions, but so completely deserted by the inhabitants that he could only find two Indians to assist the men in carrying maize: every soldier, therefore, was compelled to take a load of greens and fowls, and in this way the detachment returned to our camp with a good supply of provisions, and without having encountered any disaster. This was all the damage our men did, although they had so many opportunities of doing more, Cortes having most strictly forbidden any wanton outrage, that there might not be a repetition of what happened on the island of Cozumel.

We were overjoyed with the provisions; for when man can satisfy his appetite, he forgets half his sufferings. Gomara mentions another expedition in this place, which, he says, Cortes himself undertook, with 400 men, to explore the interior of the country: but here again he must have been misinformed; for there was no other made than the one I have just mentioned. In the meantime Cortes was not inactive, but did all in his power to gain the adherents of Diego Velasquez: one was presented with some of the gold we had made,—for with gold mountains are removed; another was silenced by considerable promises. He likewise set the whole of them at liberty, excepting Juan Velasquez de Leon and Diego de Ordas, who were lying bound in chains on board a vessel: however, both these were also shortly after released, and they became true friends to him, of which they subsequently gave sufficient proofs. Gold, indeed, was not spared on this occasion, for they were only to be tamed by that means. As soon as greater union was thus restored, it was resolved that we should march for the township Quiahuitzlan, which I have above mentioned. Our vessels were also at the same time to set sail and run into the harbour, lying about four miles from the latter place.

Our march lay along the coast, and on our route we killed a large fish which had been thrown on shore; we then came to a pretty deep river, on whose banks the town of Vera Cruz at present lies: this we crossed by means of some old canoes we found here, and by ferryboats; I, however, swam across. On the opposite bank of the river lay several small townships, subject to one more extensive called Sempoalla. This was the home of the five Indians who came to Cortes in the character of ambassadors, and who were called by us *lopelucios*. We found the idol-temples stained with spots of blood, the apparatus for perfuming and sacrificing, a quantity of parrot feathers, and several packages of paper stitched one over the other, resembling our Spanish linen. We nowhere met any Indians; for as they had never before seen people like unto us, nor any horses, they had all run away from fear, so that we were forced to go hungry to bed. The next day we marched inland in an easterly direction: of course we had not the least knowledge of the road we were taking, and we turned at a venture into a beautiful meadow, where we found wild deer grazing. Pedro de Alvarado chased one of these on his brown mare, and managed to wound it with his lance; but the animal escaped over some heights.

In the meantime twelve Indians made their appearance, inhabitants of the district, where we were encamped for the night, bringing with them some fowls and maize-bread, which, they told Cortes, by means of our interpreter, had been sent us by their *cazique*, who had likewise desired we should visit his township, which lay at a distance of one sun, say a day's march, from our present station. Cortes returned them sincere thanks for their great kindness, and we marched on until we came to a small township, where a short time previous several human beings had been sacrificed. As the kind reader would be disgusted with hearing of the numbers of male and female Indians we found butchered along every road and in every village we passed through, I will be silent on that head, and merely add that a supper was provided for us in the small village where we had arrived. Here we also learnt that the road to Quiahuitzlan, which latter lay on a hill, passed through Sempoalla, where we next arrive.

CHAPTER 45

We March into Sempoalla

After we had slept in the village, where the twelve Indians had quartered us, and accurately ascertained the road we were to take to Quiahuitzlan, we left very early in the morning for that place. Cortes sent six of the Indians before us to acquaint the *caziques* of Sempoalla that we were approaching, and to beg permission to visit them. The six other Indians remained behind as our guides. The whole of us marched forward in the best order, while our cannon and other arms were ready for use at a moment's notice; besides this sharp-shooters were always in advance, all strong active fellows, whom as well as the horse no one could elude.

We were not further than three miles from Sempoalla, when we were met by twenty Indians who came to welcome us in the name of their *cazique*. These carried in their hands pine-apples, most deliciously scented, and of a deep red colour, which they presented to Cortes and the others who sat on horseback, adding that their ruler awaited us in his quarters, for on account of his corpulency he had been prevented from coming out to meet us himself. Cortes thanked them kindly for their attentions, and we marched forward. As we passed along the houses of the town we were greatly surprised, for a town of such magnitude we had not yet met with. And when we saw that all around had the appearance of a luxurious garden, and that the streets were filled with people of both sexes, we returned most fervent thanks to God for having allowed us to discover such a country. The vanguard of our horse was naturally very much in advance, and had arrived in the great square and up to the dwellings where our quarters were prepared. As the walls a few days previous had been newly plastered with lime, (which these Indians prepare uncommonly well,) and the sun was shining full upon them at the time, one of our horse soldiers came galloping up to Cortes at full speed to inform him that the walls here were built of silver. Aguilar and Doña Marina immediately saw that this was lime fresh laid on; which of course created abundance of laughter. We never omitted on subsequent occasions to remind the man of it, joking him that everything white appeared to him like silver.

When we arrived at our quarters the fat *cazique* came out in the courtyard to receive us. The man was, indeed, excessively corpulent, wherefore I shall always distinguish him thereby. He paid Cortes the greatest respect, and perfumed him according to the custom of the country, who then embraced him in return. After these welcomes we were shown into our quarters, which were very comfortable, and so spacious that there was sufficient room for us all. Food was next set before us, among which there was maize-bread and several basketsful of plums, of which there were great quantities, these being just then in season. As we were greatly famished, and had not for a length of time seen such quantities of provisions at once, some of us called the place Villariciosa (luxurious town), and others Sevilla. Cortes gave strict orders that the inhabitants should not be molested in the slightest degree, and also that none of us should leave our quarters.

It being announced to the fat *cazique* that we had finished dining, he sent word to Cortes that he was desirous of paying him a visit, and immediately after he arrived with a considerable number of distinguished personages, who wore heavy golden ornaments and richly-worked mantles. Cortes rose to meet them at the entrance of our quarters, and received them most kindly. After the first compliments were passed the fat *cazique* handed a present to him which he had brought, consisting in golden trinkets and cotton stuffs, but of little value. The *cazique* constantly repeated: "*lopelucio, lopelucio*, accept this in favourable kind; if we had more to give we should have brought it."

Cortes desired Doña Marina and Aguilar to acquaint him how grateful he was for so much kindness, and he had merely to inform him in what way he in return could be of service to him and his people. We were the vassals of the great emperor Charles, who had dominion over many kingdoms and countries, and who had sent us out to redress wrongs wherever we came, punish the bad, and make known his commands that human sacrifices should no longer be continued. To all this was added a good deal about our holy religion.

After the fat *cazique* heard this he sighed deeply, and complained most bitterly about Motecusuma and his governors. It was not long ago that he had been subdued by the former, and robbed of all his golden trinkets. His sway was so excessively oppressive, that he durst not move without his orders; yet no one had sufficient courage to oppose him, as he possessed such vast towns and countries, such numbers of subjects and extensive armies. Cortes answered that he would relieve him of the oppression under which he groaned, but for the present moment he could not occupy himself with such matters. He had first of all to pay a visit to his *acales*, (so ships are termed in their language,) and prepare our quarters in Quiahuitzlan, where they would further talk the matter over. The fat *cazique* said he was perfectly satisfied with this, and the next morning we left Sempoalla. Four hundred Indian porters, who, in this district, are termed *tamenes*, were sent to accompany us. Each of these porters is capable of carrying a weight of fifty pounds to a distance of twenty miles. We were all highly delighted that each of us had a man a piece to carry our baggage; for previously every one had to carry his own knapsack, the five or six Cuba Indians we had with us being of little use. Doña Marina and Aguilar said that according to the custom of this country the *caziques* were bound in times of peace to lend their porters to any one who required them. From this moment we always demanded them wherever we came. After the first day's march we staid the night at a small township not far from Quiahuitzlan. It was wholly uninhabited, and the people of Sempoalla furnished us with food for supper. Gomara allows Cortes to pass several days at Sempoalla, and then form the confederacy and rebellion against Motecusuma. This, together with the account he gives of the number of Cuba Indians we were said to have brought with us, is wholly false; for, as I have stated, we left Sempoalla immediately on the following morning after our arrival. Where and what caused the different tribes to revolt I will afterwards relate. For the present we shall make our entry into Quiahuitzlan.

Chapter 46
We March into Quiahuitzlan

The next morning about ten o'clock we arrived in the principal township Quiahuitzlan, which is built on the steep declivity of a rock, and would certainly be difficult to take if defended. We put no trust in the peace which reigned through the country, and marched in the best order with the greatest precaution. Our troops were preceded by the cannon, that it might be ready at hand if required. Here it was that Alonso de Avila, a severe and haughty man, ran a soldier named Alonso of Villanueva, who had only one arm, through the empty sleeve of his coat, with the point of his lance, because he marched out of the ranks. From that moment we termed the man the one-armed of Villanueva. However, I shall likewise be accused of marching out of the ranks, if I relate such trifles: I cannot deny it, and will, therefore, immediately fall in again. We arrived in the midst of the town without meeting any one, and were not a little surprised at this circumstance, as the inhabitants had left that very morning, when they found we were approaching their dwellings. On the most elevated point of the fortress there was an open space in front of the cues and large houses of their idols; and here we first met with fifteen well-dressed Indians, who were carrying perfuming pans. With these they went up to Cortes, perfumed him and all who were near at the time, bid us welcome, and most humbly begged forgiveness for not having come out to meet us, and confessed that fear of ourselves and horses had prevented them, and that they had first wished to know who we were. We had now only to make ourselves comfortable, they added, and that very evening they would see that all the inhabitants returned to their houses.

Cortes thanked them most kindly for their good reception, and told them many things about our holy religion and our great monarch, as was customary with us wherever we came. He also presented them with a few green glass beads and other trifles we had brought from Spain; they supplying us with fowls and maize-bread in return.

While the first welcomings were going on it was announced to Cortes that the fat *cazique* of Sempoalla was approaching in a sedan, supported by numbers of distinguished Indians. Immediately upon his arrival he renewed his complaints against Motecusuma, in which he was joined by the *cazique* of this township and the other chief personages. He related so much of the cruelties and oppression they had to suffer, and thereby sobbed and sighed so bitterly that we could not help being affected. At the time when they were subdued, they had already been greatly ill used; Motecusuma then demanded annually a great number of their sons and daughters, a portion of whom were sacrificed to the idols, and the rest were employed in his household and for tilling his grounds. His tax-gatherers took their wives and daughters without any ceremony if they were handsome, merely to satisfy their lusts. The Totonaques, whose territory consisted of upwards of thirty townships, suffered like violence.

Cortes consoled them as well as he could by means of our interpreters. He promised and assured them that he would put an end to such oppression and ill usage. It was particularly for this object that his majesty had sent us to their country; they should, therefore, keep up their spirits, and they would soon see what he was about to do for their good. This in some measure seemed to comfort them; though Cortes was unable wholly to allay the fear in which they stood of the great Motecusuma.

We soon had proof of this on the very spot; for, during our discourse with these *caziques*, some Indians belonging to the district announced that just then five Mexican tax-gatherers had arrived. At this information the *caziques* turned quite pale with fear; they left Cortes and hastened to receive the unexpected guests, for whom an apartment was immediately cleared and dinner set on table. Cacao in great quantities was in particular served up to them, which is the principal beverage of the Indians. As the house of the *cazique* was in the neighbourhood, the Mexicans passed by our quarters; but behaved with such reserve and so haughtily, that they neither addressed Cortes nor any of us. They wore richly-worked mantles and *maltatas* similarly manufactured, which were then still in fashion among them. The hair of their head was combed out quite glossy and tied up in a knot in which were stuck some sweet scented roses.

Every one carried a stick with a hook, and had an Indian slave with a fan to keep off the flies. They were accompanied by a great number of distinguished personages from the country of the Totonaques, who remained around them until they arrived in their quarters and had sat down to dinner. After this was finished they sent for the fat *cazique* and the other chiefs of the townships, and scolded them under severe threats for having received us. They had no business with us, added they; this was by no means the wish of their master Motecusuma, without whose command and permission they ought not to have provided us with quarters, nor given us any golden trinkets. They would have to pay dearly for all this; at present, however, they must find twenty Indians and an equal number of females, in order that by sacrificing them they might appease the gods for the evil service which had thus been rendered.

Cortes, who observed how restless every one appeared, desired Doña Marina and Aguilar to explain the reason of all this, and who the strange Indians were. Marina knew all that had passed, and told him accordingly; upon which he sent for the fat *cazique*, with the chiefs of the townships, and questioned them himself as to who the strangers were whom they treated so ceremoniously? They answered, that these were tax-gatherers of the great Motecusuma, who had remonstrated with them for having received us without his previous permission, and now required twenty persons, of both sexes, for a sacrifice to the god of war, in order that he should grant them the victory over us. They had likewise been assured, that Motecusuma would take us prisoners and turn us into slaves.

Upon this Cortes consoled and bid them take courage, assuring them he would punish the Mexicans for it, as both he himself and his troops were willing, and had the power to do so.

Chapter 47

Rebellion Against Motecusuma

Cortes further said to the *caziques*, they were aware he had already assured them that the emperor, our master, had specifically commissioned him to punish all those who did evil, and in particular, no longer to suffer kidnapping nor human sacrifices.

As the Mexican tax-gatherers now required human beings of them for those sacrifices, he would take and keep them prisoners until Motecusuma should learn the reason why he had done so, and was made acquainted with the other violent measures they were accustomed to commit against them, their wives and daughters.

The *caziques* were excessively alarmed that Cortes should require this at their hands, and durst not venture to lay hands on the tax-gatherers of the mighty Motecusuma. But Cortes exhorted them for such a length of time that they at last took courage, seized their persons, and fastened them, in their fashion, to long poles, by collars, which went round the neck, so that they could not even move themselves. One of them, who made resistance, was whipped into the bargain.

Upon this Cortes commanded the *caziques* no longer to obey the mandates of Motecusuma, nor to pay him tribute, and to make these his wishes known to all those tribes with whom they were allied and friendly, adding that they should inform him, whether there were tax-gatherers in other districts, that he might also send to take them prisoners.

The rumour of all this quickly spread through the whole country, as the fat *cazique* despatched messengers to that end, while the chiefs, who had accompanied the Mexican tax-gatherers, hastened back to their townships to relate the wonderful news. When the Indians learnt this astounding, and to them so important an occurrence, they said to one another, that, such great things could not have been done by men, but only by *teules*, which sometimes mean gods, sometimes demons, here in the former sense; which was the reason they termed us *teules*, from that moment; and I beg the reader to observe, that whenever in future I speak of *teules* in affairs relating to us, that we are meant thereby.

All the *caziques* were of opinion that we should sacrifice the prisoners, that they might not return to Mexico and relate what had befallen them. Cortes, however, strictly forbade this, and placed a strong watch over them. About midnight he ordered the sentinels into his presence, and said to them: "Pay particular attention to what I say. Take two of the most active of the prisoners, now in our hands, and bring them into my quarters. This must be done with great circumspection, so that the Indians of this township may know nothing of it."

When the two men were brought before Cortes, he did as if he was unconscious they were Mexicans, and questioned them, by means of interpreters, as to whence they came, and why they had been taken prisoners? To which they answered, "that the *caziques* of Sempoalla, and of this township, had seized upon their persons in secret understanding with us." Cortes, however, positively assured them, that he was totally ignorant of the whole matter, and was very sorry it should have happened. He immediately ordered food to be given them, and otherwise to be kindly treated, and commissioned them to acquaint their monarch, Motecusuma, that we were all his sincerest friends and most devoted servants. That they might not suffer any further ill treatment, he added, they should be set at liberty and he would severely reprimand the *caziques*, by whom they had been imprisoned. He was ready to render them any service in his power, and he would likewise release their three companions; they themselves, however, had better get out of sight as quickly as possible, that they might not be retaken by the inhabitants and killed. Both the prisoners said, they should be very thankful for their liberty, but were afraid of falling again into their enemies' hands, as they were compelled to pass through their country. Cortes therefore ordered six sailors to take the Mexicans in a boat to a certain point on the coast, twelve miles distant, where they would be out of the Sempoallan territory. All this was dexterously managed, and when daylight appeared the *caziques* and other chiefs were not a little surprised to find only three prisoners remaining. These they insisted should be sacrificed, but Cortes feigned to be highly incensed at the escape of the two, and said he was determined to guard the others himself.

To this end he ordered chains to be brought from our vessels, with which the prisoners were bound, and in that way taken on board, where their chains were taken off again. They received the kindest treatment, and were assured they would be sent back to Mexico in a very short time.

The *caziques* of Sempoalla, Quiahuitzlan, and those from the country of the Totonaques, now assembled and explained the position in which they were placed at present, as no doubt Motecusuma, upon the first intelligence of the imprisonment of his tax-gatherers, would put his army in motion and fall upon them, the consequence of which would be their total extirpation.

But Cortes assured them, with the most pleasing smile on his countenance, that he and his brothers who were with him would be their protection, and he who should dare to molest them, should forfeit his life. Upon this the *caziques*, one and all, promised to unite their whole armed force to ours against Motecusuma and his allies. On this occasion Diego de Godoy drew up a formal deed of their subjection to the sceptre of his majesty the emperor, and notice was sent of this to the different townships of the province. As there was no further talk of tribute, and tax-gatherers no longer made their appearance, these people were almost out of their senses for excessive joy in having shaken off the Mexican yoke.

Chapter 48
Villa Rica de la Vera Cruz

After we had thus formed an alliance with the thirty townships of the Totonaque mountains, which had revolted from Motecusuma and submitted of their own free will to the sceptre of our sovereign, we immediately hastened to profit by the circumstance and found Villa Rica de la Vera Cruz. The spot we made choice of lay at about two miles distance from the fortress of Quiahuitzlan, in the valley beneath. We first of all marked out the ground for the church, the market, the magazines and other public buildings belonging to a town. We then set off part of the ground to form a fortress, and nothing could exceed the assiduity with which the walls of the foundation were carried up, the woodwork completed, the turrets and loopholes constructed with the parapets. Cortes himself put the first hand to it, carried a basket filled with stones and earth on his shoulders, and worked at the foundations. The *caziques* and all of us followed his example, and every part of the work was carried on with like vigour. Some were mixing mortar, fetching water, burning chalk, baking bricks and tiles, others prepared the food and cut wood. The smiths hammered hard at the nails and other ironwork. In short, from the highest to the lowest showed the greatest activity, while the Indians lent us such efficacious aid, that in a short time the church and other buildings were quite finished, and the fortress nearly so.

In the meantime Motecusuma received the intelligence at Mexico, that his tax-gatherers had been imprisoned by our allies; that the latter had renounced obedience to him, and that all the Totonaque townships had revolted. He was excessively enraged against Cortes and the whole of us, and ordered one of his powerful chiefs to make war upon the tribes which had revolted, and extirpate them to a man. Against us he would march in person at the head of an immense army, commanded by many generals. While preparations for this purpose were being made, the two prisoners whom Cortes had liberated arrived in Mexico. When Motecusuma learnt that Cortes had restored them to liberty, and himself sent them to Mexico with the commission to offer his services to their monarch, the Almighty softened down the hardness of his heart, and he resolved to make inquiries as to what our intentions were. To this end he despatched two of his young nephews, accompanied by four aged men, who were *caziques* of distinction, to our quarters, sending with them a present consisting in gold and cotton stuffs. These men were commissioned to thank Cortes for the liberation of his two tax-gatherers, but at the same time to make heavy complaints respecting these tribes who had presumed to revolt from him, merely because we had taken them under our protection, and now refused all further obedience and to pay tribute. At present he was merely withheld from putting his threat into execution of exterminating them totally, out of consideration for us, since we inhabited their dwellings; for, in our persons he recognized that people whose arrival in this country had been foretold by his ancestors, and who were of the same lineage with himself. However, they would not long rejoice in their treachery, and he should know how to deal with them at some future period.

Cortes received these messengers very kindly and accepted their present, which was worth above 2000 *pesos*. He assured them that he as well as all the rest of us were friendly disposed, and ready to serve Motecusuma, and that it was in this spirit we had taken the three other tax-gatherers under our protection, who were now immediately brought forth from our vessels, clothed and delivered up to the ambassadors. Neither did Cortes on his part suppress the complaints he had to make against Motecusuma, for he told them, that Quitlalpitoc, his governor, had passed a night in our quarters, and had been uncourteous enough not to call upon him. He was, certainly, convinced that such behaviour had not been commanded by Motecusuma, but had emanated from the natural ill-breeding of the man. Honourable treatment, however, had so much worth in our estimation, that for this reason only had we paid a visit to the townships where we now were. Motecusuma, therefore, ought to pardon the people for our sakes. But as to their complaints respecting the refusal to pay tribute, it was to be imagined that they could not serve two masters at once, as they had, during our stay here, sworn allegiance to our emperor. For the rest, he and his companions would shortly wait upon Motecusuma himself, when these matters could be altogether amicably adjusted.

After this and other declarations, Cortes presented both these distinguished young personages and their four venerable companions, who were men of the first consequence, with blue and green coloured beads, paying them the greatest possible respect.

As the meadows in this neighbourhood were well adapted for cavalry exercise, Cortes desired Alvarado, who had an excellent brown mare, and our other good riders, to go through the different manoeuvres, by which we quite won the hearts of these messengers, who returned highly satisfied to Mexico. About this time Cortes lost his horse; for which reason Ortiz, the musician, and Bartolome Garcia, the mountaineer, gave up their dark brown horse to him, which was one of the best among the whole troop.

For the rest, our allies in the mountains and the inhabitants of Sempoalla had stood in no little awe of Motecusuma, as they believed nothing less than that he would instantly invade their country with a great army to extirpate them. But, when they found that even several of his relatives arrived, bringing presents, and that they comported themselves so submissively to Cortes, they began more and more to fear us, and the *caziques* said to one another, these must necessarily be *teules*, as even Motecusuma himself stood in awe of us and sent us presents. If they had previously formed a great idea of our power, it was now vastly augmented by this unexpected circumstance.

Chapter 49

A Mexican Attack

After the Mexican messengers had taken their leave, the fat *cazique* with several other distinguished personages from among our allies called upon Cortes, and begged of him to repair to a township called Tzinpantzinco, two days' journey, or about from thirty-two to thirty-six miles from Sempoalla; as a number of Mexican warriors had assembled there, destroying their fields and plantations, falling upon their subjects, and doing all manner of mischief. Cortes manifested great sympathy for them, but scarcely knew what answer he should give, as he had promised them every assistance. He, therefore, desired them to retire, until he should have considered the matter a little.

After he had bethought himself for a short time, he turned smilingly round to us who were standing near him and said: "Methinks, gentlemen, we already pass here for great heroes; indeed, after what has happened with the tax-gatherers these people must look upon us as gods, or a species of beings like their idols. Now, I am of opinion it is best to strengthen them in this notion; and that they may think that one single man of us is sufficient to dislodge the Mexicans from the fortress of Tzinpantzinco, we will send thither old Heredia of Biscay. The malignancy of his features, his huge beard, his half-mangled countenance, his squinting eyes and lame leg, constitute him the most fitting person for this object, besides which he is a musketeer."

Cortes then sent for the man and said to him: "You must go with the *caziques* to the river which flows about a mile from this spot. When you have arrived there do as if you were thirsty, and wished to wash your hands; then fire off your musket. This shall be a signal for me to send some one after you, who will, in my name, desire you to return. All this is done in order that the Indians may suppose us to be deities, and as you have not one of the most pleasing countenances, I trust they will take you by preference to be some idol."

Heredia, who had served many years in Italia, perfectly well knew how to perform his part, and gladly undertook this matter. Cortes now ordered the fat *cazique*, and the other chief Indians who were expecting succours from us, into his presence again, saying to them: "I send this my brother with you to drive the Mexicans out of the fortress, and to bring those whom he does not kill prisoners to me."

When the *caziques* heard this they stood in utter amazement, not knowing whether Cortes was in earnest; but finding he did not change countenance, they began to convince themselves that this was really his intention, and marched away in company of Heredia. When he had arrived between the mountains he loaded his musket and shot it off in the air, that it might be heard by every Indian in the district. The *caziques* themselves sent notice to the different townships, that they had a *teule* with them, and were marching to Tzinpantzinco in order to kill the Mexicans there.

I have mentioned this laughable circumstance, that the reader may see what artifices Cortes employed to throw dust into the eyes of the Indians. Of course, when Heredia arrived at the river he was recalled; the *caziques* returning with him, to whom Cortes said, he had formed a different plan. His friendship for them was so great, that he would accompany them himself with some of his brothers, in order to take a survey of the country and the fortress. They had only to furnish four hundred porters to convey the cannon, and to return to us next morning early. All this was accordingly done, and as soon as daylight had broken forth, we moved forward, four hundred in number, with fourteen horse and a sufficient number of matchlocks and *arquebuses*.

On this occasion some of Diego Velasquez's adherents again began to murmur, declaring that Cortes might proceed further with those who wished to follow him; but as for themselves they were determined to return to Cuba.

How this matter terminated we shall see in the following chapter.

Chapter 50
Disaffection

Next morning when our petty officers went round to our different quarters and called upon the men to march out with their arms and horses, the partisans of Velasquez insolently answered, that they would take no further part in any expedition, but wished to return home to their possessions in Cuba. They had already lost enough, by allowing themselves to be led away by Cortes to join him in the first instance; they now, however, would desire him to fulfil the promise, which he had made in the camp on the downs, namely, to grant those their discharge who wished to return to Cuba, and provide them a vessel and the necessary provisions.

Seven men now declared they were positively determined to return home; Cortes, therefore, desired they should be brought before him, and asked them, "Why they wished to play him such a vile trick?" They answered in rather an angry tone, "That they could not help feeling astonished, he should think of founding a colony with a handful of men in a country full of towns possessing many thousands of inhabitants. They were suffering from indisposition, quite tired of roving about, and desired to return to their settlements in Cuba; he ought, therefore, to grant them their discharge according to promise."

To this Cortes answered, in the mildest manner possible, that he had made such promise indeed; but, that they would be acting in a manner forgetful of their duty to desert the standard of their captain at a time when he was meditating an expedition: at the same time he commanded them to embark themselves immediately, and provided them with a vessel, *cassave*-bread, a bottle of oil, a quantity of vegetables, and such things as ships generally take on distant voyages. One of these men, a certain Moron of Delbayamo, had a well-trained horse, and exchanged it most profitably with Juan Ruano for some valuable property the latter had at Cuba.

When these men were about to set sail, the rest of our troops, headed by the *alcaldes* and *regidors* of the town of Vera Cruz, repaired to Cortes and begged of him to issue an order that no one should leave the country, an order which both the service of God and his majesty required, declaring that they considered every one merited death who could think of such a thing, surrounded as we were by such numerous enemies, nor could we look upon them in any other light than men who wished to desert their commander and his standard in the midst of battle and in the moment of the greatest danger. Cortes, nevertheless, did as if he was desirous of discharging the malcontents, but soon after countermanded this order. All they got for their pains was contempt and disgrace, while Moron in the bargain was done out of his horse, which Juan Ruano had no wish to return him. Upon this Cortes gave orders for our march, and we arrived without any accident in Tzinpantzinco.

Chapter 51
At Tzinpantzinco

The first day we marched twenty miles, and arrived at Sempoalla, where we passed the night: here 2000 Indian warriors, divided into four troops, stood ready to join us. The second day, towards nightfall, we arrived at the plantations in front of Tzinpantzinco, and took the road leading into that fortress, which wound up between large and steep rocks. The inhabitants were most likely apprized of our approach; for immediately eight Indians of distinction and several *papas* came out to us, making signs of peace, and asked Cortes, with tears in their eyes, why we were going to kill them, as they had done nothing against us? We bore the character of doing good only wherever we might come, and of putting a stop to the oppression of nations, and for that reason had even imprisoned the tax-gatherers of Motecusuma: between the warriors of Sempoalla, who accompanied us, and themselves there existed an inimical feeling, already of ancient date, respecting a dispute of territory and boundaries, and these people had no other object in view than to plunder and destroy them, under our protection: there was, indeed, generally speaking, a Mexican garrison in their township, which, however, had returned home, upon the news that we had imprisoned the tax-gatherers; they, therefore, begged of us not to proceed any further, and to be merciful towards them.

When these representations were made known to Cortes through our interpreters, he immediately ordered Alvarado and Christobal de Oli, with us who were nearest to him, to march off to the Sempoallans and command them not to advance any further. Though we used the utmost expedition to fulfil these orders, yet we already found them plundering the plantations. This made Cortes excessively angry; he ordered the chiefs of the Sempoallans into his presence, and severely remonstrated with them for such behaviour: he commanded them, with heavy threats, to bring him all the plunder, and not to set a foot into the town. They had trumped up a false story to us, he told them, merely to be enabled, under our protection, to plunder their neighbours and then to sacrifice them, whereby they had deserved death. Our emperor had not sent us to this country to commit such crimes, and they had better mind not again to fall into such guilt, as none of them would escape alive if it happened again.

After this earnest reproof, the *caziques* and chiefs of Sempoalla brought the prisoners and the turkey-fowls they had captured: the first, Cortes ordered to be set at liberty, and the latter were restored to their owners; upon which he commanded the Sempoallans, in a very angry tone, to return to their camp and there remain for the night.

The *caziques* and *papas* of Tzinpantzinco, with other inhabitants of the surrounding neighbourhood, having witnessed this act of justice, and seeing altogether how friendly Cortes was disposed, and the good deeds which he manifested, were the more susceptible of the things he told them about our holy religion,—respecting the abolishment of their human sacrifices and kidnapping, the discontinuation of other abominations and obscenities, with other matters salutary to their well being. They appeared so well inclined that they assembled the inhabitants of the surrounding districts, and formally declared themselves vassals of the emperor, our master. On this occasion, likewise, numerous complaints were made against Motecusuma, which all terminated with instances of his oppression similar to what we had heard from the Sempoallans and Quiahuitzlans.

The next morning very early Cortes sent for the chiefs and *caziques* of the Sempoallans. In fear and anxiety had they passed the while, in consequence of his anger for having attempted to deceive us with a pack of lies. He brought about a reconciliation and good understanding between them and the inhabitants of Tzinpantzinco, which was never afterwards interrupted. Upon this we again put ourselves in motion, and marched back to Sempoalla, but took a different route over two townships friendly with the Tzinpantzincans, where we rested ourselves, as we were greatly fatigued, and the sun was excessively hot. In one of these townships, a certain Mora, of Ciudad-Rodrigo, took some fowls out of an Indian hut, which so greatly incensed Cortes that he ordered a rope to be tied around the fellow's neck, and would have had him hung up if Alvarado, who was standing next to Cortes, had not cut the rope in two with his sword, and thus released the poor devil, who had the fear of death before his eyes.

I have merely mentioned this trait to convince the curious reader how exemplary Cortes acted, and of the necessity of being strict under similar circumstances. Mora subsequently lost his life in a battle we fought on a mountain in the province of Guatimala. After we had left these two townships in peace, we found the fat *cazique* with the chiefs of Sempoalla in some huts which they had constructed for us, where they were waiting our arrival with various kinds of provisions which they had brought with them. Although Indians, they readily perceived what a good and holy thing is justice, and that Cortes' declaration of our having come into these countries to put an end to all oppression, perfectly agreed with his conduct on our entry into Tzinpantzinco; they, therefore, became the more united to us. We passed the night in these huts, and returned next morning, in company of our Indian friends, to Sempoalla. Indeed, the only wish of the Sempoallans was now, that we should never leave their country again, fearing Motecusuma would send an army about their ears; they, therefore, proposed to Cortes, since such a close and friendly alliance now subsisted between us, and we could look upon each other as brothers, that we should choose wives from among their daughters and relatives, that our posterity might descend from one and the same stock. In order that this more intimate connexion might be brought about, they immediately made a good beginning by presenting us with eight females, all daughters of *caziques*: one of these, the niece of the fat *cazique*, was given to Cortes, and Puertocarrero was presented with the daughter of another powerful *cazique*, whom they called Cuesco. All these young women were finely dressed out after the fashion of the country: they wore beautiful shifts, had golden chains about their necks, golden rings in their ears, and had other Indian females to wait upon them.

When the fat *cazique* presented these, he said to Cortes, "*Tecle*, (which signifies sir, in their language,) these seven women are intended for your chief officers, and this my niece, who herself holds dominion over a country and a people, I have destined for you." Cortes joyfully accepted of the young women, and returned thanks to the chiefs, remarking, at the same time, that he should gladly recognize in these women, the bonds of brotherly union between us. But now they should likewise renounce their idols, and no longer bring them human sacrifices. It grieved him sorely whenever he reflected on the monstrous heresy in which they lived; henceforth he would neither see nor hear of these abominations, of human sacrifices and unnatural offences: then only could a permanent and brotherly union subsist between us. Above all things the women must be converted to Christianity, before we could think of taking them. Further, all unnatural crimes must be put a stop to, and young men must cease to go about in female garments, to make a livelihood by such cursed lewdness. Indeed, hardly a day passed by that these people did not sacrifice from three to four, and even five Indians, tearing the hearts out of their bodies, to present them to the idols and smear the blood on the walls of the temple. The arms and legs of these unfortunate beings were then cut off and devoured, just in the same way we should fetch meat from a butcher's shop and eat it: indeed I even believe that human flesh is exposed for sale cut up, in their *tiangues*, or markets.

"All these atrocities," added Cortes, "must cease from this moment; then only could our union be sincere, and should we be able to make them lords over additional countries." To this the *caziques*, the *papas*, and all the other personages answered, "That it would be impossible to abolish their idols and the human sacrifices: for everything that was good they received from these idols; they made their seeds grow and granted them all necessaries; but with regard to the unnatural crimes, they would strive in future to put an end to them."

This unsatisfactory answer made a most disagreeable impression on Cortes and all of us; for, indeed, we could no longer bear to look upon their barbarities and the dissolute life which they led. Cortes spoke a long time to us upon the subject; he brought many holy and useful lessons to our mind, and observed "That we could do nothing which would be more beneficial to this people, and more to the glory of God, than to abolish this idolatry with its human sacrifices. It was certainly to be expected that the inhabitants would rise up in arms, if we proceeded to destroy their idols: we should, however, make the attempt, if even it were to cost us our lives."

Upon this we all arrayed ourselves as if we were preparing for battle, and Cortes acquainted the *caziques* that we were now going out to destroy their idols. When the fat *cazique* heard this he ordered the other chiefs to call out the warriors in their defence, and when we were about to mount up a high temple where the sacrifices were made,—I forget now how many steps led to the top,—he and the other chiefs became outrageously furious. They went menacing up to Cortes, and asked him, "Why he was going to destroy their gods? such an insult they would not suffer; it would be their and our destruction."

Cortes now also lost patience, and answered, "He had already told them several times they should not sacrifice to these monsters, who were nothing more than deceivers and liars. There was now, therefore, no alternative left him than to lay violent hands on them himself, and hurl them from their bases. He must look upon them as his worst enemies, and not as friends, since they would put no faith in his advice. He was well aware what design their chiefs and armed warriors had in hand; his forbearance was at last exhausted, and any opposition would cost them their lives."

These threats were most intelligibly interpreted to the Indians by Doña Marina, who also put them in mind of Motecusuma's army, which every moment might fall upon them. They, therefore, turned the question another way, and declared, "That they were not worthy of laying hands on their gods. If we durst venture to do so, they supposed we must, for we could not resist the temptation; but they would never give their consent."

They had scarcely done speaking when more than fifty of us began to mount the steps of the temple. We tore down the idols from their pediments, broke them to pieces, and flung them piecemeal down the steps. Some of these idols were shaped like furious dragons, and were about the size of young calves; others with half the human form; some again were shaped like large dogs, but all were horrible to look at.

When the *caziques* and *papas* thus beheld these monsters lying crumbled on the ground, they set up a miserable howl, covered their faces, and begged forgiveness of the idols in the Totonaque language, as they were unable to protect them against the *teules*, nor durst they attack us for fear of Motecusuma. It did not, however, end here, for their armed warriors who had now come up began to fly their arrows at us. Finding matters had taken such a turn, we seized the fat *cazique*, six *papas*, and several of the chief personages; and Cortes declared to them, that if the attack was not instantly staid they should all forfeit their lives. Upon this the fat *cazique* commanded his men to desist, and when quiet was somewhat restored they began to negotiate about terms of peace, which was concluded as shall shortly be related.

In this place I have only further to add, that our march to Tzinpantzinco was the first expedition Cortes made towards the interior of New Spain, and that it turned out greatly to our advantage. The historian Gomara here again tells his fables of the many thousands of human beings we destroyed at Tzinpantzinco; the curious reader, however, may sufficiently convince himself from my account what little faith is to be placed in his history, however beautiful the style may be in which it is written.

Chapter 52

An Altar to the Blessed Virgin

After peace had been restored between us, the *caziques*, *papas*, and other chiefs, Cortes ordered the fragments of the idols we had destroyed to be carried away and burnt. These orders were executed by six *papas* who came forth from a particular house, into which they carried the broken pieces and burnt them. The dress of these priests consisted in a long black cloak, white cassock, without sleeves, which hung down to the feet, and in a species of hood, which some wore greater, some less in size. Their dress was completely clogged together with blood, with which they were besmeared from head to foot, and impeded in their walk: they likewise smelt most offensively of sulphur and putrid flesh. We subsequently learnt that these *papas* were sons of distinguished personages. They were forbidden to marry, but were wholly given to unnatural offences, and fasted on certain days. Generally speaking, I never saw them eat anything else than the seeds of the cotton tree; they may, however, have partaken of other food for all I know.

When the idols were burnt, Cortes said everything that was edifying to the Indians by means of our interpreters. "Now," he said, "we could look upon them as our true brothers, and lend them every powerful assistance against Motecusuma and the Mexicans, he having already acquainted the former that he was no longer to make war upon them, nor to exact tribute. Instead of their idols, he would give them our own blessed Virgin and Sainte, the mother of Jesus Christ, in whom we believed, and to whom we prayed, that she might intercede and protect them in heaven."

The Indians listened with great good nature to this and many other things, which Cortes explained to them, concerning our holy religion. Every mason in the town was now set to work to bring chalk, which was in great abundance here, to clean away the blood from the walls of the cues, and plaster them well over. The day following this work was finished and an altar erected, which was covered with cotton cloth. The Indians were likewise ordered to bring a quantity of their splendid and sweet-scented roses with small branches of trees. Of these a garland was plaited, which was constantly to be renewed, that the place might remain pure and undefiled. Four *papas* were selected by Cortes to take charge of this; but their hair was previously shorn off, which they wore, as I have before remarked, very long and bristly; their dirty cloaks were taken off, and white ones put on, which, with the other part of their dress, they were in future to keep perfectly clean. In order, however, that they might have some one to look over them in their new occupation, Cortes nominated Juan de Torres, an old lame invalid of Cordova, to dwell near the altar, in the capacity of anchorite. The carpenters likewise made a cross which we erected on an elevated base, well plastered over with lime.

The next morning early father Olmedo said mass. A regulation was also made that in future the copal of this country should be used instead of our usual incense, and the inhabitants were taught to make wax candles from the wax of the country; of which, up to this moment, they had made no manner of use: these candles were always to be kept burning on the altar. The principal *caziques* of the district and village attended mass. But the chief ornaments there were the eight Indian females, who in the meantime had remained with their parents and relatives. These were now baptized after an edifying discourse had preceded the ceremony. The niece of the fat *cazique*, a very ugly woman, was named Doña Catalina, and presented to Cortes, who accepted her with every appearance of delight. The daughter of Cuesco, on the other hand, was most beautiful for an Indian female, and received the name of Doña Francisca, and fell to the lot of Puertocarrero. The six remaining young women, whose names I have totally forgotten, were given to some other of our soldiers.

The mass and baptismal ceremony being concluded, the *caziques* and principal personages took their leave, and from this moment the best feeling subsisted between us, for they were highly delighted that Cortes had accepted their daughter. We, therefore, returned to our new town Vera Cruz amidst the most joyous professions of friendship, and we shall soon see what happened there.

The good reader, however, may feel assured that nothing of any consequence further took place at Sempoalla than what I have related, and that herein Gomara and the other historians have completely erred.

Chapter 53
Arrival at Vera Cruz

We arrived at Vera Cruz, in company of the most distinguished personages of Sempoalla, on the same day that a ship had run in there from Cuba. The captain's name was Francisco de Saucedo, but we always called him the gallant, from his extravagance in beautifying his outward person, being altogether a perfect fop. He was said to have been at one time butler to the admiral of Castile, and was born at Medina de Rioseco. Along with him were ten soldiers, and a certain Luis Marin, a most distinguished officer, who afterwards became one of our chief commanders in the Mexican campaigns. Both the former had horses, one a stallion, and the other a mare. These men brought us intelligence that Diego Velasquez had obtained authority from Spain to trade and found colonies wherever he liked, and was appointed *adelantado* of Cuba. All this pleased his adherents excessively, in particular the latter preferment.

The building of the fortress having solely occupied us for a length of time, and now in such a forward state that we could lay the woodwork, we began to grow tired of doing nothing. Almost the whole of us, therefore, addressed Cortes in a body: representing to him, that we had now been three months in this country, and high time we should just convince ourselves how much truth there was in the boasted power of Motecusuma, of which so much had been said: we would gladly risk our lives in it, and therefore begged he would make preparations for this expedition. But, previous to commencing our march, we ought first to give some proof of our most humble submission to his majesty our emperor, by forwarding him a complete account of everything that had befallen us since our departure from Cuba. We also proposed that all the gold we had bartered for, and the presents sent by Motecusuma, should be forwarded to his majesty.

In answer to which Cortes said, that our ideas accorded exactly with his own, and that he had already spoken to the same effect to several of the cavaliers. There was merely one circumstance which caused him to hesitate, namely, that if each person took the portion of gold which fell to his share, too little would remain to be worthy of his majesty's acceptance. For this reason he commissioned Diego de Ordas and Francisco de Montejo, who were thorough men of business to see what they could make out of those men whom they might expect would demand their share. This was accordingly done, and they represented to every one that we were desirous of sending his majesty the emperor a present in gold, which, considering it was the first, ought indeed to be something valuable. In order, however, to make this possible, nothing remained but that each one should give up his share of the gold which had been made up to this moment. A great number of officers and soldiers had already signed their hands to that effect; yet every one was at liberty to act herein as he thought proper. Here was the paper, which every one who chose could put his hand to.

Every one, without exception, signed his name to the document, and agents were chosen to be despatched to Spain. These were Alonso Puertocarrero and Francisco de Montejo, to whom Cortes himself had already given above two thousand *pesos*. The best vessel of our squadron, furnished with the necessary provisions and manned with fifteen sailors, was selected to convey them. The charge of the vessel was given to two pilots, one of whom was Anton de Alaminos, from his being so well acquainted with the passage through the Bahama channel, and the first who had ventured that road. Upon this all of us, in common, drew up an account of our adventures expressly for his majesty, relating everything that had happened to us, and Cortes himself, as he assured us, likewise wrote a very circumstantial narrative, which, however, was not given us to read.[1] The account was signed by all the authorities of the new town and ten soldiers, of which I myself was one. But there was likewise another account drawn up by all the officers and soldiers, the contents of which will be fully explained in the following chapter.

1. Most probably Cortes' despatches of the 16th of July, 1519, which were lost.

Chapter 54

A Letter to the Emperor

This account very properly opened with those distinguished marks of respect which were due to our great emperor and master. Then followed a complete account of our expedition, from the day of our departure from Cuba up to our arrival on the coast of Mexico, and the day the account was drawn up. We did not omit to state that we had merely been induced to join the expedition from a promise that we were going to found a colony, and how Diego Velasquez had given Cortes secret instructions merely to confine himself to the trade of barter. That Cortes, conformably to this, had indeed wished to return to Cuba with the gold we had made; that, however, we had compelled him to remain here and found a colony, for which purpose we had elected him captain-general and chief justice, until we should receive his most gracious majesty's pleasure on this head. We had, moreover, promised him a fifth part of all the gold that should remain after deducting the fifths for his majesty. We then mentioned the name of Francisco Hernandez de Cordoba, as the first discoverer of this country; the expedition which followed upon that under Juan de Grijalva; of our landing on the island of Cozumel, and of our fortunate discovery of Geronimo de Aguilar, and other things. We described our negotiations with the great Motecusuma, mentioning his power and riches, of which the things he had given us to present to his majesty, consisting in the sun of gold and moon of silver, and the *casque* of gold dust, as it is found in the mines, as also the other articles of solid and manufactured gold, were small proofs.

After this we spoke about the extent of the country, its population, the arts, customs, and religion of the inhabitants, of whom we sent four as a sample, whom we had liberated from a wooden cage at Sempoalla, where they were being fattened for a sacrificial feast.

We then mentioned something about ourselves; how we were in all 450 armed men in the midst of so many warlike tribes; how our expedition had merely for its object to serve God and his majesty; and, in the position we were now placed, how much depended upon a man being at our head who was acquainted with the country, and in whom we could repose all trust. We most humbly begged of his majesty not to confer the command of this country upon any one of his officers; from its extent and vast riches, it was worthy of being ruled by a royal prince or some other great personage. We all feared that the archbishop Don Rodriguez de Fonseca, whom his majesty had entrusted with the government of Indian affairs, had destined the command to one of his own creatures, namely, a certain Diego Velasquez, who was then viceroy of Cuba; this favour, however, was entirely owing to the presents which the bishop received from Velasquez, consisting in the most valuable townships of his imperial domains wherever any gold was to be found. As his majesty's most humble and faithful servants, we could not neglect to bring this under his imperial notice, and we had resolved to wait until our agents had thrown themselves at his majesty's feet to hand over our letters, and his majesty should have acquainted them with his imperial wishes, which we, whatever they might be, would honour in the very dust. If the archbishop Fonseca in the meantime sent any one to take the command, we should not obey him until we had informed his majesty of it, wherever he might be. We begged of his majesty, for the present, to confer the command on Cortes. This prayer we accompanied by such high-flown praise of Cortes,—how faithful and devoted he was to his majesty; that we elevated him to the very skies. This closed the letter, which was drawn up with great discernment, and divided into chapters. This letter was signed by all the officers and soldiers who belonged to Cortes' party. We also took the precaution of keeping other copies.

After the letter was quite finished, Cortes desired to read it, and when he found how faithfully the account was drawn up, and himself so highly praised, he was vastly pleased, returned us hearty thanks, and promised us golden mountains. He, however, observed, that it would be better to make no allusion to the fifth part of the gold which we had promised him; also to suppress the names of the first discoverers of the country. Indeed, we subsequently learnt that Cortes, in his account, never mentioned a word either about Cordoba, or of Grijalva, but reserved all the honour and merit to himself.

Nevertheless the men were not wanting among us who answered the objections made by Cortes, saying it was our bounden duty to narrate every circumstance to his majesty as it had really taken place.

Our agents took charge of the letters, and were bound down by a promise not to touch at the Havannah under any pretence whatever, nor run into the harbour of El Marien, where Francisco de Montejo had possessions. This was done that Velasquez might receive no intelligence of our doings. They certainly promised, but neglected to observe these orders, as will be seen.

Everything being now ready for their departure, father Olmedo said mass, and we commended them to the guidance and protection of the Holy Ghost. On the 26th of July, 1519, they set sail from San Juan de Ulua, and arrived pretty soon at the Havannah. Here Francisco de Montejo left our chief pilot Alaminos no peace, persuading him to sail along the coast in the direction of his settlement, where he pretended he would take in a fresh supply of *cassave*-bread and bacon. Puertocarrero was greatly displeased with this conduct; however, the landing was effected. The night following a sailor swam secretly on shore, and forwarded Diego Velasquez letters from his adherents, giving him an account of all that had passed. We afterwards learnt that Montejo himself had sent this man, who, besides this, spread the news everywhere along the route he journeyed. We shall now see what steps Velasquez took upon this.

Chapter 55

Diego Velasquez's Agents

Diego Velasquez received intelligence of everything we had done, partly by the letters which had been secretly conveyed to him, and were said to be of Montejo's own writing, and partly from the sailor, who swam on shore for that purpose. When he heard of the valuable present which we sent to his majesty, and of the agents we had selected for the purpose, he grew excessively angry, and threw out the most heavy curses against Cortes, against his own private secretary Duero, and the treasurer Almador de Lares. He then immediately ordered two small but very swift sailing vessels to be fitted out, and furnished with as great a number of men and firearms as could be got together at the moment. These vessels were given in command of two officers named Gabriel de Rojas and Guzman, who were ordered to repair to the Havannah, and to capture the vessel which conveyed our agents and the gold.

Both vessels arrived, after two days' sail, in the Bahama roads, and made every inquiry of the fishermen and coasters whether they had seen a ship of considerable tonnage pass that way. All the accounts they received went to show that she must have left the roads, as the wind had constantly been favourable: they, therefore, tacked up and down a considerable time, but, discovering no trace of her, they re turned to Santiago.

If the first accounts had made Diego Velasquez dispirited, he was now the more so when he found the ship had escaped. His friends now advised him to send some one to Spain to lay his complaints before the president of Indian affairs, with whom he stood in great favour. Velasquez also laid a formal accusation against Cortes and all of us, in the royal court of audience at Santo Domingo, and also before the Hieronymite brethren, who were viceroys of that island. These brothers were then three in number, father Luis de Figueroa, father Alonso de Santo Domingo, and father Bernardino de Mancañedo: they lived together in the cloister of Mejorada, eight miles from Medina del Campo. The answer they gave Diego Velasquez was not very consoling; for, when they found, from our papers, what great things we had done, they declared that no reproach could be made either to Cortes or his troops: we had merely addressed the emperor our master, and sent him a present of such considerable value as had not been seen in Spain for a length of time, (this they might say in all justice, for Peru was then still unknown;) on the contrary, we had merited a most noble remuneration at his majesty's hands.

Besides coming to this decision, the Hieronymite brothers commissioned the licentiate Zuazo, who was either purposely sent to Cuba for this purpose, or at least had arrived there only a few months previous, to examine into this affair of Velasquez on the spot itself. The turn which this matter had taken completely prostrated his spirits for many days together. At last he again aroused himself, and gave orders to fit out every ship in the island, and to enlist officers and men: his intention was to send out such a powerful fleet as would soon overcome Cortes and the whole of us: indeed he spared no trouble; he travelled himself from place to place, and from one settlement to another, and where he could not call in person, he at least sent letters, and invited all his friends to join the armament. In this way he succeeded, after the space of eleven or twelve months, to fit out a fleet of eighteen sail, carrying 1300 soldiers and sailors: for, as the affair was carried on with great party spirit, his relations and every distinguished person of Cuba, as well as every one who had a commendary, considered themselves bound to take part in the undertaking. The command of this fleet was given to a cavalier named Pamfilo de Narvaez, a man of high stature and great bodily strength, with a voice amazingly powerful, and an imperious look in his countenance: he was a native of Valladolid, very wealthy, and had married a widow at Cuba named Maria de Valenzuela, who possessed several lucrative Indian townships.

For the present, however, we will leave this expedition to itself, and turn to our agents, who had most favourable weather for their voyage, and arrived safe at the place of destination, as we shall see in the following chapter. The good reader will do me the justice to consider, with respect to the irregular mode of narrating which I appear to pursue, that I am bound to mention the occurrences in this my history in the order they follow each other.

CHAPTER 56

Our Success at Court

Our agents had a most favourable voyage to the Havannah, and thence through the Bahama roads: their further course was equally prosperous, and they very soon arrived at the Tercera isles, and from there to Sevilla, where they hired a carriage and posted to the imperial court residence, at that time in Valladolid. Here the archbishop Fonseca governed at will, he being, moreover, president of Indian affairs, and the emperor then still very young, and residing in Flanders.

Our agents waited upon the archbishop, in the full expectation of being well received with thanks. They handed over to him the letters with the details of our adventures, also the presents, with the valuable things, and begged of him to forward all this to his majesty by a courier, whom they would accompany themselves. However, instead of meeting with a kind reception, they were very coolly received, and dismissed with a few dry and harsh words. They begged of him to mention the great services which Cortes and his men had rendered his majesty, and repeatedly urged him to send the letters and presents to the emperor, that he might learn everything as it had really taken place. He, however, answered in a very haughty tone, desiring them not to give themselves any further trouble: he would fully inform his majesty of what had taken place; not, however, according to their story, but conformably to truth; that, namely, we had rebelled against Velasquez. This was followed by many other sharp rebukes.

About this time also, Benito Martin, chaplain to Velasquez, arrived in Valladolid, preferring heavy accusations against Cortes and all of us, which set the archbishop more and more against us. Francisco de Montejo had not the courage to step forward and defend our cause; but Puertocarrero, as cousin to the earl of Medellin, durst presume the more: he therefore took up the question, and most urgently begged of the archbishop to give them a quiet hearing, and not to answer them so harshly. They demanded nothing further of him than to forward the presents to his majesty; they had a right to ask this, for we were servants of the crown, and merited a remuneration, but not the remarks he had allowed himself to make.

These words so greatly incensed the archbishop, that he ordered Puertocarrero to be thrown into prison, on account of some previous affair which had come to his ears; he having, namely, three years ago, carried off a married woman, named Maria Rodriguez, of Medellin, and taken her to India. Such was the first reception which our presents and services met with in Spain, and nothing remained for our agents but to hold their tongues for the present, and wait until a more favourable time and opportunity should present itself. The archbishop now forwarded his account to the emperor, who was then in Flanders, in which he extolled the merits of his creature Velasquez to the very skies, saying everything that was bad of Cortes and all of us; nor did he mention one single word about our letters.

Upon this Puertocarrero, Montejo, Martin Cortes, the father of our general, the licentiate Nuñez, who was reporter to the royal council, and a near relation to Cortes, determined to despatch a courier of their own to the emperor in Flanders. They fortunately possessed duplicates of all our despatches and letters, as also a list of all the presents we had destined for his majesty.

With these papers they likewise sent a separate letter to the emperor with complaints against the archbishop and the whole of his doings with Diego Velasquez. In this resolution they were backed by other cavaliers who were at variance with the archbishop, who, upon the whole, had many enemies on account of his haughty behaviour and the abuse he made of the important offices he filled. And as the great services we had rendered to God and his majesty, in whom we had alone reposed our trust, were looked upon in a favourable light, it also happened that his majesty made the strictest inquiries into the whole affair. His majesty was so highly pleased with what we had done, that the dukes, marquisses, earls, and other cavaliers, for days together spoke of nothing but Cortes, our courageous behaviour, our conquests, and of the riches we had sent over. It was owing to this as well as to the unfaithful and distorted account which the archbishop had drawn up respecting these matters, and particularly because he had not sent all the presents, but kept the major part to himself, that he fell from that moment into his majesty's displeasure. In the meantime the archbishop's agents in Flanders had sent him information of all that had passed, which vexed him in no small degree, and if previously he had blackened Cortes and all of us to his majesty, he now boldly accused us of high treason. But the Lord very soon bridled his rage; for two years after he received his dismissal, and then in his turn experienced the curse of malice and contempt. We, on the contrary, were looked upon as loyal men who had rendered services to the crown, as shall be mentioned in the proper place. For the present the emperor informed our agents, that he would himself shortly visit Spain to investigate the matter more closely and reward us. Our agents, therefore, awaited his majesty's arrival in Spain.

Before I proceed any further with my narrative, I must answer one question, which several cavaliers have very justly put to me; namely, how it was possible for me to relate these things, as I was not present myself, but making the campaign in New Spain, when our agents were despatched with the letters and presents, and met with this ill treatment from the archbishop of Rosano? To which my answer is, that our agents forwarded to us, the true conquistadores, verbatim all that had passed between them and the latter, as also the favourable decision which the emperor came to in our behalf; of which Cortes sent copies to all the towns where we happened to be stationed, to show us how favourably everything had terminated, and what a great enemy we had in the archbishop. After this digression we will return to our quarters in New Spain, and see what happened there in the meantime.

Chapter 57

Conspiracy

The suspicions of Velasquez's adherents were again aroused at the departure of our agents, and the following occurrence took place a few days after. A conspiracy was set on foot by Pedro Escudero, Juan Cormeño, Gonzalo de Umbria, a pilot, the priest Juan Diaz, Bernardino de Coria, (who afterwards became a citizen of Chiapa, and was father of a certain Centeno,) and some seamen of Gibraleon. All these were excessively embittered against Cortes; some because he had refused to grant them the promised discharge to return to Cuba; others because they had lost their share of the gold by the present which had been sent to the emperor; and the seamen because they could not forget the lashes which he had given them on the island of Cozumel for stealing the flitches of bacon. They had determined to seize upon one of our small vessels, to sail to Cuba, and acquaint the viceroy Diego Velasquez that he had merely to send to the Havannah and the possessions of Montejo in order to capture our agents with all the riches. We concluded from this that the conspirators had been counselled by persons of authority among our officers, since they knew that Montejo, notwithstanding the strict injunctions which he had received to the contrary, had landed at his commendary. The affair was already so far advanced that the conspirators had sent on board the necessary provisions of *cassave*-bread, oil, dried fish, water, and such like, and were about to set sail, when one of them, Bernardino de Coria, began to repent, called upon Cortes at midnight, and discovered the whole plot to him.

Cortes first of all made an accurate inquiry into the names and number of the conspirators, as also into the reasons and the way they intended carrying out the plot; he then ordered the sails, the compass, and the rudder to be taken from the vessel which was to have conveyed them. Upon which he closely examined the conspirators, when they immediately made a full confession, and mentioned the names of others who were implicated. These names were for the present very prudently suppressed, and proceedings were merely taken against those who stood most prominent in the affair. A council of war having been held with all the usual formalities, Pedro Escudero and Juan Cormeño[1] were sentenced to be hung; the pilot Gonzalo de Umbria to have his feet cut off, and the sailors to receive two hundred lashes each. If father Juan had not been a priest he would likewise have shared a similar fate; as it was he merely suffered for a time the dread of suspense which indeed must have been terrible enough. I shall never forget how Cortes cried out, with a sigh, and deeply affected, at the moment he signed the death-warrants: "What a fortunate thing if I were unable to write; then should I neither be able to sign a death-warrant!" This same exclamation likewise frequently falls from judges who have to decide over life and death; in which expression, however, they merely repeat the words of the barbarous emperor Nero, when in the commencement of his reign he showed so goodly a disposition.

The sentences being executed, Cortes immediately set out for Sempoalla, having previously ordered that 200 men, with all our horse, should follow him. The distance to this place was a good twenty miles. Pedro de Alvarado was absent during this time, having three days beforehand been sent with 200 men into the mountains in search of provisions, which were extremely scarce. Orders were, therefore, left behind for him to march to Sempoalla on his return, where arrangements would be made for our further route to Mexico. Alvarado, consequently, was not present when the executions took place.

---

1. Torquemada (Mon., Ind. i, iv, c. 25) gives some additional circumstances respecting this conspiracy; among other things he says, that the pilot Cermeno was so remarkably nimble, that if two of the tallest men held up a lance as high as they could horizontally, he would bound over it with ease by means of another lance. Also that his sense of smelling was so acute that he could scent the land at a distance of sixty miles when at sea; but adds, *"aunque no olio esta muerte;"* yet he could not smell the nature of his death.

Chapter 58

Destroying Our Ships

While preparations were going on at Sempoalla for our march into the interior numerous consultations were held with Cortes respecting everything connected with it, we, his trustworthy adherents, proposed that all the vessels should be run on shore, in order at once to cut off all possibility of further mutiny, when we should have advanced far into the interior of the country. In which case, likewise, the pilots and sailors would be of greater use to us than by idling their time away in the harbour. I am well aware that the idea of destroying our vessels originated with Cortes himself, and that he merely shoved it on our shoulders for this reason, that if payment for the vessels should be demanded of him, he could throw the blame on us, and say that all was done at our own request; so that we both individually and collectively should have to assist in repaying the damages. This resolution was immediately adopted, and Cortes ordered the *alguacil*-major, Juan de Escalante, a young man of very great courage, and who was a close adherer to him, utterly hating Diego Velasquez because he had neglected to give him any considerable commendary in Cuba, to take all the anchors, ropes, sails, in short everything that might be of use to us out of the vessels, and run the latter all on shore, with the exception of the boats. The pilots, the old ships' masters, and those seamen who were unable to make the campaign with us, were to remain behind in the town, and employ themselves in catching fish with our two drag-nets in the harbour, where the former were in great abundance.

Juan de Escalante punctually obeyed these orders, and arrived in Sempoalla with an additional company formed of the sailors, of whom several became very excellent soldiers. The next thing Cortes did was to call all the *caziques* of the mountain tribes together, who had revolted from Motecusuma, and formed an alliance with us. He gave them to understand that they were to assist in the building of the church, the fortresses, and houses of our new town. "This man," continued he, taking Juan de Escalante by the hand, "is my brother; him you must obey in everything; and to him you must apply if you require assistance against the Mexicans. He will himself at all times march out in your defence." The *caziques* in reply, said, "They were ready to obey him in everything," and perfumed Juan de Escalante after their fashion, which I can still well remember he unwillingly submitted to. For the rest he was a man you could trust in all matters, and who fully possessed the confidence of Cortes; for which reason the latter entrusted him with the command of the town and harbour, as one in whom he could place implicit reliance, in case, during his absence, Diego Velasquez should set anything on foot against him.

Gomara here relates, that Cortes ordered the vessels to be sunk, and that he did not disclose his intentions to us of visiting the great Motecusuma himself at Mexico. But we Spaniards are, indeed, not the people who require so much pressing to move forward, or who desire to sit quietly down in a place where neither advantage nor military honour is to be gained. Gomara also says, that Pedro de Irico was the person left behind in command of Vera Cruz. This, however, is quite erroneous, for it was Juan de Escalante who was appointed commander and *alguacil*-major of New Spain. Pedro de Irico, indeed, would scarcely have been entrusted with the command of a company, much less, therefore, with such an important post. Nothing should be given to a man that does not belong to him, and nothing should be taken from him to which he is entitled.

Chapter 59

Marching to Mexico

After the vessels had been run ashore before our eyes, and we the officers and soldiers were one morning after mass all standing around Cortes, the discourse turned upon various military topics, when he begged our attention for a few minutes, as he had some proposal to make to us. He then addressed us at great length, as near as possible, to the following effect. We already knew of the campaign which was in contemplation. It was of such a nature, that the aid of Jesus Christ, our Lord, only could bring us forth victorious from all the battles and engagements which awaited us; but, notwithstanding all the trust we reposed in God, we should not ourselves be wanting in courage and activity; should we be worsted, which Almighty God forbid, considering our small numbers we could expect no other assistance than from above, and that of our own arms, as we had no longer any vessels to return to Cuba. Cortes then adduced many beautiful comparisons from history, and mentioned several heroic deeds of the Romans. We answered him, one and all, that we would implicitly follow his orders, as the die had been cast, and we, with Caesar, when he had passed the Rubicon, had now no choice left; besides which, everything we did was for the glory of God and his majesty the emperor.

After this speech, whose penetrating eloquence and charming powers I am unable to repeat, Cortes ordered the fat *cazique* into his presence, and reminded him of the care and reverence which was due from him to the church and the cross. For himself he was now about leaving for Mexico; he added, to oblige Motecusuma, for the future to abolish all robbery and the human sacrifices. He also told him he should require two hundred porters to transport our cannon, and fifty of his best warriors to accompany us.

When we were about to put ourselves in motion a soldier arrived from Vera Cruz, whom Cortes had despatched there to fetch more men. He brought a letter from Juan de Escalante, announcing that a vessel had been seen off the coast, to which he had made various signals by means of smoke and other things; had hung out white flags and rode up and down the coast on horseback dressed in scarlet, to attract the attention of those on board. He did not doubt for an instant but all this had been observed by the men on-board, yet they made no signs of running into the harbour. He had made inquiries along the coast as to where the vessel had put in, and found she was lying at anchor in the mouth of a small river, at the distance of about nine miles; he therefore awaited Cortes' orders as to what further steps he was to take. As soon as Cortes had read the letter he gave the command of all the troops, then at Sempoalla, to Alvarado conjointly with Gonzalo de Sandoval. This was the first time Sandoval had been put in command, for those military qualities, by which he so greatly distinguished himself all the rest of his life, now began to develop themselves. Properly speaking, the command ought to have devolved upon Alonso de Avila, which therefore created ill blood between him and Sandoval. Upon this Cortes mounted horse, selected four of our cavalry, and fifty of the most nimble-footed men amongst us, and marched to Vera Cruz, where we arrived that very night.

Chapter 60

Taking Prisoners

As soon as we had arrived at Vera Cruz, Juan de Escalante came up to Cortes and told him, it would be best to make off for the strange vessel that very night, otherwise she might heave anchor and steer for the wide ocean. Cortes himself might take his rest and allow him to manage the affair with twenty men.

To this Cortes answered, he could not rest as long as there was any thing to be done, and he was determined to go in person with the men he had brought along with him. We accordingly set off on our march along the coast, without even tasting a morsel of food before we left. On our road we soon captured four Spaniards, who had been ordered to take possession of the country in the name of Francisco de Garay, viceroy of Jamaica. They had been sent on shore by an officer named Alonso Alvarez de Pinedo, who a few days previous had left a settlement on the banks of the Panuco. One of the four Spaniards, named Guillan de la Loa, had drawn up a formal deed of having taken possession of the country, which was signed by the three others.

After the prisoners had made this disclosure to Cortes, he inquired of them under what pretence Garay had sent them out to take possession of the country? To which they gave the following answer. In the year 1518, when the fame of our having discovered this country, under Cordoba and Grijalva, and of the twenty thousand *pesos* which it produced Diego Velasquez, had spread through the whole of the West Indies, Anton de Alaminos and another pilot who had made the voyage of discovery with us, persuaded Garay to petition his majesty, that the discovery of all the countries which might lie to the north of the River St. Peter and Paul might be granted to him. Trusting to the patrons he had at the court of Madrid, he despatched his house-steward, Torrolva, to Spain, who managed to obtain for him the appointment of *adelantado*, and vice-regent of all countries north of the river just mentioned. Garay, in consequence of this appointment, fitted out three vessels with two hundred and seventy men, besides horses and the necessary provisions. The command of these he entrusted to an officer named Alonso Alvarez Pinedo, who at present was lying at a distance of about 280 miles from this place, in the River Panuco, where he intended to found a colony. For the rest, added the prisoners, they had merely obeyed the commands of that officer, and were therefore not answerable for anything they had done. Cortes was very much pleased with these fellows, on account of the disclosure they had made; he tried to gain them over to his interest, and inquired of them, if it were possible to capture the vessel? Guillan de la Loa, the most distinguished of the prisoners, thought it might be done, and he, with his comrades, would hail the ship's shallop on shore. This they accordingly tried, but, notwithstanding all their shouting and signals, no one moved from the vessel. No doubt we must have been observed by them, for the captain knew all about us, and he had particularly cautioned his men to be upon their guard, not to fall into the hands of Cortes. We had now, therefore, no other course left than to try to entice the shallop on shore by some other stratagem. For this purpose Cortes desired the prisoners to take off their clothes, and four of our men to put them on, who were to remain behind. The rest of us marched back along the road we had come, and halted behind a mountain, as soon as we were out of sight of the vessel. Here we remained until midnight, when all was dark around; we then, without the least noise, put ourselves in motion, and made for the landing-place, in the neighbourhood of which we concealed ourselves, so as to be invisible to any one excepting our four disguised soldiers.

As soon as daylight had broken forth, the latter made signals to the vessel with their cloaks and hats; upon which the shallop put off with six sailors, two of whom had water-bottles in their hands, and immediately stepped on shore. We watched until the four others should have done the same. Our four disguised men were in the meantime washing their hands, and doing everything else to hide their faces. Those in the shallop cried out, "What the deuce are you about there? why don't you come on board?" One of our men then answered, "Come on shore for a few minutes, and see what the place is like!" They found, however, the voice to be that of a stranger, and put off with the shallop to the vessel again, notwithstanding all the signals our men were making. We others were very desirous of sending a few musket-shots after them, but Cortes would not permit us, saying, we ought to allow them to go off quietly, and he would communicate with their commander himself. All the prisoners we made, therefore, were the four above-mentioned, and the two who had stepped out of the shallop, and we returned to Vera Cruz without having tasted a morsel of food. Such are the true particulars of the whole matter, and not as Gomara relates, who even makes Garay himself present on this occasion, though he did not visit these parts in person until some time after, having sent the three officers with the vessels before him. I shall speak more particularly of this in the proper place.

Chapter 61

The Battles We Fought

After we had got all in readiness for our march to Mexico, we held a consultation as to the route we should take. The chiefs of Sempoalla preferred the road through the province of Tlascalla, as the inhabitants were friendly with them and deadly enemies of the Mexicans. They had likewise equipped forty of their best warriors to accompany us, who, indeed, proved of the greatest utility to us on this journey. They also gave us 200 porters to convey our cannon; for, at that time, we poor soldiers had no other baggage than our weapons, with which in hand we stood, walked, and slept: we had not even any other covering to our feet than light shoes, but we were always ready for battle. It was about the middle of the month of August, 1519, that we broke up our quarters at Sempoalla. During our march we observed the strictest order, while our sharp-shooters and a great number of our most active men were always in advance. On the first day we arrived in the township of Xalapa, and from there to Socochina, which is very strongly situated, the access to it being very dangerous, and surrounded by numerous trained vine trees.[1] Doña Marina and Aguilar told the inhabitants a good deal about our holy religion, and how we were subjects of the emperor Don Carlos the Fifth, who sent us out to bring them back from kidnapping and sacrificing human beings. As they were in friendship with the Sempoallans, and paid no tribute to Motecusuma,

1. It may appear astonishing to some that grape trees should have been found here, as it is well known that this tree was introduced from Europe into the West Indies; yet it is certainly true that the Spaniards found the wild vine growing in the New World. Oviedo, in his valuable work entitled *'Historia general y natural de las Indias,'* says, "These wild vines bear good black grapes, and I have often eaten them myself. I say good, for considering the wild state in which they grow, they are really good. These grapes are found throughout the whole of the West Indies, and I do believe that all other vines have originated from these wild trees."

we found them very well inclined towards us, and we received hospitable treatment. We erected a cross in every township, and explained its signification to the inhabitants, and what great veneration was due to it. From Socochina we marched over a high mountain, through a pass, to Texutla: here, likewise, the inhabitants were friendly to us, because they refused to pay any further tribute to Motecusuma. It was from this township that we first arrived into a rugged and wild mountain district; the population ceased, and, in the very first night, we had excessive cold, with hail showers; add to which, our provisions were totally gone, and the wind so keen which blew across the snow mountains, that we shook again with the frost: indeed, no one can wonder at this, for we had come so suddenly from the hot climate of Cuba, the town of Vera Cruz, and the neighbouring coast, into a cold country. Whatever calamity might befall us, we had only our weapons for protection, and were, moreover, totally unaccustomed to the cold. From this place we arrived at another mountain pass, where we found some houses and huge temples for human sacrifices; near these, heaps of wood were piled up for the use of the idol-worship. Neither did we here again meet with any food, the weather continuing bitterly cold.

Our route now lay across the territory of the township Xocotlan. We sent before us two Indians of Sempoalla to the *cazique*, to acquaint him of our approach, and beg of him to give us an hospitable reception. As the inhabitants of this district were subject to Motecusuma, everything wore a different aspect, and we marched forward with the utmost precaution and in close array. For the rest, we were as much pleased with this spot as with many a Spanish town, on account of the numerous and beautifully whitewashed balconies, the dwellings of the *caziques*, and the elevated temples wholly built of stone and lime. We, therefore, called it Castilblanco, which name it still retains; for a Portuguese soldier, who was among our troops, assured us, the place was very like the town of Casteloblanco in Portugal. The *cazique*, on receiving information of our arrival, came out to meet us with the principal inhabitants. His name was Olintecle, and he led us into his habitation, where he gave us but little to eat, and that with bad will.

After the repast, Cortes, by means of our interpreters, put all manner of questions to the *cazique* respecting the affairs of his monarch. Motecusuma, and we learnt a good deal about the great armies which were stationed in the conquered provinces, besides those on the boundaries themselves, and the provinces which bordered on them. He spoke of the great and strong city of Mexico, how it lay in the midst of the waters, and that it was only by means of bridges and canoes that a person could go from one house to another: every house was provided with a balcony at the top, and was so completely isolated by means of moats, that they might separately be considered as so many castles, and, as such, capable of defence. The town was approached by three roads, each of which was cut through in four or five several places, to admit the water; across these sections, wooden bridges were built: it was merely requisite to break down these bridges, and all access to Mexico was cut off. Lastly, the *cazique* also mentioned the great quantity of silver and gold, the numerous precious stones and great riches of Motecusuma; in fact, there was no end to the praises he bestowed upon his monarch.

Cortes and all of us were vastly astonished at everything the man related of Motecusuma's power and greatness. However, instead of being thereby disheartened, we only the more earnestly desired to try our fortune against the fortresses and bridges, for such is the very spirit of a Spanish soldier; while the impossibility of which Olintecle spoke seemed to us a mere nothing. Mexico was, indeed, strongly fortified, and even more so than mentioned by the *cazique*: a person ought to have seen it himself to form an idea of it,—a description can convey none. For the rest, added the *cazique*, Motecusuma is accustomed to obedience from every one, and he feared Motecusuma's resentment when he should learn that we had entered the township without his permission, and had been provided with provisions.

Upon which Cortes, by means of our interpreters, spoke to him as follows: "I give you to understand that we have come here from very distant countries, by command of our emperor and master Don Carlos, who has among his numerous vassals many powerful princes, to acquaint your great Motecusuma that he shall no longer permit kidnapping and human sacrifices, nor conquer any more territories, and that he must obey the commands of the emperor our master. In the same way I also declare to you Olintecle, and the other *caziques* now present that you must relinquish those human sacrifices, no longer eat human flesh, and abstain from committing unnatural offences and other abominations customary with you; for such are the commandments of the God in whom we believe, and whom we adore, from whom come life and death, and who will once receive us into his heaven."

As the Indians made no answer to all this and many other things he said of our holy religion, Cortes turned to us, and said, "I think, gentlemen, we can do nothing further here than erect a cross:" to which father Olmedo answered, "I think, sir, that even this would be doing too much at present, for these people, as subjects of Motecusuma, are neither afraid nor shy of us, and would undoubtedly destroy the cross. What we have disclosed to them concerning our religion is sufficient until the time they shall be susceptible of understanding more of it."

In compliance with this advice, no cross was erected here.

On this expedition we had a large dog with us, the property of Francisco de Lugo. As the animal did nothing but bark the whole night, the *caziques* asked our friends of Sempoalla whether it was a lion or a tiger which we employed for the purpose of tearing the Indians to pieces? The Sempoallans answered that we indeed let it loose upon those who attacked us. They gave similar answers to questions concerning our cannon, telling them we loaded these with stones, and killed every one therewith at whom we shot: that our horses were as nimble as deer; that they galloped against whomsoever we desired. "Certainly these must be *teules*!" said Olintecle and the other chiefs. "That they are indeed as you see them now before you, (continued the Sempoallans,) therefore take great care not to arouse their displeasure. Whatever you may do, they are sure to know: they penetrate your very thoughts, and have even imprisoned the tax-gatherers of your great Motecusuma, and commanded the inhabitants of the mountains and us of Sempoalla not to pay any more tribute. They have likewise torn down our *teules* from the temples, and placed theirs there instead. The tribes of the Tabasco and Tzinpantzinco were conquered by them; and, however powerful Motecusuma may be, he nevertheless sent them presents. Now they have visited you, and you have given them nothing; therefore you cannot too speedily correct the mistake you have made."

From this it may be seen that our confederates perfectly understood how to boast of us: nor was it long before the *caziques* brought us four chains, three neck ornaments, and a few lizards, all of gold, though of an inferior quality; besides this there was a package of cotton cloths, and four women to bake our bread. Cortes thanked them very kindly for these presents, and offered to render them services in return.

One certain spot in this township I never shall forget, situated near the temple. Here a vast number of human skulls were piled up in the best order imaginable,—there must have been more than 100,000; I repeat, *more than 100,000*. In like manner you saw the remaining human bones piled up in order in another corner of the square; these it would have been impossible to count. Besides these, there were human heads hanging suspended from beams on both sides. Three *papas* stood sentinel on this place of skulls, for which purpose, it was told us, they were particularly appointed.[2] Similar horrible sights we saw towards the interior of the country in every township, and even in Tlascalla.

Cortes inquired of the *cazique* Olintecle, which was the best and most easy road to Mexico. "That one," answered the *cazique*, "over Cholulla, which is a very large town." Our friends of Sempoalla, however, advised us not to take that road, as the inhabitants of Cholulla were a treacherous people, and Motecusuma had always a strong garrison in that town. We had better choose the road over Tlascalla was their opinion; for there the inhabitants were their friends, and sworn enemies to the Mexicans. This advice was followed by Cortes, and the Almighty blessed his choice. Before our departure we required an additional twenty of their best warriors to join our ranks, which were accordingly granted us by the *cazique*.

The next morning we commenced our march to Tlascalla, and first arrived in the small township of Xacatcinco. From this place we sent before us to the Tlascallans two of the principal men of Sempoalla, who well knew how to blazon forth our praise, and were upon intimate terms of friendship with the latter. We gave them a letter to these, although we knew they could not read it, and a Flanders hat surmounted by a coloured feather, as they were worn at that time. I will relate in the following chapter what further took place.

2. Of the township of Xocotlan, Torquemada gives some further account, from which we learn more of the condition of the country at the time of the conquest. Olintecl, he says, was lord of 20,000 subjects, and he had thirty wives, who were attended upon by one hundred female servants. The township contained thirteen temples, full of various shaped idols made of stone, to whom were sacrificed men, women, children, pigeons, and quails. Here the Mexican monarch had a garrison of 5000 men, and couriers were stationed at particular distances from each other all the way from the town to the city of Mexico. These nimble pedestrians were always in pairs, that all news might be conveyed to the metropolis with the utmost speed.

Chapter 62
Our March on Tlascalla

On our march from Castilblanco we were, if possible, doubly precautious. Our sharp-shooters were always in advance, the cavalry kept surrounding our troops, our muskets were loaded, the matches lighted, and, in short, we were ready for action at a moment's notice.

We first arrived in the small township of Xacatcinco, where the inhabitants presented us with a golden chain for the neck, some packages of cotton stuffs, and two Indian females. As above remarked, we despatched two distinguished personages of Sempoalla to Tlascalla, who were to announce our approach, and say we came as friends, and hoped they would receive us as such. We found it the more necessary to send this message, as we learnt in Xacatcinco, that the whole of Tlascalla was up in arms against us. They were already informed of our having left that place, and concluded from the number of warriors we had with us out of Sempoalla and Xocotlan, tributary to Motecusuma, that we came with hostile intentions. They had quite concluded we were going to act like the Mexicans, who always, under some fraudulent pretence or other, marched into their country when intent upon plunder.

When, therefore, the messengers arrived with our letter and the Flanders hat, and were about to deliver our commission, they were even refused a hearing, and immediately thrown into prison. We awaited their return for two days, during which time Cortes explained to the inhabitants as usual, the nature of our holy religion, who our emperor was, the sinfulness of human sacrifices, and the other abominations they practised. He also demanded twenty of their warriors to accompany us.

These they readily furnished us, and after we had commended ourselves to the protection of the Almighty, we broke up our quarters on the third day and marched for Tlascalla. On our route we were met by our two messengers, who had been secretly released by their friends. All Tlascalla was making warlike preparations against us. They appeared quite downcast, and durst scarcely inform us of what they had seen and heard. Having at last taken courage, they related how they had been immediately seized and thrown into prison, and what terrible threats had been thrown out against us and themselves. "Now we will rise up," it had been told them, "and destroy those whom yon term *teules*. We shall soon see whether they are so courageous as you have mentioned. We will devour both you and them together, for you are come under fraudulent pretences, and at the instigation and in the spirit of the traitor Motecusuma."

The messengers might say what they liked in contradiction to this it was all to no purpose. When Cortes and we others heard this lofty language, and how they awaited us completely equipped for war, we did not think altogether so light of the matter; nevertheless, we one and all cried out, "Well, then, since it cannot be otherwise, forward! for good or ill luck." We commended ourselves to the protection of God, and unfurled our standard, which was borne by the ensign Corral. The inhabitants of the small township, where we passed the night, informed us, that the Tlascallans would march against us to prevent our entering into their country. Of this opinion were also our friends of Sempoalla.

As we were marching along, our only discourse was how we should attack the enemy. Our cavalry was to gallop up three abreast, with lances fixed, and run the Indians full in the face. At the same time they were to be particularly upon their guard that the enemy did not lay hold of the lances with their hands; should such, however, be the case, the rider was to keep the tighter hold of his lance, give his horse the spur, and either by a sudden jerk wrest it out of the enemy's grasp, or drag him along with it.

The reader will perhaps ask, why we took these precautions though we had not yet come in sight of the foe? I can answer this with Cortes' own words, who spoke to us as follows: "You are aware, gentlemen, of the smallness of our numbers, we must, therefore, be the more upon our guard, and fancy the enemy will each moment fall upon us. Nor is this sufficient, we must imagine ourselves already fighting, as if the battle was begun. Every soldier is fond of catching hold of the enemy's lance with his hand, but considering the smallness of our numbers, we must now particularly guard ourselves against it. For the rest, you are not in need of my advice, for I have always found that you do things much better than I am able to instruct you."

Under similar discourses we had already advanced about eight miles, when we came up to an enormous entrenchment, built so strongly of stone, lime, and a kind of hard bitumen, that it would only have been possible to break it down by means of pickaxes, and if defended would have with difficulty been taken. We halted on purpose to inspect this fortification, and Cortes inquired of the Xocotlans, for what purpose it stood there. They told him that it was built by the Tlascallans, on whose territory we were now entering, against the great Motecusuma, with whom they were continually at war, to protect them against his hostile incursions.[1]

After we had examined this structure for some time, and each expressed his opinion upon it, Cortes cried out, "Let us follow our standard, gentlemen! It bears the figure of the holy cross, and in that sign we shall conquer." To which we unanimously added: "Forward! whatever may happen; for God is our only strength."

We now continued our march onwards in the cautious manner above mentioned, and had not proceeded far when our vanguard observed at no very great distance about thirty Indians, who had been sent out to reconnoitre; this was immediately communicated to us. They had broad swords, which are used with both hands, the edges of which are made of hard flint, and are sharper than our steel swords. They were also armed with shields, lances, and had feathers stuck in their hair. Cortes ordered some of our cavalry to go in among them, and try, if possible, to capture one, but not to inflict any wounds. These were followed at a distance by five others, to assist them should they fall into an ambush; the rest of our army marched direct for the narrow pass, but with the utmost circumspection, as our friends had assured us that we should undoubtedly meet with a large body of the enemy in some hiding place or other. When the thirty Indians above mentioned found our cavalry approaching them, and saw how they beckoned to them with their hands, they began to retreat slowly, and arranged themselves again in order, whenever our men attempted to take any of them prisoners. They defended themselves right valiantly with their swords and lances, wounding several of our horses. The

1. Of this fortification Torquemada gives a different account. He says it was a wall of twenty feet in thickness, that it could be defended from the top; had only one entrance, defended by other works within, and was built by a *cazique* of the country, whom he calls Yztacmixtitlan, to protect the boundaries of his country against the incursions of the Tlascallans.

blood of our men now also began to boil, who, in return, killed five of the Indians. At that moment a swarm of more than 3000 Tlascallans rushed furiously from an ambush, pouring forth a shower of arrows upon our cavalry, who now immediately closed their ranks. At the same time we fired among them with our cannon, and so at last we obliged the enemy to give ground, though they fought bravely and with a good deal of manoeuvring. On our side we had four wounded, of whom one died a few days after, if I still remember rightly. Seventeen of the enemy lay dead, and the number of their wounded was very considerable. As it was growing very late they continued to retreat, and we to follow them.

As soon as we had passed over the mountain we came into a plain, and found numerous plantations of maize and *maguey*,[2] from which the inhabitants make their wine. We took up our night's quarters near a brook, and for want of oil we dressed the wounds of our men with the fat of a corpulent Indian who had been killed. We made our supper off young dogs, which we found here in great numbers; for, although the inhabitants had left all their plantations and taken the dogs with them, these animals during the night time had come back to their old places again; and we were thus able to catch a good many, and so procured ourselves some very delicious joints. The whole of this night we kept a most vigilant look-out. We placed outposts in all quarters; our horses stood ready saddled and bridled, and the rounds were regularly made. I will, however, break off here, and relate our further battles in the next chapter.

2. *Agava Americana.*

Chapter 63

Battles With the Tlascallans

The next morning, after we had commended ourselves to God in prayer, we broke up our quarters. Each company marched in close order, and our cavalry were to be particularly upon their guard; were either to advance suddenly, or fall back upon us, according as circumstances might be, and at all events to watch that our ranks were nowhere broken, and that no one strayed from his own company.

After we had marched onwards for some time we came up with two large bodies of the enemy, amounting to about 6000 men. They set up a most terrific noise with their drums and trumpets, and yelled awfully. They then let fly their arrows, threw their lances at us, and upon the whole were most daringly valiant. Cortes now ordered us to halt, and despatched three Indians, whom we had made prisoners the day before, to the enemy, requesting them to stay hostilities, as we were very desirous of looking upon them as brothers and friends. At the same time he ordered one of our warriors, Diego de Godoy, who was the royal secretary, to pay particular attention to everything that should take place, in order that if any reproach were made us for having destroyed any of the Indians, he might give evidence, and be able to prove that we on our side had shown every disposition for peace.

The prisoners went off with this message to the enemy, but not the slightest notice was taken of it; on the contrary, they attacked us so furiously that we could no longer look idly on. "Forward! St. Jacob is with us! On to the enemy!" cried Cortes; and in an instant we greeted the Indians so sharply with our firearms, that numbers were immediately killed and wounded; among the former three chiefs. After this first volley they fell back to about the distance of a musket-shot, where they took up their position. Here an army of above 40,000 warriors, commanded by their general-in-chief Xicotencatl, lay in ambush. Their standards bore his colours, white and variegated. As the ground here was full of deep cavities our cavalry were completely useless, until by using the greatest precaution they managed to pass over these. This was not done without considerable risk, for the enemy plied their bows and lances with great dexterity, having, moreover, the advantage of the higher ground. The stones from their slings were no less annoying; but all this only lasted until we had gained the level ground. For now we richly rewarded them for their pains, and killed great numbers. Yet we durst not venture to open our ranks; for the instant any one stepped out to assist any other soldier or officer he was that moment dangerously wounded. We were, therefore, obliged to keep our ranks firmly closed, and by degrees had to contend with more than twenty different divisions, which was, indeed, pretty hot work. Besides all this the Indians kept continually throwing sand in our faces to blind us. Here, indeed, the great mercy of God alone could save us. The chief object of the enemy was to capture one of our horses, in which they did not altogether fail; for, as Pedro de Moron on his well-trained mare, attended by three others of our cavalry, was attempting to break through the enemy's ranks, the Indians wrenched the lance out of his hand, and fell furiously upon him with their broad swords, wounding him severely. They gave his mare such a terrific cut with the same weapon in the neck, that the animal instantly fell down dead. If Moron's three companions had not immediately hastened to his assistance, he would have shared his horse's fate; for this gave our whole company time to come up.

I must again repeat, that the worst was, we had to keep ourselves so close together in order not to run the danger of being cut off, which of course greatly encumbered our movements. Nevertheless, we were obliged to open our ranks to rescue the mare and Moron whom they were already dragging off half dead. The mare we were obliged to relinquish, though we managed to cut the girth asunder in order at least to save the saddle. In this battle we had nine wounded. As for the enemy I believe on this occasion we killed four of their chiefs. We pushed forward shoulder to shoulder, and made considerable havoc with our swords. The enemy retreated, carrying off the dead mare, which was subsequently cut into pieces to be sent into every township of Tlascalla. As we afterwards learnt, the horse's shoes, the Flanders hat, and the letter we sent them, were brought as an offering to their idols. The mare belonged to Juan Sedeño, who, on the previous day, was wounded in three several places, and had, therefore, lent her to Moron.

This Moron was a capital horse soldier, and died a few days after; at least, I do not remember to have seen him again after this battle.

We had fought for a good hour, and our firearms must have done considerable destruction among the enemy who stood so crowded together. Every man among us did his duty, and we fought away like brave warriors, for in all truth we were placed in greater jeopardy this time than we had ever been before. Numbers of the Indians lay dead on the field of battle; among whom were eight of the principal chiefs, all sons of old *caziques*, who dwelt together in the chief town of the country. At last our enemies retreated in good order, which we were glad enough to see, for we could scarcely stand any longer from overfatigue, nor durst we think of following the enemy. Add to which, the ground was greatly to our disadvantage, partly on account of the number of straggling houses, partly on account of a species of pits in which many of the inhabitants dwelt. This battle was fought on the first two days of September, 1519, near the village of Tehuacacinco, and we returned fervent thanks to God for having rescued us from such great peril and for the victory we had gained.

After the battle, we fell back to some temples, which were very high, and large enough to serve us for castles. We dressed the wounds of our men with the fat of Indians, as we had done on previous occasions. Five of our horses were wounded, and fifteen men, of whom one subsequently died. Upon this we took our suppers, and made a good meal off the number of dogs and fowls which we found in the dwellings. Before, however, we lay down to rest, we posted our sentinels, and continually patrolled during the night: not before all these things were properly ordered did we lie down, and slept till morning.

For the rest, we made fifteen prisoners, among whom were two of the most distinguished personages; but we could never discover how many we killed or wounded, as it was customary with the Tlascallans immediately to carry off the wounded and dead from the field of battle.[1]

---

1. To this custom of the Tlascallans of carrying off their killed and wounded from the field of battle, the historian de Solis partially attributes Cortes' great success in these battles; for as a great number of the enemy were constantly occupied in this work, they naturally offered a less formidable front, and considerable openings were made in their ranks.

Chapter 64
Tehuacacinco

As the battles we fought had greatly fatigued us, besides that several of our men and horses were wounded, we made a day of rest, repaired our crossbows, and supplied ourselves with arrows. The next morning Cortes said to us, "It would be no harm if our horse were to gallop up and down the country a little; the Tlascallans might otherwise think we had had enough of it in the last battle: we must show them that we are constantly at their heels." And indeed it was better that we began ourselves than wait until we should be attacked, that the enemy might not suppose we had been too greatly weakened, and had lost our courage. Besides this, the country round about was quite level, and thickly populated. We therefore ordered out seven horse, some crossbow-men, and several musketeers, in all 200 men, without including our confederates. Every possible precaution had been previously made to secure our camp. On our march through the townships we captured twenty Indians of both sexes, but in no way molested them. Our allies, however, who were barbarous characters, could not refrain from setting fire to many houses where they had found quantities of fowls and young dogs. After we had again returned to our quarters, Cortes ordered the fetters to be taken off the prisoners, and food to be given them. Doña Marina and Aguilar then addressed them very affectionately, and gave to each some glass beads, adding, at the same time, that in future they should not be so foolish, but make peace with us, as we were very desirous of looking upon them as brothers, and would protect them as such.

We also set the first two Indians at liberty whom we had captured, and gave them a letter with the commission to tell the chief of the provinces that we were not come in any way to injure the Tlascallans, but merely wished to take the road through their country to Mexico, there to have an interview with Motecusuma.

Both these delegates punctually followed our orders, and arrived at the headquarters of Xicotencatl, which lay, if I remember rightly, about six miles from our camp, in the township of Tehuacinpacingo. Having, in the absence of the father, fulfilled our commission to the younger Xicotencatl, he told them, we had only to come to his father's township, there they would make peace, after they had satiated themselves with the flesh of our bodies, and had honoured their gods with the sacrifice of our blood and hearts. The next morning we should behold his answer with our own eyes.

As the last battles were still fresh in our memories, we did not exactly relish the haughty answer with which our delegates returned. Cortes, nevertheless, received them most kindly, perceiving, from their return, that they no longer stood in awe of us; and with the view that they should once more be despatched as messengers of peace, he gave them some additional strings of beads. For the rest he made the most minute inquiries respecting the commander Xicotencatl, and the number of his troops, and found that the latter were much more numerous than in the last battle: he had now five chiefs under him, each of whom commanded 10,000 men. These troops were enumerated in the following manner: First of all came the 10,000 men of Xicotencatl's division; next a similar number under another powerful *cazique* called Maxixcatzin; then a like number under the distinguished *cazique* Chichimeclatecl; 10,000 under the *cazique* of Topoyanco, named Tecapaneca; and an equal number under the *cazique* Quaxobcin;—altogether thus 50,000 men. Each troop had its standard and arms, the latter being a large white bird, with outspread wings, as if preparing to fly, and resembled an ostrich.[1] Besides this, every chief had his particular insignia of war and colours, in the same way as our Spanish dukes and earls. At first we did not believe anything of all this, but found afterwards that it was perfectly true; and since we were human beings, and feared death, we all confessed to father Olmedo and the priest Juan Diaz, which occupied them the whole of the night: neither did we fail to offer up fervent prayers to the Almighty to grant us victory. Under such like occupations the following day broke forth on which we were to fight the battle, of which I shall speak in the next chapter.

1. This is a very remarkable observation of Bernal Diaz, for the ostrich with outspread wings is also found on the ancient Persian monuments; and this bird, it is well known, is not common to the New World. If we add to this circumstance the repeated questions which were put to the Spaniards by the inhabitants of New Spain, as to whether they came from the region where the sun rises, there is reason for supposing that the tradition which came down to them from their forefathers was not altogether vague; namely, that a people would come from the east and take possession of their country.

Chapter 65
Battling the Tlascallans Again

It was the following morning, on the 5th of September, 1519, that we equipped ourselves for battle. Our horse were first arranged in order, then the foot soldiers, and even our wounded were forced to go along with us, if only to swell out our numbers, and do what lay in their power. The crossbow-men received orders that some were merely to load, while others fired, and this always in platoons. The musketeers received similar orders, and the remaining portion of our men, who were armed with swords and shields, were principally to strike at the enemy in the region of the belly, in order to stop them from venturing so near to us as they had the time before. Every one was also particularly cautioned not to leave the ranks. It was also the particular duty of our cavalry not to leave each other in the lurch, always to attack in full gallop, and only aim at the face and eyes. The ensign Corral received a guard of four men, and in this way we sallied forth from our camp, with our standard flying.

We had scarcely proceeded a quarter of a mile when we found the fields covered with warriors; they had large feather-knots on their heads, waved their colours, and made a terrific noise with their horns and trumpets: indeed, the pen that would wish to describe everything we saw here, would not find it such an easy task! this was indeed a battle of as fearful and dubious an issue as well could be. In an instant we were surrounded on all sides by such vast numbers of Indians, that the plain, here six miles in breadth, seemed as if it contained but one vast body of the enemy, in the midst of which stood our small army of 400 men, the greater part wounded and knocked up with fatigue. We were also aware that the enemy had marched out to battle with the determination to spare none of us, excepting those who were to be sacrificed to their idols. When, therefore, the attack commenced, a real shower of arrows and stones was poured upon us; the whole ground was immediately covered with heaps of lances, whose points were provided with two edges, so very sharp that they pierced through every species of cuirass, and were particularly dangerous to the lower part of the body, which was in no way protected. They fell upon us like the very furies themselves, with the most horrible yells; we employed, however, our heavy guns, muskets, and crossbows, with so much effect, and received those who pressed eagerly upon us with such well-directed blows and thrusts, that considerable destruction was made among their ranks, nor did they allow us to approach so near to them as in the previous battle: our cavalry, in particular, showed great skill and bravery, so that they, next to the Almighty, were the principal means of saving us.

Indeed our line was already half broken; all the commands of Cortes and our other officers to restore order and form again were fruitless, the Indians continually rushing upon us in such vast crowds that we could only make place with sword in hand to save our line from being broken. Our only safety was owing to the great number of the enemy itself; for they stood so closely crowded that each shot we fired must have done great execution among them. They left themselves altogether no room to manoeuvre in, while many of the chiefs, with their men, were not even able to mix at all in the engagement. Besides this, disagreements and inimical feelings had arisen out of the previous battle between the commander-in-chief Xicotencatl and another chief, the son of Chichimeclatecl. Xicotencatl had accused the latter of not having done his duty, who, in reply, said, he had discharged it better than he; so that in this battle neither lent the other any assistance, and Chichimeclatecl had even commanded Huexotzinco not to take any part in the combat. To all this must be added, that the enemy had been taught in the former battle to fear our horse, cannon, swords, and crossbows, not to forget the courage we displayed. It must likewise be borne in mind that a merciful God had lent us extraordinary powers during the engagement. As Xicotencatl met with no obedience from two of his principal officers,—we, on the contrary, fighting on the more bravely, and killing great numbers of their men, who, as well as the wounded, were immediately hurried from the field of battle, so that we never came to see any of their killed,—the Indians at length grew exasperated against those two chiefs who had thus left them in the lurch, and now fought with less vigour. It is, however, probable that one of their chief commanders had fallen, for they retreated in good order: our cavalry, indeed, pursued them a short distance in full gallop, but were soon compelled to return, from fatigue.

As soon as we had got rid of this vast crowd, we returned most fervent thanks to the Almighty. We had, however, only lost one man, but, on the other hand, sixty of us were wounded, with all our horses. I myself carried off two wounds, one of which was on my head from the stone of a sling, and the other by an arrow piercing my ankle; but neither of them were so bad as to compel me to leave the battle, or disable me from doing duty. This, however, was the same case with the majority of my comrades; for, if a wound was not dangerous, they still continued to perform duty, as the number of those who came off whole would have been too small to make head against the enemy. We now returned to our quarters, overjoyed at our victory, and offered up fervent thanks to God. We buried our dead in one of the subterranean dwellings, that the Indians might not discover us to be mortal as well as themselves, but still continue to fancy us gods: we, therefore, heaped up a quantity of earth over the spot, that even the stench of the decomposing body might not betray the dead. The fat of the Indians, as before, served us to dress our wounds. Oh, the distress we suffered here! We had neither oil for our wounds nor salt to our food. To all this was added the misfortune of having nothing to shelter us from the keen wind, which blew across the Sierra Nevada, and made us shake again with cold. We, nevertheless, kept up our spirits, and this night we slept more soundly than on the previous one, as we had better regulated our outposts and the patrols.

CHAPTER 66

Seeking Peace

In the last battle we had taken three distinguished personages prisoners. These Cortes sent with the two others whom we had previously taken, and once before despatched with a message to the *caziques* of Tlascalla, desiring them in our name to make peace with us, and allow us to march through their country to Mexico, as we had before requested of them. If they still refused, we would exterminate them all. It would, however, grieve us if they drove us to such extremities, as we were well inclined, and would gladly look upon them as brothers; nor should we have done thus much if they themselves had not driven us to it. Besides this, Cortes said many other kind things to gain their friendship.

The delegates arrived betimes in the chief town of Tlascalla, and delivered their message in a full assembly of the *caziques*, whom they found conversing with several old men and *papas*. Every one still appeared very downcast on account of the unfavourable issue of the battle, the loss of their chiefs, their sons and relations who had fallen; and at first would not even listen to our messengers. At last they came to the resolution to consult all the astrologers, *papas*, and fortune-tellers, a species of conjurors whom they call *tacalnaguas*. These being assembled, they were desired to discover by their witchcraft and enchantments, what sort of people we were, and whether it was possible to overcome us if they continued to harass us night and day. They were also to give a decisive answer as to whether we were really *teules*, that is to say evil spirits, as the inhabitants of Sempoalla had assured them; and lastly, what nourishment we took. All this they were most minutely to investigate.

The soothsayers, conjurors, and *papas*, who were in great numbers, immediately began their exorcisms and enchantments, after their fashion; and they pretended to have discovered, by means of their art, that we were human beings made of flesh and bone; that we ate dogs, fowls, bread and fruits, as they did, if we could get them; and that we did not devour the Indians, and much less the hearts of those we had slain. Our friends of Sempoalla, namely, had told them all manner of foolish things about us; not only that we were *teules*, but that we devoured the hearts of the Indians; that the flashes of our bombards, shot off like lightning; that our dog was a tiger or a lion, and that we let loose our horses upon the Indians when we wished to kill them. But the worst thing these soothsayers and *papas* affirmed was, its being impossible to conquer us excepting during the night-time, for we were helpless as soon as the sun, from which we received all our strength, had gone down.

This affirmation seemed a capital hint to the *caziques*, they therefore sent orders to their captain-general, Xicotencatl, to fall upon us as soon as possible with a large force during night-time. This, Xicotencatl did not fail to do. He drew out ten thousand of his bravest troops, marched towards our quarters, and fell upon us from three several points at once, with the utmost fury. They made this attack with perfect assurance, believing they had merely to show themselves and they should be able to capture us immediately, and sacrifice us to their idols. But the Almighty had ordered things differently. For, however silently they approached, they found us perfectly upon our guard, as the outposts and patrols had come running in at the first noise they heard and given the alarm. As, moreover, we were accustomed to sleep in our clothes with our weapons in our hands, the horses always ready bridled and saddled, and our cannon loaded, we gave the enemy such a rough reception with our muskets and crossbows, and cut among them so vigorously with our swords, that they soon had enough of it and turned their backs. The country before us was quite level, and the moon shone bright, so that our cavalry were able to follow the flying enemy to a considerable distance. Next morning we found about twenty of them dead and wounded, so that their loss must have been considerable, and they experienced, no doubt, that this fighting at night-time was not exactly so pleasant. It is also said they were so exasperated against the soothsayers and *papas*, that two of them were butchered for a sacrifice. In this night's combat we lost one of our friends of Sempoalla, and two of our men besides a horse were wounded. The number of prisoners we made were four. The kind reader may well conceive that we were not a little overjoyed that this affair terminated so fortunately. We fervently thanked God for the assistance he had lent us, buried our friend of Sempoalla, dressed our wounds, and lay ourselves down to rest for the remaining part of the night; but not without previously taking every precaution to secure our camp as usual. It was only the following morning we were able to discover our true condition. There was not one among us who had not, up to this moment, received one, two, or three wounds, and all were more or less weakened by fatigues and hardships. Xicotencatl continued to hover around us, and we had already lost fifty-five of our men, some of whom were killed on the field of battle, others had died of disease and from excessive cold. Twelve of our men were knocked up with fatigue, and even our commander-in-chief himself and father Olmedo were suffering from fever. But no one can wonder at this; for among all the hardships we had to undergo, we never durst for one moment leave our heavy weapons out of our hands; to all these discomforts was added the severity of the weather, and particularly our great want of salt, which we could find no means of obtaining. It was also natural that we should begin to think what would be the final issue of this campaign, and if we once got out of the present snare where we were next to bend our steps; for the idea of penetrating into Mexico appeared to us perfectly laughable, when we considered the great power of that state. If even we succeeded in making the same good terms with the people of Tlascalla as we had done with the Sempoallans, what would become of us if we ever came to an engagement with the great armies of Motecusuma? We were totally ignorant as to how matters stood in our fortress at Vera Cruz, and our men there knew as little what had become of us. Certainly there were among us plenty of valiant cavaliers and soldiers of great courage in battle, who showed no less wisdom in our councils, nor did Cortes ever speak or do anything without previously consulting them. With the historian Gomara it is always thus: Cortes did this, Cortes did that, Cortes was there, Cortes left there; just as if all this had been a mere nothing. If even, as Gomara affirms, Cortes had had an iron frame, he could not possibly have been everywhere, and have done everything himself. What good is it to make use of such expressions? He could only say, that Cortes was an excellent captain, as indeed he was, and this would have been enough! I was forced to make this remark, for besides the protection which the Almighty lent us in all our undertakings, his blessing was upon the arm of us soldiers and the advice we gave Cortes, and it was only in this way all things could have terminated so well.

I will not, however, detain the reader with this preamble of great deeds, for it has little to do with the principal object of this history. I am more pleased to relate, that we unanimously swore to protect his person, and begged of him, that as God had rescued us out of such extreme danger and spared our lives, to set our prisoners at liberty and send them again to the *caziques*, and desire of them to conclude peace with us, adding, that we should pardon what had taken place, as also the death of the horse.

Neither must I omit to mention the fine manly spirit which Doña Marina, though one of the daughters of the country, showed upon every occasion. We heard nothing the whole day long but of being butchered and devoured by the inhabitants; she had with her own eyes beheld how we had been completely surrounded by our enemies in the recent battles; how we were all wounded and suffering from disease; yet she never appeared disheartened; but, on the contrary, displayed a courage much beyond that of her sex. When the prisoners were about departing, again to make offers of peace to the enemy, she and Aguilar gave them every instruction as to what they were to say; that peace was to be concluded within the space of two days, otherwise we would march forward, lay waste the whole country, force our way into their towns, and put every living being to the sword. I must, however, again return to Gomara, who never mentions a single word about our killed and wounded, or the hardships we underwent; as if everything of itself turned to our advantage. Indeed, those who furnished him with the account must have been badly informed themselves. Did it never once occur to him, that his work would be highly interesting to all of us conquistadores, and that we would not repress the truth when we had read it?

But to return to my narrative, our delegates went straightway to the chief town of Tlascalla, where the elder Xicotencatl abode. If I still remember rightly, we sent a letter with them, although we knew the Indians could not understand it; there was likewise an arrow with the letter. They found the two chief *caziques* in council with the other principal personages. I will give their answer in the following chapter.

Chapter 67

Still Seeking Peace

The two chief *caziques* to whom our messengers addressed themselves were Maxixcatzin and the elder Xicotencatl, father of the captain-general of the same name, who was commonly termed the younger. They fulfilled their commission, and the *caziques* remained for a time silent and undecided, when the Almighty inclined their hearts to conclude a peace with us. They called a meeting of all the *caziques* and chief personages who had weight in the townships, as also of their friends from the province of Huexotzinco. All having met in the township of Maxixcatzin and the elder Xicotencatl, which held the first rank, the latter who were men of good understanding addressed the meeting to the following effect. Though we may not, perhaps, give the exact words, yet, from what we afterwards learnt, it was to this effect: "Brothers and friends! You yourselves know how often these *teules*, who are now in our country, ready to fight at a moment's notice, have offered us peace, and assured us that they have come as friends to our assistance. Nor can you have yet forgotten the numbers of prisoners they have taken, though they never do them any harm, but always restore them to liberty. Thrice have we attacked them with the whole of our forces, both by day and by night, but we have not been able to conquer them. On the contrary, they have killed many of our subjects, numbers of our sons, relations, and chiefs in these battles. They now again request us to come to terms of peace, and those of Sempoalla who are encamped with them, assure us they are enemies to Motecusuma and the Mexicans, and have commanded them and the tribes of the Totonaque mountains not to pay any more tribute to him. We all very well know that the Mexicans for a space of more than one hundred years have annually made incursions into our country. Indeed, they have completely shut us up within our own territory. We cannot get beyond to fetch salt for our victuals, nor cotton for our clothing. If any one of us ever ventures beyond the mountains, he very seldom returns home alive. The treacherous Mexicans and their allies kill all our people that fall into their hands, or at least make slaves of them. Our *tacalnaguas*, soothsayers, and *papas* have told us their opinion of these *teules*; that they are very powerful and courageous we have experienced ourselves. We feel, therefore, inclined to make peace with them. Whether they are men or *teules*, in both cases an alliance with them will be useful to us. Let us, therefore, despatch four of our chiefs to their camp with good provisions, and show them love and an inclination to make peace, that they may assist and protect us against our enemies. We will invite them into our country, and present them with females from among our countrywomen, that we may become one people with them; for, according to the assurance of the messengers whom they have sent to offer us peace, they have women with them." The *caziques* upon hearing this proposition all declared they were agreeable to it, and resolved that a treaty for peace should be set on foot, and the captain-general Xicotencatl and the other commanders should be ordered to stay all hostilities; for which end they instantly despatched messengers. The younger Xicotencatl, however, would by no means listen to these orders, but evinced excessive grief and used harsh language. "As affairs stood there was no need of suing for peace," he said. "Many of the *teules* were already killed, besides one of their horses; he would fall upon us the night following and destroy us all."

When the elder Xicotencatl, Maxixcatzin, and the other *caziques* received this answer, they were so exasperated, that they immediately sent orders round to all the officers and the whole army not to obey Xicotencatl in anything which related to an attack upon us, and altogether to stay all hostilities against us. Neither would Xicotencatl submit to these orders, so that it was found necessary to send the four old men, who were appointed to make a treaty of peace between us, the Tlascallans and inhabitants of Huexotzinco, to these refractory fellows in order to bring them to reason. These four men, however, stood in such awe of the young hothead that they neglected to fulfil their commission.

As two or three different occurrences took place at the same time, I must relate what comes first in order, and give an account of our excursion to another township which lay in the neighbourhood.

Chapter 68

Marching to Zumpanzingo

After two days had passed by without our doing anything worthy of notice, we proposed to Cortes that we should make an excursion to a township situated about four miles from our encampment, to the inhabitants of which we had fruitlessly made overtures of peace. We determined upon taking them by surprise during night-time; not with the intention of injuring, killing, wounding, or taking the inhabitants prisoners, but merely to procure provisions, frighten them a little, and make new offers of peace according as circumstances might be. This township was called Zumpanzingo, and was the chief of many smaller ones. The district Tecodcungapacingo, where we had taken up our quarters, stood likewise under it; the whole country round about moreover being covered with straggling houses and villages. Cortes fell in with this proposal, and we accordingly commenced our march shortly before daybreak with all our men who were best able to bear the fatigue, six of our cavalry, ten crossbow-men, and eight musketeers. The command was taken by Cortes himself, although he was suffering from the tertian ague. For the rest all necessary precautions were taken for our camp.

We had marched to a distance of about six miles before daylight appeared, and the wind which blew across the snow mountains was so keen, that we shook again with cold. Our horses likewise felt the frost very sensibly. Two of them indeed got the gripes and trembled like aspen leaves, at which we were greatly concerned, for we thought they would have died. Cortes therefore ordered them back to our camp. We arrived in front of Zumpanzingo before sunrise. The inhabitants, having observed our approach, had fled from their dwellings. Their minds full of the most horrible ideas they had formed of us, they kept crying out to one another to beware of the *teules*. They kill all, it was said, and spare neither young nor old. Finding how greatly they feared us, we halted in a courtyard until daylight had fully broken forth, that we might not injure any of the people in the dark. On the summit of the highest temples in the township we observed some *papas* and other old men of distinction, who, when they found we remained quiet without doing the least harm, took courage and came down to Cortes. They commenced by making excuses for not having sent us provisions, or any one with offers of peace, though we had demanded both of them. They assured us that no one was to blame for all this but the commander Xicotencatl, who had forbidden them, and was at that moment stationed in the immediate neighbourhood. They could not help feeling afraid of this man, as he had all their warriors as well as all those out of the land of Tlascalla under his banners. Cortes answered them by means of our interpreters, Doña Marina and Aguilar, whom we carried along with us wherever we went. They were told to allay their fears, and desire the *caziques* of the chief township to come and make peace with us, as war would only bring misfortune down upon them.

This was the message which the *papas* were to deliver; for we had not yet received any answer from the other ambassadors whom we had sent to the chiefs of Tlascalla, neither had their four distinguished personages yet arrived. Previous to their departure the *papas*, however, brought us more than forty fowls and turkeys, besides two women to bake our bread. Cortes thanked them very kindly for this present, and demanded twenty Indians to carry them to our camp. These immediately came forward without evincing any signs of fear, carried the provisions and remained with us until evening. After presenting them with a few trifles they returned highly delighted to their homes. As we did no one any injury, the inhabitants greatly extolled our kind behaviour; the *papas* and chief personages also informing the captain-general, Xicotencatl, that they had given us provisions and two females; which grieved him sorely. The same information was sent to the elder *caziques*, who were delighted when they learnt how we could have destroyed them all during the night, but that instead of doing any harm we had only made offers of peace. They, therefore, ordered provisions to be sent us daily, with everything else we might require. The orders to the four principal personages who were commissioned to make terms of peace with us were also renewed; they now no longer delayed, but repaired to our quarters and brought us provisions and other presents. We then returned to our camp, much pleased with the victuals and the Indian females.

Chapter 69

Return from Zumpanzingo

On returning to our headquarters from Zumpanzingo with a good supply of provisions, and delighted with the peace we had concluded with the inhabitants, we met with nothing but complaints and discontent. We heard of nothing else than the imminent dangers we were daily exposed to in this campaign; nor did our arrival mend matters. Foremost among the discontented were those again who possessed settlements and Indian commendaries at Cuba, nor did they confine themselves to murmuring in secret, but seven of them, whose names, for honour's sake, I will refrain from mentioning, confederated together, and repaired to the quarters of Cortes. One of them was chosen spokesman. He was a man eloquent in address, and perfect master of the subject he was about to speak on.

He began in the kindly tone of giving advice, and desired Cortes to consider our wounds, how disabled and knocked up we were by the excessive hardships we had to undergo day and night, by constant battling, patrolling the country, standing at the outposts, and reconnoitring about. They had calculated, he said, that we had already lost fifty-five of our men since our departure from Cuba. Neither did we know how matters stood with our garrison at Vera Cruz. Though the Almighty had everywhere granted us victory, it was merely out of the abundance of his mercy towards us. It was not right to calculate too long upon his mercy and forbearance, for that would be tempting him. The pitcher goes to the well until it is broken, and one morning or other we should undoubtedly be sacrificed to the idols. God in his mercy might certainly avert this; but then also it was necessary we should return to Vera Cruz and there remain quiet, where we should be surrounded by our friends and allies, the tribes of the Totonaque mountains, until we had fitted out a vessel and sent to Diego Velasquez and to the islands for a fresh supply of men and other necessaries. What a good thing if our vessels had been preserved, or at least a couple, in case of accident. But, alas! he had followed the advice of men who did not consider the instability of fortune, and who had totally destroyed the last means of escape.

"May God forbid," said they, "that you and those whose advice it was, may not yet have to rue it. The measure of our miseries is already full; our condition begins to be insupportable, and the life we lead is worse than that of beasts of burden. When these have gone their day's journey, their load is taken off, food is given them, and they are allowed to take rest; we, on the contrary, are always under arms, nor do we ever take our clothes off. He might compare the histories of the Romans, of Alexander the Great, and of the most celebrated generals," continued they, "and he would find that none of them ever destroyed a fleet, when similarly situated as we were, a mere handful of men amidst numerous and warlike tribes. He would have to answer for his own death and the destruction of us all. He should at least attempt to save ours and his own life, and march back to Vera Cruz, while we were still at peace with the country. They would gladly have mentioned all this earlier to him; but the vast numbers of the enemy by which we had been daily surrounded had given them no opportunity; this, however, was now at last presented them by the quiet demeanour of the foe. For the rest, the enemy would certainly return, the three days which Xicotencatl had allowed to pass by was merely in expectation of a fresh supply of men. We could not think of coming to another trial of strength as we had done up to this moment."

These and other representations they made to Cortes, and held up their heads pretty high the whole time. As, however, all was said under the guise of giving good advice, Cortes answered them very mildly, as nearly as possible in these words: "Much of what you have been representing to me has not escaped my own notice; but, what I have seen above all things, and of which I have gained the most convincing proofs, is this, that the whole world could not produce Spaniards who are so brave, and fight so courageously, and who could bear hardships as well as we do. Indeed, we should have been inevitably lost if we had not continually held our weapons in our hands, kept patrolling and watching day and night, and boldly encountered all weathers. We are indebted to our safety by having manfully borne these and other greater hardships. The Almighty certainly lent us his aid, yet I cannot imagine to myself a greater piece of heroism, when I bring back to my recollection the vast crowds of the enemy, how they locked us in on all sides with their troops, and fell upon us with their broad swords, particularly in that battle where they killed one of our horses. At that critical moment I learnt more of your noble character than on any former occasion. And since the Almighty rescued us out of that battle I have gained the hope that our future endeavours will be crowned with success. I can call you to witness, that I was never found for an instant to lack courage in any of the dangers I have shared with you; nor have you, I must add, ever proved unworthy of the trust I reposed in you."

It was perfectly true what Cortes said of himself, for he was always found foremost in battle.

"Neither must you forget, gentlemen," continued he, "that up to this moment the Almighty has lent us his protection, and we may confidently hope he will not desert us in future, for, from our first arrival in this country we have announced his holy religion to the different tribes according to the best of our abilities and destroyed the idols. We may also, in trusting to God and our mediator the holy apostle Peter, consider the war in this province at an end, since Xicotencatl and the other chiefs no longer show themselves, because they fear us on account of the destruction we made among their troops in the late battles, or it may be they are unable to rally their men again. The inhabitants of Zumpanzingo willingly furnish us with provisions, while the surrounding tribes continue peaceably in their villages. With regard to our vessels, it was, indeed, requisite they should be destroyed, and if I did not consult all of you on the occasion I had sufficient reason for pursuing that course after the occurrence on the downs, which, however, I will not enter into here. The course you advised me to adopt on the former occasion, and your present discontent, both emanate from the same bad feeling; but you should remember that there are several cavaliers among our troops who are not of the same opinion with yourselves, who request and counsel that we should continue as heretofore to repose our trust in God alone, and faithfully fulfil our duties in his holy service. You are, however, perfectly justified in saying that the most renowned generals of Rome even cannot boast of such military exploits as we can. Future historians will also have to relate, if God be willing, greater things of us than of them. We shall continually be reaping harvests of glory, because strict justice and Christian feeling are everywhere our guides, and also because our endeavours are exerted in the service of God and of our emperor. You cannot, gentlemen, have weighed the matter well if you suppose we could save ourselves by a retreat: for the instant these people were to observe this, and though we should depart from them in profound peace, the very stones of the ground would be raised up against us. And in the same way the Indians now stare at us as if we were beings of a superior order, or rather gods, as they term us, they would then consider us cowards and poltroons. We might, you say, settle ourselves quietly down among our allies, the tribes of the Totonaque mountains! To which my answer is, that even they would rise up against us immediately they perceive we are turning back without marching on to Mexico; for if we leave them, and they refuse to pay tribute to Motecusuma as heretofore, he will send his armies against them not merely to subdue, but to compel them to declare war with us; and if they are not desirous of being annihilated, what other course could they pursue? In this way, where we had thought to have friends, we should be preparing ourselves enemies. What reflections would the powerful Motecusuma make, and what judgment would he pass upon our previous speeches and the messages we sent him if we were to turn back? He would think we had been jesting with him. Thus you see, gentlemen, it looks bad one way and worse another. The most prudent step we can take for the present is to maintain our ground here in this thickly populated valley where we can obtain provisions in abundance. To-day we have fowls, to-morrow dogs, and thus, thank God, we shall always have plenty of food. Salt and warmer clothing are really at present the only great privations we suffer. You further state, that we have lost fifty-five men since our departure from Cuba from famine, cold, fatigue, disease, and from wounds: that our numbers are very small, and all of us more or less suffering from ill health. But, on the other hand, you must remember that God has given us the power of numbers, and that war is ever accompanied by loss of men and horses. To-day we have provisions, the next day none. And you must also bear in mind that we are not come into this country to seek repose, but to fight valiantly about whenever it may be necessary. I, therefore, beg of you, gentlemen, who are cavaliers, and who have up to this moment behaved so courageously, and whom despondency so ill suits, to drive from your minds all remembrance of Cuba and everything you have left behind there. Show yourselves brave soldiers as you have hitherto, for next to God, who is our strength, all depends upon the valour of our arms."

With this answer the deputies repaired to their partisans, who all declared they could not contradict anything our general had stated, and remarked that we had certainly departed from Vera Cruz with the full intention of marching to Mexico; but that at present we were better informed as to the strength of that city and its numerous troops. The Tlascallans themselves never mentioned the Mexican name but with terror. We said the Sempoallans were at peace with us, but we had as few certain proofs of that as of the state of affairs in Mexico. Up to this moment we had altogether suffered so much that if we were once again so furiously attacked as we had been in the late battles, we should be unable to stand against them. Suppose even they were to remain quiet for the present, our march to Mexico would, nevertheless, be a monstrous undertaking; and they were surprised at the man who could desire it and issue commands to that effect. To all this Cortes replied rather angrily: "Even then it is better to die like a brave warrior, as the poets say, than to live a coward!" We others who closely adhered to our general, and had consented to the destruction of our vessels, and appointed him captain-general, agreed with all he had said, and desired him in a loud voice not to trouble himself any further about their talk and complaints, but to order everything, with the aid of God, as circumstances might require, and to rely on our faithful assistance.

Herewith an end was put to all their cabals. They certainly continued their murmurings against Cortes, and cursed us who adhered to him, and the Sempoallans for having proposed this route; making altogether use of language which little beseemed them; but for the time being they remained quiet, and obeyed our general even to a wink.

In the meantime the elders of Tlascalla again sent peremptory orders to Xicotencatl not to attack us, but to send us provisions and repair to our camp in person to conclude a treaty of peace with us. This was the desire of all the *caziques* and principal personages of Huexotzinco and Tlascalla. A message was at the same time forwarded to each of his officers, commanding them not to obey him in anything which had not reference to a conclusion of peace. These orders were despatched no less than three successive times to Xicotencatl, information having been received that he was not only determined to lend a deaf ear to these injunctions, but to fall upon us the very next night, for which purpose he had assembled 20,000 warriors. Thus ever presumptuous and haughty, he now again refused to listen to their commands, and we shall see in the following chapter how this terminated.

CHAPTER 70

Xicotencatl's Attack

The *caziques*, Maxixcatzin and the elder Xicotencatl, with all the chief personages of the principal town of Tlascalla, had now for the fourth time issued orders to their captain-general not to approach our camp, and commanded the other officers not to accompany him unless he called upon us to make peace. Xicotencatl lay in our immediate neighbourhood, and was terribly exasperated at this; yet he determined to send us forty Indians with provisions, consisting in fowls, bread, and fruits.[1] This present was also accompanied by four disgusting old Indian females and a quantity of copal and parrot feathers.

We, of course, concluded that these people came with peaceable intentions. They perfumed Cortes when they were brought into his presence, and thus addressed him, without observing the courtesies customary among them: "These presents are sent you by the general Xicotencatl, that you may eat, in case you are *teules*, as the people of Sempoalla have assured us. If you require a sacrifice with them, kill these four women, and devour their flesh and their hearts. As we do not know what your wish is on this head we have not sacrificed them for you. But if you are human beings, be contented with the fruit and the fowls; and if you are kind-hearted *teules*, take the copal and the parrot feathers as an offering."

Cortes answered, by means of our interpreters, that he was desirous of making peace, not war, which he had already made known to them. He was come into their country to beg of them, in the name of our Lord Jesus Christ, and of our great emperor Don Carlos, to

1. During this war the Tlascallans frequently sent provisions to Cortes' troops. This they did partly out of pride, that it might not be said they conquered the Spaniards by famine; partly that the latter might not become meagre in body, but that their flesh might taste savoury when they sacrificed them to their gods, so sure were these brave warriors of victory!

abstain from human sacrifices. We were all human beings made of flesh and bone like themselves, and not *teules*, but Christians. We killed no one, excepting when we were attacked, then, indeed, we destroyed our enemies, whether it happened to be day or night. He was very thankful for the provisions, but now they should likewise have the good sense to send us messengers of peace.

We readily perceived that these people whom Xicotencatl had despatched to us were spies, who came to gain the necessary information respecting the accesses to our camp, and the number of our troops, of the horses and the cannon, and everything else. They remained with us the whole day and following night. From time to time some returned to Xicotencatl, and others again arrived in their stead. All this greatly surprised our friends of Sempoalla, as it was not customary with them to stay night and day in an enemy's camp without some particular design. This accordingly aroused their suspicions, which were further confirmed by some hints which fell from two old men of Zumpanzingo that Xicotencatl stood ready with a large army to fall upon us unawares. At first they had laughed at the idea, thinking it a mere piece of bragging, and had, therefore, not mentioned it to Cortes. Doña Marina, to whom they had made this known, immediately brought the intelligence to our general, who, to fathom this matter more deeply, ordered two of the Tlascallans, who appeared to be honest fellows, to be seized, when they confessed that Xicotencatl had sent them as spies into our camp. These men were then liberated, and several others seized, who all gave the same answer, adding, that their commander Xicotencatl was merely waiting their information to fall upon us the following night with the whole of his troops.

After Cortes had convinced himself of the true state of affairs, he commanded us to be upon our guard, and to hold ourselves ready for action; he also imprisoned seventeen other of the spies, some of whom he ordered to have their thumbs cut off, others the whole hand, and to be sent back in that condition to Xicotencatl, with the information, "That this was his mode of punishing such messengers. He might now come whenever he liked in the night or by daytime, we would wait for him here two whole days: if we had not been peaceably inclined, we should ourselves have attacked and annihilated both his army and himself long before this: it was now, however, high time he should desist from his folly, and send us a sincere token of peace."

The unfortunate beings who had thus been dismembered, arrived in Xicotencatl's headquarters just as he was on the point of marching off with his whole army to fall upon us in the dark. When he saw his spies before him in that condition, and learnt why they had been so treated, his pride and conceit fell at once. To this was added, that a certain chief, with whom he had quarrelled on account of the late battles, had left the camp with the men under his command.

Chapter 71
Peace Negotiations

We now despaired of concluding the peace we so greatly desired, and therefore began to prepare for battle. We cleaned and sharpened our weapons, provided ourselves with arrows, and were making other preparations for an engagement, when one of our outposts came suddenly running up with the tidings that a number of Indians of both sexes were advancing along the principal road of Tlascalla, straightway to our quarters, laden with packages. One of our horse had rode up to watch their movements more closely, and now also came galloping up with the news that the procession was fast approaching our camp, and merely halted from time to time to take a little rest.

Cortes and all of us were highly delighted with this piece of news, for we hoped they were coming with tidings of peace, which, indeed, was really the case. He issued orders that no alarm should be sounded, and for all of us to remain quiet in our huts as if we were unconscious of their approach. When the Indians had arrived at our camp, four principal personages stepped forth from among the porters, who had been commissioned by the elder *caziques* to conclude a treaty of peace with us. They made the sign of peace, which consisted in bending the head forwards; they then walked straightway to the hut which Cortes inhabited. They first touched the ground with their hands, and then kissed it, bowed themselves three times, and perfumed with copal. They then began as follows: "All the *caziques* of Tlascalla, with their subjects, allies, friends, and confederates, make peace and friendship with Cortes and his brothers, the *teules*. They beg forgiveness for having commenced hostilities, instead of uniting in friendship with them, which had merely been done under the impression that we were friends of Motecusuma and the Mexicans, who had been their most deadly enemies from time immemorial;

and what had strengthened them in this suspicion was, our being accompanied by such numbers of the tribes who were tributary to that monarch, who was accustomed to fall into their country under various pretences, and carry off their wives and children. They had this time again feared some foul stratagem was on hand, and therefore had put no faith in our ambassadors. They had not commenced the attack in the first instance when we marched into their country, neither was it done at their instigation or command, but assured us it was the Chontal-Otomies, a rude and wild mountain tribe, who imagined they would have been easily able to overcome our small numbers, carry us off prisoners, and send our hearts to the Tlascallan chiefs, in order to gain their good wishes. They now came to beg forgiveness, and would daily bring us a sufficient supply of provisions. They hoped we would accept of these they now brought with the same kind feeling in which they were offered. In the space of two days the chief commander Xicotencatl, with the other *caziques*, would call himself, and further prove how fervently the whole of Tlascalla desired to make peace and friendship with us."

After the chiefs had done speaking, they again bowed themselves, touched the ground with their hands, and kissed it. Cortes, with great dignity and earnestness depicted in his countenance, returned them the following answer through our interpreters: "He had certainly great cause to refuse them a hearing, or to make any compact of friendship with them; for, upon our first entering into their country, he had offered them peace, and announced that he intended to assist them against their enemies the Mexicans; yet they would not believe him, and had even been upon the point of killing our ambassadors, and had made three murderous attacks upon us; and, by way of a finish, had also sent spies into our camp. In the battle we had fought with them, we could have killed many more of the troops; and we even grieved for those whose lives had thus been sacrificed, but we had been driven to it. He had resolved to carry the war into the very town where the old *caziques* dwelt; but as they now came to sue for peace, he was willing to receive them kindly in the name of our emperor, and was also pleased to accept of the provisions which they had brought. They should now tell their chiefs to repair hither in person, or send him some better warranty of peace. If they refused to come, he would put his army in motion, and attack them at their very doors. They were, moreover, to approach our camp during daytime only, for if they came at night, we would put them all to the sword without mercy."

After Cortes had given them this answer, he presented the messengers with blue beads for the *caziques*, in token of peace. They then took leave, and turned off to some Indian dwellings which lay in the neighbourhood, leaving there the Indian females whom they had brought along with them to prepare the bread, fowls, and a dinner for us; besides this there were twenty Indians who furnished the wood and water for cooking; and indeed they prepared us a most delicious meal. Being now convinced that they earnestly desired peace, we returned hearty thanks to God, who had thus ordered things: indeed it was high time, for we were all in a terrible state of exhaustion, and were sick of a war to which there seemed no end, as the good reader may well imagine.

With respect to these proceedings, Gomara has again mixed up many untruths. One time he makes Cortes mount up to the top of a mountain, and thence look over the township of Zumpanzingo, and yet it lay quite close to our camp, and he must have been blind indeed who could not see it straight before him. He also relates that the soldiers said things which I will not repeat here, though he would make one believe he had all from good authority. There is not the slightest foundation for all his assertions. There never was a commander in this world who was so strictly obeyed as Cortes, nor will it ever again fall to the lot of any man to be so. No such thought ever entered the minds of our men, excepting on the occasion which I have related above. Even the representations which were made to Cortes, mentioned in the preceding chapter, were all given in the tone of advice. Those who made them did so with a good intention, and imagined they were in the right, and though they differed with him in opinion, they paid him strict obedience. Is it, then, any wonder that a general should listen to good advice from intelligent soldiers, particularly when his troops are so awkwardly situated as ours were? I am only sorry when I reflect that all Gomara's untruths will be credited, because his style of writing is so eloquent.

CHAPTER 72

Ambassadors from Motecusuma

After the Almighty, in his great mercy, had granted us the victory in the battles against the Tlascallans, our fame was spread to every district, and even reached the ears of the mighty Motecusuma, in the great city of Mexico. If we had been previously looked upon as *teules*, or a species of gods, their idea of our bravery now became the more exalted, and terror seized the whole country when we had broken the great power of the Tlascallans with such a handful of men, and compelled them to sue for peace.

And so it also happened that the powerful king of Mexico, Motecusuma, either in the great goodness of his heart, or because he began to fear our approach to his metropolis, despatched five men of distinction to our camp in the land of Tlascalla to welcome us on our arrival, and to assure us of the excessive delight he felt at the great victories which we had gained over such numerous armies. This message was accompanied by a valuable present in gold trinkets of various workmanship, worth about 1000 *pesos*, and of packages of cotton stuffs as much as twenty men could carry. He likewise wished us to know that it was his desire to become a vassal of our emperor, and the great pleasure he felt to find that we were so near his metropolis, that he was every way well disposed towards Cortes and all the *teules* his brothers: he likewise wished to know from us what annual tribute in gold, silver, jewels, and cotton stuffs he was to forward to our great emperor, which would save us the trouble of coming to Mexico: he should, indeed, be pleased to see us, but our march there would be a terrible one, through a sterile and rocky country, and the fatigues which we should have to undergo grieved him the more when he considered the impossibility to remove those difficulties out of our way.

To this Cortes answered, that he was very thankful for such kind feeling, as also for the presents, and the offer to pay tribute, but he must beg of the ambassadors not to leave again before we had reached the metropolis of Tlascalla, when he would deliver to them his answers for their monarch.

The real fact was, he did not feel well enough just then, as the day previous he had taken a purgative of *manzanilla*,[1] which latter is found on the island of Cuba, and is very wholesome when its use is rightly understood.

1. This name Oviedo gives to the fruit of a tree, which he calls *macanna*, growing in Cuba. (Hippomane Mancinella of Linn.) From the same fruit, according to this historian, the inhabitants prepare the deadly poison in which they dip the points of their arrows.

Chapter 73

Captain-General Xicotencatl

Cortes was still discoursing with the ambassadors of Motecusuma, and about to dismiss them, to retire to rest, for the fit of ague was again coming upon him, when it was announced that the general Xicotencatl was approaching, with several *caziques*. They were clothed in cloaks, white and parti-coloured, that is, one half of the cloak was white and the other coloured, for these were their national colours in time of peace. The number of distinguished personages who accompanied Xicotencatl amounted altogether to about fifty. When they had arrived in Cortes' quarters, they paid him the most profound reverence, after their fashion, and burnt a quantity of copal before him. Cortes received them most friendly, and desired them to take place near him; upon which Xicotencatl said, "He came, in the name of his father, of Maxixcatzin, and of all the *caziques* of the republic of Tlascalla, to beg of us to admit them to our friendship: he, at the same time, in their name, came to do homage, and promise obedience to our emperor and master, and to beg forgiveness for having taken up arms against us. They had done this because they were ignorant as to who we were: indeed, they believed we had been sent by their enemy Motecusuma, who had often before used fraud and treachery to enter their country for the sake of plunder, and they now thought he contemplated another attack upon them: they, therefore, considered themselves bound to advance boldly into the field to protect their persons and their country. They were, however, very poor, and possessed neither gold, silver, jewels, nor cotton stuffs: they were in want of salt to savour their victuals, as Motecusuma would not allow them to stir out of their country to procure it. Their forefathers had certainly possessed some gold and precious stones, but this had from time to time been delivered up to Motecusuma, to prevent their total destruction. All this had happened a long time ago, and now they had nothing left wherewith to make us a present. It was not their fault, but their poverty, yet they were well disposed."

After this preamble Xicotencatl brought various other accusations against Motecusuma and his allies. "The latter," he said, "were all hostile to their country, and left them no peace. They had certainly, up to this moment, defended themselves bravely at all times, but found that all their endeavours were fruitless against us, although they had renewed the conflict three several times; we were invincible. Hard experience at length taught them who we were, and they now desired to become our friends, and the vassals of the great emperor Don Carlos; for, they were convinced, that in alliance with us, they would be able to live in security and peace with their wives and children, and not be each moment exposed to the incursions of the treacherous Mexicans."

Xicotencatl made various other offers of his services in the name of his country. This Xicotencatl was a tall man, broad shouldered, and well built, with a large fresh coloured face, full of scars, as if pitted with the smallpox. He may have been about thirty-five years of age, and was earnest and dignified in his deportment. Cortes thanked him most sincerely, saying, "he would acknowledge them as vassals of our emperor, and would, for the future, look upon them as our friends."

Upon this Xicotencatl begged he would repair to the metropolis of his country, where all the *caziques*, elders, and *papas* were expecting us with impatience. Cortes answered, that he would comply with his request as soon as possible; for the present he had still some business to transact with the ambassadors of Motecusuma, and as soon as he had finished this he would visit them. He then continued to address them in a harsher tone of voice, and mentioned the repeated attacks they had made upon us. He would certainly bear them no malice, and freely forgave all the past, but they must sacredly observe the peace which he had granted them, and show no inconstancy in their conduct. If they did he would assuredly destroy their town and put all the inhabitants to the sword, and no longer listen to them, but carry on a war of extirpation to the very last. Xicotencatl, and all the distinguished personages who were with him, assured Cortes they would faithfully abide by their promise, and that they were ready to offer themselves as hostages in proof of their sincerity. Upon this followed various other discourses between Cortes, Xicotencatl, and the principal men of his suite. We presented them with blue beads for themselves, the elder Xicotencatl and most of the other *caziques*, with the assurance that we intended soon to visit their metropolis, which we desired they would announce to their countrymen.

The Mexican ambassadors were present during the whole of this interview, and heard the friendly offers which the Tlascallans made us of their services; and were not at all pleased with the peace we had concluded, and easily foresaw it would prove disadvantageous for their country. When, therefore, Xicotencatl had taken his leave, they remarked rather smilingly to Cortes, that he should not repose any trust in their assurances of friendship and kind offers. All this was sheer deceit, and nothing but treachery was hidden in their sentiments. They merely wished thereby to entice us into their town, when they could fall upon us unawares and destroy us all. We should remember how often they had attacked us with their whole army, but finding open force of no avail, they now, after so many of their numbers had been killed and wounded, would try their chance with fine words and a pretended show of peace.

To this Cortes answered with an air of determination, that he no way troubled himself about their intentions. If their suspicions proved true he would put the Tlascallans all to death. They might attack him by night or day, in the open field or in the town, it was all the same to him, and to convince himself as to how matters really stood he was determined to visit their metropolis. When the Mexican ambassadors found him thus determined, they begged of him to remain for at least another six days in his present quarters, that they might first send messengers to communicate with Motecusuma, and would return again with his answer in the time specified.

To this Cortes consented, partly on account of his ague, partly because he thought the warnings the Mexicans had given him might not be altogether so unfounded as he imagined. In that time he could also gain more certain proofs of the real intentions of the Tlascallans.

As everything now wore a peaceable aspect, and the whole country from the town of Vera Cruz up to our present quarters, was inhabited by friendly tribes and our allies, Cortes ventured to forward a letter to Juan de Escalante, who had remained behind there in garrison. He desired him to complete the buildings, and then gave him an account of the great victories we had gained since our arrival in Tlascalla, and how we had compelled the inhabitants to sue for peace. He also desired him to make a day of thanksgiving, and in every way to favour our allies of the Totonaque mountains. Lastly, he requested him to send two bottles of wine which he had buried in a certain corner of his quarters there, and some holy wafers, as we had none left. Escalante sent a speedy answer with the things Cortes required. It may easily be imagined how joyously this news was received at Vera Cruz, without my spending many words upon it.

During these days we erected a majestic cross in our quarters, and Cortes had one of the temples in our neighbourhood cleansed and fresh plastered by the inhabitants of Zumpanzingo, and some other Indians. But, to return to our new friends, the *caziques* of Tlascalla; the postponement of our visit greatly distressed them, yet they continued to send us fowls and figs,[1] which were now just in season, and a daily supply of provisions. This they did with the best of good will, nor would they ever take anything in return; on the contrary, they daily more earnestly begged of Cortes not to delay his visit any longer. Our general, however, was desirous of waiting the six days for the return of the Mexican ambassadors, and he each time put off the Tlascallans with some friendly excuse.

The Mexicans faithfully kept their word, and at the expiration of the above-mentioned time six distinguished personages arrived from Mexico with a rich present from Motecusuma, in value above 3000 *pesos*, consisting in gold trinkets of various workmanship, two hundred pieces of cotton stuffs, interwoven with feathers and other productions of Mexican art.

When they handed over these presents to Cortes they informed him that Motecusuma was greatly delighted at the successful state of our affairs. For the rest he requested us most urgently not to bring any Tlascallans into his dominions, for whatever purpose it might be, and upon the whole not to trust them. They were merely watching to rob us of our gold and other valuables, as they were quite poverty-struck themselves, and possessed no fine cotton cloaks. This evil design they cherished the more fervently, as they knew that we were on friendly terms with them, and had received presents in gold and cotton stuffs. Cortes accepted these presents with every appearance of delight, and thanked them, with the assurance that he would render Motecusuma good services in return. If he should discover that the Tlascallans really bore treachery at heart they would have to

1. These figs, Bernal Diaz calls Tuna, which is the Cactus Tuna of Linnaeus.

pay very dearly for it. He, however, trusted that such thoughts were remote from their minds, and he would now repair thither in person to see how much truth there was in their statement.

In the midst of this discourse several messengers arrived from Tlascalla, bringing Cortes information that all the old *caziques* of the country were on their road to pay us a visit, and conduct us into their city. On learning this, Cortes requested the Mexican ambassadors to stay with us three days before they departed again to their monarch with his answer; for that, at present, he was about to grant terms of peace to the Tlascallan chiefs.

CHAPTER 74

An Invitation to Tlascalla

The old *caziques* ofTlascalla finding that we did not arrive in their city, determined to call upon us themselves, and set out, some on foot and some in sedans and a species of hand-barrow. Besides those I mentioned above, (Maxixcatzin and the blind Xicotencatl, the elder,) there were Guaxolacima, Chichimeclatecl, and Tecapaneca ofTopoyanco. Their suite was composed of several distinguished personages. When they arrived in presence of Cortes they paid him the profoundest respect, making him and us who stood around three deep bows. They likewise perfumed with copal, touched the ground with their hands, and kissed it.

The elder Xicotencatl then addressed Cortes as follows:

"*Malinche! Malinche!* often have we begged of you to forgive the hostile attacks we made upon you. We have already explained to you that we imagined you were in league with Motecusuma. Indeed, if we had known before what we now do, instead of refusing you admission, we would not only have marched out to meet you by the shortest route with a quantity of provisions, but have come to the very coast where your vessels lie, in order to conduct you hither. But, as you have now pardoned all this, I am come with all the *caziques* to beg of you to accompany us immediately to our city, and to construct in good part the reception which we intend to give you there according to the best of our abilities. Stay all other business for the present, *Malinche,* we beg of you, and go with us now. We greatly deplore that the Mexicans should have attempted to poison your mind with all manner of falsehoods respecting us, and that this should alone have withheld you from paying us a visit. We are quite accustomed to their slanders. You must not believe them, no, nor even listen to them, for all their actions and words are full of deceit."

To which Cortes said, with serenity depicted on his countenance, "He knew years ago that we should one time visit this country. They were a brave people, and he was astonished they should have treated us as enemies. With regard to the Mexicans who were now present, they were merely waiting his commands to return to their monarch Motecusuma. He joyously accepted of their invitation to visit their city, and thanked them for the provisions they had sent, and also for all their other kind offers; they might depend upon our services in return. The reason why he had not visited them before this was solely owing to our want of men to transport the *tepuzques*," so they termed our cannon. When they heard this, they appeared exceedingly pleased, and immediately cried out, "How! was it nothing but this, and you would not tell us?" And, sure enough, scarcely half an hour elapsed before there were 500 porters on the spot, so that next morning early we were enabled to set out for the metropolis of Tlascalla. We marched forward as usual, with the heavy guns, the horse, the crossbow-men, and musketeers, in close order. Cortes had also requested the Mexican ambassadors to accompany us, in order that they might convince themselves that the people of Tlascalla were sincere. To allay their apprehensions, he assured them they should live in his own quarters, and not be molested.

Before, however, I proceed with my narrative, I must explain how it happened that Cortes was termed *Malinche* by all the tribes through whose territories we had passed. I myself in future will call him by that name, excepting there where it would be improper. This name was given to him because our interpretress Doña Marina was always about his person, particularly when ambassadors arrived, and in our negotiations with the several *caziques*, as on those occasions she interpreted for both parties. They therefore called him the captain of Marina, and contracted that appellation in the word *Malinche*.[1] This name was likewise given to Juan Perez de Artenga of Puebla, because he always accompanied Doña Marina, and to Geronimo de Aguilar for a similar reason. The former of these two even retained the name of Juan Perez *Malinche*. Our entry into the metropolis of Tlascalla took place twenty-four days after we had crossed the confines of the country, the 23rd day of September, in the year of our Lord 1519.

1. For Marina, as appears from several passages in Torquemada and other writers, was called by the inhabitants Malintziu.

Chapter 75
Our March to Tlascalla

When the *caziques* found that our baggage was moving forward, they hastened before us to make the necessary preparations for our reception, and to adorn our quarters with green boughs. We had arrived within a mile of their city when they again came out to meet us, accompanied by their daughters, nieces, and other distinguished personages, in which those of the same kin or same family or tribe kept together. Without that of Topoyanco, which held the fifth degree, there were four tribes. The inhabitants of the other townships also kept flocking up, all distinguished by the national colours of their respective dresses, which, for want of cotton, were very prettily and neatly manufactured of coloured *nequen*. Next came the whole body of *papas*, of whom there were great numbers in the temple service. They carried the pans with glowing embers, and perfumed us. Some of them had on long white cloaks, after the fashion of surplices with capes, as worn by our canons. The hair of their heads was long and matted together, so that it would have been an impossibility to have put it in any shape or order without cutting it off: besides this, it was completely besmeared with blood, which trickled down over their ears, for they had been sacrificing that very day. The nails of their fingers were uncommonly long, and they held down their heads on approaching us, in token of humility. It was told us that these men were greatly revered for their religion. The principal personages now gathered themselves around Cortes' person, and formed a guard of honour. When we entered the town, the streets and balconies could scarcely contain the numbers of men and women who had come out to see us: delight was depicted on every countenance, and twenty baskets full of roses were brought us, of various colours and sweetly scented, which were presented to Cortes and the other soldiers whom they considered officers, and particularly to those who sat on horseback. In this way we gradually arrived to some spacious courtyards, where quarters had been prepared for us. Here Xicotencatl the elder and Maxixcatzin took Cortes by the hand and conducted him into his apartments. For each of us there was a separate bed, filled with a species of dried grass, and covered with cloaks of *nequen*. Our friends of Sempoalla and Xocotlan were quartered in our vicinity in a similar manner. Cortes then requested that the ambassadors of Motecusuma might lodge with him. We soon discovered that good-will and friendly feeling were universal towards us here, and we therefore somewhat relaxed in our ordinary precautions. The officer whose duty it was to post our sentinels and order the patrols, remarked to Cortes, that, as everything wore such a friendly aspect there, our usual watchfulness would not be required. "This may be very true," answered our general, "yet we will not relinquish that excellent custom. Though the people here may be very good, we must not trust too much to this peace, but always be upon our guard as if we expected each moment to be attacked. Many a general has been ruined by carelessness and over-confidence. We, who are a mere handful of men, and have been precautioned by Motecusuma himself, though he may not exactly have been in earnest, must be ready for action at a moment's notice."

The two chief *caziques*, the elder Xicotencatl and Maxixcatzin, were very much hurt at the military precautions we took, nor did they strive to hide their feelings from Cortes, but spoke to him as follows: "*Malinche*, if we are to draw a conclusion from the steps you are taking, you either look upon us as your enemies, or at least you place no confidence in us and the treaty of peace which has been concluded between us. You post sentinels and order your men to patrol the streets as formerly, when both armies stood in hostile array against each other. This you have not done of your own accord, *Malinche*, but because the Mexicans have secretly whispered to you fears of treachery, wishing thereby to estrange you from us. Believe us, you cannot put any faith in what they say. You are now in the midst of us; everything we have is at your service—our own persons and our children; and we are ready to suffer death for you. Ask for as many hostages as you like, and you shall have them."

Cortes and all of us admired and were moved at the kind and graceful manner in which the old men expressed themselves. Our captain said he required no hostages; he had merely to make use of his eyes to convince himself that all was perfectly safe. These military precautions were ever customary with us, and they were not to take umbrage on that account. He thanked them for their kind intentions, and promised to render them great services in return.

After this explanation, other persons of distinction arrived with a quantity of provisions, consisting of fowls, maize-bread, figs, and vegetables. We had, indeed, everything in the greatest abundance during the whole of the twenty days we lay in this town.

CHAPTER 76

Mass With the Caziques

The next morning early Cortes ordered an altar to be constructed, and mass to be said, as we now again had a supply of wine and holy wafers. Father Olmedo lying ill of the fever, which had greatly weakened him, the priest Juan Diaz officiated for him: Maxixcatzin, the elder Xicotencatl, and several other *caziques* were present.

After mass, Cortes retired to his quarters. Those among us who were always about his person accompanied him: we were also followed by the old *caziques* and our interpreters, who were indispensable in such company. The elder Xicotencatl now informed Cortes that it was the general wish of the inhabitants to make him a present, if agreeable to him. Cortes answered that he should at all times be most happy to receive one: they accordingly spread some mats on the floor, and over these a few cloaks, upon which they arranged five or six small pieces of gold, a few stones of trifling value, and several parcels of manufactured *nequen*, altogether a very poor present, and not worth twenty *pesos*. The *caziques*, on presenting these things to Cortes, said to him, with a smile on their countenance, "*Malinche*! we can easily imagine that you will not exactly experience much joy on receiving a present of such wretched things as these; but we have told you before that we are poor, possessing neither gold nor other riches, as the deceitful Mexicans, with their present monarch Motecusuma, have by degrees despoiled us of everything we had. Do not look to the small value of these things, but accept them in all kindness, and as coming from your faithful friends and servants." These presents were at the same time accompanied by a quantity of provisions.

Cortes accepted of all this with every appearance of delight, and assured the old men that, since these things came from them, and were given with such great good will, they had more value in his estimation than a whole house full of gold, and that he accepted of them in that light. These words he accompanied with numerous other kind sayings and assurances of the esteem he entertained for them.

The *caziques* had also agreed among themselves to present us the most beautiful of their daughters and nieces. The old Xicotencatl, therefore, again addressed Cortes: "In order, *Malinche*, that you may have a still clearer proof of our good feeling towards you, and to show you how glad we are to do anything which we imagine may please you, we have resolved to give you our daughters in marriage, that they may have children by you. We should like to be completely fraternized with such good and brave men as you are. I myself have a daughter, who is very beautiful, and has never been married, whom I have destined for you."

Maxixcatzin and most of the other *caziques* continued in the same strain, begging of us to take their daughters for our wives. These requests were accompanied by various other proffers of friendship, and Maxixcatzin and Xicotencatl passed the whole day with us: the latter was blind with age; in order, therefore, to form to himself some idea of Cortes, he drew his hand over his hair, his face, his beard, and the whole of his body.

Cortes answered, with respect to the women, that he himself and all of us were very grateful for them, and that we should take the first opportunity of rendering them a kindness in return.

"What is your opinion," said Cortes, turning to father Olmedo, "would this not be the proper moment to desire these people to abolish their idols and the human sacrifices? From fear of the Mexicans, they will undoubtedly do anything we require of them." "It will be time enough," answered the priest, "when they bring us their daughters: then we shall have the best opportunity of telling them that we cannot accept of them until they have promised to abstain from their human sacrifices. If they comply, it is well; if they refuse, we know what our duty and our religion require of us."

Chapter 77

The Caziques and Their Daughters

The day following, the old *caziques* came and brought five young women with them, who, for Indian females, were in every sense handsome, and neatly dressed. Each had, in addition, a young woman as maid in waiting, and all were daughters of *caziques*. On this occasion, Xicotencatl thus spoke to Cortes: "*Malinche*, this is my daughter; she is still a virgin, and has never been married: take her to yourself, and give the others to your officers."

Cortes received the young women from his hand, and appeared very pleased, declaring that he would now consider these females as our own, but desired that they should, for the present, remain with their fathers. The *caziques* inquired the reason of this, when Cortes replied: "I have no other reason than that I am bound first to fulfil my duty to the God whom we adore, and to the emperor our master, which is to require of you to abolish your idols, the human sacrifices, and other abominations practised among you, and exhort you to believe in him in whom we believe, who alone is the true God." Besides this, he told them many other things concerning our holy faith, which Doña Marina and Aguilar explained right well to them. Similar discourses took place on every occasion: Cortes at the same time showed them the image of the holy Virgin, holding her inestimable Son in her arms, and he explained to them how that represented the blessed Virgin Mary: she was now high in the heavens above, and was the mother of our Lord Jesus Christ, whom she held in her arms, conceived by the Holy Ghost; that she was a virgin before, after, and during his birth. She was our mediator with her heavenly Son, our God.

To this he added many other things concerning our holy religion, and concluded by saying: "If you are, indeed, our brothers, and you are really inclined to conclude a lasting peace with us, and if we are to take and keep your daughters as affectionate husbands should do, they must abandon their horrible idols, and believe in the Lord God whom we adore. They would soon discover the beneficial effect of this; blessings would be showered down upon them, the seasons would be fruitful, and all their undertakings would prosper; after death their souls would be transplanted to heaven, and partake of eternal glory; for, by the human sacrifices which they made to their idols, who were nothing but devils, they would be led to hell, where eternal fire would torment their souls." For the present Cortes said nothing further to them respecting their idols, as he had often before spoken to them concerning these.

In answer to all this, they said to Cortes: "*Malinche*, we have heard all this from you on former occasions, and willingly believe that this your God and this illustrious woman are right good beings. But you should reflect how very recently you have arrived in our country, and you have but just entered our city. You should certainly give us time to learn more of your doings, manner of behaviour, and nature of your gods; and when we shall have satisfied ourselves respecting their qualities, we shall certainly make choice of those we consider best. How can you ask us to abandon our gods whom we have adored for so many years, and prayed and sacrificed to them? But if we should even do so to please you, what would our *papas*, our young men, yes, even our boys, say to it? Believe us, they would all rise up in arms. The *papas*, indeed, have already spoken to our *teules*, who have told them not to abolish our human sacrifices, nor any other of our ancient customs, otherwise they would destroy our whole country by famine, pestilence, and war."

We might conclude from this straightforward and fearless answer, that it would be useless to insist any longer on this point, and that they would rather allow themselves to be killed than abolish their human sacrifices. Even father Olmedo, who was a profound theologian, found himself compelled thus to address Cortes on the subject: "My opinion is, sir, that you should no longer urge this matter with these people. It is not acting right to force them to become Christians. I could likewise wish that we had not destroyed the idols at Sempoalla. This I am convinced ought not to be done until the people have gained some knowledge of our holy religion. What, indeed, do we gain by pulling down their idols from the temples? They have merely then to repair to another temple. But, on the other hand, we should never cease to exhort them with our pious lessons. In this way the time will certainly arrive, when they will find that our intentions and our advice are good."

In this same strain the three cavaliers Alvarado, Leon, and Lugo likewise spoke to Cortes; assuring him that father Olmedo was in the right, and that they perfectly agreed with him, that it would be inadvisable again to touch upon this point with the *caziques*.

Here, accordingly, the subject was dropped, and Cortes confined himself to ordering the idols to be taken down from a temple which had been recently built in the neighbourhood. The latter to be cleansed and fresh plastered, and the image of the blessed Virgin to be placed on it. To this the *caziques* readily consented, and when all was finished mass was said, and the daughters of the *caziques* were baptized. Xicotencatl's daughter was named Doña Louisa,—when Cortes took her by the hand and presented her to Alvarado, saying, at the same time, to Xicotencatl, that he to whom he had given her was his brother and a chief officer under him, who would certainly treat her well, and with whom she would live happily; to this Xicotencatl said he was perfectly agreeable.

The niece or daughter of Maxixcatzin received the name of Doña Elvira. She was very beautiful, and was presented, if I still remember rightly, to Leon. The others were given to Oli, Sandoval, and Avila, who all subjoined their Christian names to theirs as if they had been young ladies of noble birth.

Upon this it was also explained to the *caziques* why we always erected two crosses wherever we formed a camp and passed the night: assuring them amongst other things that their gods feared them. All this the *caziques* listened to with great attention. But before I continue my narrative I must add a few words about Xicotencatl's daughter, Doña Louisa, who was given to Alvarado.

The whole of Tlascalla took the greatest interest in her welfare, and honoured her as a woman invested with command. Alvarado, who was a bachelor, got a son by her, who was named Don Pedro; and also a daughter, Doña Leonora, who is now the wife of Don Francisco de la Cueva, a cavalier of distinction, and a relation of the duke of Albuquerque. She is already the mother of four or five sons, all valiant cavaliers. She is an excellent lady, and a daughter worthy of such a father, who, as every one knows, is *comptoir* of Santiago and chief justice and viceroy of Guatimala; nor is she less worthy of the house of Xicotencatl, for the latter ranked very high in Tlascalla, and was looked upon as a king.

Chapter 78

Information About Mexico

Cortes one day took the *caziques* aside, and put several questions to them respecting the situation and affairs of Mexico. Xicotencatl, as the more intelligent and distinguished personage, answered his queries, and Maxixcatzin, who was likewise a man of high rank, assisted him from time to time.

"Motecusuma," said Xicotencatl, "had such a vast army, that when he intended to conquer any large township, or of falling into any province, he invariably ordered 100,000 warriors into the field. They, the Tlascallans, had often experienced this in the many wars which they had waged with the Mexicans for upwards of 100 years."

When Cortes here interrupted them with the question: "How they had managed to escape from being in the end subdued by such a vast army?" They replied, "That they had, indeed, often been worsted by the Mexicans, and lost many of their men, who were either killed in battle, or taken prisoners and sacrificed to the idols; but that they likewise had slain numbers of the enemy and taken many of them prisoners. Neither did the Mexicans ever approach so unobserved, but that they received some previous notice of their movements. In these cases they made every effort that lay in their power; could always depend on the assistance of the Huexotzincans; and, according to circumstances, either assailed the enemy or pursued a system of defence. Besides this, another circumstance was greatly in their favour, namely, that the Mexicans were excessively hated in all the provinces and among all the tribes which Motecusuma had subdued and plundered, and that the warriors who were forced to serve in his army fought with reluctance and with little courage. In this way, then, they defended their country as well as they could. The greatest overthrow they ever experienced was from the Cholullans, whose town lay about a day's march from Tlascalla. The inhabitants there were a most deceitful set. In that town it was that Motecusuma usually assembled his troops, whence they generally commenced their march during night-time."

Maxixcatzin here observed, "That Motecusuma had strong garrisons in every town, besides the warriors who marched out from the metropolis to the field of battle. Every province was compelled to pay him tribute, consisting in gold, silver, feathers, precious stones, cotton stuffs, as well as Indians of both sexes: some of whom he took into his service, and some were sacrificed. He was altogether such a powerful and wealthy monarch, that he accomplished and obtained everything he desired. His palaces were filled with riches and *chalchihuis* stones, on which he seized wherever he came. In short, all the wealth of the country was in his possession."

They then gave such an account of the magnificence and splendour of his court, that if I here felt inclined to repeat what they told us, I should never finish; also of the number of his wives; some of whom he now and then gave in marriage to his relations; the great strength of his metropolis, how it lay in the midst of a lake, and the great depth of the latter. Several causeways, they added, led to this city, which were intersected in various places, over which wooden bridges were built, under which canoes could pass; but, if they were removed, the space between every two sections became an island, and all entrance to the town was completely cut off. Nearly the whole of the houses of the city were built in the water, and it was only possible to get from one building to another by means of drawbridges or canoes. Balconies were attached to each house, which were provided with a kind of breastwork, so that the inhabitants were able to defend themselves from the tops of the houses. Yet the whole town was well supplied with sweet water from the spring of Chapultepec, which lay about two miles from the town, whence the water was partly conveyed to the houses by means of pipes, partly in boats through the canals, and then retailed to the inhabitants.

With respect to the weapons employed by this nation, they consisted in two-edged lances, which they threw by means of a thong, and would penetrate through any cuirass. They were likewise excellent shots with the bow and arrow, and carried pikes with blades made of flint, which were of very skilful workmanship and as sharp as razors. Besides these, they carried shields, and wore cotton cuirasses. They likewise employed a great number of slingers, who were provided with round stones, long pikes, and sharp swords, which are used with both hands.

To explain all this they brought forth large pieces of *nequen*, on which were depicted their battles and their art of warfare. When Cortes and we others considered we had gained sufficient information of these things, the discourse turned on subjects of greater importance. Our friends told us how and whence they came into this country, and how they had settled themselves there; how it came that, notwithstanding their vicinity to the Mexicans, they resembled each other so little, and lived in perpetual warfare with each other. The tradition was also handed down from their forefathers, that in ancient times there lived here a race of men and women who were of immense stature with heavy bones, and were a very bad and evil-disposed people, whom they had for the greater part exterminated by continual war, and the few that were left gradually died away.

In order to give us a notion of the huge frame of this people, they dragged forth a bone, or rather a thigh bone, of one of those giants, which was very strong, and measured the length of a man of good stature. This bone was still entire from the knee to the hip joint. I measured it by my own person, and found it to be of my own length, although I am a man of considerable height. They showed us many similar pieces of bones, but they were all worm-eaten and decayed; we, however, did not doubt for an instant, that this country was once inhabited by giants. Cortes observed, that we ought to forward these bones to his majesty in Spain by the very first opportunity.

The *caziques* also mentioned another tradition which had come down from their forefathers. A certain god, to whom they paid great honours, had informed them that there would one time come from the rising of the sun, out of distant countries, a people who would subject and rule over them. If we were that people they should feel delighted, for we were courageous and good-hearted. This old prophecy was also brought up when we were negotiating terms of peace with them, and they had chiefly offered us their daughters in order to bring about a relationship between us and themselves, and to obtain assistance against the Mexicans; this they had communicated to their idols.

We were all greatly astonished at this account, and inquired of each other in amazement, whether all they told us could be true. Cortes said to them, "That we came, indeed, from the rising of the sun. The emperor, our master, had purposely sent us, that we might become their brothers, as he had had some previous knowledge respecting their country. May God in his mercy grant," continued Cortes, "that we may be the means of saving you from eternal perdition!" To which we all added, "Amen!"

The good reader will now, no doubt, have heard sufficient of our discourses with the people of Tlascalla. And I myself shall be glad to cut them short here, as I have many other things to relate besides these.

Among others, in particular, the burning mountain of Huexotzinco, which, at the time we were in Tlascalla, happened to be emitting more flames than usual, and Cortes and all of us, to whom a volcano was something new, regarded it in astonishment. Diego de Ordas, one of our chief officers, entertained the bold idea to inspect this wonder more minutely, and begged leave of our general to ascend the mountain, who granted this request.

Ordas took two of our men with him, and desired some of the chief personages of Huexotzinco to accompany him. They certainly did not refuse, but tried to deter him by assuring him, that when he should have ascended the Popocatepetl, for so they termed this volcano, half way, he would not be able to advance further on account of the trembling of the earth, and the flames, stones and ashes which were emitted from the crater. They themselves never durst venture higher than to where some temples were built to the *teules* of Popocatepetl. And indeed they left Ordas when he arrived at that spot. The latter, however, boldly continued to ascend with our two soldiers until he had reached the summit.

While they were still ascending, the volcano began to emit huge flames of fire, half burnt and perforated stones, with a quantity of ashes; and the whole mountain shook under their feet to the very foundation. They then halted for an hour, until they found that the smoke and fire gradually began to diminish and less ashes to fall; they then continued to ascend until they reached the crater, which was perfectly round and about a mile in diameter. From this elevation they could plainly discern the great city of Mexico, with the whole of its lake, and the surrounding townships; for this mountain only lies about forty-eight miles from Mexico.

After Ordas had well viewed everything and sufficiently enjoyed and wondered at the sight of Mexico and its suburbs, he again returned with the two soldiers and the Indians of Huexotzinco to Tlascalla. The inhabitants there considered this undertaking to be extremely venturesome, and even we ourselves who had never seen a burning mountain before, were perfectly astonished at the account which Ordas gave Cortes of his hazardous enterprise. Indeed at that time it might well be termed hazardous! Subsequently, to be sure, several other Spaniards and Franciscan monks ascended to the mouth of this volcano, but Ordas was nevertheless the first who had ventured. When, therefore, he afterwards again returned to Spain, he begged permission of his majesty to bear a volcano in his coat of arms. These arms are at present borne by his nephew of the same name, living at Puebla. As long as we remained in this country we never again saw the mountain throw out so much fire, or heard of its making such a heavy rumbling noise, as on this occasion, and not until the year 1539 did it burst out again.

Enough, however, of this mountain; we now pretty well know what it is. Subsequently we saw many other volcanoes, as those of Nicaragua and Guatimala; after which that of Huexotzinco is scarcely worth noticing. I have still to mention that in Tlascalla we found houses built of wood, in the shape of cages, in which numbers of Indians, of both sexes, were confined, and fattened for their sacrifices and feasts. We never hesitated a single moment to break them down and liberate the prisoners. These unfortunate beings, however, never durst leave our side, and this was the only means of saving them from being butchered. From this moment Cortes gave orders to break open these cages wherever we came, for we found them in every township. We all showed our horror of these atrocities, and earnestly reproved the *caziques* for it, who then promised no longer to kill and devour human beings. I say they promised, but that was all, and if we were but an instant out of sight the same barbarities were committed. It is now, however, high time to think of our march to Mexico.

Chapter 79

We Determine to March to Mexico

We had now been seventeen days in Tlascalla, and had heard so much during that time respecting the immense treasures of Motecusuma, and the splendour of his metropolis, that Cortes resolved to hold a consultation concerning our march to Mexico, with all those officers and soldiers amongst us whom he presumed were inclined to advance further on. In this council of war it was agreed that we should commence our march thither without delay; various opinions, however, were expressed on the occasion in our camp. Many maintained that it would be acting over-rashly to venture with a mere handful of men into a strongly fortified city, whose monarch had such vast numbers of warriors at his command. But Cortes declared that all arguing on this point was useless; we could not alter the resolution we had come to, and we had on every occasion expressed our desire to pay our respects personally to Motecusuma. When those who were averse to this step saw his determination, and that the majority of us warriors were devoted with our very hearts to him, crying out, "Forward, now or never!" they ceased to make any further opposition. Those who opposed us were those again who had possessions in the island of Cuba; we other poor soldiers were ready to sacrifice our very existence in battle, and to undergo all manner of fatigues for God and our sovereign. When Xicotencatl and Maxixcatzin were convinced that it was our determination to march to Mexico, they grew anxious on our account. They urgently dissuaded Cortes from it, and warned him not to put the slightest trust in Motecusuma, nor altogether in any of the Mexicans,—to put no faith in his show of veneration, his courteous and humble talk. All their professions of friendship, said they, and even their very presents had treachery at the bottom; for what they give at one moment they take away at another. They advised us to be upon our guard night and day; for they were perfectly assured that the Mexicans would fall upon us when we were least prepared to defend ourselves. Neither were we to spare life to any of them, if it should come to a battle;—to the young man that he might not again take up arms against us, to the old man that he might not do us injury by his counsel.

They gave us many similar precautions, and our captain assured them how grateful he was for it, and otherwise showed them every possible kindness, made them and the other *caziques* various presents, and divided among them a great portion of the fine stuffs which had been presented to him by Motecusuma. Cortes at the same time remarked to the *caziques*, that it would be the best possible thing if peace and friendship could be brought about between themselves and the Mexicans, that they might no longer continue in the disagreeable necessity of making shift with other things for want of cotton, salt, and other wares.

To this Xicotencatl immediately replied, "That with the Mexicans a treaty of peace was a mere formality: enmity, nevertheless, always clung fast to their hearts. It was the characteristic of this people to plot the foulest treacheries under the semblance of profound peace. No reliance could be placed on their promises, their words were empty sounds, and he could not remind and beg of us too often to be upon our guard against the snares of this vile people."[1]

Next came into consideration the route we should take in our march to Mexico. Motecusuma's ambassadors, who still remained with us, and wished to act as our guides, maintained that the best and most level road lay through the town of Cholulla, whose inhabitants, as subjects of Motecusuma, would be ready to lend any assistance.

We were also unanimously of opinion that this was the road we ought to take; but the *caziques* of Tlascalla, on the contrary, were quite downcast, when they learnt our determination, and maintained that we ought to march over Huexotzinco, whose inhabitants were their

---

1. In all the conferences which Cortes had with the Tlascallan chiefs, they showed an excessive hatred to the Mexicans, from which the Spaniards derived great advantages: Gomara, however, would make it appear that the Mexicans could at any time have given the Tlascallans a total overthrow if they had felt so inclined, but that they considered it better policy to attack them from time to time, when they wanted victims for their sacrifices; and then also the younger warriors of Mexico could have frequent opportunities of learning the art of war near to the metropolis, without marching to the distant boundaries of the empire for that purpose. This supposition of Gomara, however, is not founded on anything like fact.

relatives and friends, and that we ought not to take our road through Cholulla, where Motecusuma was accustomed to form his vile stratagems. Their arguments, however, were of no avail: Cortes adhered to his resolution of marching over that town. His reason for taking that road was because this town, according to general report, was thickly populated, had many beautiful towers, and large cues and temples, and lay in a beautiful valley, surrounded by extensive townships well stocked with provisions. Indeed, at that time even, Cholulla, when viewed at a distance, had the appearance of our great city of Valladolid of Old Castile. At Cholulla, moreover, we should have our friends of Tlascalla in the immediate neighbourhood; we could not, therefore, select a more proper spot to form our plans of reaching the city of Mexico without coming into contact with the great body of its troops. For in all truth, if God had not mercifully assisted us with his heavenly arm, and lent us strength in the moment of need, it would not have been possible for us to have achieved what we did!

After a long deliberation thus, the route over Cholulla was fixed upon, and Cortes sent to acquaint the inhabitants with our intentions, more particularly as, notwithstanding they dwelt so near, they had despatched no ambassadors to us, nor shown any of those attentions which were due to us who came in the name of our great monarch, who, he added, had the good of the people of Cholulla at heart. He at the same time desired that all the *caziques* and *papas* of the town should repair to our quarters, and swear allegiance to our sovereign and master, otherwise he should look upon them as our enemies.

While Cortes was despatching this message, and making other arrangements, it was announced to him that four ambassadors had arrived with presents in gold from the powerful Motecusuma, who, indeed, never despatched any messengers from his court if not provided with presents by him. He would have considered it an insult offered to us if he had not done so. I will relate in the following chapter what message these ambassadors brought.

CHAPTER 80

Motecusuma's Ambassadors

When Cortes admitted the four ambassadors into his presence they paid him and we other warriors, who stood around his person, the most profound respect, and placed before him the presents, consisting of valuable gold trinkets of various workmanship, worth about 10,000 *pesos*; and in ten packages of cotton stuffs, most beautifully interwoven with feathers: all of which our general received with a friendly smile. They then said that their monarch could not help feeling astonished that we had made such a long stay among a poor and uncivilized people, who were even not fit for slaves, but at the same time so viciously disposed, so treacherous and thievish, that some day or night when we least expected it they would murder us merely for the sake of plunder. Motecusuma begged of us rather to visit his town, where, at least, we might enjoy the good things it offered, though even these should be below our deserts, and not equal to what he could wish. We should be regularly supplied with the necessary provisions, though these had all to be brought into their city from other parts.

These expressions of friendship were merely sent by Motecusuma in order to entice us from Tlascalla, being aware that we stood in close friendship with its inhabitants, and that the *caziques* to strengthen the union had given their daughters to *Malinche* and his officers. For he would easily conjecture that nothing good could ensue to the Mexicans from our alliance with them, and this was the reason why he baited us with gold and other presents that we might enter into his territory, or that we should, at least, quit the country of the Tlascallans.

The Tlascallans were personally acquainted with these ambassadors, and they told our captain that all of them were great personages and landed proprietors, who had subjects of their own. These ambassadors Motecusuma employed on the most important matters only. Cortes returned them many thanks, in the most flattering manner, for their civilities and the expressions of friendship they made in the name of their monarch, and he desired them to say that in a short time he would pay his respects to him. He then invited them to pass some time amongst us.

About this time Cortes also sent two of our chief officers in advance to communicate with Motecusuma and view the great city of Mexico, and inspect its strong fortifications and other works of defence. These officers were Alvarado and Vazquez de Tapia. They set out on their march, and the four ambassadors who had brought the last present remained with us as hostages. Our two officers were accompanied by the other messengers who had previously arrived. At that time I was suffering from a severe wound, accompanied by fever, and could procure no medicine to relieve my sufferings, so that I cannot now recall to my memory how far these two officers proceeded on their journey: this, however, I have not forgotten, that as soon as it was known that Cortes had sent these cavaliers at a venture to Mexico, it met with universal disapprobation, and we desired that they might be recalled from their journey, as nothing could ensue from this but a mere view of that city; and a despatch was accordingly sent after them, with orders for their immediate return to our camp. They were not long returning, as Tapia had been attacked by fever on the road. When the ambassadors who accompanied them related this to Motecusuma, he was very curious to know something about the features and the height of these two *teules*, who had been on their way to Mexico, and whether they were officers. These ambassadors, it appears, informed him, that Alvarado was a man whose countenance was particularly graceful and noble, shone like the sun, and that he was an officer. They had indeed taken a faithful likeness of him, and gave him the name of Tonatio,[1] which he retained ever after among them, and signifies the *Sun, son of the Sun*. Of Tapia, that he was a man of a very stately deportment, powerful, and likewise a chief officer. Motecusuma was sorely grieved to hear of their return; his ambassadors, however, had correctly delineated their physiognomies and stature: for Alvarado was in every sense beautifully propor-

1. The name which the Mexicans gave to Alvarado was Tonatiuh, the sun. It may naturally be supposed that when the Spaniards first arrived in New Spain, they did not catch the true sound of names. Torquemada, who spent nearly the whole of his life in New Spain, is considered the most correct in this respect.

tioned in body, noble in his gait, had very pleasing features, and an amiable manner of expressing himself, so that there always appeared a smile on his countenance; in the same way Tapia, notwithstanding a certain expression of bodily strength which he had about him, had great nobleness in his carriage.

For the rest, we were not a little delighted when they reappeared in our quarters; nor did we make a secret of our opinion, that their mission had not exactly been the most prudent of Cortes' resolves. But I will say nothing further of this matter, as it has little to do with my history.

Chapter 81

Apologies from Cholulla

I mentioned in the preceding chapter that our captain had sent a message to Cholulla, inviting the inhabitants of that town to visit us in Tlascalla. When the *caziques* there received this message, they merely thought proper to send us four Indians of mean rank, and apologised for not appearing themselves, on account of indisposition. These messengers neither brought any provisions nor anything else with them, but in a few dry words offered the excuse just mentioned.

The *caziques* of Tlascalla who were present when these messengers arrived, were struck with their appearance, and remarked to Cortes that this message was a real insult to him and all of us, since these messengers were Macehuales,[1] and people of mean condition.

This circumstance induced Cortes to despatch four Indians of Sempoalla to Cholulla, telling them to acquaint the inhabitants there that he should expect an embassy from them within the space of three days, consisting of men of rank and authority. The distance between them and him was merely twenty miles, and if no one appeared within the stated time, he should consider the town of Cholulla in rebellion against us. If, however, the embassy he required did make its appearance, it was his intention to reveal matters of importance to them, for the salvation of their souls, and salutary to their whole existence; he would then also look upon them as friends and brothers, in the same way as he considered their neighbours the Tlascallans. If, however, our proposals met with their entire disapprobation, and if they did not consider our friendship worthy of acceptance, we should be far from troubling them with our presence.

When the inhabitants of Cholulla were made acquainted with this

1. Bernal Diaz writes, incorrectly, Macegales. By this word the Mexicans denoted the country people, who formed the great mass of the population, who also tilled the ground, and paid to the landowners a third part of the produce..

friendly declaration, they sent word that the reason why they could not come to Tlascalla was, because they were at enmity with the inhabitants, and were well aware how they and their ruler Motecusuma had been slandered by them: we had merely to quit the town of Tlascalla and the boundaries of that province, and if then they did not do their duty towards us, we might look upon them in the light we had threatened, and treat them accordingly.

Our captain considered this excuse perfectly reasonable, and we therefore resolved upon marching to Cholulla. When the *caziques* of Tlascalla saw that our determination was fixed, they thus addressed Cortes: "Then you rather put your trust in what the Mexicans say, than in us who are your friends? We have often impressed on your mind how particularly you should be upon your guard with the people of Cholulla, and against the power of Mexico in general; however, in order that you may have assistance in case of need, we have armed 10,000 of our warriors to accompany you."

Cortes expressed his thanks to these excellent men for their good wishes, and deliberated with us as to the policy of entering with such a large army into a country whose friendship we were desirous of gaining. After mature consideration, we came to the conclusion that 2000 men would be a sufficient number to join us, and Cortes accordingly begged our friends for so many, and the rest were thus forced to remain at home.

Chapter 82

A Brilliant Reception at Cholulla

Early one morning we broke up our quarters, and left for the town of Cholulla. We marched onward in the best order possible; for, as I have before remarked, we were always doubly on our guard wherever we suspected hostilities. The first day's march brought us to a river which flows about four miles this side of Cholulla, and we took up our night's quarters at a spot where now a stone bridge is built across the river. Here, huts and mess rooms had been erected for our accommodation.

This same night ambassadors arrived from the *caziques* of Cholulla, all personages of the first rank, to bid us welcome in their territory. They brought us provisions, consisting of fowls and maize-bread, and announced to us that all the *caziques* and *papas* would call to give us a friendly reception, and begged we would excuse them for not having come out immediately. Cortes returned them thanks through Doña Marina and Aguilar for the provisions and their kind intentions; we then laid ourselves down to rest, after we had posted the necessary sentinels and ordered the patrols.

With break of day we put ourselves in motion, and marched direct for the town, within a short distance of which we were met by the *caziques*, *papas*, and numbers of other Indians who had come out to welcome us. Most of them were clad in a species of cotton cloak, similar in shape to our *marlotas*.[1] These cloaks are also worn by the Capotecas Indians. They all appeared friendly, and well-disposed towards us. The *papas* carried along with them earthen censors, with which they perfumed our officers and those soldiers who stood nearest.

When the *papas* and other chief Indians saw the Tlascallans who had accompanied us, they begged of Doña Marina to remind Cortes

1. A small kind of cloak, a part of the old Moorish dress, still worn in Spain during festivals.

that it was not proper for their enemies to enter into the town with weapons in their hands. Cortes then ordered the officers and the whole of us to halt, and spoke to us as follows: "I am of opinion, gentlemen, that, previous to our entering into Cholulla, we should, by kind words, elicit from these *papas* and *caziques* what their real intentions are. They seem hurt that these our friends the Tlascallans should have accompanied us, and are, indeed, perfectly right in what they say; wherefore it is my intention to acquaint them, in a mild manner, with our reasons for visiting their city. You know already, from the Tlascallans, that these people are treacherous by nature; it is, therefore, most prudent we should first desire them to take an oath of allegiance to our sovereign."

He then desired Doña Marina to call the *caziques* and *papas* around him where he sat on horseback, all of us being close at his side. Three of the principal *caziques* and two *papas* immediately appeared in Cortes' presence, and addressed him thus: "*Malinche*, you must not harbour any suspicion against us for not having come to Tlascalla to pay our respects to you there, and because we did not send you any provisions. We were not wanting in good wishes towards you, but Maxixcatzin, Xicotencatl, and the whole of Tlascalla are at enmity with us. They have too grossly slandered us and our great monarch, and now they no longer abide by words, but have the audacity to be upon the point of entering, all armed, into our city, under your protection. We earnestly beg you will tell them to return to their own country, or at least command them to remain outside in the fields, and not to march into our city in such a manner. The rest of you are at liberty to enter at any time, and are perfectly welcome."

As soon as our captain was informed of this their reasonable request he sent for Alvarado and Oli, and commissioned them to beg of the Tlascallans to erect themselves huts and barracks outside the town, and not to follow us there except those of them who transported our heavy guns, and our friends of Sempoalla. These officers were, at the same time, to inform them what had occasioned these orders, and the great fear in which all the *caziques* and *papas* stood of them; that they should be duly informed of the day when we commenced our march through Cholulla to Mexico; lastly, they were desired not to grieve on account of this change.

When the inhabitants of Cholulla perceived the arrangements which Cortes had made respecting the Tlascallans, they appeared more easy; upon which Cortes acquainted them that our sovereign and master, whose subjects we were, was a powerful monarch, who had under his command many great kings and *caziques*. We were sent by him into this country to acquaint them, in his name, that, in future, they were no longer to worship idols, make human sacrifices, eat human flesh, and were to abstain from committing unnatural crimes, and all other abominations. We had come to their town because the road to Mexico lay through it, whither we were going to hold a conference with the great Motecusuma; and we were also desirous of considering them as brothers. Cortes further said that other great *caziques* had already sworn obedience and submission to our sovereign, and he hoped they would follow their example.

In answer to this, they said that we really demanded too much; we had scarcely seen them before we required of them to abolish their *teules*, which they could not think of complying with; but as regarded doing homage to our sovereign, in so far they would yield to our wishes. They accordingly made a verbal promise of allegiance, but not with the usual formalities, in presence of a royal notary; upon this we made our entry into the city of Cholulla. The tops of the houses and streets were everywhere crowded with people to gaze upon us. And who can wonder? They had never before seen men like ourselves, nor any horses! Through this mass of people we were conducted to our quarters, consisting of several large apartments, in which all of us, with our friends of Sempoalla and the Tlascallans who transported our baggage, found plenty of room, and we were immediately supplied with abundance of good victuals.

Chapter 83

Treachery

The splendid reception we met with at Cholulla was certainly well meant and honest on the part of the inhabitants, yet a most rapid change took place. Motecusuma, namely, through his ambassadors, had concocted a plan with the inhabitants to murder us all. The latter were ordered to arm themselves in all secrecy, and act in concert with 20,000 of his troops, who were already on their road, and would enter Cholulla by stealth, when they were to fall upon us unawares in a body, harass us day and night, take as many of us prisoners as they could, and send us bound to Mexico. These orders were accompanied with great promises and presents of jewels, and other precious things,—among them a golden drum. The *papas* also received instructions to sacrifice twenty of us to their idols.

All this was nicely planned, and ready to burst forth. Motecusuma's troops lay for a part hid among the woods, about two miles from Cholulla; another portion had been secretly admitted into the dwellings of the Cholullans. All were well armed, and the balconies of the houses had been strengthened by breastworks, the streets barricaded by heaps of earth, and intersected by deep holes, so as to render our horse useless. Some houses had even been filled with neck-straps, ropes made of twisted hides, and long poles, to which we were to be bound and transported to Mexico. But the Almighty had willed this otherwise, and all their designs were frustrated, as the kind reader will shortly see.

For the present we were lodged in good quarters, and received a regular and plentiful supply of provisions during the first days; and though all seemed in profound peace, we did not relax in our excellent custom of keeping a sharp look-out: and, indeed, a visible change was taking place, for, on the third day, provisions were no longer brought us, nor did any *cazique* or *papa* make his appearance among us: if any Indian did approach our quarters from curiosity, he merely came with derisive smiles, as if to convey that something unexpected was going to befall us. Cortes, perceiving this, desired the ambassadors of Motecusuma, who still remained with us, to order the *caziques* to send us provisions as usual. Some wood and water was now indeed brought us, but the old man who came with it assured us that there was no more maize left in Cholulla. That very day even other ambassadors had arrived from Motecusuma, who joined those staying with us, and delivered their monarch's message to Cortes without any show of courtesy, and in an impudent tone of voice, saying that their monarch desired we should not come to his city, as he could not provide for our sustenance there. To this they required an immediate answer, they being in a hurry to return with our reply to Mexico. As soon as Cortes saw what a sad turn affairs had taken, he spoke with much reserve, and answered the ambassadors in the most courteous manner possible, telling them how greatly he was astonished that so powerful a monarch as Motecusuma should so often change his mind: in the meantime he begged of them to postpone their return until the following day, when he would be able to say in how far we could comply with their monarch's wishes.

If my memory is correct, he likewise presented them with a few strings of glass pearls. It is, however, certain that they promised to remain until the morrow.

As soon as this conference had ended, Cortes called us all together, and told us to be particularly upon our guard, as the inhabitants, no doubt, had some evil design in hand. He then sent for the principal *cazique*, whose name has slipped my memory, and desired him, if he could not come in person, to send some one else; but received an answer that he was indisposed, and that neither he nor any other of the chiefs could come.

Cortes, perceiving this unfavourable aspect of affairs, ordered two *papas* to be brought into his presence from a large *cu*[1] adjoining our quarters, where several other *papas* had assembled together. This was accordingly done with every mark of respect due to their persons.

Cortes commenced by presenting each with a *chalchihuis*, a stone which they prize as much as we do a *smaragdus*. He then, in a most affectionate manner, inquired of them what had caused the

1. A temple where human beings were sacrificed to idols.

fear which had seized the *caziques*, the other chiefs, and the *papas*, and why they no longer called upon us, though we had sent them invitations? One of these *papas* appeared to hold a superior rank, as of a bishop, above the others; all the cues of the town stood under him, and the inhabitants paid him the profoundest veneration. This personage stated, in reply to Cortes, that the *papas* did not entertain any fear for us: if the *cazique* and other chief personages would not make their appearance, he was very willing to call upon them, and he doubted not for an instant but that they would immediately repair to our quarters.

Cortes desired him accordingly to go and call them; in the meantime he would detain the other *papa*. It was not long before this chief priest reappeared in our quarters, bringing along with him the *caziques* and the other principal personages of the district. Cortes inquired of them what cause they had had to fear us, and why they no longer sent us anything to eat? adding, that if our stay in their town was burdensome to them, we would leave the very next morning for Mexico, to pay our respects to their monarch Motecusuma: they had merely to furnish us with a requisite number of their porters to convey our baggage and the *tepuzques*, (that is, our cannon,) and to send us provisions.

The *cazique* was so embarrassed at what Cortes had said, that he scarcely durst open his mouth; but at length promised us the provisions we required, although he had been, he added, commanded by Motecusuma, his sovereign, to withhold them, and not to allow us to proceed any further on our march.

During this conference, three of our Sempoallan friends entered, and secretly acquainted Cortes that they had found deep holes in the streets adjoining our quarters, which were thinly covered over with sticks and earth, so as to be imperceptible to the eye, unless by close inspection; they had the curiosity to remove the earth from off one of these holes, and found, sticking up at the bottom, numbers of short stakes sharply pointed, and no doubt placed there to wound our horse when they fell into the holes: heaps of stones had been gathered on the tops of the houses, and the latter strengthened by breastworks made of burnt bricks. Every preparation had been made for an attack, and another street was strongly barricaded by large wooden beams. At this same moment eight Tlascallans also arrived from their quarters outside the town, and said to Cortes, "Are you ignorant, *Malinche*, of the treacherous designs which are going on in this town? We have been given to understand that the Chollullans last night sacrificed seven persons to their god of war, among them five children, in order to obtain from him a promise of victory over you. And we also know that all their goods, wives, and children have been sent out of the town."

On learning this piece of news, Cortes desired these men to return to their quarters and tell their chiefs to hold themselves in readiness to fall into the town at a moment's notice. Then, turning to the *cazique*, *papas*, and chiefs of Cholulla, he told them to allay their fears; to remain true to the promise they had made with respect to our monarch, otherwise he should find himself obliged to punish them severely: he had already acquainted them that, on the following morning, he intended to take his departure for Mexico, and he should require 2000 of their warriors to join his army, a like number having been furnished by the Tlascallans.

The chiefs, in reply, assured Cortes of their willingness to comply with his wishes; they would find him the number of warriors and porters he required; they then took their leave to make the necessary preparations, and appeared perfectly confident, for they thought we should not be able to stand against their warriors and the army of Motecusuma, which lay in ambush in the defiles, and that they should be able either to kill us or take us prisoners, as we should be unable to use our horses on account of the deep holes. They likewise ordered their men to block up all the outlets of the town, and so enclose us in the narrow streets, as we intended leaving next morning. Every one was to be particularly on his guard, and to perform his part at the right time. They would also send 2000 men in advance, and as we did not dream of what was going to take place, they would make easy work with us, take us prisoners without danger, and carry us off bound to Mexico. There was no doubt as to their success, for they had sacrificed to their god of war, and obtained a promise of victory from him.

While they were thus making sure of victory, Cortes made every effort to discover their plans, and commissioned Doña Marina to present the two *papas*, he had first spoken to, with additional *chalchihuis* stones, and acquaint them that *Malinche* was very desirous of having a second interview with them. Doña Marina was quite an adept in such matters, and succeeded by means of the presents, to induce them to accompany her into our general's quarters, who then desired them to disclose everything faithfully to him, which, as priests and men of rank, who would disgrace themselves by telling lies, they were doubly bound to do. He also assured them that the trust they reposed in him should not be betrayed, particularly as we were going to leave next day; and in order to give more weight to his words, he made them considerable promises. The *papas* then confessed that their sovereign Motecusuma could come to no resolution with himself as to whether he ought to allow us to march towards his metropolis, and that he changed his mind several times in one day. At one time he sent orders, that when we should arrive in Cholulla, we were to be treated in the most respectful manner, and they were to accompany us to his city; at another time he sent word that our march to Mexico was contrary to his wishes; and now his gods, Tetzcatlipuca and Huitzilopochtli, in whom he reposed all confidence, had advised him to kill us, or have us taken prisoners in Cholulla. The day before he had sent 20,000 warriors to this place, of whom one half was already secreted in the town, the other among the mountain defiles in the neighbourhood. These troops had been informed of our intended departure, and of the mode in which the attack was to be made upon us, as also of the 2000 men of Cholulla who were to accompany us, and how twenty of our men were to be sacrificed to the idols of Cholulla.

After Cortes had elicited all this from them, he presented both the *papas* with several of the most beautiful cloaks, enjoining them to betray nothing of what had passed between him and themselves, if they did they should certainly forfeit their lives on his return from Mexico. That very night our general called a council of war, consisting of the most sensible and experienced soldiers of our small army, to deliberate what our next step should be. Opinion, as generally happens under such circumstances, was much divided. Some proposed that we should change our route altogether and take the road over Huexotzinco. Others were of opinion that we should preserve peace at any sacrifice and return to Tlascalla. We others, however, maintained, that if we left the contemplated treachery of the Cholullans unpunished, the Mexicans would play us worse tricks in other places, and as we had once gained a footing in this vast territory, it would be better for hostilities to break out here, where, besides that, provisions were plentiful, we could do more execution than in the open field; and immediately to acquaint the Tlascallans with our determination, that they might join us in the combat.

This plan, in the end, received unanimous consent, and the following morning was fixed on for the day of our departure. We therefore fastened up our knapsacks, which indeed was no great trouble, as we had very little baggage with us. Our attack upon the Indians was to be made in the spacious square adjoining our quarters, which was surrounded by high walls, here we should be able to pay them out according to their deserts. As to the ambassadors of Motecusuma, we merely told them, that some villains of Cholulla had formed a conspiracy against us, and had attempted to lay it all to the door of their sovereign Motecusuma and his ambassadors; but that we could not for a moment give credence to this, though for the present we must beg of them not again to leave our general's headquarters, and to break off all further intercourse with the inhabitants of the town, in order to erase from our minds all suspicion of an understanding between the latter and themselves; they could also act as our guides on our march to Mexico.

The ambassadors assured us that neither their sovereign Motecusuma, nor they, were aware of anything we had mentioned to them. We, however, placed a guard over their persons, fearing they might depart without our knowledge, and relate to Motecusuma how we had discovered the conspiracy.

During the whole of this night we were particularly on our guard and all under arms, the horses were ready saddled and bridled, strong watches were posted in various places, and one patrol followed the other, as we were sure we should be attacked that night by the united forces of Mexico and Cholulla. Of this we obtained further certainty from an old Indian female, the wife of a *cazique*, who taking compassion on the youth and good looks of Doña Marina, knowing at the same time that she possessed many fine things, had induced her to follow her home to save her from the impending carnage; for, according to her account, we were all to be killed that night or the day following. This woman assured her that Motecusuma had issued the most peremptory orders to this effect, and had therefore sent an army of Mexicans, who were to join the Cholullans and spare none of us alive, excepting those they could make prisoners, who were to be sent bound to Mexico. On hearing this, the old woman added, she was induced from a compassionate feeling to disclose it to her. She advised her to pack up her goods in all haste and come and live in her house. She should have her second son for husband, the brother of the young man then present.

Doña Marina, who was altogether very shrewd, thus answered the old woman: "I am thankful indeed, good mother, for your kind warning; I would go with you this instant if I could find any one to carry away my mantles and gold trinkets, for I have a pretty good quantity of both. Wherefore I beg of you, good mother, wait a few moments here with your son, and we will leave together during the night; for these *teules* have their ears and eyes everywhere."

The old woman placed perfect confidence in what she had said, and continued chatting with her for some time. Doña Marina then put several other questions to her, as to the manner in which we were to be killed? How and when the plan had been formed? The answers which the old woman returned perfectly agreed with the account of the two *papas*. Marina then questioned her as to how she had come to the knowledge of that, which the Cholullans had thought to keep so secret? "I know all this from my husband," returned she, "who is the chief of one of the quarters of this town, and who has already joined the men under his command, to make the necessary preparations, and join the troops of Mexico in the mountain defiles. Both armies will meet and cut down all the *teules*. All this I have known three days ago, for my husband has been presented with a golden drum, and the three other chiefs with splendid cloaks and gold trinkets, with orders to take all the *teules* prisoners and send them to Mexico."

Doña Marina artfully concealed the real impression all this made upon her mind, and said to the old woman: "How delighted am I to learn that your son, to whom you intend to marry me, is a man of high rank! We have now been discoursing about matters which were intended to be kept a secret. I will now go and pack up my things; in the meantime you wait for me here, for I cannot carry all my goods alone; you, your son, my future brother, must assist me to decamp."

The old woman swallowed all this, and stationed herself at some particular spot with her son. In the meantime Doña Marina related to our general the whole of the discourse she had had with the old woman. Cortes immediately ordered the latter into his presence, and put further questions to her respecting the plans of the treacherous Cholullans. Everything she related corresponded with the account of the two *papas*; Cortes then ordered her to be detained in close custody that she might not return and disclose anything to her companions.

When morning arrived it was quite amusing to behold the air of contempt and the confidence which was depicted in the countenances of the *caziques*, the *papas*, and of the Indians in general. They appeared as if they had already caught us in a snare. They sent a larger body of their troops than we had demanded of them; yet there was sufficient room to hold all these besides our own men in the square adjoining our quarters, which may be seen to this hour as a memento of that bloody day. Though it was very early when the troops of Cholulla arrived in our quarters, yet they found us quite ready for the day's work.

The largest gate of this enclosed square was occupied by that portion of our troops who were armed with swords and shields, who were ordered not to allow egress to any Indian who bore arms. Our general had mounted his horse, surrounded by several of us as a guard to his person, and when he saw how early all the *caziques*, *papas*, and warriors had assembled in the morning, he cried out in a loud voice: "How impatient these treacherous people are to get us among the defiles and satiate themselves with our flesh: but the Almighty will order things differently from what they expect!"

He then inquired for the two *papas* who had disclosed the plot to him; and was informed that they were waiting outside with other *caziques*, and wished to be admitted; upon which Cortes sent our interpreter, Aguilar, to desire them to return home, as he had no occasion for them at that moment. This was done that no harm might befall them when we should fall upon the Indians, and as a recompense for the services they had rendered us.

Our general, seated on horseback, with Doña Marina at his side, then severely upbraided the *caziques* and *papas*. "Why had they," said he to them, "wished to murder us all the preceding night, though we had not done them the smallest injury? Had we said or done anything to justify this treacherous movement? Had he done anything more than exhorted them, as he had all the different tribes through whose territories he had passed, to abolish their human sacrifices and abstain from eating human flesh, to commit no unnatural crimes, and to lead a better life than they had hitherto? He had, further, merely spoken to them about our holy religion, and certainly thereby done them no violence. For what purpose had they collected all those long poles with the nooses and ropes in the house adjoining the large cue? Why had they during the last three days barricaded the streets, intersected the latter by deep holes, and fortified the tops of their houses with breastworks? Why had they sent away from the town their wives, children, and all their goods? All this sufficiently proved their treacherous designs, which were no longer to be concealed; they had even refused to provide us food, and in mockery had sent us merely wood and water, as if to make us believe they had no maize left. He was perfectly aware that large troops of warriors had secreted themselves in the defiles near the town, laying in wait for us when we should be on our road to Mexico. During the past night they had been joined by several other troops. In reward for our having looked upon them as brothers, and announced what our God and our sovereign had commissioned us to reveal to them, they wished to murder us, and eat our flesh, for which purpose they had already prepared the dishes, the salt, the pepper, and the tomates. If they intended to kill us, why did they not attack us boldly in the open field as beseemed brave warriors, as their neighbours the Tlascallans had done? He was fully acquainted with all their designs, how they had promised to sacrifice twenty of us to their god of war; and that they had sacrificed seven Indians three nights ago to him, that he might grant them victory over us. But all his promises were full of lies and deceit. Their gods had no power whatever over us, and their evil deeds, with all their treachery, would recoil upon themselves."

When the *caziques*, *papas*, and the other principal personages heard this, all of which Doña Marina most intelligibly interpreted to them, they confessed that what Cortes had said was perfectly correct, but added, that they were not the guilty persons, everything having been done at the instigation of Motecusuma's ambassadors, in accordance with his commands. To which Cortes answered, "That the Spanish laws did not allow such treachery to pass by unpunished, and that they would be punished for it with the loss of their lives." At this moment he ordered a cannon to be fired, which was the signal for us to fall upon them.

A great number of these people were put to the sword, and some were burnt alive, to prove the deceitfulness of their false gods. Before a couple of hours had elapsed our friends of Tlascalla came storming out of their camp into the town, and fought courageously with the troops of Cholulla in the streets, who strove to drive them back. They then dispersed themselves about the town for the sake of plunder, and taking prisoners; nor were we able to prevent them. The following day more troops arrived from Tlascalla, who committed worse depredations, so deeply rooted was their hatred against Cholulla. At length our compassion was aroused, and we ordered the Tlascallans to stay all further hostilities, and Cortes commanded all the chiefs into his presence, when he addressed them at some length, and requested them to return to their camp, which they accordingly complied with, the Sempoallans alone remaining within the town.[2]

While all this was going on, several *caziques* and *papas* arrived from other quarters of the town, who were said to have taken no part in this treacherous movement; which may, indeed, have been the case, as in this large town every quarter had its own regiment and peculiar regulations. These people begged Cortes and all of us to pardon them, as the real traitors had now received their deserved punishment. In this prayer they were joined by our friends, the two *papas*, who had first discovered the plot to us, and the old wife of the Indian chief, who was to have been Doña Marina's mother-in-law.

Cortes at first appeared very little disposed to listen to their prayers; but at length he sent for the two ambassadors of Motecusuma, whom we had kept in close confinement. He began by telling them, that though the whole town, with all its inhabitants, had merited total destruction, he would, nevertheless, substitute mercy for justice in consideration of their monarch Motecusuma, whose subjects they were; but he expected they would in future show a better disposition towards us, and give us no further cause to renew such a scene as had just taken place, otherwise they would undoubtedly forfeit their lives. He next sent for the *caziques* of the Tlascallan camp, and ordered them to liberate the prisoners they had taken, as they had now sufficiently revenged themselves. It was with difficulty we could persuade the Tlascallans to comply with this, for they maintained that the Chollulans had deserved a good deal more at their hands for the many times they had suffered from them; how-

2. Cortes, in his despatches to the emperor, mentions that three thousand Chollullans were killed on this occasion; but Torquemada gives double the number, which is nearer the truth, particularly as Gomara agrees with him. Respecting this massacre, Torquemada gives the following remarkable account: The Chollullans, he says, expected that their god Quetzalcohuatl would come to their assistance with some miracle. They believed that at any time, by removing part of the white plaster from the temple, a strong flood of water would instantly burst out, and they were therefore very particular in repairing any little damage that might happen in this way to the temple, by means of chalk mixed with the blood of children two and three years of age, killed for the purpose. It was on this temple that the Chollullans defended themselves with the greatest obstinacy; but the victory soon declaring in favour of the Spaniards, the inhabitants began to loosen the plaster off the outside, firmly believing that a deluge of water would instantly burst forth, and drown the assailants; when finding themselves disappointed in their expectations, they complained bitterly to their god for not rendering them any assistance; refused, however, to capitulate; and numbers flung themselves headlong from the top of the temple, to seek death that way.

ever, as it was Cortes' wish, they liberated a great number of their captives; but carried off a great deal of booty, consisting in gold, cloaks, cotton, salt, and other matters.

Cortes then brought about a reconciliation between these two tribes, and as far as I know, the good understanding which grew up between them was never after disturbed. He then desired the *caziques* and *papas* to order all the inhabitants into the town again, and to open the *tiangues*[3] or markets, at the same time assuring them that no further harm should befall them. The chiefs accordingly promised that all the inhabitants should return to the town within the space of five days, as most of them had fled to the woods; and added, that they feared Cortes would elect a *cazique* to whom they might be averse in the room of him who had been killed in the recent attack. Our general, however, merely inquired who the rightful successor was according to their laws; and on being informed the late *cazique*'s brother, he appointed him governor.

As soon as the town was again filled with people, and the markets frequented as usual, Cortes assembled the *papas*, chiefs, and the principal inhabitants, and explained to them the nature of our holy religion, and showed them the necessity of abolishing their idolatry and human sacrifices, and their other abominations. He likewise showed them the delusion they lived under with respect to their idols, which were nothing but evil spirits from whom they could expect nothing but falsehood. They should remember how these had lately promised them the victory over us, and how all their promises had terminated. They should, therefore, pull down and destroy those lying and deceitful idols, or leave that work to us, if they declined doing it themselves. At present he desired they would clear and fresh plaster one of their temples, that we might fit it up for a chapel and erect a cross there. These words seemed to cheer them up a little, and they gave a solemn promise to destroy their idols, but continually postponed the fulfilment whenever we put them in mind of it. On this matter father Olmedo set Cortes' mind at ease, by assuring him it would be of little use if even the Indians did abolish their idols, unless they had previously received some notion of our religion and faith. We ought first to see what impression our march into Mexico would make upon them.

3. Torquemada sometimes writes this word Tianquitz, sometimes *Tiangues*, but we find it also written Tianquiztli. By the terminating syllable most likely some particular market is meant; for it is peculiar to the Mexican language to modify the meaning of words in that manner.

Time alone could be our surest guide as to our further proceedings. For the present we had done sufficient by admonishing them to piety, and by erecting a cross there.

Respecting the town of Cholulla, I have further to remark; that it lay in a valley, and was surrounded by the townships Tepeaca, Tlascalla, Chalco, Tecamachalco, Huexotzinco, and so many others that I am unable to enumerate them all. The country furnished quantities of maize and various leguminous plants, and particularly *maguey*, from the sap of which the inhabitants make their wine.[4] In the town itself various kinds of earthenware pots are made, embellished with black and white colours, which are burnt in; with these it supplies Mexico and the neighbouring provinces. In this respect Cholulla is equally celebrated in this country, as the towns Talavera and Valencia are in Spain. At that time Cholulla had above a hundred very high towers, the whole of which were cues or temples, on which the human sacrifices were made and their idols stood. The principal cu here was even higher than that of Mexico, though the latter was, indeed, magnificent and very high.[5] It is said to have contained one hundred courts, and an idol of enormous dimensions, (the name of which I have forgotten,) which stood in great repute, and people came from various parts to sacrifice human beings to it and bring offerings for the dead.[6] I well remember when we first entered this town, and looking up to the elevated white temples, how the whole place put us completely in mind of Valladolid.

I must now say a few words respecting the troops which Motecusuma had despatched here. These lay in ambush in the immediate vicinity of the town, and had planted stakes in the ground, and dug deep holes to render our cavalry incapable of acting. But when they were informed of what had taken place there, they immediately returned to Mexico to bring the intelligence to Motecusuma. However rapidly their departure may have been, we, nevertheless, were immediately apprized of it by the two distinguished personages who were with us. Motecusuma was excessively vexed and grieved at the news, and instantly ordered a number of Indians to be sacrificed to his warrior god Huitzilopochtli, that he might reveal to him whether he should

4. Termed by the inhabitants Pulque.

5. An interesting account of this remarkable building, of which considerable remains are still to be seen, is given by Humboldt, in the *'Atlas Pittoresque.'*

6. It was the god Quetzalcoatl, of whom also an account will be found in the above-mentioned work of Humboldt.

obstruct our march to Mexico, or allow us peaceable entrance into his metropolis. Two whole days did he spend with his *papas* in devotional exercises, and in sacrificing human beings to his idols, and at length was advised by them to send us ambassadors to apologise for the occurrence at Cholulla. He was further to allow us to march into Mexico, under every show of friendship; but when we had entered the town to deny us provisions and water, break down the bridges, shut us in, and put us all to the sword. If they attacked us in a body, and from all sides at once, not one of us could escape. Not till then were the great sacrifices to be instituted, as well in honour of the warrior-god Huitzilopochtli, who had given the oracle, as in that of the god of hell, Tetzcatlipuca. Our legs, thighs, and arms were to be eaten at their feast, and our entrails, with the remaining part of our bodies, were to be thrown to the serpents and tigers, which they kept confined in wooden cages, as will be mentioned in the proper place.

It may well be imagined that the chastisement we gave the inhabitants of Cholulla spread like wildfire through the whole of New Spain. If, previously, the battles of Potonchan, Tabasco, Cingapacinga, and Tlascalla, had spread the fame of our invincible courage, and obtained for us the name of *teules* or gods of a fearful nature, we were now looked upon as divinities of a superior order, from whom nothing could be kept a secret, and the greatest veneration was consequently paid to us.

The kind reader has now, no doubt, heard enough of this occurrence at Cholulla, and I myself would gladly break off here, but must add a word or two about the wooden cages we saw in this town. These were constructed of heavy timber, and filled with grown-up men and little boys, who were fattening there for the sacrifices and feasts. These diabolical cages Cortes ordered to be pulled down, and sent the prisoners each to their several homes. He likewise made the chiefs and *papas* promise him, under severe threats, never again to fasten up human beings in that way, and totally to abstain from eating human flesh. But what was the use of promises which they never intended to keep?

These are, among others, those abominable monstrosities which the bishop of Chiapa, Las Casas, can find no end in enumerating. But he is wrong when he asserts that we gave the Chollullans the above-mentioned chastisement without any provocation, and merely for pastime. I can, however, produce as witnesses to the contrary the pious Franciscan friars who were the first monks our emperor despatched thither after the conquest of New Spain. These venerable men were purposely sent to Cholulla to make the minutest investigation into this affair. They gained all their information from the elders and *papas* of the town itself, and they were fully convinced that everything had really taken place as I have related above: and, indeed, if we had not made an example here, we should have lived in constant alarm, as we were completely surrounded by Mexican and Chollulan troops, who were everywhere lying in ambush. If we had been destroyed at that time, New Spain would certainly not have been so speedily conquered; a second armament would not so easily have found its way there; and if it had, there would have been hard work with the Indians who defended the coasts; and they would have continued in their idolatrous worship. I have myself heard the very pious Franciscan brother Toribio Motelmea[7] say that it would certainly have been better if we could have avoided spilling so much blood, and the Indians had not given us the cause to do so; but it had this good effect, that all the inhabitants of New Spain became convinced that their idols were nothing but deceitful demons, and they experienced how much happier they were when they discontinued to worship them or sacrifice to them; and it is a fact, that the inhabitants of Cholulla, from that moment, cared very little about their idols: they took down the large one from the principal cu, and either hid it somewhere or destroyed it altogether: we, at least, never saw that one again, and they placed another there in its stead.[8]

7. The name is correctly written Motolinia. This was the excellent brother Toribio Benavente, who so greatly exerted himself in converting the Indians to Christianity. He adopted the name of Motolinia on his arrival in New Spain, and the word means, *O! the poor man!* which the Indians exclaimed when they first beheld the meanness of his attire.

8. Respecting the castigation of the inhabitants of Cholulla, Las Casas, (Brevissima *Relacion de la destrucyon de las Indias*) asserts, though merely from hearsay, that Cortes, while cutting down the Indians, repeated this verse:

Miro Nero de Tarpeya,
A Roma como se ardia,
Gritos dan Niños y' viejos,
Y el de nada se dolia.

A translation of these lines will be found in a subsequent note.

CHAPTER 84

Negotiations With Motecusuma

We had now lain a fortnight in Cholulla, and any further stay there would have been waste of time. All the inhabitants had returned to their dwellings, and the markets were again filled with goods and merchants; peace had been concluded between them and their neighbours the Tlascallans; a cross erected, and much of our holy faith explained to the inhabitants. Besides this, we discovered that Motecusuma had sent spies into our quarters to gain intelligence as to our future plans, and whether we really intended marching to his metropolis. His two ambassadors, who were still with us, also forwarded him due information, from time to time, of all that was going on.

Our captain now called a council of war of those officers and soldiers in whom he could place implicit confidence, and of whose wisdom and courage he entertained the highest respect. In this council it was resolved we should despatch a most friendly and flattering message to Motecusuma, as near as possible to the following effect: "We had now, in compliance with the commands of our sovereign, journeyed over many seas, and through far distant countries, solely for the object of paying our personal respects to him, the monarch of Mexico, and of disclosing things to him which would prove of the greatest advantage to him. We chose the road over Cholulla because his ambassadors had proposed that route, and had assured us that the inhabitants were his subjects. We met with the best of receptions, and were well treated during the first two days of our stay there, when we discovered that a vile conspiracy had been set on foot to destroy us all; which, however, could not prove otherwise than a failure, as we were endowed with the faculty of knowing things beforehand, and it was utterly impossible to do anything without our knowledge: we had, therefore, punished a number of those who had concocted that treacherous movement, but we had, at the same time, abstained from punishing all those who had taken part in it, in consideration that the Cholullans were his subjects, and from the deep veneration we entertained for his person, and the great friendship we bore him. It was, however, to be regretted that the *caziques* and *papas* should have unanimously declared that all had been done at his commands, and planned by his own ambassadors. Of this, however, we had not believed a single word, as it seemed impossible to us that so great a monarch, who always styled himself our friend, could have consented thereto. On the contrary, we expected from him that, in case his gods had whispered to him to treat us hostilely, he would have attacked us in the open field, although it was all the same to us whether we were to fight about in a town or in the open field, or during night or daytime, as we easily overthrew those who ventured to attack us. As we were fully convinced of his friendship, and were very desirous to make his personal acquaintance, and to discourse with him, we intended marching to Mexico to lay our monarch's commission before him."

When Motecusuma received this message, and found that we in no way considered him implicated in the occurrence which had taken place at Cholulla, he again, as we were told, began to fast with his *papas*, and to sacrifice to his gods, of whom he wished to know whether he was to admit us into his metropolis or not. They pronounced in the affirmative, as, when we were once there, he would be able to slay us at his pleasure. His chief officers and *papas* were of the same opinion, and thought that, if he did not admit us into the city, we might commence hostilities against his subjects, and call in the assistance of the Tlascallans, the Totonaque, and other tribes who were at enmity with the Mexicans, and in alliance with us. To obviate all this, the surest way would be to follow the wise counsel which Huitzilopochtli had given.

The day had now arrived which had been fixed for our departure, and, just as we were about to break up our quarters, other ambassadors arrived, with presents from Motecusuma.

Chapter 85

A Present of Gold

When Motecusuma was made acquainted with what we said concerning our friendship towards him, and the confident manner in which we had expressed ourselves, he again felt embarrassed, and was amazed at the idea that nothing could be concealed from us, and that he might attack us whenever he liked, within the city walls or in the open field, by day or by night, it was all the same to us. He thought of our war with the Tlascallans, of the battles we had fought at Potonchon, Tabasco, Cingapacinga, and Cholulla, and grew quite perplexed and dispirited. He several times altered his resolutions, until at last he determined upon sending us six of his principal courtiers with a present in gold and trinkets of various workmanship, worth altogether above 2000 *pesos*, besides several packages of cotton stuffs most beautifully manufactured.

When these messengers were introduced into Cortes' presence, they touched the ground with their hands, and kissed it, and thus addressed our general, with signs of the deepest veneration: "*Malinche*! our ruler and monarch, the mighty Motecusuma, sends you this present, and begs you will accept of it with the same kind feeling he bears you and your brothers: he at the same time desires us to express his regret for the late occurrence at Cholulla, and to assure you it would be pleasing to him if you would castigate that evil-minded and lying people more severely, since they had wished to heap the infamy of their vile proceedings upon him and his ambassadors. We might (they continued) rest assured of his friendship, and repair to his metropolis as soon as we should think proper. Being as we were men of vast courage, and the ambassadors of so great a monarch, he would receive us with due honours, and only regretted that, owing to the situation of his metropolis in the midst of a lake, he should not be able to furnish our table with the victuals he otherwise could wish. The greatest respect would everywhere be paid us, and he had also sent orders to the different townships we should pass through to furnish us with everything we required." Besides these, there were many other civilities they mentioned in their monarch's name.

Cortes, to whom our interpreters had explained this message, accepted the present with every appearance of delight. He embraced the ambassadors, and presented them with various articles of cut glass. Every officer and soldier amongst us congratulated himself upon this favourable turn which affairs had taken, and at the monarch's invitation to visit Mexico,—for our desire to see that city daily grew upon us, particularly upon those who had no possessions in Cuba, and had accompanied the previous expeditions under Cordoba and Grijalva.

Cortes returned the ambassadors a kind answer to all they had said, and arranged that three of them should remain with us to show us the road, while the others were despatched to Mexico, to acquaint their monarch that we had already set out on our march thither.

When the two old *caziques* of Tlascalla found that Cortes was earnestly bent on marching to Mexico, they appeared excessively grieved, and reminded Cortes how frequently they had warned him, and could not do so too often, to dissuade him from marching into a town of such vast extent and power, and which possessed various means of carrying on a murderous war. The Mexicans would certainly, one day or other, fall upon us unawares, and it would be a wonder if we escaped alive out of their hands. To convince us how well they were inclined towards us, they would, however, gladly furnish us with 10,000 of their warriors, under the command of their most able generals, with a sufficient supply of provisions.

Cortes thanked them for their kind offers, and explained to them that it would not be proper to enter Mexico at the head of so large an army, particularly as the hatred between themselves and the Mexicans was so excessive. One thousand men was all he required to transport our cannon and baggage, and clear the road before us.

These 1000 men were immediately upon the spot, all strong and fine young fellows, and we were just upon the point of commencing our march when the *caziques* and chiefs of Sempoalla, who had remained with us all this time, and rendered us such valuable services, called upon Cortes and hoped he would return with them to Sempoalla. They were determined, they said, not to march over Cholulla to Mexico, as they were quite convinced it would be ours and their destruction; theirs, because they were the most distinguished personages of Sempoalla, who had not only been the chief means of inducing their countrymen to refuse all further obedience and to pay tribute to Motecusuma, but also of seizing his tax-gatherers.

Cortes, in answer to this, desired them to allay their fears; he was sure no harm would befall them, for, if they marched along in our company, who would dare to molest either? He therefore begged of them to alter their determination, and remain with us, and promised them all manner of riches. But all his entreaties, added to Marina's friendly advice, were fruitless, and they refused to accompany us: upon which Cortes cried out, "God forbid that we should force these people, who have rendered us such valuable services, to go with us against their inclination!" He then ordered several packages of the very finest cotton stuffs to be divided among them, and likewise sent the fat *cazique* two packages for himself and his nephew Cuesco, who was also a powerful *cazique*. He wrote, at the same time, to his lieutenant Juan de Escalante, who was *alguacil*-major of Vera Cruz, mentioning all that had befallen us, and that we were on our march to Mexico. He particularly cautioned him to keep a sharp look out upon the inhabitants of the country, desired him by all means to hasten the completion of the fortress, and to take the inhabitants there under his protection against the Mexicans, and also not to suffer our men to molest them in any way. This letter was given in charge of the Sempoallans, and we then commenced our march forward with every military precaution.

Chapter 86

Our March to Mexico

On our march from Cholulla, we adopted our usual precautions. A few of our cavalry were always in advance to explore the territory, and these were closely followed by a number of our best foot to assist them in case of an ambush, and to clear any obstruction from the road. Our cannon and muskets were ready loaded, while our cavalry rode three and three together on the flanks of our troops to lend immediate assistance should anything occur, all the rest of our men marching in close order. I am very particular in mentioning all this that my readers may convince themselves of the great precautions we observed on this march.

On the first day we arrived at a spot where there were a few scattered dwellings on a rising ground, subject to Huexotzinco, and, if I mistake not, bear the name of Iscalpan, and lie about nine miles from Cholulla. Here we found all the *caziques* and *papas* of Huexotzinco assembled, who were friendly with the Tlascallans. They had brought along with them other tribes from the neighbourhood of the volcano, and presented Cortes with a quantity of provisions and a few trinkets of gold, begging him, at the same time, not to consider the small worth of the latter, but the good will with which they were given. They then one and all dissuaded him from marching to Mexico, representing to him the strength of the city, the vast numbers of warriors there, and all the dangers we should be exposed to. Seeing, however, that they could not alter our determination, they instructed us as to the road we should take, and told us that, as soon as we had laid back the mountain pass, we should come to two broad roads, one of which led to Chalco, the other to Tlalmanalco, both of which townships were subject to the Mexican empire. One of these roads was in excellent condition, and passable, and in so far it would be the best we could take; the other had been rendered impassable by numbers of large pine and other trees which had been felled and thrown across the road to prevent our marching that way. A little way further up the mountain, the good road along which it was supposed we would march had been intersected and palisaded, and Mexican troops were lying in ambush there, and others had been stationed in this pass to fall upon us and put us to the sword. They therefore advised us to leave the good road, and turn into the one leading to Tlalmanalco, which had been rendered impassable by the fallen trees. They would lend us sufficient hands to clear away the latter, in which they would be assisted by the Tlascallans who were with us.

Cortes returned them many thanks for their present and good advice, assuring them he was determined, with the assistance of Providence, to continue his march, and would take the road they had pointed out.

The next morning very early we again moved forward, and, towards noon we reached the summit of the mountain, where we found the two roads exactly as described by the inhabitants of Huexotzinco. Here we halted for a short time to reconsider what had been told us respecting the Mexican troops which we should find stationed in the pass. Cortes then inquired of the two Mexican ambassadors which of the two roads they would advise him to turn into,—the one which had been blocked up by a fall of timber, or the smooth road? They told him into the latter, because it led to Chalco, a town of considerable magnitude, where we should meet with a good reception, as it was subject to Motecusuma; the other road, blocked up by the trees, was very dangerous in places, and was rather round about, leading, moreover, to a township much inferior to Chalco. Cortes, however, determined for the other road, and we marched through the mountains in the closest possible order. Our Indian friends set diligently to work to clear away the heavy trees, and even to this day many of the latter are still to be seen lying on the roadside. When we had reached the summit of the mountain, it began to snow so fast that the ground was soon covered with it. We now began to descend, and we took up our night's quarters in some scattered huts, which had the appearance of taverns for the accommodation of Indian merchants. We likewise found abundance of food here, and, notwithstanding the severity of the weather, we posted our sentinels as usual, and made regular patrols.[1]

---

1. It was here probably that Cortes was nigh being shot by one of his own sentinels. Late at night he visited the outposts himself, and one of the sentinels was just upon the point of firing at him, when Cortes fortunately made himself known.

The next morning we broke up our quarters, and arrived, about the hour of high mass, in the township of Tlalmanalco, where we met with very kind and hospitable treatment. Immediately upon the news of our arrival, numbers of people gathered about us from the neighbouring townships of Chalco, Amoquemecan, Ayotzinco, and from various other small places whose names I have forgotten. The last-mentioned town has a harbour, where canoes ply up and down. These tribes made us a present in common, consisting in gold, worth about 150 *pesos*, two packages of cotton stuffs, and eight females. "*Malinche*," said they, in handing these over to Cortes, "may it please you to accept of the present we have here brought you, and from this moment we hope you will look upon us as your friends!"

Cortes received it with every appearance of delight, and promised to assist them whenever they might require his aid. While we were thus standing around him, he desired father Olmedo to give them some notion of the Christian religion, and to admonish them to abolish their idol-worship, with which the father complied, and made similar disclosures to them as we had done to the inhabitants of the other townships we had visited. They acknowledged that all was very good which he told them, and that they would consider that matter more maturely at some future period. We likewise spoke to them about the vast power of our emperor, and how he had sent us to this country to put an end to all robbery and oppression.

We had scarcely touched this string when they began to throw out bitter accusations against Motecusuma and his tax-gatherers, but out of the hearing of the Mexican ambassadors. The Mexicans, they said, robbed them of everything they possessed; abused the chastity of their wives and daughters, before their eyes, if they were handsome, and carried them forcibly away to toil hard in base servitude. They themselves were compelled to transport wood, stones, and maize, both by water and by land, to the monarch's extensive maize plantations, and to relinquish the produce of their own land for the maintenance of the great temple: in short, their complaints knew no end, and, owing to the many years which have since elapsed, I cannot now remember them all.

Cortes, in the most affectionate manner, gave them every consolation in his power, which Doña Marina interpreted to them exceedingly well, adding, however, that, at present, our general could not redress their wrongs. They would have to bear with these hardships for some time yet, when they would certainly be released from this state of oppression. He then requested two of their principal personages to repair in all secrecy, with four of our friends from Tlascalla, to the spot where the other road had been intersected, mentioned by the inhabitants of Huexotzinco, to ascertain how matters stood, and if any troops were stationed there. But the *caziques* assured our general that it was not necessary to repair thither for that purpose, as all the palisades had been taken away, and the hole filled up again. The Mexicans had, indeed, cut through a dangerous pass some six days ago, and stationed a strong body of troops there to prevent our passing that way; but, since that time, they had been advised by their god of war to allow us to march forward unmolested, and not to attack us until we should be within the city, and then to kill us all. The *caziques* likewise begged of us to remain with them, and they would provide us with everything we might require. "Believe us," they added, "you must not go to Mexico, for we know how great the strength of that city is, and what large bodies of troops are there: if you once enter that city, you will all be put to death."

Cortes replied to this well-meant advice with the serenest countenance in the world, and assured them that neither the Mexicans nor any other people had the power to deprive us of life,—this was in the hands of the God in whom we believed. We had to fulfil our commission to Motecusuma, to all the *caziques* and *papas*, and were therefore determined to march straightway to Mexico. We should only require twenty of their men to accompany us. He would do his utmost for them, and, immediately upon his arrival there, demand justice for them; and that neither Motecusuma nor his tax-gatherers should oppress them as heretofore.

These promises spread an expression of joy over the countenance of every Indian present, and the twenty men whom Cortes required, instantly joined us; and, just as we were about to leave, other ambassadors arrived from Motecusuma, whose message I will relate in the next chapter.

Chapter 87

A Message From Motecusuma

As I have before said, we were about to continue our march, when four distinguished Mexicans arrived in our quarters, with a message from Motecusuma, accompanied by a present in gold and cotton stuffs, and thus addressed Cortes, after they had shown the usual signs of veneration: "*Malinche*! our sovereign, the mighty Motecusuma, sends you this present. He desires us to express his sorrow for the many hardships which you have been compelled to undergo on your tedious journey from such distant countries to behold his person. He now likewise, again renews the offer to pay you a quantity of gold, silver, and *chalchihuis* stones, in shape of tribute to your monarch, and as a present to you and the other *teules* who are with you; but, at the same time, he again begs of you not to advance any further, but to return from whence you came. He promises to send abundance of gold, silver, and jewels, for your emperor, to the harbour on the sea coast; he will present you with four loads of gold, and your companions with one each:[1] but he altogether forbids you to enter into Mexico, as all his troops are under arms to oppose you; add to which, the only access to the metropolis is by one narrow causeway, and we could not supply you with provisions there."[2]

Besides these, the ambassadors offered many other reasons in order to dissuade us from advancing any further. However unpleasant this disclosure might sound in his ears, Cortes, nevertheless, embraced the ambassadors most affectionately, and accepted the presents, the value of which I cannot now remember. I must also remark that

1. Clavigero says, that a Mexican load was equal in weight to fifty Spanish pounds, or eight hundred ounces, and values the gold which Motecusuma offered to Cortes on this occasion at above three millions of ducats!

2. Torquemada (Monarch. Ind. lib. iv) gives many reasons why Motecusuma was so undecided as to whether he should allow the Spaniards to enter his metropolis.

Motecusuma never sent any message to us which was not accompanied by some present in gold.

On this occasion Cortes again told the ambassadors that he was surprised how their master, who had styled himself our friend so very many times, and was so powerful a monarch, could so often change his mind. Desire a thing one day, to countermand it the next. With respect to his offer of the gold for our emperor and ourselves, we were thankful for his kind intentions, as also for the presents they now brought with them, and he would certainly some day render him valuable services in return. He would ask them himself if it would be acting right after we had advanced within such a short distance of his metropolis, to turn back without fulfilling our monarch's commission? Motecusuma should place himself in our position and consider, if he had sent ambassadors to a monarch of his own rank, how he would like it, if they returned home after arriving almost at his palace, without once seeing that monarch or fulfilling their commission to him? How would he receive these ambassadors when they appeared before him? Would he not look upon them as cowards and spiritless beings? Our emperor, at least, would not look upon us in any other light, and treat us accordingly if we returned so to his court. We had now no choice left, and we must get into his metropolis one way or other. In future, therefore, we begged their monarch would not send any more ambassadors with such messages. He, Cortes, was determined to see and speak to Motecusuma himself personally, to acquaint him with the object of our mission. All we required of him was merely an audience, for the moment our stay in his metropolis became irksome to him we would leave and return to the place whence we had come. With regard to the alleged scarcity of provisions, we were accustomed to content ourselves with little. He had better, therefore, make up his mind to receive our visit, as we could not possibly relinquish our purpose of seeing Mexico. With this answer Cortes sent the ambassadors back to their monarch, and we continued our march. As we had been so often warned by the people of Huexotzinco and Chalco, and we were aware that Motecusuma had been advised by his idols and *papas* to allow us to enter the city and then fall upon us, we became more thoughtful, for we were likewise mortals and feared death. We were now, therefore, doubly upon our guard, more particularly as the country was thickly populated; and we made short days' marches. We arranged the manner in which we were to enter the city, and commended ourselves to the protection of God, and we felt confident hopes, that as the Lord Jesus had up to this moment watched over us in all our perils, he would also shield us against the power of Mexico.

We took up our night's quarters in Iztapalapan, where we found an excellent supper awaiting us. This town lay half in the water and half on the dry land, on the slope of a small hill, where, at present, a public-house is built.

After Motecusuma had learnt our answer to his message, he despatched his nephew Cacamatzin, prince of Tezcuco to us, in great pomp, to bid us welcome. The first intimation of this prince's approach was brought in by our outposts, who announced to our general that a great number of Mexicans were advancing, arrayed in their most splendid mantles and showed signs of peace. It was still early in the day, just as we were about to break up our quarters, and Cortes consequently ordered us to halt, until we should learn the purport of this visit.

At this moment four distinguished personages came up to him, and made signs of the profoundest veneration, and announced to him that Cacamatzin, prince of Tezcuco, and nephew to Motecusuma, was approaching, and they begged that Cortes would await his arrival, as he would come almost immediately. It was indeed not long before this prince made his appearance in such splendour and magnificence as we had not yet seen in any of the Mexican chiefs. He was seated in a beautiful sedan, which was decorated with silver, green feathers, and branches made of gold, from which hung quantities of precious stones. This sedan was supported on the shoulders of eight distinguished personages, who, we were assured, were likewise *caziques* over townships.

When the procession had arrived in front of Cortes' quarters, they assisted the prince out of the sedan, and swept clean every inch of ground before him, and then introduced him into the presence of our commander. After the usual compliments, Cacamatzin addressed Cortes as follows: "*Malinche*! I and these chiefs are come here to wait upon you, and to provide all those things for you and your companions which you may require, and to conduct you to the quarters we have prepared for you in our city. All this is done at the command of our monarch, the powerful Motecusuma."

When we contemplated the splendour and majesty of these *caziques*, and particularly of the nephew of Motecusuma, we could not help remarking to each other, if these appear in so much splendour what must not the power and majesty of the mighty Motecusuma himself be![3]

---

3. Other writers say, that several of the Spaniards could not be persuaded for a length of time that it was not the monarch himself.

When Cacamatzin had done speaking, Cortes embraced him, and said many fine things to this prince and the great personages around him, and presented the former with three pieces of polished stone, of a pearly hue, containing various figures in different colours;[4] and the other chiefs with blue glass beads. He then again thanked him for the attentions which Motecusuma had thus far shown him, and inquired what day he should be able to thank Motecusuma in person?

This conference being ended, we continued our march; we were accompanied by the *caziques* who had come out to meet us and their numerous suite, with all the inhabitants of the surrounding neighbourhood, so that we could scarcely move along for the vast crowds of people.

The next morning we reached the broad high road of Iztapalapan, whence we for the first time beheld the numbers of towns and villages built in the lake, and the still greater number of large townships on the mainland, with the level causeway which ran in a straight line into Mexico. Our astonishment was indeed raised to the highest pitch, and we could not help remarking to each other, that all these buildings resembled the fairy castles we read of in Amadis de Gaul; so high, majestic, and splendid did the temples, towers, and houses of the town, all built of massive stone and lime, rise up out of the midst of the lake. Indeed, many of our men believed what they saw was a mere dream. And the reader must not feel surprised at the manner in which I have expressed myself, for it is impossible to speak coolly of things which we had never seen nor heard of, nor even could have dreamt of, beforehand.

When we approached near to Iztapalapan, two other *caziques* came out in great pomp to receive us: one was the prince of Cuitlahuac, and the other of Cojohuacan; both were near relatives of Motecusuma. We now entered the town of Iztapalapan, where we were indeed quartered in palaces, of large dimensions, surrounded by spacious courts, and built of hewn stone, cedar and other sweet-scented wood. All the apartments were hung round with cotton cloths.

After we had seen all this, we paid a visit to the gardens adjoining these palaces, which were really astonishing, and I could not gratify my desire too much by walking about in them and contemplating the

4. Bernal Diaz says, *"Tres piedras que se llaman margaritas."* Margarita is Spanish for a pearl; yet it is evident our old soldier is not speaking of pearls here, and most likely what he calls stones were nothing more than coloured Venetian glass, which was formerly held in great estimation; for in the next chapter he further describes these stones by *"piedras de vidrio,"* stones of glass.

numbers of trees which spread around the most delicious odours; the rose bushes, the different flower beds, and the fruit trees which stood along the paths. There was likewise a basin of sweet water, which was connected with the lake by means of a small canal. It was constructed of stone of various colours, and decorated with numerous figures, and was wide enough to hold their largest canoes. In this basin various kinds of water-fowls were swimming up and down, and everything was so charming and beautiful that we could find no words to express our astonishment. Indeed I do not believe a country was ever discovered which was equal in splendour to this; for Peru was not known at that time. But, at the present moment, there is not a vestige of all this remaining, and not a stone of this beautiful town is now standing.[5]

We had not been long here before the *caziques* of this town, and of Cojohuacan arrived with a present, worth about 2000 *pesos*, for which Cortes returned them many thanks, and showed the *caziques* every possible kindness, and explained, by means of our interpreters, many important things to them relative to our holy religion, and the great power of our emperor.

Iztapalapan was at that time a town of considerable magnitude, built half in the water and half on dry land. The spot where it stood is at present all dry land; and where vessels once sailed up and down, seeds are sown and harvests gathered. In fact, the whole face of the country is so completely changed that he who had not seen these parts previously, would scarcely believe that waves had ever rolled over the spot where now fertile maize plantations extend themselves to all sides; so wonderfully has everything changed here in a short space of time!

---

5. Cortes, in his despatches, gives even a more glowing description of this charming spot; a strong proof that Bernal Diaz has not said too much of it.

Chapter 88

Our Reception by Motecusuma

The following morning we left Iztapalapan accompanied by all the principal *caziques* above mentioned. The road along which we marched was eight paces in breadth, and if I still remember ran in a perfectly straight line to Mexico. Notwithstanding the breadth, it was much too narrow to hold the vast crowds of people who continually kept arriving from different parts to gaze upon us, and we could scarcely move along. Besides this, the tops of all the temples and towers were crowded, while the lake beneath was completely covered with canoes filled with Indians, for all were curious to catch a glimpse of us. And who can wonder at this, as neither men like unto ourselves, nor horses, had ever been seen here before!

When we gazed upon all this splendour at once, we scarcely knew what to think, and we doubted whether all that we beheld was real. A series of large towns stretched themselves along the banks of the lake, out of which still larger ones rose magnificently above the waters. Innumerable crowds of canoes were plying everywhere around us; at regular distances we continually passed over new bridges, and before us lay the great city of Mexico in all its splendour.

And we who were gazing upon all this, passing through innumerable crowds of human beings, were a mere handful of men, in all 450, our minds still full of the warnings which the inhabitants of Huexotzinco, Tlascalla, and Tlalmanalco, with the caution they had given us not to expose our lives to the treachery of the Mexicans. I may safely ask the kind reader to ponder a moment, and say whether he thinks any men in this world ever ventured so bold a stroke as this?

When we had arrived at a spot where another narrow causeway led towards Cojohuacan we were met by a number of *caziques* and distinguished personages, all attired in their most splendid garments. They had been despatched by Motecusuma to meet us and bid us welcome in his name; and in token of peace they touched the ground with their hands and kissed it. Here we halted for a few minutes, while the princes of Tetzcuco, Iztapalapan, Tlacupa, and Cojohuacan hastened in advance to meet Motecusuma, who was slowly approaching us, surrounded by other grandees of the kingdom, seated in a sedan of uncommon splendour. When we had arrived at a place not far from the town, where several small towers rose together, the monarch raised himself in his sedan, and the chief *caziques* supported him under the arms, and held over his head a canopy of exceedingly great value, decorated with green feathers, gold, silver, *chalchihuis* stones, and pearls, which hung down from a species of bordering, altogether curious to look at.

Motecusuma himself, according to his custom, was sumptuously attired, had on a species of half boot, richly set with jewels, and whose soles were made of solid gold. The four *grandees* who supported him were also richly attired, which they must have put on somewhere on the road, in order to wait upon Motecusuma; they were not so sumptuously dressed when they first came out to meet us. Besides these distinguished *caziques*, there were many other *grandees* around the monarch, some of whom held the canopy over his head, while others again occupied the road before him, and spread cotton cloths on the ground that his feet might not touch the bare earth. No one of his suite ever looked at him full in the face; every one in his presence stood with eyes downcast, and it was only his four nephews and cousins who supported him that durst look up.

When it was announced to Cortes that Motecusuma himself was approaching, he alighted from his horse and advanced to meet him. Many compliments were now passed on both sides. Motecusuma bid Cortes welcome, who, through Marina, said, in return, he hoped his majesty was in good health. If I still remember rightly, Cortes, who had Marina next to him, wished to concede the place of honour to the monarch, who, however, would not accept of it, but conceded it to Cortes, who now brought forth a necklace of precious stones, of the most beautiful colours and shapes, strung upon gold wire, and perfumed with musk, which he hung about the neck of Motecusuma. Our commander was then going to embrace him, but the *grandees* by whom he was surrounded held back his arms, as they considered it improper. Our general then desired Marina to tell the monarch how exceedingly he congratulated himself upon his good fortune of having seen such a powerful monarch face to face, and of the honour he had done us by coming out to meet us himself. To all this Motecusuma answered in very appropriate terms, and ordered his two nephews, the princes of Tetzcuco and Cojohuacan, to conduct us to our quarters. He himself returned to the city, accompanied by his two other relatives, the princes of Cuitlahuac and Tlacupa, with the other *grandees* of his numerous suite. As they passed by, we perceived how all those who composed his majesty's retinue held their heads bent forward, no one daring to lift up his eyes in his presence; and altogether what deep veneration was paid him.

The road before us now became less crowded, and yet who would have been able to count the vast numbers of men, women, and children who filled the streets, crowded the balconies, and the canoes in the canals, merely to gaze upon us? Indeed, at the moment I am writing this, everything comes as lively to my eyes as if it had happened yesterday; and I daily become more sensible of the great mercy of our Lord Jesus Christ, that he lent us sufficient strength and courage to enter this city: for my own person, I have particular reason to be thankful that he spared my life in so many perils, as the reader will sufficiently see in the course of this history: indeed I cannot sufficiently praise him that I have been allowed to live thus long to narrate these adventures, although they may not turn out so perfect as I myself could wish.

We were quartered in a large building where there was room enough for us all, and which had been occupied by Axayacatl, father of Motecusuma, during his life-time. Here the latter had likewise a secret room full of treasures, and where the gold he had inherited from his father was hid, which he had never touched up to this moment. Near this building there were temples and Mexican idols, and this place had been purposely selected for us because we were termed *teules*, or were thought to be such, and that we might dwell among the latter as among our equals. The apartments and halls were very spacious, and those set apart for our general were furnished with carpets. There were separate beds for each of us, which could not have been better fitted up for a gentleman of the first rank. Every place was swept clean, and the walls had been newly plastered and decorated.[1]

1. Of this building Torquemada says, it contained apartments in which one hundred and fifty Spaniards slept, each in a separate bed; and that, notwithstanding the magnitude of the building, every place was kept remarkably clean; the floors were covered with mats, and the walls were hung with tapestry of cotton decorated with feathers, and in every room there was a fire, which threw out a delightful perfume.

When we had arrived in the great courtyard adjoining this palace, Motecusuma came up to Cortes, and, taking him by the hand, conducted him himself into the apartments where he was to lodge, which had been beautifully decorated after the fashion of the country. He then hung about his neck a chaste necklace of gold, most curiously worked with figures all representing crabs. The Mexican *grandees* were greatly astonished at all these uncommon favours which their monarch bestowed upon our general.

Cortes returned the monarch many thanks for so much kindness, and the latter took leave of him with these words: "*Malinche*, you and your brothers must now do as if you were at home, and take some rest after the fatigues of the journey," then returned to his own palace, which was close at hand.

We allotted the apartments according to the several companies, placed our cannon in an advantageous position, and made such arrangements that our cavalry, as well as the infantry, might be ready at a moment's notice. We then sat down to a plentiful repast, which had been previously spread out for us, and made a sumptuous meal.

This our bold and memorable entry into the large city of Temixtitlan-Mexico[2] took place on the 8th of November, 1519. Praise be to the Lord Jesus Christ for all this. If, however, I have not exactly related every circumstance that transpired at the moment, the reader must pardon me for the present.

2. The real name was Tenuchtitlan, and it was not known by any other name when Cortes first visited the country; for Mexico was a more modern name for this city.

Chapter 89

A Visit From Motecusuma

After Motecusuma had dined, and was informed that we had likewise left table, he set out from his palace in great pomp, accompanied by a number of his *grandees* and all his relations, to pay us a visit. Cortes, being apprized of his approach, advanced to the middle of the apartment to receive him. Motecusuma took him by the hand, while others brought in a species of chair of great value, decorated, according to Mexican fashion, with gold beautifully worked into various shapes; the monarch then invited our general to seat himself next to him.

Motecusuma then began a very excellent discourse, and, first of all, expressed his delight to entertain in his kingdom and city such courageous cavaliers as Cortes and all of us were. A couple of years ago he had received intelligence that some other officer had made his appearance in the province of Champoton; and a year later, of a second, who had been off the coast with four vessels. He had long desired to see Cortes, and, since his wishes were now fulfilled, he was ready to render us any services, and provide us with everything we might require. He was now convinced that we were those people of whom his earliest forefathers had spoken,—a people that would come from the rising of the sun and conquer these countries. After the battles we had fought at Potonchan, Tabasco, and those against the Tlascallans, which had been represented to him by pictures, all further doubt had vanished from his mind.[1]

---

1. Cortes, in his despatches to the emperor, says that the monarch spoke as follows to him: "We have long known, from the historical books of our forefathers, that neither I, nor the inhabitants of this country, originally belonged to it, but that our forefathers came from distant countries. We also know that the tribe we belong to was brought hither by a monarch to whom it was subject; but this king returned to his own country, nor did he return to visit his people till several years had elapsed, after they had married the daughters of the land, and got large families by them. The monarch came with the view of leading them back to their old continued on next page)

To which Cortes answered, that we should never be able to repay him for all the kindnesses he had shown us. We indeed came from the rising of the sun, and were servants and subjects of a powerful monarch, called Don Carlos, who had numerous distinguished princes among his vassals. Our monarch had received intelligence of him, Motecusuma, and of his great power, and had expressly sent us to his country to beg of him and his subjects to become converts to the Christian faith, for the salvation of their souls; and that we only adored one true God, as he had previously, in some degree, explained on the downs to his ambassadors Teuthlille, Cuitalpitoc, and Quintalbor, all of which, however, would be more fully explained to him at some future period. When this discourse was ended, Motecusuma presented to our general various kinds of valuable gold trinkets, and a smaller portion of the same kind to each of our officers, with three packages of cotton stuffs, splendidly interwoven with feathers; and to every soldier two similar packages. All this he gave with every appearance of delight, and in all he did he showed his excellent breeding. He likewise inquired, after the presents had been distributed, whether we were all brothers, and subjects of our great emperor? To which Cortes replied in the affirmative, assuring him we were all united in love and friendship towards each other. In this way a pleasant discourse was kept up between Motecusuma and Cortes, though it was of short duration, as this was the monarch's first visit, and he was unwilling to be too troublesome thus early. He then ordered his house steward to provide us the necessary provisions, consisting in maize, fowls, and fruits, and also grass for our horses; to furnish women to grind our corn with stones, and bake the bread: after which the monarch took leave of us with great courtesy, Cortes and all of us conducting him to the door.

Our general now issued strict commands that no one should stir from headquarters until we had gained some certain knowledge as to how matters really stood.

---

country again; however, they not only refused to accompany them, but would no longer acknowledge him as their king. We have always firmly believed that descendants of this monarch would one time or other make their appearance among us, and obtain the dominion of the country. As you, according to your assurances, come from the rising of the sun, we doubt not, after what you have told us of your great monarch, who sent you here, that he is our rightful sovereign; and we have the more reason to believe this, since you tell us that he had some previous knowledge of us."

Chapter 90

Our General Visits Motecusuma

The next day Cortes determined to visit Motecusuma in his own palace. He therefore first sent to inquire after his health, and whether it would be agreeable to the monarch to receive a visit from him. Our general took with him four of our principal officers, namely, Alvarado, Leon, Ordas, and Sandoval, besides five soldiers, of whom I was one.

When our arrival was announced to Motecusuma, he advanced to the middle of the apartment to meet us, being solely attended by his nephew, as the other *grandees* were only allowed to enter his apartments upon very important occasions. After the first compliments had passed between the monarch and our general, they shook hands, and Motecusuma conducted Cortes to an elevated seat, and placed him at his right hand. The rest of us were also desired to sit down on chairs which were brought in for us. Cortes then, by means of our interpreters, addressed Motecusuma at considerable length: "He said that all his and our wishes were now fulfilled, as he had reached the end of his journey, and obeyed the commands of our great emperor. There only now remained to disclose to him the commandments of our God. We were Christians, believing in one true God only, Jesus Christ, who suffered and died for our salvation. We prayed to the cross as an emblem of that cross on which our Lord and Saviour was crucified. By his death the whole human race was saved. He rose on the third day, and was received into heaven. By him, heaven, earth, and sea, and every living creature was formed: and nothing existed but by his divine will. Those figures, on the contrary, which he considered as gods, were no gods, but devils, which were evil spirits. It was very evident how powerless and what miserable things they were, since in all those places where we had planted the cross, those gods no longer durst make their appearance. Of this

his ambassadors were fully convinced, and he himself would, in the course of time, be convinced of this truth. He begged he would also pay particular attention to something else he had to communicate." Here Cortes very intelligently explained to him how the world was created, how all people were brothers, and sons of one father and mother, called Adam and Eve; and how grieved our emperor was to think that so many human souls should be lost, and sent to hell by those false idols, where they would be tormented by everlasting fire; for this reason he had sent us hither to put an end to so much misery, and to exhort the inhabitants of this country no longer to adore such gods, nor sacrifice human beings to them; and also to abstain from robbery and committing unnatural offences. In a very short time our emperor would send to this country men of great piety and virtue, of whom there were numbers in our country, and who would explain these things more fully to them. Of all this we were merely the first messengers, and could only beg of them to support us in our labours, and assist us in their completion.

As Motecusuma was about to answer, Cortes stopped short, and, turning to us, said, "Verily, I am determined they shall comply with this, and let this be the commencement of our work!"

Motecusuma, in reply, expressed himself as follows: "*Malinche*! What you have just been telling me of your God has, indeed, been mentioned to me before by my servants, to whom you made similar disclosures immediately upon your arrival off the coast. Neither am I ignorant of what you have stated concerning the cross and everything else in the towns you passed through. We, however, maintained silence, as the gods we adore were adored in bygone ages by our ancestors. We have, once for all, acknowledged them as good deities, in the same way as you have yours, and therefore let us talk no further on this subject. Respecting the creation of the world, we likewise believe it was created many ages ago. We likewise believe that you are those people whom our ancestors prophesied would come from the rising of the sun, and I feel myself indebted to your great emperor, to whom I will send a present of the most valuable things I possess. It is now two years ago that I received the first intelligence of him by some vessels which appeared off my coast belonging to your country, the people on board of which likewise called themselves subjects of your great emperor. Tell me, now, do you really all belong to the same people?"

Cortes assured him we were all servants of the same great emperor; that those vessels were merely sent out in advance to explore the seas and the harbours, to make the necessary preparations for our present expedition.

Motecusuma likewise remarked that then even he had contemplated allowing some of those men to penetrate into the interior of his country, from his great desire to see them, and had intended to pay them great honours. Since the gods had now fulfilled his greatest desires, and we now inhabited his dwellings, which we might look upon as our own, we could rest from our fatigues, and enjoy ourselves, and we should not want for anything. Although he had sometimes sent us word not to repair to his metropolis, he had done so with great reluctance. He had been forced to act so on account of his subjects, who stood in great awe of us, and believed that we whirled fire and lightning around us, and killed numbers of men with our horses; that we were wild and unruly *teules*, and such like nonsense: as he had now gained personal knowledge of us, and convinced himself that we were likewise formed of flesh and bone, and men of great understanding, with great courage, he entertained even a more elevated opinion of us than he had previously, and was ready to share all he possessed with us.

Upon this, Cortes assured him that we felt ourselves vastly indebted to him for the very kind feeling he evinced on our behalf.

Motecusuma, who was always of a merry disposition, though never, for an instant, forgetful of his high station, now continued in a more humorous style, as follows: "I am perfectly well aware, *Malinche*, what the people of Tlascalla, with whom you are so closely allied, have been telling you respecting myself. They have made you believe that I am a species of god, or *teule*, and that my palaces are filled with gold, silver, and jewels. I do not think, for an instant, that reasonable men as you are can put any faith in all their talk, but that you look upon all this as nonsense: besides which, you can now convince yourself, *Malinche*, that I am made of flesh and bone as you are, and that my palaces are built of stone, lime, and wood. I am, to be sure, a powerful monarch; it is likewise true that I have inherited vast treasures from my ancestors; but with regard to anything else they may have told you respecting me, it is all nonsense. You must just think of that as I think of the lightning and burning flames which you are said to whirl about in all directions."

To this Cortes answered, likewise laughingly, "We knew, from old experience, that enemies neither tell the truth nor speak well of each other. We had, however, long ago convinced ourselves that there was not another such a noble-minded and illustrious monarch as himself in this quarter of the world, and that the great idea our emperor had formed of him was well founded."

During this discourse, Motecusuma secretly desired his nephew to order his house-steward to bring in some gold trinkets and ten packages of fine stuffs, which he divided among Cortes and the four officers who were present. We five soldiers obtained each two gold chains for the neck, in value about ten *pesos* each, besides two packages of cotton stuffs.

The gold which Motecusuma gave away upon this occasion was estimated at above 1000 *pesos*. But what was more, everything he gave away was given with the best of good will, and with an air of dignity which you might expect in so great a monarch.[1]

As it was already past noon, Cortes began to fear that any longer stay might be troublesome to the monarch, and said to him, in rising from his seat, "We are daily becoming more and more indebted to your majesty for so many kindnesses; at present it is time to think of dinner."

The monarch, in return, thanked us for our visit, and we took leave of each other in the most courteous manner imaginable. We now returned to our quarters, and acquainted our fellow-soldiers with the kind reception the monarch had given us.

1. Torquemada relates that the monarch had made minute inquiries of the interpreters respecting the rank of each Spaniard, and that the value of the presents he intended to give them was to be according to their respective ranks.

Chapter 91

About Motecusuma

The mighty Motecusuma may have been about this time in the fortieth year of his age. He was tall of stature, of slender make, and rather thin, but the symmetry of his body was beautiful. His complexion was not very brown, merely approaching to that of the inhabitants in general. The hair of his head was not very long, excepting where it hung thickly down over his ears, which were quite hidden by it. His black beard, though thin, looked handsome. His countenance was rather of an elongated form, but cheerful; and his fine eyes had the expression of love or severity, at the proper moments. He was particularly clean in his person, and took a bath every evening. Besides a number of concubines, who were all daughters of persons of rank and quality, he had two lawful wives of royal extraction, whom, however, he visited secretly without any one daring to observe it, save his most confidential servants. He was perfectly innocent of any unnatural crimes. The dress he had on one day was not worn again until four days had elapsed. In the halls adjoining his own private apartments there was always a guard of 2000 men of quality, in waiting: with whom, however, he never held any conversation unless to give them orders or to receive some intelligence from them. Whenever for this purpose they entered his apartment, they had first to take off their rich costumes and put on meaner garments, though these were always neat and clean; and were only allowed to enter into his presence barefooted, with eyes cast down. No person durst look at him full in the face, and during the three prostrations which they were obliged to make before they could approach him, they pronounced these words: "Lord! my Lord! sublime Lord!" Everything that was communicated to him was to be said in few words, the eyes of the speaker being constantly cast down, and on leaving the monarch's presence he walked backwards out of the room. I also remarked that even princes and other great personages who come to Mexico respecting lawsuits, or on other business from the interior of the country, always took off their shoes and changed their whole dress for one of a meaner appearance when they entered his palace. Neither were they allowed to enter the palace straightway, but had to show themselves for a considerable time outside the doors; as it would have been considered want of respect to the monarch if this had been omitted.

Above 300 kinds of dishes were served up for Motecusuma's dinner from his kitchen, underneath which were placed pans of porcelain filled with fire, to keep them warm. Three hundred dishes of various kinds were served up for him alone, and above 1000 for the persons in waiting. He sometimes, but very seldom, accompanied by the chief officers of his household, ordered the dinner himself, and desired that the best dishes and various kinds of birds should be called over to him. We were told that the flesh of young children, as a very dainty bit, was also set before him sometimes by way of a relish. Whether there was any truth in this we could not possibly discover; on account of the great variety of dishes, consisting in fowls, turkeys, pheasants, partridges, quails, tame and wild geese, venison, musk swine, pigeons, hares, rabbits, and of numerous other birds and beasts; besides which there were various other kinds of provisions, indeed it would have been no easy task to call them all over by name. This I know, however, for certain, that after Cortes had reproached him for the human sacrifices and the eating of human flesh, he issued orders that no dishes of that nature should again be brought to his table. I will, however, drop this subject, and rather relate how the monarch was waited on while he sat at dinner. If the weather was cold a large fire was made with a kind of charcoal made of the bark of trees, which emitted no smoke, but threw out a delicious perfume; and that his majesty might not feel any inconvenience from too great a heat, a screen was placed between his person and the fire, made of gold, and adorned with all manner of figures of their gods. The chair on which he sat was rather low, but supplied with soft cushions, and was beautifully carved; the table was very little higher than this, but perfectly corresponded with his seat. It was covered with white cloths, and one of a larger size. Four very neat and pretty young women held before the monarch a species of round pitcher, called by them Xicales, filled with water to wash his hands in. The water was caught in other vessels, and then the young women presented him with towels to dry his hands. Two other women brought him maize-bread baked with eggs. Before, however, Motecusuma began his dinner, a kind of wooden screen, strongly gilt, was placed before him, that no one might see him while eating, and the young women stood at a distance. Next four elderly men, of high rank, were admitted to his table; whom he addressed from time to time, or put some questions to them. Sometimes he would offer them a plate of some of his viands, which was considered a mark of great favour. These grey-headed old men, who were so highly honoured, were, as we subsequently learnt, his nearest relations, most trustworthy counsellors and chief justices. Whenever he ordered any victuals to be presented them, they ate it standing, in the deepest veneration, though without daring to look at him full in the face. The dishes in which the dinner was served up were of variegated and black porcelain, made at Cholulla. While the monarch was at table, his courtiers, and those who were in waiting in the halls adjoining, had to maintain strict silence.

After the hot dishes had been removed, every kind of fruit which the country produced was set on the table; of which, however, Motecusuma ate very little. Every now and then was handed to him a golden pitcher filled with a kind of liquor made from the *cacao*, which is of a very exciting nature. Though we did not pay any particular attention to the circumstance at the time, yet I saw about fifty large pitchers filled with the same liquor brought in all frothy. This beverage was also presented to the monarch by women, but all with the profoundest veneration.

Sometimes during dinner time, he would have ugly Indian humpbacked dwarfs, who acted as buffoons and performed antics for his amusement. At another time he would have jesters to enliven him with their witticisms. Others again danced and sung before him. Motecusuma took great delight in these entertainments, and ordered the broken victuals and pitchers of *cacao* liquor to be distributed among these performers. As soon as he had finished his dinner the four women cleared the cloths and brought him water to wash his hands. During this interval he discoursed a little with the four old men, and then left table to enjoy his afternoon's nap.

After the monarch had dined, dinner was served up for the men on duty and the other officers of his household, and I have often counted more than 1000 dishes on the table, of the kinds above mentioned. These were then followed, according to the Mexican custom, by the frothing jugs of *cacao* liquor; certainly 2000 of them, after which came different kinds of fruit in great abundance.

Next the women dined, who superintended the baking department; and those who made the *cacao* liquor, with the young women who waited upon the monarch. Indeed, the daily expense of these dinners alone must have been very great!

Besides these servants there were numerous butlers, house-stewards, treasurers, cooks, and superintendents of maize-magazines. Indeed there is so much to be said about these that I scarcely knew where to commence, and we could not help wondering that everything was done with such perfect order. I had almost forgotten to mention, that during dinner-time, two other young women of great beauty brought the monarch small cakes, as white as snow, made of eggs and other very nourishing ingredients, on plates covered with clean napkins; also a kind of long-shaped bread, likewise made of very substantial things, and some *pachol*, which is a kind of wafer-cake. They then presented him with three beautifully painted and gilt tubes, which were filled with liquid amber, and a herb called by the Indians tabaco. After the dinner had been cleared away and the singing and dancing done, one of these tubes was lighted, and the monarch took the smoke into his mouth, and after he had done this a short time, he fell asleep.[1]

About this time a celebrated *cazique*, whom we called Tapia, was Motecusuma's chief steward: he kept an account of the whole of Motecusuma's revenue, in large books of paper which the Mexicans call *amatl*. A whole house was filled with such large books of accounts.[2]

---

1. Respecting the custom of smoking among the Mexicans, Humboldt gives the following, in his work on New Spain: "The Mexicans called tobacco *yetl*, which they not only considered a remedy against toothache, cold in the head, and bowel complaints, but they likewise used it as a luxury, by smoking and snuffing it. At Motecusuma's court it was used as a narcotic, not only after dinner, but also after breakfast, to produce a comfortable nap, as is still the custom in many districts of America. The leaves were rolled together like cigars, and then stuck in tubes made of silver, wood, or of shell."

2. The revenue of Motecusuma we know consisted of the natural products of the country, and what was produced by the industry of his subjects. Respecting the payment of tribute, we find the following story in Torquemada: "During the abode of Motecusuma among the Spaniards, in the palace of his father, Alonso de Ojeda one day espied in a certain apartment of the building a number of small bags tied up. He imagined at first that they were filled with gold dust, but on opening one of them, what was his astonishment to find it quite full of lice? Ojeda, greatly surprised at the discovery he had made, immediately communicated what he had seen to Cortes, who then asked Marina and Aguilar for some explanation. They informed him that the Mexicans had such a sense of their duty to pay tribute to their monarch, that the poorest and meanest of the inhabitants, if they possessed nothing better to present to their king, daily cleaned their persons, and saved all the lice they caught, and that when they had a good store of these, they laid them (continued on next page)

Motecusuma had also two arsenals filled with arms of every description, of which many were ornamented with gold and precious stones. These arms consisted in shields of different sizes, sabres, and a species of broadsword, which is wielded with both hands, the edge furnished with flint stones, so extremely sharp that they cut much better than our Spanish swords:[3] further, lances of greater length than ours, with spikes at their end, full one fathom in length, likewise furnished with several sharp flint stones. The pikes are so very sharp and hard that they will pierce the strongest shield, and cut like a razor; so that the Mexicans even shave themselves with these stones. Then there were excellent bows and arrows, pikes with single and double points, and the proper thongs to throw them with; slings with round stones purposely made for them; also a species of large shield, so ingeniously constructed that it could be rolled up when not wanted: they are only unrolled on the field of battle, and completely cover the whole body from the head to the feet. Further, we saw here a great variety of cuirasses made of quilted cotton, which were outwardly adorned with soft feathers of different colours, and looked like uniforms; *morions* and helmets constructed of wood and bones, likewise adorned with feathers. There were always artificers at work, who continually augmented this store of arms; and the arsenals were under the care of particular personages, who also superintended the works.

Motecusuma had likewise a variety of aviaries, and it is indeed with difficulty that I constrain myself from going into too minute a detail respecting these. I will confine myself by stating that we saw here every kind of eagle, from the king's eagle to the smallest kind included, and every species of bird, from the largest known to the little *colibris*, in their full splendour of plumage. Here were also to be seen those birds from which the Mexicans take the green-coloured feathers of which they manufacture their beautiful feathered stuffs. These last-mentioned birds very much resemble our Spanish jays, and are called by the Indians *quezales*. The species of sparrows were

---

in bags at the feet of their monarch. Torquemada further remarks, that his reader might think these bags were filled with small worms (*gasanillos*), and not with lice; but appeals to Alonso de Ojeda, and another of Cortes' soldiers, named Alonso de Mata, who were eyewitnesses of the fact." This story, no doubt, is founded on something like truth, and most probably these bags were filled with the *coccus* cacti, the famous cochineal insect, then unknown to the Spaniards, who might easily have mistaken them in a dried state for lice.

3. This weapon, called by the Mexicans *maquahuitl*, was much dreaded by the Spaniards; and the historian Acosta relates that the Mexicans would cut off the head of a horse with it at one blow.

particularly curious, having five distinct colours in their plumage—green, red, white, yellow, and blue; I have, however, forgotten their Mexican name. There were such vast numbers of parrots, and such a variety of species, that I cannot remember all their names; and geese of the richest plumage, and other large birds. These were, at stated periods, stripped of their feathers, in order that new ones might grow in their place. All these birds had appropriate places to breed in, and were under the care of several Indians of both sexes, who had to keep the nests clean, give to each kind its proper food, and set the birds for breeding. In the courtyard belonging to this building, there was a large basin of sweet water, in which, besides other water fowls, there was a particularly beautiful bird, with long legs, its body, wings, and tail variously coloured, and is called at Cuba, where it is also found, the *ipiris*.

In another large building, numbers of idols were erected, and these, it is said, were the most terrible of all their gods. Near these were kept all manner of beautiful animals, tigers, lions of two different kinds, of which one had the shape of a wolf, and was called a jackal; there were also foxes, and other small beasts of prey. Most of these animals had been bred here, and were fed with wild deer flesh, turkeys, dogs, and sometimes, as I have been assured, with the offal of human beings.

Respecting the abominable human sacrifices of these people, the following was communicated to us: The breast of the unhappy victim destined to be sacrificed was ripped open with a knife made of sharp flint; the throbbing heart was then torn out, and immediately offered to the idol-god in whose honour the sacrifice had been instituted. After this, the head, arms, and legs were cut off and eaten at their banquets, with the exception of the head, which was saved, and hung to a beam appropriated for that purpose. No other part of the body was eaten, but the remainder was thrown to the beasts which were kept in those abominable dens, in which there were also vipers and other poisonous serpents, and, among the latter in particular, a species at the end of whose tail there was a kind of rattle. This last-mentioned serpent, which is the most dangerous, was kept in a cabin of a diversified form, in which a quantity of feathers had been strewed: here it laid its eggs, and it was fed with the flesh of dogs and of human beings who had been sacrificed. We were positively told that, after we had been beaten out of the city of Mexico, and had lost 850 of our men, these horrible beasts were fed for many successive days with the bodies of our unfortunate countrymen. Indeed, when all the tigers and lions roared together, with the howlings of the jackals and foxes, and hissing of the serpents, it was quite fearful, and you could not suppose otherwise than that you were in hell.

I will now, however, turn to another subject, and rather acquaint my readers with the skilful arts practised among the Mexicans: among which I will first mention the sculptors, and the gold and silversmiths, who were clever in working and smelting gold, and would have astonished the most celebrated of our Spanish goldsmiths: the number of these was very great, and the most skilful lived at a place called Escapuzalco, about four miles from Mexico. After these came the very skilful masters in cutting and polishing precious stones, and the *chalchihuis*, which resemble the emerald. Then follow the great masters in painting, and decorators in feathers, and the wonderful sculptors. Even at this day there are living in Mexico three Indian artists, named Marcos de Aguino, Juan de la Cruz, and El Crespello, who have severally reached to such great proficiency in the art of painting and sculpture, that they may be compared to an Apelles, or our contemporaries Michael Angelo and Berruguete.[4]

The women were particularly skilful in weaving and embroidery, and they manufactured quantities of the finest stuffs, interwoven with feathers. The commoner stuffs, for daily use, came from some townships in the province of Costatlan, which lay on the north coast, not far from Vera Cruz, where we first landed with Cortes.

The concubines in the palace of Motecusuma, who were all daughters of distinguished men, were employed in manufacturing the most beautiful stuffs, interwoven with feathers. Similar manufactures were made by certain kind of women who dwelt secluded in cloisters, as our nuns do. Of these nuns there were great numbers, and they lived in the neighbourhood of the great temple of Huitzilopochtli. Fathers sometimes brought their daughters from a pious feeling, or in honour of some female idol, the protectress of marriage, into these habitations, where they remained until they were married.

The powerful Motecusuma had also a number of dancers and clowns: some danced in stilts, tumbled, and performed a variety of other antics for the monarch's entertainment: a whole quarter of the city was inhabited by these performers, and their only occupation consisted in such like performances. Lastly, Motecusuma had in his

4. Alonso Berruguete, a Spanish artist, who rose to great eminence in painting, architecture, and sculpture. He received great protection from Charles the Fifth, who employed him in considerable works in the Alhambra of Granada and elsewhere.

service great numbers of stone-cutters, masons, and carpenters, who were solely employed in the royal palaces.[5] Above all, I must not forget to mention here his gardens for the culture of flowers, trees, and vegetables, of which there were various kinds. In these gardens were also numerous baths, wells, basins, and ponds full of limpid water, which regularly ebbed and flowed. All this was enlivened by endless varieties of small birds, which sang among the trees. Also the plantations of medical plants and vegetables are well worthy of our notice: these were kept in proper order by a large body of gardeners. All the baths, wells, ponds, and buildings were substantially constructed of stone-work, as also the theatres where the singers and dancers performed. There were upon the whole so many remarkable things for my observation in these gardens and throughout the whole town, that I can scarcely find words to express the astonishment I felt at the pomp and splendour of the Mexican monarch.

In the meantime, I am become as tired in noting down these things as the kind reader will be in perusing them: I will, therefore, close this chapter, and acquaint the reader how our general, accompanied by many of his officers, went to view the Tlatelulco, or great square of Mexico; on which occasion we also ascended the great temple, where stood the idols Tetzcatlipuca and Huitzilopochtli. This was the first time Cortes left his headquarters to perambulate the city.

---

5. Bernal Diaz, unfortunately, gives no description of Motecusuma's palace; we will therefore give Torquemada's account of this remarkable building. He himself, however, never saw it, but chiefly gained his information from the Mexicans themselves, who may have exaggerated a little: Motecusuma's palace had twenty doors, which either opened into the large square or into the principal streets of the city; it had three large courts, and in one of them was a tank, supplied with water by the aqueduct of Chapultepec. The palace contained a number of halls, and a hundred rooms twenty-five feet long and as many broad, each provided with a bath. Everything was built of stone and lime. The walls were covered with beautiful stones, marble, jasper, porphyry, and a block stone, which is so highly polished that you might use it for a looking-glass; besides these, there was a white stone, almost transparent. All the woodwork was made of white cedar, palm, cypress, pine, and other fine woods, adorned with beautiful carved-work. In one of the apartments, which was one hundred and fifty feet long and fifty broad, was Motecusuma's chapel, which was covered with plates of gold and silver almost the thickness of a finger, besides that it was decorated with innumerable emeralds, rubies, topaz, and other precious stones.

Chapter 92

The Temple of Huitzilopochtli

We had already been four days in the city of Mexico, and neither our commander nor any of us had, during that time, left our quarters, excepting to visit the gardens and buildings adjoining the palace. Cortes now, therefore, determined to view the city, and visit the great market, and the chief temple of Huitzilopochtli: he accordingly sent Geronimo Aguilar, Doña Marina, and one of his pages named Orteguilla, who, by this time, understood a little of the Mexican language, to Motecusuma, to request his permission to view the different buildings of the city. Motecusuma, in his answer to this, certainly granted us permission to go where we pleased, yet he was apprehensive we might commit some outrage to one or other of his idols: he, therefore, resolved to accompany us himself, with some of his principal officers, and, for this purpose, left his palace with a pompous retinue. Having arrived at a spot about half way between his palace and a temple, he stepped out of his sedan, as he would have deemed it a want of respect towards his gods to approach them any otherwise than on foot. He leant upon the arms of the principal officers of his court; others walked before him, holding up on high two rods, having the appearance of sceptres, which was a sign that the monarch was approaching. He himself, whenever he was carried in his sedan, held a short staff in his hand, one half of gold, the other of wood, very much like that used by our judges. In this way he came up to the temple, which he ascended, in company with many *papas*. On reaching the summit he immediately began to perfume Huitzilopochtli, and to perform other ceremonies.

Our commander, attended by the greater part of our cavalry and foot, all well armed, as, indeed, we were at all times, had proceeded to the Tlatelulco: by command of Motecusuma, a number of *caziques* had come to meet us on our road there. The moment we arrived in this immense market, we were perfectly astonished at the vast numbers of people, the profusion of merchandise which was there exposed for sale, and at the good police and order that reigned throughout. The *grandees* who accompanied us drew our attention to the smallest circumstance, and gave us full explanation of all we saw. Every species of merchandise had a separate spot for its sale. We first of all visited those divisions of the market appropriated for the sale of gold and silver wares, of jewels, of cloths interwoven with feathers, and of other manufactured goods; besides slaves of both sexes. This slave market was upon as great a scale as the Portuguese market for negro slaves at Guinea. To prevent these from running away, they were fastened with halters about their neck, though some were allowed to walk at large. Next to these came the dealers in coarser wares—cotton, twisted thread, and *cacao*. In short, every species of goods which New Spain produces were here to be found; and everything put me in mind of my native town Medina del Campo during fair time, where every merchandise has a separate street assigned for its sale. In one place were sold the stuffs manufactured of *nequen*; ropes, and sandals; in another place, the sweet *maguey* root, ready cooked, and various other things made from this plant. In another division of the market were exposed the skins of tigers, lions, jackals, otters, red deer, wild cats, and of other beasts of prey, some of which were tanned. In another place were sold beans and sage, with other herbs and vegetables. A particular market was assigned for the merchants in fowls, turkeys, ducks, rabbits, hares, deer, and dogs; also for fruit-sellers, pastry-cooks, and tripe-sellers. Not far from these were exposed all manner of earthenware, from the large earthen cauldron to the smallest pitchers. Then came the dealers in honey and honey-cakes, and other sweetmeats. Next to these, the timber-merchants, furniture-dealers, with their stores of tables, benches, cradles, and all sorts of wooden implements, all separately arranged. What can I further add? If I am to note everything down, I must also mention human excrements, which were exposed for sale in canoes lying in the canals near this square, and is used for the tanning of leather; for, according to the assurances of the Mexicans, it is impossible to tan well without it. I can easily imagine that many of my readers will laugh at this; however, what I have stated is a fact, and, as further proof of this, I must acquaint the reader that along every road accommodations were built of reeds, straw, or grass, by which those who made use of them were hidden from the view of the passers-by, so that great care was taken that none of the last-mentioned treasures should be lost. But why should I so minutely detail every article exposed for sale in this great market? If I had to enumerate everything singly, I should not so easily get to the end. And yet I have not mentioned the paper, which in this country is called *amatl*; the tubes filled with liquid amber and tobacco; the various sweet-scented salves, and similar things; nor the various seeds which were exposed for sale in the porticoes of this market, nor the medicinal herbs.

In this market-place there were also courts of justice, to which three judges and several constables were appointed, who inspected the goods exposed for sale. I had almost forgotten to mention the salt, and those who made the flint knives; also the fish, and a species of bread made of a kind of mud or slime collected from the surface of this lake, and eaten in that form, and has a similar taste to our cheese.[1] Further, instruments of brass, copper, and tin; cups, and painted pitchers of wood: indeed, I wish I had completed the enumeration of all this profusion of merchandise. The variety was so great that it would occupy more space than I can well spare to note them down in; besides which, the market was so crowded with people, and the thronging so excessive in the porticoes, that it was quite impossible to see all in one day.

On our proceeding to the great temple, and passing the courtyards adjoining the market, we observed numbers of other merchants, who dealt in gold dust as it is dug out of the mines, which was exposed to sale in tubes made of the bones of large geese, which had been worked to such a thin substance, and were so white that the gold shone through them. The value of these tubes of gold was estimated according to their length and thickness, and were taken in exchange, for instance, for so many mantles, *xiquipiles*[2] of *cacao*[3] nuts, slaves, or other merchandise.

On quitting the market, we entered the spacious yards which surround the chief temple. These appeared to encompass more ground than the market-place at Salamanca, and were surrounded by a double wall, constructed of stone and lime: these yards were paved with large

---

1. This slimy substance the Mexicans called *tecuitlatl*, or excrement of stone. It was made into various shapes, and dried in the sun.

2. According to Torquemada, this word expressed the number 8000 of anything, whether of cacao beans, troops, or other matters.

3. Cacao nuts should be cacao beans; they were used by the Mexicans as small coin, and even to this day, according to Humboldt, they form the smallest coin among the inhabitants of New Spain.

white flag-stones, extremely smooth; and where these were wanting, a kind of brown plaster had been used instead, and all was kept so very clean that there was not the smallest particle of dust or straw to be seen anywhere.

Before we mounted the steps of the great temple, Motecusuma, who was sacrificing on the top to his idols, sent six *papas* and two of his principal officers to conduct Cortes up the steps. There were 114 steps to the summit, and, as they feared that Cortes would experience the same fatigue in mounting as Motecusuma had, they were going to assist him by taking hold of his arms. Cortes, however, would not accept of their proffered aid. When we had reached the summit of the temple, we walked across a platform where many large stones were lying, on which those who were doomed for sacrifice were stretched out. Near these stood a large idol, in the shape of a dragon, surrounded by various other abominable figures, with a quantity of fresh blood lying in front of it. Motecusuma himself stepped out of a chapel, in which his cursed gods were standing, accompanied by two *papas*, and received Cortes and the whole of us very courteously. "Ascending this temple, *Malinche*," said he to our commander, "must certainly have fatigued you!" Cortes, however, assured him, through our interpreters, that it was not possible for anything to tire us. Upon this the monarch took hold of his hand and invited him to look down and view his vast metropolis, with the towns which were built in the lake, and the other towns which surrounded the city. Motecusuma also observed, that from this place we should have a better view of the great market.

Indeed, this infernal temple, from its great height, commanded a view of the whole surrounding neighbourhood. From this place we could likewise see the three causeways which led into Mexico,—that from Iztapalapan, by which we had entered the city four days ago; that from Tlacupa, along which we took our flight eight months after, when we were beaten out of the city by the new monarch Cuitlahuatzin; the third was that of Tepeaquilla. We also observed the aqueduct which ran from Chapultepec, and provided the whole town with sweet water. We could also distinctly see the bridges across the openings, by which these causeways were intersected, and through which the waters of the lake ebbed and flowed. The lake itself was crowded with canoes, which were bringing provisions, manufactures, and other merchandise to the city. From here we also discovered that the only communication of the houses in this city, and of all the other towns built in the lake, was by means of drawbridges or canoes. In all these towns the beautiful white plastered temples rose above the smaller ones, like so many towers and castles in our Spanish towns, and this, it may be imagined, was a splendid sight.

After we had sufficiently gazed upon this magnificent picture, we again turned our eyes toward the great market, and beheld the vast numbers of buyers and sellers who thronged there. The bustle and noise occasioned by this multitude of human beings was so great that it could be heard at a distance of more than four miles. Some of our men, who had been at Constantinople and Rome, and travelled through the whole of Italy, said that they never had seen a market-place of such large dimensions,[4] or which was so well regulated, or so crowded with people as this one at Mexico.

On this occasion Cortes said to father Olmedo, who had accompanied us: "I have just been thinking that we should take this opportunity, and apply to Motecusuma for permission to build a church here."

To which father Olmedo replied, that it would, no doubt, be an excellent thing if the monarch would grant this; but that it would be acting overhasty to make a proposition of that nature to him now, whose consent would not easily be gained at any time.

Cortes then turned to Motecusuma, and said to him, by means of our interpretress, Doña Marina: "Your majesty is, indeed, a great monarch, and you merit to be still greater! It has been a real delight to us to view all your cities. I have now one favour to beg of you, that you would allow us to see your gods and *teules*."

To which Motecusuma answered, that he must first consult his chief *papas*, to whom he then addressed a few words. Upon this, we were led into a kind of small tower, with one room, in which we saw two basements resembling altars, decked with coverings of extreme beauty. On each of these basements stood a gigantic, fat-looking figure, of which the one on the right hand represented the god of war Huitzilopochtli. This idol had a very broad face, with distorted and furious-looking eyes, and was covered all over with jewels, gold, and pearls, which were stuck to it by means of a species of paste, which, in this country, is prepared from a certain root. Large serpents, likewise, covered with gold and precious stones, wound round the body of this monster, which held in one hand a bow, and in the other a bunch of

4. In the large work of Ramusio, entitled *'Raccolta delle Navigazioni e Viaggi,'* there is a very interesting account of the city of Mexico. There we find that this market was about three times larger than the one at Salamanca, and surrounded by porticos. Every five days was a great market day, and from forty to fifty thousand people come to buy and sell there.

arrows. Another small idol which stood by its side, representing its page, carried this monster's short spear, and its golden shield studded with precious stones. Around Huitzilopochtli's neck were figures representing human faces and hearts made of gold and silver, and decorated with blue stones. In front of him stood several perfuming pans with copal, the incense of the country; also the hearts of three Indians, who had that day been slaughtered, were now consuming before him as a burnt-offering. Every wall of this chapel and the whole floor had become almost black with human blood, and the stench was abominable.

On the left hand stood another figure of the same size as Huitzilopochtli. Its face was very much like that of a bear, its shining eyes were made of *tetzcat*, the looking-glass of the country. This idol, like its brother Huitzilopochtli, was completely covered with precious stones, and was called Tetzcatlipuca. This was the god of hell, and the souls of the dead Mexicans stood under him.[5] A circle of figures wound round its body, resembling diminutive devils with serpents' tails. The walls and floor around this idol were also besmeared with blood, and the stench was worse than in a Spanish slaughter-house. Five human hearts had that day been sacrificed to him. On the very top of this temple stood another chapel, the woodwork of which was uncommonly well finished, and richly carved. In this chapel there was also another idol, half man and half lizard, completely covered with precious stones; half of this figure was hidden from view. We were told that the hidden half was covered with the seeds of every plant of this earth, for this was the god of the seeds and fruits: I have, however, forgotten its name, but note that here also everything was besmeared with blood, and the stench so offensive that we could not have staid there much longer. In this place was kept a drum of enormous dimensions, the tone of which, when struck, was so deep and melancholy that it has very justly been denominated the drum of hell. The drum-skin was made out of that of an enormous serpent; its sound could be heard at a distance of more than eight miles. This platform was altogether covered with a variety of hellish objects,—large and small trumpets, huge slaughtering knives, and burnt hearts of Indians who had been sacrificed: everything clotted with coagulated blood, cursed to the sight, and creating horror in the mind. Besides all this, the stench was everywhere so abominable that we scarcely knew how soon to get away from this

5. With regard to Mexican mythology, Bernal Diaz is, perhaps, not quite so correct in general. The *abbé* F. S. Clavigero, who wrote a history of Mexico, in two volumes quarto, is more intelligent in this respect.

spot of horrors. Our commander here said, smilingly, to Motecusuma: "I cannot imagine that such a powerful and wise monarch as you are, should not have yourself discovered by this time that these idols are not divinities, but evil spirits, called devils. In order that you may be convinced of this, and that your *papas* may satisfy themselves of this truth, allow me to erect a cross on the summit of this temple; and, in the chapel, where stand your Huitzilopochtli and Tetzcatlipuca, give us a small space that I may place there the image of the holy Virgin; then you will see what terror will seize these idols by which you have been so long deluded."[6]

Motecusuma knew what the image of the Virgin Mary was, yet he was very much displeased with Cortes' offer, and replied, in presence of two *papas*, whose anger was not less conspicuous, "*Malinche*, could I have conjectured that you would have used such reviling language as you have just done, I would certainly not have shown you my gods. In our eyes these are good divinities: they preserve our lives, give us nourishment, water, and good harvests, healthy and growing weather, and victory whenever we pray to them for it. Therefore we offer up our prayers to them, and make them sacrifices. I earnestly beg of you not to say another word to insult the profound veneration in which we hold these gods."

As soon as Cortes heard these words and perceived the great excitement under which they were pronounced, he said nothing in return, but merely remarked to the monarch with a cheerful smile: "It is time for us both to depart hence." To which Motecusuma answered, that he would not detain him any longer, but he himself was now obliged to stay some time to atone to his gods by prayer and sacrifice for having committed *gratlatlacol*, by allowing us to ascend the great temple, and thereby occasioning the affronts which we had offered them.

"If that is the case," returned Cortes, "I beg your pardon, great monarch." Upon this we descended the 114 steps, which very much distressed many of our soldiers, who were suffering from swellings in their groins.[7] The following is all I can communicate with respect to the size or circumference of this temple; but previously reckon upon

6. This note refers to the idol, half hidden from view, of which Bernal Diaz has forgotten the name; it was probably the goddess Centeotl, sometimes called Tonacajohua.

7. The Spanish is, *"Estavan malos de bubas ó humores, les dolieron los muslas de baxar!" bubas* I have everywhere translated by the general term of swellings in the groin, though it is quite evident, from the 68th letter of Petrus Martyr ab Angleria, (*De Rebus Oceanicis el Novo orbe decades tres*) that this disease was the syphilis, which was then spreading so dreadfully.

the reader's kind indulgence, if I should make any misstatement; for at the time when all these things were going on, I was thinking of anything but writing a book, but rather how best to fulfil my duty as a soldier, and to act up to the commands of our general Cortes. However, if I remember rightly, this temple occupied a space of ground on which we should erect six of the largest buildings, as they are commonly found in our country.[8] The whole building ran up in rather a pyramidical form, on the summit of which was the small tower with the idols. From the middle of the temple up to the platform there were five landings, after the manner of barbicans, but without any breastworks. A perfect idea of the form of this temple may be gained from the pictures which are in the possession of several of the Conquistadores, (I have one myself,) which every one must have seen by this time. The following is what I learnt respecting the building of this temple. Every inhabitant had contributed his mite of gold, silver, pearls and precious stones thereto. These gifts were then buried in the foundations, and the ground sprinkled with the blood of a number of prisoners of war, and strewed with the seeds of every plant growing in the country. This was done in order that the gods might grant the country conquest, riches, and abundant harvests. The reader will here naturally ask the question: how we got to know that its foundations were thus filled with gold, pearls, silver, precious stones, seeds, and sprinkled with human blood, as this building had stood there for the space of one thousand years? To this I answer, that subsequent to the conquest of this large and strongly fortified city, we found it to be a positive fact; for when new buildings were being erected on the place where this temple stood, a great part of the space was fixed upon for the new church dedicated to our patron Saint Santiago, and the workmen, on digging up the old foundations to give more stability to the new ones, found a quantity of gold, silver, pearls, *chalchihuis* stones, and other valuable things. A similar discovery was made by a citizen of Mexico, to whom also a portion of this space had been allotted for building-ground, but the treasure was claimed for his majesty; and parties went so far as to commence a lawsuit about it, I cannot however now recollect how it terminated. Besides all this, the accounts of the

8. The best-informed writers agree with Bernal Diaz as to the vast extent of this temple. It was so extensive, says Torquemada, that an arrow shot from a crossbow would not reach the length of one of its sides. A few lines lower he says, that each of these sides was three hundred and sixty feet long! The wall which surrounded this huge temple was entirely built of hewn stone.

caziques and grandees of Mexico, and even of Quauhtemoctzin himself, who was alive at that time, all correspond with my statement. Lastly, it is also mentioned in the books and paintings which contain the history of the country.[9]

With respect to the extensive and splendid courtyards belonging to this temple I have said sufficient above. I cannot, however, pass by in silence a kind of small tower standing in its immediate vicinity, likewise containing idols. I should term it a temple of hell; for at one of its doors stood an open-mouthed dragon armed with huge teeth, resembling a dragon of the infernal regions, the devourer of souls. There also stood near this same door other figures resembling devils and serpents, and not far from this an altar encrusted with blood grown black, and some that had recently been spilt. In a building adjoining this we perceived a quantity of dishes and basins, of various shapes. These were filled with water and served to cook the flesh in of the unfortunate beings who had been sacrificed; which flesh was eaten by the *papas*. Near to the altar were lying several daggers, and wooden blocks similar to those used by our butchers for hacking meat on. At a pretty good distance from this house of horrors were piles of wood, and a large reservoir of water, which was filled and emptied at stated times, and received its supply through pipes underground from the aqueduct of Chapultepec. I could find no better name for this dwelling than the house of Satan!

I will now introduce my reader into another temple, in which the *grandees* of Mexico were buried. The doors of which were of a different form, and the idols were of a totally different nature, but the blood and stench were the same.

Next to this temple was another in which human skulls and bones were piled up, though both apart; their numbers were endless. This place had also its appropriate idols; and in all these temples, we found priests clad in long black mantles, with hoods shaped like those worn by the Dominican friars and choristers; their ears were pierced and the hair of their head was long and stuck together with coagulated blood. Lastly, I have to mention another temple at no great distance from this place of skulls, containing another species of idol, who were said to be the protectors of the marriage rights of the men, to whom likewise those abominable human sacrifices were made. Round about this large courtyard stood a great number of small houses in which the *papas* dwelt, who were appointed over the ceremonies of the idol-worship.

9. Bernal Diaz is here speaking of the Mexican picture writing or hieroglyphics.

Near to the chief temple we also saw an exceedingly large basin or pond, filled with the purest water, which was solely adapted for the worship of Huitzilopochtli and Tetzcatlipuca, being also supplied by pipes underground from the aqueduct of Chapultepec. There were also other large buildings in this neighbourhood, after the manner of cloisters, in which great numbers of the young women of Mexico lived secluded, like nuns, until they were married. These had also two appropriate idols in the shape of females, who protected the marriage rights of the women, and to whom they prayed and sacrificed in order to obtain from them good husbands.

Although this temple on the Tlatelulco, of which I have given such a lengthened description, was the largest in Mexico, yet it was by no means the only one; for there were numbers of other splendid temples in this city, all of which I am unable to describe. I have to remark, however, that the chief temple at Cholulla was higher than that of Mexico, and was ascended by 120 steps: also the idol at Cholulla stood in greater repute; for pilgrimages were made to it from all parts of New Spain, to obtain forgiveness of sins. The architecture of this building was also different, but with respect to the yards and double walls they were alike. The temple of the town of Tetzcuco was also of considerable height, being ascended by 117 steps, and had broad and beautiful courtyards, equal to those of the two last mentioned, but differently constructed. It seems indeed quite laughable that each province and every town should have its own peculiar idols, which, however, never interfered with each other, and the inhabitants severally sacrificed to them.

Cortes, and the whole of us at last grew tired at the sight of so many idols and implements used for these sacrifices, and we returned to our quarters accompanied by a great number of chief personages and *caziques*, whom Motecusuma had sent for that purpose.

Chapter 93

The Treasure of Motecusuma's Father

Our general and father Olmedo readily perceived that Motecusuma would never give his consent to our erecting a cross on his chief temple, nor that we should build a chapel there. We had, upon our arrival in Mexico, fitted up some tables as an altar; but we were not satisfied with this, and therefore begged of Motecusuma's house-steward to order his masons to build us a church in our quarters, who referred us to the monarch himself, upon which Cortes sent him with our interpretress and the page Orteguilla to Motecusuma, who immediately gave his consent and issued orders accordingly.[1]

In three days our church was finished, and a cross planted in front of our quarters. Mass was now regularly said every day as long as our wine lasted, which indeed was very short, as Cortes and father Olmedo, during their illness in Tlascalla, had used the wine destined for the mass. Nevertheless we went daily to church and prayed on our knees in front of the altar and before the holy images; because it was our Christian duty, and that Motecusuma and his grandees might notice it, and become accustomed to these holy things, from seeing us kneel down in devotion before them, particularly when we repeated the Ave Maria.

Wherever we went it was our custom to examine everything about us, and consequently we searched every corner and nook in our quarters; and so it happened, as we were looking for a proper spot to erect our altar, that two of our men, one of whom was Yañez our carpenter, found the traces of a doorway in the wall of one of the apartments, which had been carefully walled up and neatly plastered over; and as we all very well knew that the treasure of Motecusuma's father was

1. This passage fully proves the kind disposition of the monarch, for he even overcame his religious scruples to please the very men who came to take his kingdom from him.

secreted somewhere in our quarters, these two men soon conjectured that this doorway might be the entrance to the treasury. Yañez communicated his suspicions to the chief officers, Leon and Lugo, who were relatives of mine; and at last it got to the ears of Cortes. The consequence was, that the doorway was in all secrecy broken open, and Cortes, with some of our officers, entered the hidden apartment.

Their expectations were fully realized; for they found here such a vast quantity of trinkets, thick and thin plates of gold, *chalchihuis*, and other precious things heaped up together, that they were perfectly astounded and were almost speechless at the sight of such immense riches. This matter soon became known to all of our men, who now also paid a visit to this secret treasure. I also followed their example, and as at that time I was still a young man, and had never before beheld such vast treasures, I concluded that the whole of the remaining part of the world, put together, could not produce such a vast collection of riches. However, all our officers and soldiers unanimously agreed to leave everything untouched, and that the doorway should be walled up again as before, nor was Motecusuma to be informed of our discovery.

As all of us, officers as well as privates, were men of experience, full of energy and very determined, who never lost sight that the Lord Jesus Christ had assisted us with his divine hand in all our undertakings, we deputed four officers and twelve of our most trustworthy and faithful soldiers, myself being among the number, to Cortes, and represented to him how we were cooped up in this strong city, as if we had been caught in a net or cage. We begged of him to remember the bridges and causeways, how we had been cautioned in every town we passed through against Motecusuma, and were assured that Huitzilopochtli had advised him to allow us to enter the city quietly, and when once there to fall upon us unawares and destroy us all. He ought to remember the inconstancy of the human mind in general, and of the Indians in particular; and not trust to the kindness and friendship which Motecusuma showed us. All this might change in an instant, and if Motecusuma did not exactly fall upon us with sword in hand, he had merely to cut off our supply of provisions and water, or break down some of the bridges, and we should be lost. He, Cortes, ought to consider what a large body of warriors always surrounded the monarch, and how powerless we should be and ill able to defend ourselves, since all the houses stood in the water. We could not count upon the assistance of our friends the Tlascallans, as they would be totally cut off from us.

Taking all this into consideration our opinion was, that we had no other resource left by which we could place our own lives in safety than by seizing the monarch's person without delay. All the gold this monarch had given us, all we had seen in the treasury of his father, and all the fine provisions he had set before us, could not induce us to hide our sentiments. These reflections harassed us night and day, and if some of our men did appear heedless as to our present position, these were merely a few narrow-minded folks, who, on account of the vast quantity of gold after which their mouths watered, were unable to see the death which stood before them.

Cortes, in reply to their representations said: "Do not imagine, gentlemen, that I either sleep so peaceably, or that what you have just been stating has not also caused me much anxiety. But we ought first to weigh well whether you think we are sufficiently strong in numbers for so bold an attempt as to take this mighty monarch prisoner in his own palace, amidst his body-guard and other warriors. I cannot see how we can manage this matter without running the risk of being attacked by his troops."

Our four officers, namely, Leon, Ordas, Sandoval, and Alvarado, said, that the only way would be by some means or other to entice the monarch out of his palace, then to conduct him to our quarters, and then inform him that he was our prisoner. If he offered any resistance or made any noise, then to knock him down at once. If Cortes himself objected to have any hand in it, they begged he would give them permission to carry it out themselves. There was as much danger on one side as on the other; but it was certainly more advisable to take the monarch prisoner than to wait until he made war upon us; for what chance of escape should we then have?

To all this was added, that several of us had of late remarked, that Motecusuma's house-steward appeared to become haughty in his manners, and that he did not supply our table so abundantly as on the first few days. Lastly, our friends of Tlascalla had secretly informed Aguilar that the Mexicans, for the last two days, appeared to have some evil design on hand.

One hour was thus spent in deliberating as to whether we should take Motecusuma prisoner, and the manner in which it was to be done. At last we came to the resolution of seizing the monarch's person on the following day, and Cortes gave his full consent. The whole of that night was spent in prayer with father Olmedo, to ask the Almighty's support in this holy cause.

The following morning two Tlascallans arrived secretly in our quarters, with a letter from Vera Cruz, announcing to Cortes that Juan de Escalante had been slain with six other Spaniards in an engagement with the Mexicans. A horse had likewise been killed, and all the Totonaques who had joined him had been slain. All the mountain tribes as well as the Sempoallans had turned against us. They would neither any longer furnish the town with provisions nor assist in building the fortifications, and the garrison scarcely knew what to be about in its present distress.

After this overthrow, the belief that the Spaniards were *teules* had altogether vanished. The Totonaque tribes, as well as the Mexicans, began to throw out threats, and the profound veneration in which they before held us was now changed for utter contempt.

God only knows what a terrible sensation this news created among us. It was the first defeat we had sustained in New Spain, and the good reader may easily see from this how rapidly the wheel of fortune turns from good to bad. She had but just seen us enter this great metropolis, and meet with a splendid and triumphant reception. We already believed we were on the sure road to wealth, from the many presents which Motecusuma gave us daily. We had had a peep into Axayacatl's treasure; we had, up to this moment, been regarded as *teules* who could not fail to come off victorious in battle. This delusion had now flown all at once. We appeared, like all other men, vincible, and the Indians had already began to be insolent and haughty in their demeanour towards us.

We had now the more reason to strike some determined blow, and we therefore resolved to get possession of Motecusuma's person some how or other, if we were even to forfeit all our lives in the attempt.

I will, however, first relate the battle in which Escalante and the six other Spaniards lost their lives.

Chapter 94

The Mexican Battle

The reader will remember, some chapters back, how we lay quartered in the township of Quiahuitzlan, and that several of the confederate tribes, friendly with Sempoalla, assembled around us there. Above thirty townships, on this occasion, at the command of Cortes, refused to pay any further tribute to Motecusuma, and threw off his yoke. It was during that time also that the Mexican tax-gatherers were imprisoned by the Sempoallans, at our instigation. After all this had taken place we broke up our quarters at Sempoalla and began our march towards Mexico, leaving Juan de Escalante behind, as governor of Vera Cruz, who received particular instructions to protect our allies.

Motecusuma had garrisons in every province of his empire, which were always stationed on the confines. Such garrisons, for instance, lay in Xoconoctico, for the protection of Guatimala and Chiapa, another in Coatzagualco, a third in Mechoacan, and a fourth on the confines of Panuco, between Tuzapan and a township lying on the north coast, which was called Almeria.[1] When the garrison of the latter place demanded the tribute of Indians with the provisions from the neighbouring townships, they refused to pay it, (as they were in alliance with Sempoalla, and had assisted Escalante in the building of the fortress,) and gave for reason that *Malinche* had so commanded it, and that the powerful Motecusuma had consented thereto.

The Mexican chiefs, however, were not to be put off with this answer, and declared they would destroy every township which refused to pay the tribute, and carry off the inhabitants as slaves, as they were bound to obey the commands which Motecusuma had recently issued.

On hearing these threats the Totonaque tribes applied to Escalante for assistance against the Mexicans, who were coming to plun-

1. The Mexican name of this township was Nauhtlan.

der them. Escalante accordingly sent off messengers to the Mexican chiefs, commanding them to leave those tribes at peace, as that was the wish of their monarch, Motecusuma, with whom we stood on very friendly terms; and if they refused compliance with his commands he would march into the field against them in person, and treat them as enemies.

The Mexicans received these threats with utter contempt, and returned the haughty answer, "that they would meet him on the field of battle!" Escalante, who was a man of great courage, and very prompt in what he did, issued orders to our mountain allies to equip themselves for battle, and he selected those from among his own men who were in the best health, and most able to bear fatigue.

In this way he marched out against the Mexicans, with two cannon, a small supply of powder, three crossbow-men, two musketeers, besides forty Spanish soldiers and above 2000 Totonaques. The Mexicans were double the number of our Totonaque auxiliaries, who, besides this, had become intimidated by former battles; so that they left Escalante in the lurch after the very first attack. Escalante now forced his way to Almeria, which he set fire to. Here he halted for a short time, as he was dangerously wounded. In the several engagements which here took place Escalante lost one horse, and one of his men, named Arguello, a young man of amazing bodily strength, with a wild-looking countenance, a large head, and black curly beard, who was carried off alive by the Mexicans. Six others of his men were likewise dangerously wounded; the only alternative, therefore, which Escalante had left was to return to Vera Cruz, where he and six others of his men died three days after their arrival.

This is exactly what took place at Almeria; and not as Gomara relates, who says, that all this happened under Pedro de Ircio, who had marched out on this occasion with a few men to Panuco, in order to found a colony there; though we had scarcely sufficient troops in Vera Cruz to place the necessary sentinels; how much less, therefore, could the thought have entered our mind to send out a colony to Panuco? Besides which, Ircio was not an officer at that time; no, nor even a corporal; had altogether nothing to do with the whole affair, being at the time with us in Mexico. In the same way Gomara tells his tales about our imprisoning Motecusuma, without for a moment reflecting that several of the Conquistadores were still alive; who, when they had perused his work, would be able to say so and so such a thing happened, and not otherwise.

We must now turn to the Mexican generals, and relate how they announced their victory to Motecusuma, and sent him the head of Arguello, who most likely died on the road of his wounds. We afterwards learnt that Motecusuma was quite horror-struck at the sight of this enormous head with the thick curly beard. He could not bear to look at it, and would not allow the head to be brought near any of the temples in Mexico, but ordered it to be presented to the idols of some other town; yet he inquired how it came that his troops, which had been many thousands in number, had not been able to overthrow such a handful of *teules*? His captains replied, that notwithstanding all their courageous fighting they had not been able to make the Spaniards give way, because a great Spanish *tecleciguata*[2] had stood at their head, who had filled the Mexicans with fear, and animated the *teules* by her speeches.

Motecusuma was convinced that this illustrious warrior was the Virgin Mary, who, we had told him, with her heavenly Son, whom she held in her arms, was our strong rock.

This wonderful apparition I did not behold with mine own eyes, as I was at the time in Mexico. However, several of the Conquistadores spoke of it as a fact; and may it please God that it was so. It is, however, certainly true that the blessing of the Virgin Mary was always upon us.

2. The Mexican name for goddess.

CHAPTER 95

The Imprisonment of Motecusuma

After we had come to the determination of seizing the person of Motecusuma, and had been on our knees the whole night in prayer, to supplicate the Almighty's assistance in this bold attempt, and that it might redound to the glory of his holy religion, we made the necessary arrangements when morning came for that purpose.

Every one received orders to be ready to march out at a moment's notice, and the horses were to be kept saddled. It is not necessary for me to repeat here that our arms were always in readiness; for they were never out of our hands either day or night; while our *alpargates*, the only covering we had to our feet, were never taken off.

Our general now sallied forth, accompanied by our five chief officers, Alvarado, Sandoval, Lugo, Leon, and Avila; besides our interpreters, Marina, and Aguilar. Cortes and his officers were completely armed; yet this would not appear strange to Motecusuma, as he had never seen them otherwise whenever they paid him a visit. Cortes, as on the former occasion, sent some one before him to announce his approach, that Motecusuma might not perceive any change in our behaviour, and feel no uneasiness at our unexpected visit. His conscience, however, was not altogether easy, on account of the affair which had taken place at Almeria, and he had a misgiving that it would bring down evil upon him. Yet he sent word that our visit would be agreeable to him.

After Cortes had entered his apartment, and the usual compliments had been passed, he thus addressed Motecusuma: "I am greatly astonished that a prince of such power, who styles himself our friend, should have commanded his troops, which lie on the coast near Tuzapan, to take up arms against my Spanish troops, and presume to demand a certain number of men and women for the sacrifices from those townships which have put themselves under the protection of our emperor. But this is not all; they have plundered those places, and even killed one of my brothers, and a horse."

Cortes very prudently omitted to mention the death of Escalante and the six others; for Motecusuma at that time knew as little of that as his generals who had commanded on the occasion.

"How very differently we acted on our side!" continued Cortes. "I had put implicit reliance in your friendship, and desired my officers in every way to comply with your wishes. You, on the contrary, have commanded your officers the very opposite. You once likewise sent a large body of troops to Cholulla to destroy us all there. At that time, from the friendship I bore you, I would not notice to you that I was aware of that. At the present moment your generals have the audacity to plot in secret to put us all to death. However, notwithstanding all this treachery, I will refrain from making war upon you, which would only end in the total destruction of this city; but in order that peace may be maintained between us, you must make a small sacrifice, which is, to follow us quietly into our quarters, and take up your abode there. There you will receive the same attention, and be treated with the same respect as if you were in your own palace. But if you make any alarm now, or call out to your attendants, you are a dead man; and it is for this reason only that I have this time brought these officers with me."

Motecusuma was seized with such sudden terror at these words, that he remained speechless for some time. At length, however, he took courage, and declared he had never given any one orders to take up arms against us. He would that instant send for his generals, and learn from them the truth of the whole matter, and give exemplary punishment. For this purpose, he loosened the seal and mark of Huitzilopochtli, which he always wore around his wrist. This he only did when he issued orders of the first importance, and that those who had the seal might be immediately obeyed. He was quite astonished, he said, we should presume to take him prisoner, and lead him away out of his palace against his wishes. No one had a right to demand that of him, he added; and altogether he felt no inclination to comply with our request.

Cortes, in answer to this, gave him very good reasons for our having come to this determination; but Motecusuma continually brought in stronger reasons why he should not comply; and was resolved not to leave his palace.

As this dispute had now lasted above half an hour, our officers began to lose all patience, and said to Cortes with great warmth, "What is the use of throwing away so many words? He must either quietly follow us, or we will cut him down at once. Be so good as to tell him this; for on this depends the safety of our lives. We must show determination, or we are inevitably lost."

These words were uttered by Juan Velasquez in a loud and harsh tone of voice. When, therefore, Motecusuma heard this, and perceived the dark looks of the officers, he asked Marina what the man had said who spoke so loud.

Marina, who was uncommonly shrewd, and well knew how to help us out with a good answer, said, "Great monarch, if I may be allowed to give you advice, make no further difficulties, but immediately follow them to their quarters. I am confident they will pay you every respect, and treat you as becomes a powerful monarch. But if you continue to refuse, they will cut you down on the spot."

Motecusuma then turned to Cortes, and said: "*Malinche*, since then you repose no trust in me, take my son and my two legitimate daughters as hostages; only do not disgrace me, by demanding my person. What will the *grandees* of my empire say, if they see me taken prisoner?"

Cortes, however, said that his own person would be the only guarantee of our safety, and that there was no other means of quieting our fears. At last Motecusuma, after a good deal of altercation, made up his mind to go quietly with us.

As soon as he had declared this his intention, our officers showed him every possible civility, and hoped that he would excuse the grief they had occasioned him, and desired him to acquaint his generals and his bodyguard that he had chosen, of his own free will, to take up his abode in our quarters; and also upon the advice of Huitzilopochtli and his *papas*, who considered it necessary for his health, and for the safety of his life.

His rich and splendid sedan was then brought in, which he commonly used when he left his palace with his whole suite, and he followed us to our quarters, where we took every precaution to secure his person. Every one of us strove hardest to make him happy, and procured him every entertainment we could think of, to make his confinement as pleasant as we could.

Shortly afterwards all the Mexican *grandees*, with his nephew, called upon him, to inquire the reason of his imprisonment, and ask him if they should commence hostilities against us? But Motecusuma told them he wished to do himself the pleasure of passing a few days with us, and that this change of abode was of his own free choice. He would make his wishes known to them as soon as he found reason to complain. They might allay their fears, and keep the metropolis quiet, and not trouble themselves any further about him. The determination he had thus taken was fully consented to by Huitzilopochtli, as many priests, who had purposely consulted him, had admitted.

These are the true circumstances relative to the imprisonment of Motecusuma. He was always surrounded by the whole of his household, and had all his wives with him, and continued to bathe himself daily, as he had been accustomed to, in his own palace. He was likewise always attended by twenty of his generals and counsellors, nor did he show the least signs of grief on account of his confinement. Disputes from the most distant parts were laid before him, as usual, for his decision; the tribute was collected, and he continued to attend to the most important affairs of state as before. His subjects paid the same veneration to his person, and the most distinguished princes who waited on him, or came upon business, always took off their fine garments, to put on a meaner dress of *nequen* cloth, and came so, barefoot, into his presence. Neither did they enter at the principal gate, but sought for some side door, and approached with eyes downcast, and made three prostrations, and pronounced the words Lord, my lord, great lord! They then acquainted him with their business, by means of pictures drawn on *nequen* cloth; and made use of thin sticks, with which they pointed to the different objects, to explain what they wanted, or the nature of the lawsuit they came about.

Motecusuma had constantly two old distinguished *caziques* at his side, who, as judges, gave their opinion in every case, after due deliberation; and the monarch then, in few words, gave his decision. The parties then, without uttering a syllable, or turning their backs to him, left the apartment with three deep bows; and on arriving outside, they again put on their fine garments, and took a stroll in the metropolis.

After some time had elapsed, the generals who had fought against Escalante were brought in prisoners to the monarch. What he told them on this occasion I do not know; but he sent them to Cortes to pronounce judgment on them himself. These unfortunate men confessed they had merely acted up to the commands of their monarch, which was, to levy the tribute by force of arms; and if the *teules* should protect the rebels, to attack them also, and put them to the sword.

Cortes acquainted Motecusuma with what these men had said, but declared that the monarch had sufficiently exculpated himself from any guilt in the affair. According to the laws of our emperor, that man suffered death who had killed another, whether he deserved killing or not; however, his love for Motecusuma was so great, that he would rather take the responsibility of this matter upon himself than allow it to rest with him; but as he still seemed anxious about it, our general made no further ceremony with these Mexicans, but sentenced them to death, and they were burnt alive in front of Motecusuma's palace.[1]

And that no impediment might be thrown in the way while these sentences were being put into execution, Cortes ordered chains to be put on Motecusuma. At first he certainly did not approve of this at all, but, in the end, quietly submitted, and grew even the more tractable afterwards. When the executions had taken place, Cortes approached him, with five of our officers, and himself took off his chains again, with the assurance that he loved him more than a brother. He likewise told him, however great a monarch he might be at present, that additional countries should be annexed to his empire, and he was at liberty to visit any of his other palaces whenever he felt inclined.

At these words Motecusuma became affected, and big tears rolled down his cheeks; and though he felt that all was mere empty sound he had heard, he nevertheless thanked Cortes for his kindness, adding, that at present he felt no inclination to go anywhere.

His nephews, relations, and *grandees* daily stormed him with petitions to allow them to make war upon us, and release him from confinement. And, indeed, it required all his persuasion to prevent them from rising up in arms immediately. If he were once, said they, outside of our quarters, they would take forcible possession of his person. The whole of the inhabitants in his metropolis would rise up in arms, and if then he would not join them, they would care little about him, and elect a new king. Motecusuma, however, succeeded in silencing them by the assurance that Huitzilopochtli had himself advised him to bear with his confinement.

To account for Motecusuma thus quietly submitting to his confinement, I must here remark that Cortes ordered Aguilar to acquaint him secretly that if even our general himself gave his consent to his liberation, it would be of no avail, as all our officers and soldiers would oppose it. Cortes feigned to be unconscious of all this, and embraced the monarch under the assurances of sincere friendship. He likewise

1. Bernal Diaz only mentions three of these generals by name: Quetzalpopoca, Coatl, and Quiahuitle, which we thought better to insert here. When Quetzalpopoca, says Torquemada, was brought into the presence of the Spaniards, and asked whether he was a vassal of Motecusuma, he replied: "Is it possible in this world to be the vassal of any other monarch."

gave him his page Orteguilla, who had already gained some knowledge of the Mexican language, the monarch having expressed a wish to have a Spanish attendant. This young man was of the greatest utility both to Motecusuma and ourselves, the monarch learning many things from him relating to Spain, and we again a good deal of the discourses which passed between the former and his generals: he was in every way attentive to the monarch, who became exceedingly fond of him. On the whole, Motecusuma appeared perfectly content with the civilities we showed him, and he continually felt greater delight in our company; for whenever any one of us passed by him, he immediately entered into discourse with us: we were quite at our ease with him, even when Cortes was present, and took off our helmets in his presence, which, as well as our weapons, we never laid aside; and the monarch always treated us with great respect.

The severe example which Cortes had made of the Mexican generals had had its full effect. The news thereof ran like wildfire through the whole of New Spain; the tribes along the coast, by whom our troops of Vera Cruz had been defeated, were seized with terror, and again offered their services to the garrison there.

I must now beg the kind reader to pause a moment upon the heroic deeds we performed, and consider their magnitude! First of all, we destroy all our vessels, and thereby cut off all hopes of escaping from this country. We then venture to march into this strong city, though we were warned against it on all sides, and assured we should merely be allowed a peaceable entrance to be the more easily destroyed. We then have the audacity to imprison the monarch of this vast empire, the powerful Motecusuma, in his own metropolis, in his very palace, amidst his numerous troops. At last, we even fearlessly burn some of his generals to death in front of his own palace, and throw the monarch himself in chains while this was being executed! Even now, in my old age, the heroic deeds we then accomplished come vividly to my memory. I imagine I see all passing before me now, but must also acknowledge that, although we had our hands full, we were aided by Divine Providence. When again on earth will be found such a handful of soldiers, in all scarcely 550, who would dare to penetrate, at a distance of above 6000 miles from their native country, into the heart of such a strong city, larger than Venice, take its very monarch prisoner, and execute his generals in his very presence? These things, indeed, ought to be deeply pondered on, and not mentioned so briefly as I here have done! But it is time I should continue my history.

Chapter 96

Alonso Grado—Lieutenant of Vera Cruz

After the execution of the Mexican generals, and Motecusuma had become pacified again, Cortes despatched one of our officers, named Alonso de Grado, a very active, handsome, and sensible man, to Vera Cruz, with the appointment of lieutenant, who, besides being an excellent musician, was a capital penman.

This Grado was one of those who had always opposed our march to Mexico, and particularly on the occasion when the intrigues were set on foot by the discontented during our stay in Tlascalla: he then insisted on our return to Vera Cruz, and, upon the whole, spoke in severe terms against our general. He was very expert in various matters, and was successful in his undertakings, and hence again obtained the command of Vera Cruz, though he was not a very good soldier. Cortes, well acquainted with the man's character, that he was not one of the most courageous, said to him, in giving him the appointment, rather jokingly, "Your desire of going to Vera Cruz, Alonso de Grado, is about to be fulfilled. There you must continue the building of the fortress with assiduity; but have nothing to do with any warlike movements: it might end equally disastrous for you as it did for Juan de Escalante!"

While Cortes was thus addressing him, he winked his eye to those who were present, as much as to say if he were required on the field of battle, we should have to drag him there by the hair of his head.

When Grado's appointment and instructions were about to be drawn up, he likewise begged Cortes to confer on him the appointment of *alguacil*-major, which Escalante had enjoyed with that of lieutenant. Our commander, however, told him it had already been conferred upon Sandoval, but, in a short time, he would give him some further appointment. He particularly desired him to watch over the interests of the inhabitants of Vera Cruz as a father, and not allow any harsh measures to be practised against the Indian population. Lastly, he desired him to order the smith at Vera Cruz to make two heavy iron chains, and to forward them, with the anchors we had taken out of our vessels, immediately to Mexico.

Alonso de Grado's conduct, however, very little corresponded with the instructions he had received. His behaviour towards the Spanish garrison at Vera Cruz was haughty to a degree. He required the men to wait upon him, as if he had been a *grandee*, and demanded golden trinkets and beautiful females from the thirty surrounding tribes which were friendly with us. He no way troubled himself about completing the fortress, and spent all his time in feasting and gambling. He went even further than this, and gave way to his former ill-will towards Cortes, by seeking to gain his friends and others over to the interest of Diego Velasquez, and proposed that if the latter himself, or any one sent by him, should appear off the coast, to make common cause with him, and deliver up possession of the country to him.

Cortes was duly apprized of all this, and sadly repented in the choice of this man, whose character and artful disposition, however, he had known beforehand.

As Cortes was still afraid that Diego Velasquez might somehow or other obtain information of the purport of our mission to the emperor, and not merely frustrate our designs, but also send out an armament against us, he considered it necessary to send a trustworthy man to Vera Cruz. His choice fell upon Sandoval, who became *alguacil*-major of the town after the death of Escalante. Sandoval was accompanied by Ircio, the same who, Gomara affirms, founded a settlement in Panuco. This Ircio had been groom to the Earl of Ureña, and likewise to Don Pedro Giron, and knew well how to entertain Sandoval with the various adventures of his life: hereby he succeeded in gaining the intimate friendship of this excellent man, who was innocence itself, and, by degrees, he obtained a captaincy. He, however, repaid him with ingratitude, and calumniated him so grossly that he might have been punished according to law, but Sandoval contented himself by giving him a severe reprimand.

I will, however, leave this subject, and relate that Sandoval, immediately upon his arrival at Vera Cruz, fulfilled Cortes' orders, took Grado prisoner, and sent him under a strong escort of Indian auxiliaries to Mexico. Sandoval very soon gained the good wishes of the whole garrison, for he began his work by providing food for the sick, and treating the inhabitants with every possible kindness, and was most particular in promoting the interests of the surrounding townships which were friendly with us. In the same way he set diligently about the completion of the fortress, and every way proved himself an active and vigilant commander, who afterwards, as will be seen, rendered vast services to Cortes and all of us.

I must now return to Grado, who soon arrived at Mexico in custody of our Indian auxiliaries. His request to obtain a hearing from Cortes was not only refused, but he was thrown into a wooden cage which had just been constructed. I can still well remember that the wood of this cage smelt strongly of garlic and onions. However, our prisoner was obliged to pass two whole days in it; yet, like a clever fellow, who is never at a loss, he found means to soften Cortes' resentment by making him solemn promises of future obedience, and not only obtained his liberty again, but, from that moment, as I witnessed myself, became very intimate with our general, who, however, never again entrusted him with any military command, but employed him in matters which suited his talents. Subsequently he appointed him auditor of the army accounts, which Avila had previously filled, and whom Cortes had despatched, as his attorney, to St. Domingo, as will subsequently be seen.

Before I close this chapter, I have to observe that Cortes desired Sandoval, on his arrival at Vera Cruz, to send him the two smiths of that town, with all their apparatus, a quantity of iron, besides the two heavy iron chains which were already finished; and likewise a supply of sails, some rigging, pitch, and a compass; all of which Cortes required for the brigantines which he intended building to navigate the lake of Mexico.

Chapter 97

Motecusuma's Confinement

Our general was a man who thought of everything, and strove as much as possible to enliven the monarch in his confinement, that he might not feel the weight of his misfortune too deeply. Cortes, therefore, every morning after we had said prayers, visited the monarch with four of our principal officers, to inquire after his health and after his wants, and otherwise to amuse him in every way; in which they succeeded so well that Motecusuma one day himself declared his confinement was not irksome to him, as our gods had given us the power to take him prisoner, and Huitzilopochtli had allowed it.

Sometimes also Motecusuma played at a certain game with Cortes, which the Mexicans call the game of *totoloc*: it is played with small round glossy balls, which here were made of gold, and are pitched at a certain mark, also of the same metal: five throws finished the game, and the stakes were for valuable gold trinkets and jewels. I still remember once when Motecusuma and Cortes were playing at this game, Alvarado scoring for Cortes, and a distinguished *cazique* (his nephew) for the monarch, that Alvarado continually scored one too many for Cortes. This was observed by Motecusuma, who said, with a pleasing smile, that he was not exactly pleased when Tonatio (so they termed Alvarado) marked the game for Cortes, for he was guilty of *ixoxol* in scoring, which means that he scored falsely, by continually marking one more than he ought.

Cortes, and we others who happened to be on duty at the time in the apartment, could not resist laughing at the observation of the monarch. And why, it will be asked, did we find that expression so amusing? Because Alvarado, notwithstanding the handsome and refined man he was, could not resist the temptation of scoring falsely, and had been discovered. However, all the gain was divided among those present; for what Cortes won he presented to the monarch's nephew and his servants; Motecusuma dividing his gains among those who happened to be on duty at the time.[1] And not a day passed that he did not present Velasquez de Leon, who was very kind to him, and was captain of the guard, and those who were on duty, with valuable gold trinkets and manufactured stuffs.

One night a sailor, named Truxillo, stood sentinel in the monarch's apartment. This fellow was very stout and strongly-built; he happened to forget himself, for a moment, in a way which, out of respect for the reader, I will not describe more minutely here. Motecusuma, who was a monarch of refined manners, happened to hear it at the moment, and considered himself grossly insulted. He inquired of his page Orteguilla who the low-bred fellow was? Orteguilla replied that the man was a sailor, and that such persons were little acquainted with good manners. It was upon this occasion also that Orteguilla explained to him the rank of every individual soldier, who were cavaliers and who were not, and many other things the monarch wished to know. Motecusuma, however, had not forgotten the insult which the sailor had offered to his person, for daylight had scarcely broken forth when he sent for him, and reproached him for his disrespectful behaviour, and advised him to mend his manners for the future; but sweetened down this lecture by presenting him with some gold trinkets, worth about five *pesos*. This kind treatment, however, had little effect on the rough sailor, who repeated his filthy conduct the following night, in the hopes of getting a second present when morning came. Motecusuma, however, disdained speaking to him any more, but complained to the captain of the guard, and desired that the fellow might be severely reprimanded and never allowed again to stand sentinel there.

Something similar happened to a soldier named Lopez, who was an excellent crossbow-man, and had a fine figure, though otherwise a man of little understanding. As he was one night on duty in the monarch's apartment, and the corporal came to make the rounds, he remarked to the latter, "A curse upon this dog, I am sure this standing sentinel at night will be my death!"

Motecusuma heard these words, and considered his feelings

1. Alvarado, who sometimes also played a game with Motecusuma, showed little generosity, according to other writers. If he lost, he paid with *chalchihuis* stones; if he won, he was paid with bars of gold, each worth at least fifty ducats. Motecusuma frequently lost in one evening from forty to fifty of such gold bars to Alvarado; but the more he lost, the more good-humoured he appeared.

deeply wounded. When, therefore, Cortes came in the morning to pay the monarch his usual visit, he complained bitterly to him about the insult that had been offered him. Cortes was exceedingly vexed, and was so enraged with Lopez that he ordered him to be whipped. From that day every one who stood sentinel in the monarch's apartment maintained a respectful silence; though, as far as regarded myself and others of my companions who often stood sentinel in the same apartment, we needed no instructions as to how we were to behave in the presence of such a great monarch, who soon got to know all our names and peculiarities, was exceedingly kind towards us, and often distributed gold trinkets among us, besides manufactured cottons and pretty females. At that time I was yet a young fellow, and whenever I stood sentinel in the monarch's apartment, I always behaved with the greatest respect, and uncovered my head on passing by him. This drew his attention towards me, and, on inquiring who I was, Orteguilla informed him that I had accompanied the two former voyages of discovery to these parts. When, therefore, Orteguilla, at my desire, hinted to him that I should be much pleased with a pretty Mexican female, he sent for me, and said, "I understand, Bernal Diaz del Castillo, that you have abundance of gold and cotton stuffs, wherefore I will now give you a pretty young female. Treat her well, for she is the daughter of distinguished parents, who will, besides, give you more gold and cotton stuffs with her."

I very respectfully thanked the monarch for his kindness, and hoped God would bless him for it. When the page interpreted my answer, he said, "Bernal Diaz appears to me to have the true feelings of a well-bred man," and ordered three small plates of gold and two additional packages of cotton stuffs to be given me.

With respect to Motecusuma's mode of life, it was his custom to say his prayers the first thing in the morning, and sacrifice to his gods: he then partook of a little breakfast, which consisted not in meat, but solely in *agi*.[2] This being finished, he gave an hour's audience to the *caziques*, who came from distant parts in great numbers to lay before him certain disputes, and obtain his judgment. The remaining part of the day was then spent in amusement, particularly with his concubines, of whom he had a great number; some of these, at times, he gave in marriage to his generals, principal favourites, and

2. A kind of soup or broth, of which the so termed Spanish pepper formed the chief ingredient.

likewise to us soldiers; as I, for instance, obtained Doña Francisca, whom you might well see was a woman of distinction. Now and then the monarch would laugh, and then again he was pensive, and seemed to reflect on his confinement.

I must once more return to the soldier whom Cortes had so severely punished for calling Motecusuma a dog. Many to whom I have related this were surprised at the severity of his punishment, as the man had not said it to the monarch's face; besides that, our numbers were so small, and that the Mexicans would be sure to hear of it. My reply to this is, that all of us, even Cortes himself, paid Motecusuma the most profound respect, and no one passed by him without uncovering his head: add to all this, he was so very kind, and so courteous in his behaviour towards us, that we should have considered ourselves bound to pay his person and good breeding every possible respect, though he had not been the monarch of New Spain.

Lastly, it must be remembered that our lives were in his hands; for, at his very wink, his subjects would have flown to his rescue. When we saw how he was continually surrounded by so many distinguished personages, and the numbers of princes who came to wait upon him from distant parts of his empire, in the same way as if he had still been at liberty in his own palace, can we at all feel surprised, then, that Cortes should so severely have punished on the spot an insult offered to this monarch? Assuredly he did nothing more than the circumstances of the moment required!

Chapter 98
Cortes' Brigantines

After the necessary materials had arrived for constructing the two brigantines, Cortes informed Motecusuma that he intended to build two small pleasure yachts to navigate the lake of Mexico, and requested him to allow his carpenters to cut wood for the purpose, and assist our ship carpenters, Martin Lopez and Alonso Nuñez, in the building of the vessels.

There was plenty of wood at a distance of about sixteen miles from the town, which could easily be transported hither. The building of these vessels went on very fast, as our men were assisted by numbers of Indians. These brigantines, therefore, were very soon completed and rigged; besides which, each was provided with an awning to keep out the heat of the sun. Both vessels turned out very good, and sailed uncommonly fast.

This Lopez was not only an excellent soldier, but also a very clever man in his profession, and subsequently built the thirteen brigantines which were of the most valuable assistance to us in the conquest of Mexico, as will be seen in the proper place.

About this time, Motecusuma expressed a wish to visit his temple, in order to make his devotions there, and sacrifice to his idols. His motive for wishing this he declared was not merely to fulfil his religious duties, but also to convince his generals, his courtiers, and particularly some of his relatives, who daily begged he would allow them to rescue him from his confinement, and commence hostilities with us, that it was his own choice to dwell with us, to which Huitzilopochtli had given his consent.

In answer to this request, Cortes said, he was afraid it would cost him his life, as his generals and *papas* might suddenly form the idea of taking forcible possession of his person on the occasion, and fall upon us, and his life would become endangered in the struggle. He was, however, no way inclined to oppose his wishes, and he might repair there early in the morning, but was not to sacrifice any human beings, as that was a great sin against the only true God, whom we had made known to him. Neither could he help remarking that it would be much more profitable to him to make his devotions before our altars and the image of the holy Virgin.

Motecusuma then assured Cortes he would not permit any human sacrifices to take place. The monarch then, with Cortes' permission, made a procession to the temple, dressed in his splendid garments, and surrounded by his most distinguished courtiers, with the usual display of pomp, preceded by the staff of honour, to announce the monarch's approach. Four of our principal officers, Leon, Alvarado, Avila, and Lugo, with 150 soldiers, accompanied him as a guard, and father Olmedo to restrain the monarch from instituting any human sacrifices.

When Motecusuma had arrived at the cursed temple of Huitzilopochtli, he was assisted out of the sedan by his nephews and other *caziques*. As the procession moved along, all the Mexican grandees kept their eyes fixed to the ground, not daring to look up in the monarch's face. At the foot of the temple he was met by a number of *papas* who assisted him in mounting the steps. The night previous, they had sacrificed four Indians; for, notwithstanding all Cortes and father Olmedo might say, they were not to be deterred, and continued those abominations. At that time, indeed, all we could do was to feign ignorance of their having taken place; for Mexico and other great towns had already been aroused into rebellion by Motecusuma's nephews, as will be presently seen.

The monarch having finished his devotions, which were of short duration, again returned with us to our quarters. He appeared now in better spirits, and presented each of us who had accompanied the procession with trinkets of gold.

Chapter 99

Motecusuma Goes Hunting

When both our brigantines were launched, and completely rigged and manned with sailors, Motecusuma expressed a wish to take a trip by water to a river where he was accustomed to go for the purpose of hunting, situated at the foot of a mountain along the banks of the lake. No one, not even his principal officers, durst visit this spot for the sake of killing game, under pain of death. Cortes answered, that, as far as regarded himself, he in no way objected, but again impressed upon his mind what he had told him on his visit to the temple: and he would advise him to make use of one of the brigantines on the occasion, which were much more safe than the canoes or pirogues.

Motecusuma was vastly pleased with this offer, and went on board the better of the two, with a great number of his principal officers: the other brigantine conveyed a son of the monarch, attended by numbers of *caziques*; and the royal huntsmen followed in the canoes of the country. Cortes took along with him Leon, Alvarado, Oli, and Avila, besides 200 of our troops, bidding them to pay particular attention to everything that passed, and narrowly watch the person of Motecusuma. Besides this, four cannon were brought on board, with the necessary powder, and our artillerymen; so that every precaution was taken. A stiffish breeze fortunately rose just as the brigantines were leaving, so that we were able to make the best use of the sails, and the monarch was greatly delighted at thus, as it were, flying across the lake: nor could the canoes, filled with the huntsmen and other Mexican chiefs, notwithstanding the number of their rowers, any way keep up with us, which amused the monarch uncommonly, and he said it showed great skill thus to be able to unite the power of the sails and the oars.

The desired river, therefore, which was not very far distant, was soon reached. Here Motecusuma created terrible destruction among the deer, hares, and rabbits, and returned highly delighted to his metropolis. When we had arrived near to Mexico, he begged our officers to fire the cannon, which gave him a new pleasure; and as we found that he was open and frank, we experienced a real pleasure in paying him the same respect as was shown him by his own *grandees*. But if I were to attempt a description of his grandeur, and the perfect submission and deep veneration which every prince of New Spain and other provinces evinced towards his person, I should, perhaps, find no end. He had merely to say the word, and everything was brought he desired, as the following instance will prove. One day, as many of us officers and soldiers were with Motecusuma, a hawk pounced upon a quail, which, with others, and numbers of pigeons, was kept by his Indian *major domo*, whose business it was to see that our quarters were always clean and tidy. This hawk succeeded in seizing its prey, and flew off with it. As we were all looking on, one of our men, Francisco de Azenedo, cried out, "O! what a fine bird! how beautifully it flies away with its prey!" We were all of the same opinion, and remarked, that this country altogether abounded with birds that might be capitally trained for hawking. Motecusuma, observing how lively we were discoursing together, was curious to know what it was, and inquired the reason of his page Orteguilla, who told him we were admiring the hawk which had pounced upon the quail, and added, that if we had such a bird in our power, we could teach it to fly from the hand, and attack a bird of any size and kill it.

Then, returned Motecusuma, I will have this same hawk caught, and we shall see whether they can teach it all they say. Upon which, we all took our caps off and thanked him for his kindness. Motecusuma then sent for his bird catchers, and commanded them to bring him the hawk above mentioned. These immediately set to work, and before the hour of Ave Maria they actually caught the bird, and presented it to Azenedo, who immediately recognized, by the plumage, that it was the identical one we had seen. We saw many similar instances, and even stronger proofs of the punctuality with which this monarch's orders were fulfilled. Even now, in his confinement, his subjects not only continued to bring him tribute from the most distant parts of New Spain, but they likewise obeyed his commands implicitly, and stood in such great awe of him, that even the birds which flew in the skies above were brought down for him if he expressed a wish that way.

It is now, however, time to relate how suddenly the wheel of fortune turned against us, by a conspiracy, which was set on foot by the inhabitants, to put us all to death.

CHAPTER 100

A Conspiracy

When Cacamatzin, the prince of Tezcuco, which, next to Mexico, was the largest town of all New Spain, was informed of his uncle Motecusuma's imprisonment, and that we seized everything we could lay our hands on,—that we had even opened the treasure of his ancestor Axayacatl, though left it entire as yet,—he determined to put an end to our dominion before we should likewise take him prisoner.

For this reason he assembled all the chiefs of Tezcuco, and with them the prince of Cojohuacan, who was his cousin, and nephew to Motecusuma; likewise the princes of Tlacupa and Iztapalapan, and another powerful *cazique*, prince of Matlaltzinco, a man of great courage, and so nearly related to Motecusuma, that many even believed the crown of right should have devolved upon him.

These powerful *caziques* accordingly, with other Mexican generals, fixed a day when all their warriors were to meet and fall upon us with their united forces. It appeared, that the prince of Matlaltzinco, who was considered to be the most courageous man in the kingdom, and who had such great pretensions to the crown, had only consented to join the conspiracy, on condition that he should be elevated to the throne. He would himself, first of all, force his way into Mexico with the whole of his army, drive us out of the city, or put us all to the sword. Cacamatzin, however, it is said, had declared that the crown would sooner devolve upon him, as nephew of Motecusuma, and that he should be able to overcome us without paying so dearly for the prince Matlaltzinco's assistance. It is nevertheless certain, that Cacamatzin, and the before-mentioned princes, agreed to meet on a certain day before Mexico, and that the troops there should, at a certain signal, rise up in arms and admit them into the city.

Motecusuma received due intelligence of all this, through the prince of Matlaltzinco, who had disagreed with Cacamatzin. The former to gain surer proofs of the whole affair, summoned all the *grandees* of Mexico into his presence; who then confessed that Cacamatzin had gained them over by presents and promises to join him in the attack upon us, and to liberate the monarch his uncle.

Motecusuma, who was extremely prudent and not willing that his metropolis should be the scene of rebellion and bloodshed, informed Cortes of the conspiracy. Our commander, however, as well as every soldier among us, was perfectly aware of what was going on, though perhaps not of all the particulars. He, therefore, proposed to Motecusuma that he should put all his troops under his command, when in concert with ours he would fall upon Tezcuco, destroy the town and lay waste the whole province.

But as Motecusuma was unwilling to fall in with this advice, Cortes sent word to Cacamatzin, that if he commenced hostilities against us it would be his death; that it was our wish to live in friendship with him and to render him good services.

Cacamatzin, however, was a young hothead, and supported in his views by a great number of chiefs, who constantly kept urging him on to fall upon us. He, therefore, sent word to Cortes that he had already heard too much of his smooth words, and desired he would send him no more of his messages; it would be quite time enough to talk with each other when their armies stood one against the other in the field of battle.

Cortes, however, sent him a second warning, and desired him to pause a little before he insulted our emperor in our persons. He would have dearly to pay for such presumptuous behaviour, and certainly be put to death.

To which this prince returned the haughty answer: He knew nothing of our emperor, and wished also he had never known anything of Cortes, since he had so grossly deceived his uncle with his vile flattery.

When Cortes received this answer he begged Motecusuma to use his own authority against the rebels, observing at the same time, that in Tezcuco there were many powerful men and relatives of his, who bore Cacamatzin ill blood, on account of his persecution and haughty behaviour towards them, and that he himself harboured one of his brothers, a young man of great promise, who had fled from Tezcuco to evade death, with which Cacamatzin had threatened him; for he could not forgive him the hopes he entertained of succeeding to the throne.

He should therefore, continued Cortes to the monarch, issue orders to the *grandees* of Tezcuco to take Cacamatzin prisoner, or by some means or other try to entice him to Mexico, where he could be seized and kept in confinement until his reason had returned. He should also transfer the sovereign power over Tezcuco upon the brother, who had fled for protection to Mexico. Moreover, Cacamatzin had already forfeited all right to sovereign power, as he had attempted to revolutionize the whole of New Spain, and by that means to make himself master of Motecusuma's throne.

The monarch now no longer hesitated, and promised to send for him, expressing, however, his doubts as to whether he would make his appearance; but if he did he would order his officers to seize his person. Cortes returned him many thanks for his ready compliance, and said: "Great monarch, if you should feel desirous of returning to your palace I myself would willingly let you go, for I now see how upright your intentions are towards us; I feel such an excess of friendship for you, that I would long ago have conducted you back to your palace with every magnificence, if it had depended solely upon me, and you yourself did not consider it good policy to stay with us, that you may not be hurried into the rebellious movement which your nephews have set on foot. Indeed, I myself should never have deprived you of your liberty if I had not been compelled to give way to my officers on that point, who think they see a guarantee of our own safety in detaining possession of your person." Motecusuma was now the more inclined to give Cortes credit for his good wishes towards him, and considered himself greatly indebted to him, and more so since Orteguilla had likewise assured him, that his imprisonment was entirely owing to our officers, and that Cortes would not be able to act according to his own wishes in this matter. Motecusuma, therefore, answered Cortes, "that he in every way preferred staying with us, until he should have gained more certain intelligence as to the real designs of his nephews." He now sent some trustworthy personages to Cacamatzin to invite him to Mexico, under the pretence that he was desirous of becoming reconciled to him. He told him, at the same time, not to feel any solicitude on account of his confinement, for it depended upon himself to leave our quarters whenever he thought proper; and *Malinche* himself had twice invited him to take up his abode in his own palace again. But he had refused to do so, that he might not go against the commandments of his gods, who had told him, through his priests, to continue our prisoner for a certain space of time, if he was desirous of preserving his life. It was therefore his interest to remain on good terms with *Malinche* and his brothers.

Motecusuma also sent similar messages to the other chiefs of Tezcuco, adding, that he had invited his nephew to Mexico, to bring about friendship between him and us again. They were therefore to thwart all attempts the young hothead might make of commencing war upon us. On the receipt of this message, Cacamatzin with his principal adherents met to consult what steps they should take. He opened the assembly with a haughty and turbulent speech, assuring them he would destroy us all within the space of four days. His uncle was a faint-hearted old woman for not having fallen upon us as he had been advised on our descending the mountain of Chalco, and when all their warriors stood in readiness. Motecusuma, indeed, had invited us into the city as if we were going to do him some good. He gave us all the gold that was collected by tribute, and we had even broken open the secret treasury of his ancestor Axayacatl. We detained the monarch himself in prison, and continually admonished him to abolish his gods and adopt ours in their stead. The injury we had done was already great, but in order to put a stop to this, and that such injustice might not remain unpunished, he begged of them to lend him their powerful aid. All he had been stating they knew to be true, and had beheld with their own eyes how Motecusuma's generals were burnt at the stake: nothing now remained but to fall upon us in good earnest.

These representations were accompanied, not only by promises when he should have ascended the Mexican throne of raising them all to great dignity, but he likewise presented them on the spot with all kinds of valuable things; assuring them he was in perfect understanding with the princes of Cojohuacan, Iztapalapan, Tlacupa, and other places, who would all join him with their troops. Even in Mexico itself he had drawn over a large number of the principal personages to his side, who would rise up in arms to assist him at a moment's notice. Nothing would be easier than to force their way into Mexico. Some of the troops were to march along the causeways, but the main body would be conveyed thither by canoes and *pirogues*. They would nowhere meet with any opposition, for his uncle was in confinement, and could issue no orders to the inhabitants of Mexico. There was no reason to fear us, for his uncle's generals had a few days ago killed several of the *teules* and one of their horses, near Almeria. Both the dead horse and head of one of the former had been shown to every one in Mexico. In the short space of one hour they would be able to capture the whole of us and feast sumptuously off our flesh.

As soon as Cacamatzin had done speaking, the generals stood gazing at each other in silence, each one waiting to hear his neighbour's answer first. At last four or five of the most distinguished personages broke silence, declaring, if they were to commence hostilities in the very metropolis of their monarch, without his command, it was their duty, first of all, to apprize him of it. If he gave his consent, they would join him heart and soul; but would consider themselves traitors, if they acted contrary to his wishes.

This answer displeased Cacamatzin uncommonly, and in the heat of his anger he threw three of the generals who thus opposed him into prison. As there were a great number of his relatives, and boisterous young men, like himself, at the meeting, the majority was for supporting him until death. Cacamatzin, therefore, sent the following answer to Motecusuma: "He might have spared himself the trouble of exhorting him to make friendship with people who had insulted him, Motecusuma, so greatly, by keeping him prisoner. They could only account for the conduct he had pursued from our being enchanters, who had bound down both his mind and energies by witchcraft, or that our gods, and the great Spanish woman, whom we termed our protectress, gave us power to accomplish everything we might wish."

Herein Cacamatzin was certainly right; for the great mercy of God and of the blessed Virgin was certainly our greatest support. This message of Cacamatzin closed thus: "It was his intention to pay both his uncle and us a visit, to our sorrow, and speak words of death to us."

Motecusuma was highly incensed at this impudent answer, and that instant sent for six of his most trustworthy generals, handed over to them his seal, with various other valuable things, and commissioned them to repair to Tezcuco, and secretly show his signet to all his relations, and those chiefs of the city whom they knew were ill inclined towards Cacamatzin, on account of his haughty behaviour, and command them to seize him, and those who supported him, and bring them to Mexico.

These officers accordingly set out immediately for Tezcuco, and fulfilled their orders so promptly, that they seized Cacamatzin in his own palace amidst his adherents, five of whom were also taken. They were bound hand and foot, thrown into canoes, which were lying ready, well manned, and so brought to Mexico.

When the officers had arrived there with the prisoners, they allowed Cacamatzin to mount his royal sedan, and so conducted him, with every respect due to his station, into the presence of Motecusuma.

In his discourse with Motecusuma, Cacamatzin showed even more audacity than before; and when the monarch learnt from the other five prisoners that he had designed to deprive him of the crown, and place it on his own head, he grew terribly exasperated. He ordered the five other prisoners to be released, but Cacamatzin to be conducted into the presence of Cortes, that the latter might take him into his own custody.

Upon this, Cortes repaired to the monarch, thanked him for this great proof of his friendship, and, with the approbation of Motecusuma, raised the brother of Cacamatzin, who, as above related, had fled for protection to Motecusuma, to the throne of Tezcuco. This was done with great pomp and ceremony, and the election of this new king was hailed by the inhabitants of that great city, and all the influential men of the province. The young king of Tezcuco received the name of Don Carlos.[1]

After the other nephews of Motecusuma, the princes of Cojohuacan, Iztapalapan, and Tlacupa, had learnt the fate of Cacamatzin, they naturally concluded that Motecusuma was informed of their having joined in the conspiracy, and they durst not come, as usual, to pay their court to him; but the former, in understanding with Cortes, likewise ordered them to be seized; and scarcely eight days had elapsed before we had the satisfaction of seeing them all securely locked in chains in our quarters.

The reader may well imagine from all this that our lives hung, as it were, by a short thread, and we heard of nothing on all sides than how we should be cut off to a man, and our bodies devoured. Here a merciful Providence was our only protection. To him we are alone indebted that the excellent Motecusuma himself should have furthered all our designs, and that his subjects, even in his confinement, should have paid implicit obedience to all his commands. We therefore every way strove to show the monarch our gratitude for his great kindness; we took every possible means to amuse him; no one was allowed for one moment to treat him with disrespect; and Cortes himself even never sat down in his presence unless he desired him to do so. We not only treated him with profound respect, but we really loved him; for in all his actions he indeed proved himself a

1. The name of the prince was Cuicuitzcatl.

great monarch. Father Olmedo from time to time would also speak to him about our holy religion. We also acquainted him with the great power of our emperor, and the immense extent of his territories. All of this he would listen to with delight; then again he would play a game at *totoloc* with Cortes, and always divided his gains among us; for liberality was a leading feature in his character.

CHAPTER 101

Motecusuma Submits

As peace was again restored to the country after the imprisonment of the petty kings, Cortes reminded Motecusuma of the offers he had made, previously to our entering Mexico, to pay tribute to our emperor; observing at the same time that he must now be sufficiently convinced of the power and the vast extent of his empire, the number of his vassals, among whom even there were distinguished sovereigns. It would be good, therefore, if he, with all his subjects, likewise acknowledged themselves vassals of our emperor; and it was customary for this act of submission to be preceded by payment of tribute.

In answer to this, Motecusuma said he was quite willing to assemble all the *grandees* of his empire, and deliberate the matter with them: and after the space of ten days the greater part of the *caziques* from the surrounding districts assembled together, with the exception, however, of the *cazique* of Matlaltzinco, who was a near relation of Motecusuma, and considered a man of uncommon bravery; at least his demeanour and bodily frame fully bespoke it, and he was looked upon as Motecusuma's successor to the throne of Mexico.

But even this man, it would appear, was seized with terror; for he sent Motecusuma word from Tula, where he was then staying, that it was impossible for him to be present at the meeting, and he was unable to pay tribute; indeed scarcely able to live himself on what his province produced him.

Enraged at this unexpected answer, Motecusuma despatched some of his generals to take the refractory prince prisoner. But as he was a very powerful *cazique*, he had, of course, numerous adherers, who sent him intelligence of the steps Motecusuma had determined to take against him; so that he had sufficient time to retreat into the interior of the country, where he was quite out of his monarch's reach.

The other chiefs, however, duly assembled at their monarch's bidding; but neither Cortes nor any of us were present at the meeting, save the page Orteguilla, from whom we learnt what follows:—Motecusuma opened the assembly by reminding the *caziques* of the ancient tradition of their forefathers, written down in their historical records, of a people that would one time come from the quarter where the sun rose, who were destined to rule this country, and put an end to the Mexican empire. That tradition referred to us, as he concluded, from the declarations of his gods. The priests of Huitzilopochtli had expressly demanded an oracle of that god on this point, and had instituted sacrifices for that purpose; but the god, contrary to his usual custom, had refused the oracle, and merely referred them to his previous declaration; wherefore they had not dared to put any further questions. We may therefore conclude, continued Motecusuma, that Huitzilopochtli meant to say we were even to take the oath of allegiance to the king of Spain, whose subjects the *teules* are. For the present we cannot do otherwise than act accordingly: we must wait to see if our gods will give a better response some time hence, we can then act as circumstances require. He therefore desired and commanded them, for their own good, cheerfully to give some proof of their allegiance to the Spanish monarch. *Malinche* had been importunate on this point, and it would not be well to refuse him. For the eight or ten years he had ruled over them they had obeyed him like faithful servants; for which reason he had enriched them, enlarged their territories, and elevated them to high dignities. They were to consider his present confinement as the will of Huitzilopochtli, who had particularly advised him to it, as he had so often assured them on other occasions.

After this reasoning and statement of Motecusuma, all present declared themselves willing to comply with his wishes, but broke out into tears, and sighed deeply, Motecusuma himself being most vehemently affected. He then immediately despatched one of his principal officers to Cortes with the information that the day following they would again meet, and take the oath of allegiance to the emperor.

The next day accordingly this was done in the presence of Cortes, of our officers, and the greater part of the soldiers. All the Mexicans seemed deeply grieved, and Motecusuma himself could not refrain from shedding tears. Even we ourselves, from the great affection we bore this monarch, became quite affected at the sight of his tears, and many of us wept as much as the monarch himself. We therefore strove, if possible, to redouble our attention towards him, and Cortes, with Father Olmedo, who was a man of great intelligence, scarcely left him for a moment; and while we employed every means to cheer him, we never lost an opportunity of exhorting him to abolish his false gods.

Chapter 102

Exploring the Gold Mines

Cortes one day, as usual, sitting with Motecusuma, the discourse, among other things, turned upon mining, and he inquired of the monarch where the gold mines and those rivers were situated where gold dust was found, and what method they pursued to collect the same, as he intended sending out two of his men for that purpose, who were great proficients in the art of mining.

Motecusuma answered, that gold was found in three different parts of the country; but more abundantly in the province of Zacatula, from ten to twelve days' journey south of Mexico. There the earth which contained the gold was washed in wooden vessels, and the gold dust sunk to the bottom. At present gold was likewise brought from the northern province of Tustepec, near to where we had landed. There it was collected from the beds of the rivers; and very productive gold mines were also worked in this province by the Chinantecs and Tzapotecs, two tribes which were not subject to him. If Cortes was desirous of sending some of his men there, he was very willing himself to despatch several distinguished officers with them.

Cortes accepted of this offer, and thanked Motecusuma for his kindness, and sent off our pilot Gonzalo de Umbria, with two miners, to Zacatula. This Umbria was the same person whom Cortes sentenced to have his feet cut off, while we were staying at San Juan de Ulua.[1] He and his companions were to return within the space of forty days. To the mines in the north he despatched an officer, named Pizarro, a young man twenty-five years of age, whom he treated as one of his own relations.

At that time Peru was still unknown, and the name of Pizarro not thought of. This young officer was accompanied by four miners and

1. According to Torquemada, Umbria was only scourged, which appears more probable.

an equal number of distinguished Mexicans. A space of forty days was likewise allowed him to return to Mexico, as he had to travel a distance of 320 miles.

Motecusuma on that occasion likewise presented Cortes with a piece of *nequen* cloth, on which all the rivers and indentures along the coast running northwards of Panuco to Tabasco, a distance of 560 miles, were very accurately described and drawn. By this chart our observation was drawn to the River Guacasualco, and as we were well acquainted with all the harbours and indentures there noted down, from our voyage under Grijalva, but knew nothing of that river, which the Mexicans described as very broad and deep, Cortes determined also to send some one there to make soundings at its mouth, and further explore the country; Diego de Ordas, a man of great intelligence and courage, offered himself for this purpose, if two of our men, and some Mexicans, might accompany him.

Cortes was at first very loth to part with him, as he was so useful to him in various ways, but at last gave his consent, to keep him in good humour. Motecusuma likewise expressed his fears about this journey, as the land of Guacasualco was not subject to him, and inhabited by a very warlike people. He cautioned Ordas to be particularly on his guard, and hoped that no reproach would be made him if any harm befell him. But if Ordas should think proper, he would order a sufficient number of his troops, which lay on the confines, to accompany him into Guacasualco. Cortes and Ordas returned Motecusuma many thanks for his kindness, and the latter then set out on his journey, accompanied by two of our men and several distinguished Mexicans.

Here again the historian Gomara commits another blunder similar to the one he previously made, respecting Pedro de Ircio, whom he sends to Panuco; for here he despatches Juan Velasquez with 100 men to form a colony in Guacasualco. In the next chapter I will give an account of what these officers saw, and the samples of gold they brought with them.

Chapter 103

Return From the Gold Mines

The first who returned to Mexico was Gonzalo de Umbria, with his companions. He brought with him about 300 *pesos* worth of gold dust, which they had collected in the township of Zacatula. There, he related, the *caziques* of the province employed numbers of the inhabitants at the rivers to wash gold out of the sand in small troughs. There were two rivers from which gold dust was collected, and if clever miners were set to work there, and the mining carried out in the same way as at St. Domingo and Cuba, they would prove very profitable.

Four distinguished chiefs of that province had accompanied Umbria to Mexico, with a present in gold trinkets for our emperor, valued at about 200 *pesos*. Cortes was as much pleased with this small quantity of gold as if it had been worth 3000 *pesos*, as he now knew for a certainty that there were rich mines in those parts. He treated the *caziques* who brought this present very kindly, gave them glass beads, and promised them all manner of good things; so that they returned home highly delighted.

Besides this, Umbria spoke about many other large townships in the neighbourhood of Mexico, and of a province on the confines, called Matlaltzinco. We could well perceive that Umbria and his companions had not forgotten themselves, for they had well stuffed their pockets with gold. This Cortes had readily foreseen, and purposely selected Umbria for that journey, to regain his friendship, and that he might forget the severe sentence which he had passed upon him.

Neither did Diego de Ordas, who had been sent to the River Guacasualco, return with empty hands. He had likewise passed through large townships, all of which he mentioned by name, and had everywhere been received with great respect. Every town he came to he had met with endless complaints from the inhabitants respecting the depredations and cruelties exercised upon them by the Mexican troops stationed on the confines. Ordas, and the distinguished Mexicans who accompanied him, had severely reprimanded the officers who commanded these troops, and threatened to acquaint Motecusuma with every circumstance, who would certainly send for and punish them with equal severity as he had Quauhpopoca for similar misconduct. These remonstrances had the desired effect, and on his further journey Ordas was only accompanied by one of his Mexican fellow-travellers. Tochel, *cazique* of the province of Guacasualco, having received information of Ordas's approach, sent out several distinguished personages to meet him. Everywhere he met with the kindest reception, for the inhabitants had learnt to know what kind of people we were, from the expedition under Grijalva.

In order to assist him in exploring this river, the *cazique* Tochel not only lent him several large canoes, but himself, accompanied by a number of his officers, had accompanied him to the River Guacasualco. At the mouth of this River Ordas found a depth of three fathoms, but higher up the river became gradually deeper, and was navigable for large vessels; and near a certain Indian village there was depth enough to carry a Spanish *carack*. In this village the inhabitants presented Ordas with some gold trinkets and a pretty Indian female. They likewise declared themselves vassals of our emperor, and complained bitterly of Motecusuma, and the cruelties exercised by his troops. It was only a short time ago they had fought a battle against the latter, and slain great numbers of them; for which reason they had named the small village where the engagement took place Cuitlonemiqui, which in their language means the *spot where the Mexican beasts fell*. Ordas thanked them very kindly for the great respect they had shown him, and presented them with some glass beads. He likewise said that the country was well adapted for the breeding of cattle, and the harbour excellently situated for trading with Cuba, St. Domingo, and Jamaica, but too far distant from Mexico, and, what was worse, full of shallows; which was the reason we seldom made use of this harbour for commerce, or transporting goods from Mexico.

With respect to Pizarro, he returned, with only one of the Spaniards who accompanied him to Tustepec, but he had been more fortunate in the discovery of gold, of which he brought with him dust of that metal to the value of 1000 *pesos*. He related that he had himself commenced washing for gold dust in the provinces of Tustepec and Malinaltepec, and neighbouring districts; for which purpose he had employed a considerable number of Indians, whom he remunerated for their labour with two thirds of the gold they found. He had likewise visited other provinces higher up in the mountains, called the country of the Chinantecs. Here he was met by a number of Indians, armed with bows, arrows, shields, and lances, of much greater length than ours. They declared that no Mexican should set foot in their territory, under pain of death, but that the *teules* were very welcome. The Mexicans consequently remained behind, and Pizarro pursued his journey with the Spaniards only. The Chinantec *caziques* then ordered a number of the inhabitants to repair to the river, to wash the gold dust from the sand. The gold dust here found is of a curly shape, and the inhabitants said that the mines, where the metal was found in that shape, were much more productive and the metal more solid. Pizarro was likewise accompanied by two *caziques* of that country, who, in the name of the inhabitants, came to make friendship with us, and declare themselves vassals of our emperor. They also brought a present in gold, and complained bitterly of the Mexicans, who were held in such utter abhorrence by them, on account of their lust after plunder, that they could not endure the sight of a Mexican, or bear to hear their name pronounced.

Cortes received Pizarro and the *caziques* with every possible kindness, and returned the latter many thanks for their present, assuring them of our friendship, and readiness to serve them at all times, and then dismissed them. That, however, they might travel in safety through the Mexican territories, he desired two distinguished Mexicans to accompany them to the confines, for which they were very thankful. Cortes then inquired of Pizarro what had become of the other Spaniards who had accompanied him. Pizarro replied, that he had ordered them to remain behind there, as the soil seemed so rich, and abounded in gold mines, and the inhabitants so peaceably inclined. He had desired them to form a small settlement there, and lay out extensive grounds for cacao, maize, and cotton plantations; also to promote the breed of cattle, and explore the gold mines of the country. Cortes greatly disapproved of his having exceeded his commands, and upbraided him severely in private, telling him that it betrayed a low disposition instantly to begin thinking of speculation in cacao plantations and breeding of cattle. Cortes then despatched a soldier, named Alonso Luis, to the Spaniards left behind, with orders for their immediate return to Mexico.

CHAPTER 104

Cortes Demands Tribute of Gold

As Diego de Ordas and the other officers whom Cortes had sent out for the discovery of gold mines had all returned with samples of that metal, and brought the most satisfactory accounts concerning the wealth of the country, our general, after long deliberation with his officers and several of the soldiers, resolved that Motecusuma should now be desired to send round to all his *caziques*, and to every township of his empire, and require them to bring in tribute to our emperor, and that he himself, as the most wealthy of his vassals, should pay the same from his own private treasures.

In answer to this request, Motecusuma said that he would forward the necessary orders for this purpose to every township; but he was compelled to inform us that many of them would be unable to fulfil those commands, who could merely contribute some trifling trinkets in gold which they had inherited from their forefathers.

Motecusuma then sent several of his principal officers to the districts where there were gold mines, desiring the inhabitants of such places to forward him the usual weight and number of gold bars they were accustomed to pay as tribute, and forwarded them two bars as a sample. He despatched similar orders to the province which stood under his relative, who behaved so refractory. This prince, however, sent him word that he would neither send any gold nor pay any attention to Motecusuma's commands, and that he had as much right to the throne of Mexico as he who thus dared to demand tribute of him.

The monarch was so incensed at this answer that he instantly despatched some of his most active officers, with his seal, to seize the rebel and bring him to Mexico. These officers were more successful than the former had been, and brought in the rebel prince prisoner. When he was led into the presence of Motecusuma, he not only evinced no fear, but was impudent to a degree, and expressed himself so disrespectfully that his conduct could only be accounted for by madness, as he, it was said, was subject to fits of insanity. Cortes, who received information that Motecusuma had given orders for his execution, begged the latter he might be sent to him, that he might take him into his own custody. The former complied with this request, and when the prince was brought into our general's presence, he spoke very kindly to him, and begged of him not to act the madman with his monarch, and assured him he would obtain his liberty again. But Motecusuma was of a very different opinion, and desired he might be heavily chained, as the other princes had been.

After the lapse of twenty days, all the officers whom Motecusuma had sent out into the provinces to collect the tribute, had returned to Mexico. He then sent for Cortes, his officers, and several of us who had been accustomed to stand sentinel in his apartment, and spoke to us as follows: "*Malinche*, and you other officers and soldiers, I consider myself greatly indebted to your emperor for his having thought it worth his while to send from such distant countries to make inquiries after me; but what more deeply occupies my thoughts is the tradition of our ancestors, which has been fully confirmed by the oracles of our gods, that, namely, the dominion of these countries was destined to devolve upon him. Receive, therefore, this gold for him; I have no more at present, as the notice to collect it was too short. With regard to myself, I have destined the whole of my father's treasure for him as my share of the tribute, which lies secreted in your quarters. I am well aware that you have inspected it, but closed up the opening as before. When, however, you transmit this treasure to your emperor, you must say in your letter, this is sent you by your faithful vassal Motecusuma. To this I will also add a few *chalchihuis*, of such enormous value that I would not consent to give them to any one save to such a powerful emperor as yours: each of these stones are worth two loads of gold. I further think of sending him three crossbows, with the small balls, and bag which contains them, all richly ornamented with jewels, which will certainly please him much. I should like to give him all I possess; now I have very little left, as I have from time to time given you the greater portion of my gold and jewels."

Cortes and all of us were astonished at this generosity and great goodness of the monarch, and we took off our caps very respectfully, and thanked him. Cortes, at the same time, assured him he would send our majesty an accurate description of all these splendid presents. Motecusuma did not delay one instant to fulfil his promise, for that very same hour his house-stewards arrived to hand us over all the treasures contained in the secret chamber. There was such a vast heap of it that we were occupied three days in taking all out of the different corners of this secret room, and in looking them over; we were even obliged to send for Motecusuma's goldsmiths from Escapuzalco to assist us. The reader may form some notion of this treasure when I tell him that, when all the articles were set apart in three heaps and weighed, the gold alone, not counting the silver and other precious things, was found to be worth above 600,000 *pesos*: in this are not included the gold plates, bars, and the gold dust contributed by the other provinces. All this treasure we ordered the goldsmiths of Escapuzalco to smelt into bars measuring three inches square.

Besides all this, Motecusuma brought another present, consisting in gold and jewels of enormous value. There were also *chalchihuis* stones of extreme beauty and size, which were considered of immense value among the *caziques* of the country. Further, there were three crossbows, with their cases set in jewels and pearls, besides a number of pictures made of feathers and small pearls, all of great value: indeed, it would be no easy task to describe all these splendid things one by one.

Upon this Cortes ordered an iron stamp to be made, about the size of a Spanish real, bearing the arms of Spain, with which the royal treasurers were to mark all the gold, with the exception of that set in jewels, which we were loth to pull to pieces. As we possessed neither scales nor weights, we cast the latter in iron, from twenty-five pounds to half a pound weight, and to four ounces; for we cared very little to weigh to a nicety of half an ounce or so. When the gold, without including the silver and jewels, was weighed, we found, as I have before stated, that it amounted to 600,000 *pesos*, though many of our men valued it at much more.

Nothing now remained but to deduct the emperor's fifths therefrom, and divide the remainder among the officers and soldiers, including those left behind at Vera Cruz. Cortes, however, was of opinion that the division should be postponed until our stock should be further increased, but most of our officers and soldiers desired that it might take place forthwith, for they asserted that above one third had already disappeared since the three heaps had been first collected together. They greatly suspected that Cortes and his principal officers had secretly taken away the greater part. The weighing of the gold, consequently, was commenced immediately, that the division might take place on the following day. In what way this was done, and how most of it fell into the hands of Cortes and others, I will relate in the following chapter.

Chapter 105

Sharing the Gold

First of all, one fifth of the treasure was set apart for the crown, and a second for Cortes, as had been promised him when we elected him captain-general and chief justice. After this had been deducted, Cortes brought in the expenses of fitting out the armament at Cuba; then the sum due to Velasquez for the vessels we had destroyed, and, lastly, the travelling expenses of our agents whom we sent to Spain. Next were deducted the several shares due to the garrison at Vera Cruz, which consisted of seventy men; then the value of the two horses which had been killed, one in the engagement with the Tlascallans, the other at Almeria.

Not until all this had been deducted were the rest of our men allowed to take their shares. Double shares were also set apart for the two priests, the officers, and the cavalry, likewise for the musketeers and crossbow-men. After these and other nibblings, there remained, for the greater part of our men, who could only claim one share, such a mere trifle, that many of them would not even accept of it, which Cortes then took himself. At that time, indeed, we thought it best to say nothing about this unjust division; for what would it have availed us had we demanded justice? Besides which, Cortes had secretly bribed some with presents and large promises, and many of the most noisy he presented with a hundred *pesos* to stop their mouths.

The portion belonging to the garrison at Vera Cruz was forwarded to Tlascalla for safe keeping. Most of our officers employed Motecusuma's goldsmiths of Escapuzalco to make them heavy chains of the gold; and Cortes, among other things, ordered a grand dinner service. Several of our soldiers, who had learnt how to fill their pockets, had other things made; and it was not long before a number of the stamped bars and trinkets came into circulation; for gambling was now commenced to a great extent, after a certain Pedro Valenciano had managed to manufacture playing cards from parchment, which were as well painted and as beautiful to the eye as those manufactured in Spain.

I will, however, show what impression this unfair division of the gold made upon our men. Among our troops there was a man named Cardenas, a sailor by profession, who had left behind him in Spain a wife and children in great want, and had the ill-luck, with many of us, to continue in poverty.

When this man beheld the great heap of gold piled up in bars, plates, besides the gold dust, and found his share of the spoil was a mere hundred *pesos*, he became excessively low-spirited. One of his friends, who had observed this, asked him the cause of his grief and heavy sighs? He answered, "Why, how the devil can I do otherwise, when I see the gold which we have so hardly earned find its way into Cortes' pockets, with his fifths, monies laid out for horses, vessels, and other such like vile trickeries, while my wife and children are perishing at home for want of food? I could even have sent them a little help when our agents went to Spain, for there was sufficient gold at that time to have divided it among us." "What gold are you speaking of?" inquired his friend. "Why," answered Cardenas, "of that which our agents took with them to Spain. If Cortes had granted me my share of that, my wife and children would not have wanted: but he employed every species of artifice to persuade us to send the whole treasure as a present to the emperor, with the exception, however, of above 6000 *pesos* to Martin Cortes, his father: I will not even mention the gold which he has secretly stowed away. We others who have fought about courageously night and day at Tabasco, Tlascalla, Zinpantzinco, and Cholulla; we who at present live in continual fear, with almost certain death before our eyes as soon as the inhabitants of this great city get it into their heads to rise up against us,—we all remain, as before, poverty-stricken, and all our remonstrances are in vain! Cortes, on the contrary, acts as if he were the emperor himself, and runs away with a fifth of our hard earnings!"

In this strain the poor fellow continued his complaints, and was of opinion that we should not have allowed Cortes to deduct a fifth for himself; and that we required no other sovereign than our own emperor.

"And are you really," returned the other, "going to embitter your happiness with such thoughts? All this will avail you nothing. You know we fare equally bad with respect to provisions, for Cortes and his officers nearly eat up all themselves; but it is of no use for us to complain, therefore drive away, all such melancholy thoughts from your mind, and pray to the Almighty that we may not meet with our total destruction in this city."

Cortes was duly apprized of all this and similar complaints; and as the discontent among the men respecting the unfair division of the gold became pretty general, he ordered the whole of us into his presence, and addressed us in a speech abounding with the sweetest sentences imaginable. He was indebted, he said, for all he had to us; that he had not required the fifth part, but the share which was promised him when we elected him captain-general, and he was quite ready to bestow something on those who stood in need. The gold we had collected up to this moment, he continued, was a trifle to that which was to come. We ought to remember what great cities were dispersed through the country, and the rich mines which were in our possession; these certainly would enrich every man in his army. In this way he continued for some time, and spoke feelingly to the heart! but, finding all this had no effect, he employed other means. Many he secretly silenced with gold, and others by great promises, and the provisions sent us by Motecusuma's orders were from this moment justly divided, so that every man among us had an equal share of food with himself. He likewise took Cardenas aside, and quieted him with a present of 300 *pesos*, and the promise that he would allow him to return home to his family with the first vessel that left for Spain. This Cardenas I shall have occasion to mention on some future occasion, for he did Cortes considerable injury in Spain during the subsequent complaints which were laid before the emperor against him.

Chapter 106

The Missing Gold

Since gold, generally speaking, is the great desire of man, and that the more he possesses of it the more avaricious he grows, it also happened here that many pieces of gold were missing from the heaps, which I have mentioned above; and as one of our officers named Leon had ordered Motecusuma's goldsmiths to make him heavy gold chains and other ornaments, the royal treasurer Gonzalo Mexia suspected something wrong, and secretly observed to him that the emperor's fifths had not been deducted from several of the bars he had sent to be smelted. Leon, who stood in high favour with Cortes, answered, that it was not his intention to return anything. The gold he possessed he had not taken himself, but had received all from Cortes before it had ever been smelted.

The royal treasurer, however, was not to be silenced by this, but affirmed, that, besides the gold Cortes had secretly taken away, and of which he had deprived his companions in arms, there was a good deal elsewhere from which the royal fifths had not been deducted, and that, in his capacity of royal treasurer, he could not suffer the emperor's interest to be thus prejudiced.

This, consequently, led to high words between both parties, so that they drew swords, and would certainly have killed each other if we had not instantly parted them; for both were high-spirited men and excellent swordsmen, and each had already wounded his antagonist.

As soon as Cortes was informed of this affair, he ordered both to be arrested and heavily chained. As, however, he always had been heart in hand with Leon, many were of opinion that all this was a mere blind to make us believe that he preferred justice to friendship; besides which it was whispered that he secretly visited him during his arrest, and assured him that he should not be confined beyond a couple of days, when he and Mexia would again be set at liberty. But all this did not go to quiet our suspicions, and now Mexia, in his turn, was reproached for not having fulfilled the duties of royal treasurer, and he was compelled by the soldiers to inquire of Cortes what had become of the missing gold?

I will, however, cut this matter short here, and return to Leon, who was confined in a room not far from the apartments occupied by Motecusuma. When Leon, therefore, who was a tall powerful man, paced up and down his room, his heavy chains dragged along the floor, so that the monarch could plainly hear the jingling noise, and he inquired of Orteguilla who the prisoner was? His page then told him that it was Leon, who had previously been captain of the guard, an appointment now filled by Oli, and told him that the reason of his confinement was on account of some gold that was missing.

When Cortes that day, as usual, paid his visit to the monarch, and the first compliments had passed between them, the latter inquired of our general how it came that such a distinguished officer as Leon should have been thrown into chains? To which Cortes answered, jokingly, that all was not as it should be with him, he having threatened, because he had not received sufficient gold, to travel around to the different towns, and demand gold of the *caziques*. Fearing, therefore, he might put his threats into execution, and kill one or other chief, he had thrown him into prison. Motecusuma, on hearing this, begged Cortes to set him at liberty again, and promised he would soon drive such thoughts from his mind by presenting him with gold from his own private treasure.

Cortes feigned great unwillingness to grant the monarch's request, but at length assured him he would comply merely on account of the affection he bore him, Motecusuma. Leon was, consequently, released, and Cortes brought about a reconciliation between him and Mexia; then despatched him with some of Motecusuma's principal officers to raise gold at Cholulla, from which place he did not return till the end of six days, and now he had more gold than ever. Mexia, however, never forgot this affair, and a coolness ever after existed between him and our general.

I have related this story, though foreign to my narrative, to show the reader what artful devices Cortes was accustomed to set on foot, and what a show he made of justice to make us fear him.

Chapter 107

A Wife for Cortes

I have often related how we strove, in every possible manner, to amuse Motecusuma in his confinement, and daily visited him in his apartments. It was on one of these occasions that the monarch said to our general, "*Malinche*! in order to prove the great affection I have for you, I must acquaint you that it is my intention to give you one of my prettiest daughters in marriage."

Cortes took his cap off, and thanked him for the honour he was going to confer upon him, and said he was already married, and that the religion and laws of our country would not allow a man to have more than one wife; but that he would accept her and treat her with the respect due to her high rank, and it was requisite she should become converted to Christianity, as the daughters of many of his grandees had been.

Motecusuma readily agreed to this, as he did in everything else we desired, save the sacrificing of human beings, which nothing could induce him to abolish; day after day were those abominations committed: Cortes remonstrated with him in every possible way, but with so little effect, that at last he deemed it proper to take some decided step in the matter. But the great difficulty was to adopt a measure by which neither the inhabitants nor the priesthood would be induced to rise up in arms. We, however, came to the determination, in a meeting called for the purpose, to throw down the idols from the top of Huitzilopochtli's temple; and should the Mexicans rise up in arms for their defence, then to content ourselves by demanding permission to build an altar on one side of the platform, and erect thereon the image of the holy Virgin with the cross.

Thus determined, Cortes, accompanied by seven officers and soldiers, repaired to Motecusuma, and spoke to him as follows: "Great monarch, I have already so many times begged of you to abolish those false idols by whom you are so terribly deluded, and no longer to sacrifice human beings to them; and yet these abominations are continued daily: I have, therefore, come to you now, with these officers, to beg permission of you to take away these idols from the temple, and place in their stead the holy Virgin and the cross. The whole of my men feel determined to pull down your idols, even should you be averse to it; and you may well suppose that one or other of your *papas* will become the victim."

When Motecusuma heard this, and saw how determined our officers were, he said to Cortes, "Alas, *Malinche*! why is it you wish to compel me to bring down total destruction on this town? Our gods are already angry with us, and who can tell what revenge they contemplate against you? I will, however, assemble all the *papas*, to know their opinion."

Cortes made a sign with his hand for the other officers to retire, and begged of Motecusuma to grant him and father Olmedo a private audience. Cortes then told the monarch he only knew one way of saving the town from open rebellion, and the idols from destruction, namely, by our being allowed to erect an altar, with the cross and Virgin Mary, on the top of the great temple. He would then pledge himself to silence the murmurs of his men, and the Mexicans themselves would soon be convinced how greatly such a change would benefit their souls, what great blessings would be showered down upon them, and how abundant their harvests would be.

To this Motecusuma likewise answered, with a deep sigh, and a countenance full of sorrow, that he would discuss the matter with his *papas*. At length, after a good deal of arguing between the *papas* and himself, we were allowed to erect an altar, with the cross and holy Virgin, on the top of the temple, opposite the cursed idol Huitzilopochtli. We returned heartfelt thanks to the Almighty, and father Olmedo, assisted by the priest Juan Diaz, and many of our soldiers, celebrated high mass.[1]

Cortes appointed an old soldier to keep watch over this altar, and begged, at the same time, of Motecusuma to order his *papas* not to obstruct the man in his duty, which was to keep the place clean, burn incense before the altar, keep the candles lighted there night and day, and decorate it from time to time with fresh branches and flowers.

I must, however, break off here, and relate something we little expected.

---

1. For a further account of what happened after the building of this altar, I must refer the reader to the oft-quoted work of Torquemada (*Monarchia*, Ind. iv, 53.)

Chapter 108

Motecusuma Advises Cortes to Quit Mexico

From the very moment we had erected this altar and cross on the great temple, and had celebrated high mass there, a storm began to gather over our heads.

About this time Huitzilopochtli and Tetzcatlipuca are said to have addressed the *papas*, and acquainted them they were desirous of leaving the country, as the *teules* had treated them with such great contempt, and that it was impossible for them to dwell in the same spot with that image and cross. If they were desirous they should remain in Mexico, they were to kill us all. These were the last words they should utter; they were to be communicated to Motecusuma and his *grandees*, and the *papas* were at the same time to put them in mind how we had melted all the gold into bars, with which previously the gods had been honoured; how we ordered things as if we had been lords of the country, and kept five powerful princes bound in chains.

All this was faithfully reported to Motecusuma, who then sent word to Cortes he should like to see him, as he had things of the utmost importance to disclose to him.

The page Orteguilla, who had been despatched to Cortes for this purpose, informed the latter that Motecusuma appeared quite changed and spiritless; that, the day previous, several *papas* and distinguished officers had had secret interviews with him, and they uttered words of which he had not understood one syllable.

Upon this, Cortes, accompanied by Oli, four other officers, and our two interpreters, immediately called upon the monarch, and, after the usual courtesies had passed between them, the latter broke out as follows: "Alas! *Malinche* and you other officers, how grieved

I am at the commands which our gods have imparted to our *papas*, myself, and my chief officers!

"They most earnestly demand of us that we shall commence hostilities with you, and put you to death, or drive you away from this country by some other means. My advice is, that you had better leave of your own accord, than allow hostilities to commence.

"This, *Malinche*, I could not help disclosing to you, that you might come to some determination or other. For myself, I have no doubt that all your lives are at stake here."

The reader may easily imagine that Cortes and his officers did not treat all this so very lightly, and that they were not a little surprised at this disclosure. No one could have suspected that affairs would have taken such a turn; but the monarch had spoken in such a positive tone as to leave no doubt on our minds that we lived in imminent danger. Cortes, however, hid his fears from the monarch, and thanked him for his information, adding, that he was sorry we had no vessels left in which we could leave the country; and that if we even did leave it, we must take him, the monarch, along with us, that he might be presented to our emperor: he therefore begged of him to amuse his priests and officers until we should have constructed three vessels on the sea-coast. And if they commenced war with us, they would undoubtedly all be killed. And that Motecusuma might convince himself that he would fulfil his promise, he desired he would despatch two of his chief officers with our carpenters to the coast to cut wood for the building of the vessels.

Motecusuma was now more dispirited than ever when he heard Cortes say that he himself must accompany us; that he was to issue the necessary orders to his carpenters, and act and not talk. Our general also desired him to call the *papas* and officers to acquaint them that it was unnecessary to raise the town into open rebellion; they might, for the present, appease the gods by offerings, but we forbade any sacrifice of human beings.

After this important disclosure Cortes left the monarch, and we now lived in constant fear of hostilities breaking out. Cortes, however, fulfilled his promise, and sent for Martin Lopez and Andreas Nuñez, described to them the size of the three vessels he wished them to build, and to march to Vera Cruz with the Mexican carpenters, where all the necessary materials, consisting in iron, rigging, tar and tow would be found. These orders were promptly obeyed. The necessary quantity of wood was cut on the coast of Vera Cruz, and the building of the vessels was commenced with all assiduity. Whether Cortes gave Lopez any secret instructions I do not know; but I cannot pass by this circumstance in silence, as Gomara mentions it likewise in his history, and maintains that all this building of the vessels was mere artifice to amuse Motecusuma. May those who know more about this matter publish the truth. There are certainly numbers of our men alive who would be able to give a true account of this. All I know is that Lopez told me in confidence, that the building of the vessels was really commenced, and that the three vessels were actually lying on the staples.

At present, however, we will leave them quietly there, and acquaint the reader that we grew much alarmed at our situation in this great city, and momentarily expected an attack upon our friends of Tlascalla, as Doña Marina had informed our general to that effect. The page, Orteguilla, shed tears all day long, and we others narrowly watched the monarch's person. I must here for the last time acquaint the reader, that whether night or day, we never took off our *gorgets* or our armour, while our arms were never for a moment out of our hands. A bundle of straw and a mat formed a couch; our horses stood ready saddled, and in short every soldier was ready for action at a moment's notice.

At night we also took the precaution of posting such numbers of sentinels, that each of us in turn, had at least one watch every night. I do not mention this in praise of myself; but I grew so accustomed to being armed night and day, as it were living in armour, that after the conquest of New Spain I could not accustom myself for a length of time to undress on going to lie down, or make use of a bed, but slept better in soldier fashion than on the softest down. Even at the present day, in my old age, I never take a bed with me when I visit the townships belonging to my commendary; and if I do take one, it is merely because the cavaliers who accompany me may not think I take no bed with me, because I have no good one. From continued watching at night it has become quite natural to me to sleep for a short time together only, and get up at intervals to gaze upon the heavens and the stars, and take a couple of turns in the open air. Neither do I wear a nightcap or wind a kerchief around my head; and thanks be to God! this has become so natural to me, that I never feel any inconvenience from it. I have merely mentioned all this to convince the reader how we, the true Conquistadores, were always obliged to be upon our guard, and what hardships we had to undergo.

Chapter 109

The Governor of Cuba Against Us

In order to explain what I am now about to relate I must refer to prior events.

I have already mentioned, in the proper chapter, that Diego Velasquez got information of our having sent agents to our emperor with all the gold and presents we had received; and also of the bad reception they had met with from the bishop of Burgos; who not only favoured Velasquez in various ways, but even commanded him to fit out an armament against us, for which he himself would be responsible to the emperor.

The governor of Cuba accordingly used the utmost exertions and assembled a flotilla, consisting of nineteen sail, on board of which were 1400 soldiers, above forty cannon, with a quantity of powder, balls, and gun-flints, besides two artillerymen, who, with the artillery stood under the immediate command of the captain Rodrigo Martin. To this was added eighty horse, ninety crossbow-men, and seventy musketeers. Fat and corpulent as he was, Velasquez had, nevertheless, in the height of his passion, visited every township in Cuba, to hasten the equipment of the flotilla, and invited every inhabitant who had either Indians, relations, or friends who could manage their estates, to join the standard of Pamfilo Narvaez, and share the honour of taking Cortes and all of us prisoners, or at least to blow out our brains. He had even advanced as far as the promontory of Guaniguanico, in the height of his zeal, though that promontory was above 240 miles from the Havannah.

Before this armament quitted the harbour, the royal court of audience at St. Domingo, and the Hieronymite brothers, who were viceroys there, were determined to look into the matter a little; as the licentiate Suazo, who was their agent in Cuba, had sent them information of the extensiveness of the armament.

As the great and valuable services which we had rendered God and his majesty were very well known at St. Domingo, as also the fact of our having sent valuable presents to our emperor, it was considered there that Velasquez was not justified in fitting out an armament to revenge himself upon us, but that his only way was to pursue us in a court of law. These impartial men well foresaw how this armament would impede the conquest of New Spain. They therefore despatched the licentiate Lucas Vazquez de Aillon, who was auditor of the court of audience at St. Domingo, to Cuba, with peremptory commands to Velasquez not to allow the flotilla to leave the harbour.

The auditor punctually fulfilled these commands, and in due form protested against the flotilla leaving the harbour; but Diego Velasquez, who had spent all his property in fitting out this armament, relied upon the good favour of the bishop of Burgos, and took no notice of the protest. Upon this Vazquez de Aillon determined upon embarking himself on board one of the vessels, to try at least if he could not prevent hostilities between Narvaez and Cortes. Many even maintained that he came to Mexico with the secret intention to side with our party, or, if we could not succeed in defeating Narvaez, himself to take possession of the country in the name of our emperor. At all events he embarked with Narvaez and arrived in the harbour of San Juan de Ulua, of which we shall hear more presently.

Chapter 110
Narvaez Arrives

When Narvaez had arrived with the flotilla off the mountains of San Martin, a north wind arose, which is always dangerous on these coasts. One of the vessels commanded by a cavalier, named Christobal de Morante, of Medina del Campo, was wrecked during night-time off the coast, and the greater part of the men perished. The other vessels, however, arrived safely in the harbour of San Juan de Ulua.

This armament, which may indeed be considered extensive, considering it was fitted out at Cuba, was first of all seen by some soldiers whom Cortes had sent out in search of gold mines. Three of these, Cervantes, Escalona, and Alonso Carretero, did not hesitate a moment to go on board the commander's ship, and are said, as soon as they stepped on board to have praised the Almighty for having rescued them out of the hands of Cortes and the great city of Mexico, where death stood daily before their eyes.

Narvaez ordered meat and drink to be set before them, and as their glasses were abundantly filled, they said to one another in his presence: "This is indeed leading a different sort of life with a glass of good wine in one's hand, when compared to the slavery under Cortes, who allows a person no rest either night or day; where a person dares scarcely say a word, and death is always staring him in the face."

Cervantes, however, who was a low buffoon, even addressed Narvaez himself, and exclaimed: "O Narvaez! Narvaez, what a fortunate man you are, that you just arrive at the moment when the traitor Cortes has heaped together above 700,000 *pesos*, and the whole of his men are so enraged with him for his having cheated them out of the greater part of the gold, that many even disdain to accept of their shares."

Such was the language which these low-minded and worthless fellows uttered, and they told Narvaez more than he was desirous of knowing. They likewise informed him that thirty-two miles further on he would come to a town we had built, called Vera Cruz, which had a garrison of sixty men, all invalids, under an officer named Sandoval, and he had merely to show himself with a few men there and they would immediately deliver up the town to him.

Motecusuma was immediately apprized of the arrival of this flotilla, and without saying a single word to Cortes despatched several of his chief officers to Narvaez, with a present in gold and other things; and commanded the inhabitants to furnish him with provisions.

Narvaez, in his message to Motecusuma, calumniated Cortes and all of us, telling him we were nothing but a parcel of thieves and vagabonds, who had fled from Spain without the knowledge of our emperor, but his imperial majesty having been informed that we were in this country committing all manner of depredations, and that we had even imprisoned its monarch, had ordered him to repair hither with his flotilla and troops, to put an end to these disorders and liberate the monarch. He had likewise received orders to put Cortes and all his men to the sword, or take them alive and send them prisoners to Spain, where death awaited them. This sober language the three soldiers, who understood the Mexican language were to translate to Motecusuma's messengers, to whom Narvaez at the same time sent a present of some Spanish goods.

Motecusuma was not a little delighted with this message, particularly when he learnt the number of Narvaez's vessels, of his cannon, and his 1300 soldiers. He, of course, thought it would be an easy matter for Narvaez to overcome us, and as his messengers had seen the three treacherous rascals who had deserted to Narvaez, he found the more reason to believe all the scandal the latter had said concerning Cortes. Besides which he received an accurate description of the whole armament from his artists, who had immediately depicted on cotton cloth everything they saw. He therefore sent a second message, accompanied by more valuable presents in gold and cotton stuffs to Narvaez, with strict commands to the inhabitants of the coast to supply him with plenty of provisions.

Motecusuma had received intelligence of the arrival of the flotilla off the coast three days before Cortes. When the latter, as usual, one day paid a visit to the monarch he found him in particular good spirits, and asked him what had occasioned it? Motecusuma replied, that he found himself in better health than he had done for some time past.

Cortes, who was very much surprised at this sudden change in the monarch, called upon him a second time that day, and now the latter began to fear our general was cognizant of the arrival of the flotilla. To remove all suspicion from his mind, therefore, he thought it better to break the news to him himself. "I have just this moment, *Malinche*," said he, "received the information that an armament of eighteen vessels, with a great number of soldiers and horses, has arrived in the harbour where you landed. Pictures of the whole armament have been transmitted to me. This, no doubt, is no news to you, and I thought from your second visit to me this day, you came to bring me the intelligence yourself, and that now there was no need for you to build new vessels. Though I may have felt hurt that you wished to keep all this a secret from me, yet, on the other hand, I am delighted at the arrival of your brothers, with whom you can now return to Spain; which thus removes all difficulties at once."

When Cortes heard this and saw the painting which the Mexicans had made of all the vessels, he exclaimed in the excess of his delight: "Praise be to God, whose assistance always comes at the right time!" Indeed the whole of us greatly rejoiced at this news, we galloped about on our horses, and fired salute after salute.

Cortes, however, began to consider it in a more serious light than he had done in the first moments, as he now plainly saw that this armament was sent out against us by Velasquez; and he communicated his suspicions to us all, and by great presents and promises he made us pledge ourselves not to act any way against his interests; which we did the more readily, as the commander of this new armament was totally unknown to us. Our joy was now excessive, not only on account of the gold which Cortes gave us from his private purse, but at the arrival of this flotilla, which we saw the Almighty had sent to us in our distress.

Chapter 111

Narvaez Demands the Surrender of Vera Cruz

After Narvaez had received every information about Vera Cruz from the three deserters, he determined to despatch thither a priest named Guevara, who was a capital hand at talking, and a certain Amaya, a man of great distinction, and a relative of Velasquez; besides a secretary named Vergara and three witnesses, whose names I have forgotten. These gentlemen were to announce his arrival, and summon the town to surrender; and, to make sure work, were provided with a copy of Narvaez appointment.

Sandoval had already been apprized of the arrival of Narvaez by the inhabitants. But as he was a man who was always upon the alert, and possessed of great penetration, he immediately guessed that the armament was fitted out by Velasquez, and that his object was to gain possession of Vera Cruz; he therefore instantly adopted every precaution, and commenced by sending all the invalid soldiers to the Indian township Papalote, merely retaining those who were in good health. He then posted watches along the road leading to Sempoalla, which Narvaez would be obliged to take if he marched to Vera Cruz. Sandoval also made his men promise him neither to surrender the town to Velasquez nor any one else, and that none of his men might forget their promise he ordered a gallows to be erected on an elevated spot outside the town.

When the outposts brought Sandoval information that six Spaniards were approaching the town, he retired into his own house to await their arrival; for he was determined not to go out to receive these guests, and had also issued orders to his men not to quit their quarters, nor exchange a single word with the strangers.

When, therefore, the priest Guevara and his companions arrived in the town, they only saw some Indians, who were working at the fortifications, but not a Spaniard to speak to; they walked straightway into the church to pray, and then repaired to Sandoval's house, which they recognized from its being the largest one in the town.

After the first greetings had passed between them, the priest began his discourse by stating to Sandoval what large sums of money Velasquez had expended on the armament which went out under the command of Cortes, who, with the whole of the men, had turned traitors to the governor; and concluded by saying, that he came to summon him in the name of Narvaez, whom Velasquez had appointed captain-general, to deliver up the town to him.

When Sandoval heard this, and the expressions which reflected dishonour on Cortes, he could scarcely speak, from downright vexation; at length he replied: "Venerable sir, you are wrong to term men traitors who have proved themselves better servants to our emperor than Velasquez has, or your commander; and that I do not now this instant punish you for this affront, is merely owing to your being a priest. Go, therefore, in the name of God, to Mexico; there you will find Cortes, who is captain-general, and chief justice of New Spain. He will answer you himself; here you had better not lose another word."

At this moment the priest, with much bravado, ordered the secretary Vergara to produce the appointment of Narvaez, and read it to Sandoval, and the others present. Sandoval, however, desired the secretary to leave his papers quietly where they were, as it was impossible for him to say whether the appointment was a lawful one or not. But as the secretary still persisted in producing his papers, Sandoval cried out to him: "Mind what you are about, Vergara! I have already told you to keep your papers in your pocket; go with them to Mexico! I promise you, the moment you proceed to read a single syllable from them, 100 good lashes on the spot. How can I tell whether you are a royal secretary or not? First show me your appointment; and if I find you are, I will listen to your papers. But, even then, who can prove to me whether your papers are true or false?"

The priest, who was a very haughty man, then cried out, "Why do you stand upon any ceremony with these traitors? Pull out your papers, and read the contents to them!"

To which Sandoval answered: "You lie, you infamous priest!" and ordered his men immediately to seize those gentlemen, and carry them off to Mexico.

He had hardly spoken, when they were seized by a number of Indians employed at the fortifications, bound hand and foot, and thrown upon the backs of porters. In this way they were transported to Mexico, where they arrived in the space of four days; the Indian porters being constantly relieved by others on the road.

These gentlemen were not a little surprised at this rough treatment; but the deeper they advanced into the country, the more astonished they grew, at the sight of the large towns and villages, where they stopped to take refreshment. They were, it is said, very doubtful within themselves whether all was not enchantment, or merely a dream.

Sandoval had sent Pedro de Solis, Orduña's son-in-law, as *alguacil*, to accompany the escort; and he likewise informed Cortes, by letter, of everything that was going on at the coast, and of the name of the captain who commanded the flotilla. The letter even arrived before the prisoners in Mexico; so that Cortes was apprized of their approach when they were still at some distance from the town.

He immediately despatched some men with a quantity of the best provisions, and three horses, for the most distinguished of the prisoners, with orders that they should be immediately released from their fetters. He likewise wrote them a letter, in which he expressed his regret that they should have met with such harsh treatment from Sandoval, and that he would give them the most honourable reception. Indeed he even went out to meet them himself, and escorted them into the town.

The priest and his companions—after they became acquainted with the vast extent of Mexico, and the number of other towns built in the lake, saw the quantity of gold which every one of us possessed, and the noble and open countenance of Cortes—were quite enchanted; and they had not been above a couple of days with us before Cortes succeeded so well to tame them, by kind words, fair promises, jewels, and bars of gold, that they, who had come like furious lions, now returned back to Narvaez as harmless as lambs, and offered to render our general every service in their power. Indeed, when they had arrived in Sempoalla, and given Narvaez an account of all they had seen, they spoke of nothing else to his men than of the policy to make common cause with us.

I will, however, break off here, and acquaint the reader with the letter which Cortes wrote to Narvaez.

Chapter 112
Cortes Writes to Narvaez

Cortes was a man who never allowed the smallest advantage to escape; and whatever difficulty he might be in, he managed to get out of it. But it must also be remembered, that he had the good fortune to command officers and soldiers on whom he could place every reliance under all circumstances, who not only lent a powerful arm in battle, but likewise assisted him with their prudent counsel. In this way, then, it was unanimously resolved in council, that a letter should be despatched by Indian couriers to Narvaez, written in the most affectionate tone, with offers of our services to him, and begging of him not to excite a rebellion in the country, which would certainly be the case if the Indians observed we were at enmity with each other. This letter was to be delivered to Narvaez before the return there of Guevara. We expressly wrote in this friendly tone, as our numbers were so very small in comparison to his, and because we were first desirous of knowing how he was inclined. Besides this, we employed other means to gain friends among Narvaez's officers, which seemed no great difficulty, as Guevara had assured Cortes that the latter were not on the best terms with their commander, and that a few bars of gold, with a few chains of the same metal, would soon pave the way. In this letter Cortes informed Narvaez how both he and all his men were rejoiced at his arrival here; in particular himself, as they were old friends. He also desired he would not connive at the liberation of Motecusuma, as the consequences would be a rebellion in the city, and throughout the whole country, which would be the destruction of both his troops and ours, as we should be overwhelmed by numbers. He could not help drawing his particular attention to this circumstance, as Motecusuma of late seemed greatly changed in his behaviour towards him, and the inhabitants were upon the point of rising up in arms, from the message which Motecusuma had received in Narvaez's name; but he was convinced that he was too prudent and sensible a man, and would not have sent such a dangerous message at such a critical period, if he had not been misled by the three scoundrels who had run over to him. To make a good finish to the letter, he begged to say that Narvaez was at liberty to dispose of his person and of his purse, and he would await his commands.

Cortes at the same time wrote to Andreas de Duero and Vazquez de Aillon, and accompanied these letters with some gold for themselves and his other friends. Aillon, besides this, privately received some other gold bars and chains. He also despatched father Olmedo to Narvaez's headquarters with a good stock of these persuasive articles, consisting in various trinkets of gold and precious stones of great value.

The first letter which Cortes had sent by the Indian courier reached Narvaez's quarters before Guevara had returned there. This Narvaez read aloud to his officers, and kept the whole time making merry at the expense of Cortes and all of us. One of his officers, named Salvatierra, even blamed him for reading the letter of such a traitor as Cortes was, to his men. Narvaez, continued he, should immediately march out against us, and put us all to death. He himself, he swore, would cut off Cortes' ears, broil them, and eat them up; and all such like folly. He said the letter ought not to be answered, and he did not care a snap of the fingers for us.

In the meantime the priest, Guevara, and his companions, had returned, and the latter gave Narvaez a circumstantial account of Cortes, showing him what an excellent cavalier he was, and what a faithful servant he had proved himself to our emperor. He spoke about the great power of Motecusuma, and the number of towns through which he had journeyed, and that Cortes would gladly submit to him. He also added, that it was for the advantage of both to remain on friendly terms with each other. New Spain was large enough to afford room for them both, and Narvaez might choose which part of the country he would occupy with his troops.

These statements, which Amaya and Guevara had accompanied by some good advice, so greatly incensed Narvaez, that he would neither see nor speak to them from that moment. The impression, however, it produced on the troops was various; for when they saw the gold these two men returned with, and heard so much good of Cortes and all of us, and heard them speak of the wondrous things they had seen, and the vast quantity of gold, and how we played at cards for gold only, many of them longed to join our corps.

Shortly after this, father Olmedo likewise arrived in Narvaez's quarters with bars of gold and secret instructions. When he called upon him to pay him Cortes' respects, and said how ready he was to obey Narvaez's commands, and remain on terms of peace with him, the latter grew more enraged than before. He even refused to listen to him, and called Cortes and all of us traitors; and when Olmedo denied this, and told him we were the most faithful of the emperor's servants, he grossly insulted him. All this, however, did not deter Olmedo from fulfilling his secret mission, and distributing the bars of gold and golden chains among those for whom Cortes had destined them; and he strove in every way to draw over Narvaez's principal officers to our side.

Chapter 113

A Prisoner to Spain

The auditor Aillon, as I have before mentioned, was most favourably inclined towards Cortes, and had purposely come to New Spain with instructions from the royal court of audience at St. Domingo and the Hieronymite brothers, who were aware of the great and important services we had rendered to God and the emperor, to promote our cause in every possible manner. After he had carefully perused Cortes' letters, and received the bars of gold, he no longer made a secret of his sentiments, but spoke without any reserve of the scandalous piece of injustice which had been perpetrated in fitting out this armament against such well-deserving men as we had proved ourselves, and was so eloquent in the praise of Cortes and his companions in arms, that the feeling in our favour became almost universal in Narvaez's headquarters. The meanness of the latter's disposition served to increase this feeling, who retained all the presents sent by Motecusuma entirely to himself, without offering any part of them either to his officers or men. Indeed, he even said haughtily to his steward, "Mind that not the smallest matter is taken away from these things; every article has been carefully noted down." When this conduct was compared with that pursued by Cortes towards his soldiers, his men almost broke out into open insurrection.

Narvaez looked upon the auditor as the cause of all this bad feeling, and brought it so sensibly home to him that no one durst give him or his adherents the smallest morsel of the provisions which were sent by Motecusuma. This circumstance of itself caused a good deal of quarrelling among the troops; but when Narvaez's principal adherents, Salvatierra, whom I have above mentioned, and a certain Juan Bono, from Biscay, with a certain Gamarra, continually added fuel to the flame, he, relying on the mighty support of Fonseca, lost sight of every consideration, imprisoned the auditor, with his secretary and all his attendants, threw them on board a vessel, and so sent them off either to Spain or Cuba.

His behaviour towards Gonzalo de Oblanco, a cavalier and a scholar, was even more severe,—when the latter boldly told him to his face that Cortes had proved himself a faithful servant to the emperor, that we all had merited a reward from his majesty, and that it was scandalous to brand us with the name of traitors, and great presumption to imprison one of his majesty's auditors, Narvaez instantly threw him into chains, and Oblanco, who was a high-spirited soul, was so hurt at this ill-treatment, that he died within the space of four days. Two other soldiers were thrown into prison merely because they had spoken well of Cortes; one of whom was Sancho de Barahona, who afterwards settled down in Guatimala.

But to return to the auditor, who was to be sent prisoner to Spain; he was scarcely at sea, when he prevailed upon the captain and pilot, by means of good words, or threats to hang them immediately on their arrival in Spain, instead of paying them for the passage, to steer for St. Domingo.

As soon as the auditor had arrived at St. Domingo, and the royal court of audience and viceroys there were informed of Narvaez's scandalous and presumptuous ill treatment of the licentiate Lucas Vazquez, they considered it in the light of an insult offered to themselves, and made heavy complaints to the supreme council of Castile. But as the bishop Fonseca was still president of that council, and, during his majesty's continued absence in Flanders, ruled affairs as he thought proper, no justice could be expected from Spain. The bishop had even the shamelessness openly to express his joy when he supposed that Narvaez had already subdued us. The bishop, himself, however, suffered from the consequences which ensued from this affair; for, when our agents in Flanders received intelligence of Velasquez's expedition, and found that it had been fitted out without his majesty's permission, and merely by authority of Fonseca, they drew great advantage from this illegal mode of proceeding during the investigation which was shortly after set on foot respecting Cortes and all of us.—The harsh treatment which the auditor Lucas Vazquez was subjected to had a bad effect upon Narvaez's troops, and many of his friends and relatives whom he regarded with a mistrustful eye, went over to Sandoval, lest they should experience similar treatment with Oblanco. Sandoval, as may well be imagined, received them with open arms, and learnt from them all that had passed in Narvaez's quarters; likewise that he contemplated sending men to Vera Cruz to take him prisoner.

Chapter 114
Narvaez marches to Sempoalla

After Narvaez had sent off the auditor prisoner, he marched with the whole of his men, the baggage, and the cannon, to Sempoalla, and quartered himself in that town, which was then very thickly populated. His first act there was to take away from the fat *cazique*, as we termed him, the cotton stuffs, gold trinkets, and other fancy articles he possessed. He likewise took the Indian females forcibly away who had been presented to us by the *caziques* of Sempoalla, and whom we had left behind with their parents and relatives, as they were daughters of distinguished personages, and much too delicate to bear the fatigues of a campaign.

The fat *cazique* had often warned Narvaez not to touch the women, or anything which Cortes had left behind in the shape of gold or cotton stuffs, as he would certainly be greatly incensed, hasten from Mexico, and not only cut off Narvaez, but also him, for suffering his property to be touched.

All the complaints this *cazique* might make respecting the depredations committed by Narvaez's troops in Sempoalla were equally fruitless. And it was of no avail for him to repeat that *Malinche* and his men had never taken the smallest thing from them, and had proved themselves altogether kind-hearted *teules*; Narvaez and Salvatierra, whose conduct in general was the most heartless, merely mocked at the *cazique*, the latter often repeating to Narvaez and the other officers, "Only just imagine in what fear these *caziques* stand of that paltry little fellow Cortes!"

May the good reader learn from this how wrong it is to speak evil of honest folks; for I am ready to swear that this very Salvatierra behaved in the most pitiable and cowardly manner when the battle was fought between Narvaez and us, and yet his build and bones were powerful enough to have defended himself right well; however, he was a mere braggadocio, and I believe he was a native of Burgos.

We must now, however, return to Cortes, and acquaint the reader that Narvaez despatched his secretary, Alonso Meta, who subsequently settled in Puebla, with three other great personages, to Mexico, commanding us and our general, by virtue of the copies of his appointment by Velasquez, to submit to him.[1]

Cortes, who received daily intelligence of what was going on in Narvaez's headquarters and at Vera Cruz, was duly informed by Sandoval how Narvaez had thrown Vazquez de Aillon into chains, and sent him to Spain or Cuba, and that, owing to such violent proceedings, five of his principal officers had come over to him, who feared, since so little respect had been paid to the person of a royal auditor, they, as Aillon's relatives, might expect worse treatment. From them Sandoval learnt everything that was passing in Narvaez's headquarters, and that it was his intention to march shortly in person to Mexico to take us all prisoners. Cortes, on receiving this intelligence, assembled his officers and all those whom he was accustomed to consult in matters of great moment, and were men entirely devoted to him. In this council it was determined we should anticipate Narvaez, and immediately march out against him. Pedro de Alvarado was to remain in Mexico, with all those who were not over-anxious to make this campaign, to guard the person of Motecusuma; and we likewise took care to leave all those behind who, as partisans of Velasquez, were not altogether to be trusted.

Cortes had fortunately ordered a quantity of maize from Tlascalla previous to the arrival of Narvaez, for the harvest had altogether failed about Mexico, owing to a continued drought: we, indeed, required a great quantity of provisions for the numbers of Naborias[2] and Tlascallan troops we had with us. This and other necessaries of life, consisting in fowls, fruits, &c., arrived at the time appointed, and were given in charge of Alvarado. We likewise took the precaution of fortifying our quarters,—we mounted four pieces of heavy cannon on the most commanding point, and left Alvarado a few falconets and all the powder we could spare, with ten crossbow-men, fourteen musketeers, and seven horse soldiers; the latter were, indeed, more than he required, as the cavalry was of little use in the courtyards attached to our quarters. The number of soldiers we left behind in Mexico was altogether eighty-three.

1. This Alonso Mata, as we afterwards see, was met on his way to Mexico by Cortes.

2. Naborias, Indian servants.

Motecusuma easily conjectured what our designs were against Narvaez; yet, though Cortes daily called upon him, he was equally upon his guard as Cortes was in not throwing out any hints of his (Motecusuma's) sending Narvaez gold and provisions. It was only at the very last that the monarch made some inquiries respecting our intended movements, which will be found in the chapter following.

Chapter 115

Motecusuma Queries Cortes' Intentions

The monarch, one day discoursing as usual with Cortes, spoke to him as follows: "*Malinche*! I have for some time past observed all your officers and soldiers going up and down in great uneasiness: even you yourself do not visit me so frequently as you were wont; and the page Orteguilla informs me that you are about to march against your brothers who have just arrived, and that you are going to leave Tonatio (so Alvarado was termed by the Mexicans) behind, to guard my person. Do tell me if there is any truth in all this? for if, in any way, I can be of service to you in this matter, it will be a great pleasure to me. I have great fears of your success, for your *teules* are too few in numbers in comparison to those just arrived. They have five times the number of troops you have; they also, as well as yourself, maintain to be Christians, and subjects of your emperor; they pay homage to the same image and cross, read the mass as you do, and everywhere spread the rumour that you have fled away from Spain from your emperor, and that he has sent them to take you back again, or put you to death. Really I scarcely know what to think of all this: one thing, however, I must tell you, to use great circumspection in what you are about to do."

In reply to this, Cortes told the monarch, with the most cheerful countenance in the world, that he had studiously avoided mentioning anything of all this up to the present moment, from his great affection towards him, to spare him the anxiety he would feel on our account. It was very true, the newly arrived *teules* were also subjects of our emperor, and Christians; but it was a falsehood to assert that we had fled away from the territory of our emperor. On the contrary, our great monarch had expressly sent us out to visit him,

Motecusuma, and make those disclosures to him, in his imperial name, which Motecusuma had heard. With regard to the numbers of those just arrived, we felt quite unconcerned, however great they might be in comparison to ours, as our Lord Jesus Christ and his blessed mother would lend us strength, and clothe us with superior power to those bad men who came with such evil designs. His emperor, continued Cortes, swayed the sceptre over so many countries and kingdoms, that the people who inhabited them were of various kinds, and differed in courage and manly spirit. We were born in the heart of Spain, which was termed Old Castile, and therefore bore the additional name of Castilians; those, on the other hand, who were now quartered at Sempoalla, came from another province called Biscay, where the inhabitants spoke a perfectly spurious language, in the same way as the Otomies do in Mexico. He need be in no apprehension about us, but might depend upon it we should very soon manage those fellows, and speedily return victorious to his metropolis. At present we merely begged of him to remain on terms of friendship with Tonatio, who would remain behind in Mexico with eighty men; and to prevent any insurrection from breaking out, and not to allow his generals and *papas* to disturb the peace; for, in case they did, he should be compelled to put them all to death on his return. He also desired he would furnish those who remained behind with the necessary provisions.

After this explanation, Motecusuma and Cortes embraced each other twice successively, while the sly Doña Marina observed to the monarch that he ought to show some signs of grief at our departure: upon which he again commenced speaking, and offered to comply with any wish Cortes might express, and promised to give him 5000 of his troops to accompany us on our march. Cortes, who well knew they would not have been forthcoming, thanked him for his kind offer, and assured him we stood in no need of his assistance, as we found our true support in the Lord our God: but begged of him to see that the image of the holy Virgin and the cross were constantly decorated with green boughs; that the church was kept clean, and wax-lights burning night and day on the altar; and not to allow his *papas* to sacrifice any human beings; and in his compliance with these things we should best be able to convince ourselves of the sincerity of his friendship.

After this Cortes told the monarch he must excuse him for breaking off the discourse now, as he had many things to regulate before commencing his march; he then once more embraced the monarch, and so they parted from each other.[1]

Cortes now ordered Alvarado and all those who were to remain behind in Mexico into his presence. He desired them to observe the utmost vigilance, and not to give Motecusuma a chance of escaping out of their hands, and commanded the soldiers to pay the most implicit obedience to Alvarado, promising, if God were willing, to enrich them all.

Among those who stayed with Alvarado was the priest Juan Diaz, and many others whom we suspected of ill will towards Cortes, whose names I do not choose to mention. We nevertheless embraced each other on leaving, and then marched out without any females or servants, with as little baggage as possible, and took the road to Cholulla. From this town Cortes sent to our friends Xicotencatl, Maxixcatzin, and the other *caziques* of Tlascalla, desiring them to send us immediately 4000 of their troops. To which they returned the answer, that if we were going to war with Indians as they were, they would gladly send us the required troops and many more; but if we intended fighting against *teules*, like unto ourselves, against cannon and horses, we were not to think ill of them if they refused our request. This answer was accompanied by as many fowls as twenty men could carry.

Cortes then sent a courier with a letter to Sandoval, desiring the latter to join him as speedily as possible with all his men; we intended to march to within forty-eight miles of Sempoalla, in the neighbourhood of the provinces of Tampanicita[2] and Mitalaguita, which are at present comprehended in the commendary of Pedro Moreno Mediana, who resides at Puebla; he particularly cautioned him to keep out of the way of Narvaez, and carefully to avoid coming to any engagement with any part of his troops.

We ourselves marched forward with every military precaution, and were ready for action at a moment's notice. Two of our most trustworthy men who were remarkably swift of foot and unwearied pedestrians, were constantly a couple of day's march in advance, and lurked along the byways, where the cavalry could not penetrate, to gain information of the Indians respecting Narvaez. Besides these we had always immediately in advance of us a small detachment of sharpshooters, to seize any of the men who strolled from Narvaez's camp,

1. According to Torquemada, Motecusuma, accompanied by a distinguished suite, conducted the Spaniards as far as Iztapalapan.

2. Probably Topaniqueta, which sounds more like an Indian name.

and if possible the latter himself. It was not long before they came up with a certain Alonso Mata, who termed himself a royal secretary, and was commissioned, he said, by Narvaez, to show us the copy of his appointment. This Mata was accompanied by four others, who were to act as witnesses on this occasion. When these people had arrived near enough they greeted Cortes and all of us in the most humble manner possible, and our general dismounted when he learnt who they were.

Alonso Mata began immediately to read his documents to us, but Cortes interrupted him, and asked him whether he was a royal secretary, and he replying in the affirmative, Cortes desired him to produce his appointment. If this was all regular, he added, he was at liberty to fulfil his commission, and he should know himself what was due from him as a servant of the emperor. But, if it was not, it was useless for him to read his papers; besides which, it was requisite the papers should contain the original appointment signed by the emperor himself, if he wished him to acknowledge his authority.

Mata was not a little staggered at being thus addressed, for he himself was well aware that he was no royal secretary. He was therefore unable to utter a single word, and those who accompanied him remained equally mute. Cortes excused their embarrassment, and desired some victuals to be set before them; and we halted for a few moments, when Cortes informed them we were marching to the township of Tampanicita, in the vicinity of Narvaez's headquarters, where, if the latter had any further communications to make, he was to be found. During the whole of this discourse Cortes showed such self-command, that he never so much as uttered a single reproachful word against Narvaez; he had also a private discourse with them, and thrust a few pieces of gold into their hands; so that they left us highly delighted, and on their return to Narvaez they could scarcely say sufficient in praise of Cortes and of us all.

While these men were still with us, many of our soldiers, for the sake of ostentation, had decorated themselves with gold chains and jewels, which spread a vast idea of our splendour. All this produced such a favourable impression in Narvaez's headquarters, that many of his chief officers desired that peace might be brought about between both generals.

In the meantime we continued our march, and arrived in Tampanicita, where Sandoval the day following likewise appeared with his small detachment, consisting of sixty men; the old and infirm of the garrison, as I have above mentioned, having been previously quartered among our allies, the Papalote Indians. He likewise brought along with him the five friends and relatives of Aillon, who had deserted from Narvaez, and had long desired to pay their respects to Cortes, who gave them the most friendly reception, and then entered into a private conversation with Sandoval, who related to him all the particulars respecting the affair with the furious priest Guevara and his companion Vergara. Sandoval likewise told him how he had sent two Spanish soldiers into Narvaez's headquarters disguised as Indians. They had the exact appearance of natives, took each a basket of cherries with them, and did as if they were desirous of selling them. They soon met with a purchaser, in the person of the *braggadocio* Salvatierra, who gave them a string of glass beads for their fruit, and fully believing they were Indians, sent them to cut some grass for his horse. It was about the hour of Ave-Maria, when they returned with a load of grass, and carried it to the shed, where the horse was tied up. They then cowered down, after the fashion of Indians, near Salvatierra's quarters, and overheard a discourse between him and several others of Narvaez's officers. Among other things they heard Salvatierra exclaim, "O! at what a fortunate time we have arrived in this country, just as the traitor Cortes has collected above 700,000 *pesos*! We shall all become wealthy; for his officers and soldiers all together cannot have a much less sum than that in their pockets."

They listened to many similar fine speeches till a late hour at night, when they stole off silently to the shed where Salvatierra's horse was fastened up, which they very quietly saddled and bridled, and so rode off with it. In the same way they managed to capture a second horse on their road home, and brought them both safely to Sandoval.

Cortes was very desirous to see those horses, but Sandoval told him he had left them with the invalid soldiers in Papalote, as he had marched along a very steep and rugged road over the mountains, where horses could not pass, which he had done that he might not fall in with Narvaez's troops.

Cortes was vastly pleased with the trick which had been played off upon Salvatierra, and the manner in which he had lost his horse, and exclaimed, "He will now threaten us with more vengeance than ever!" The following morning, we were told, when he found the two Indians, who sold him the cherries had decamped with his horse, saddle, and bridle, he threw out language really laughable, particularly when he discovered they had been disguised Spaniards belonging to Cortes' troops.

Chapter 116

Olmedo Goes to Narvaez's Headquarters

As soon as all our troops had arrived at Tampanicita, we determined to despatch father Olmedo, who was a remarkably shrewd man, to Narvaez with a letter, which, after expressing the usual courtesies, ran nearly as follows:

We all rejoiced at his arrival in this country, as we were confident that, in conjunction with such a valiant captain as he was, we should be able to render important services to God and to our emperor. It was true he had not only neglected to answer our previous letter, but had even branded us, his majesty's faithful subjects, with the name of traitors; and, by means of the message he had conveyed to Motecusuma, the whole country was about to burst out into open insurrection. We hereby begged of him to select that province which he fancied most for himself and troops; we were very willing to make room for him, and to act in every respect as beseemed faithful servants of the emperor. We had likewise requested him to forward us the original papers of his appointment, if he possessed any such, that we might convince ourselves they were signed by his majesty. However, he had not even listened to this request, but had thrown out abusive language against us, and incited the inhabitants of the country to revolt. We now again begged of him, in the name of God, and the emperor our master, to forward us his papers within the space of three days by a royal secretary, that he might read them to us; as we were ready, and also promised to act up strictly to his majesty's commands, if his documents were correct. For this purpose we had expressly come to Tampanicita, to be near his person. If he was unable to produce any such appointment direct from his majesty, and he was again desirous of returning to Cuba, he was at liberty to do so; we merely desired him to desist from stirring up the inhabitants into open insurrection, or we should consider ourselves bound to treat him as an enemy, take him prisoner, and send him in chains to the emperor, without whose authority he had commenced war upon us, and revolutionised all the towns of the country. Every drop of blood that was spilt, all destruction of property which would ensue from fire or otherwise, he would himself have to answer for.

Our reason for communicating these things to him by letter only was, because no royal secretary durst venture to convey them in person, fearing he might share a similar fate with the auditor Aillon; and we were astonished how he durst presume to act so daringly. Cortes considered himself bound in honour and justice to his majesty not to allow such a heavy offence to pass by unpunished; and he hereby summoned him, by virtue of his office as captain-general and chief-justice of New Spain, to appear before him and answer the charge preferred against him of *criminis laesae majestatis*. Lastly, he earnestly begged of him to return the cotton stuffs and gold trinkets he had forcibly taken away from the fat *cazique*; to deliver up to their parents again the Indian females who had been presented to us; and to command his men in no way to touch the property of the inhabitants.

This letter, which closed with the usual courteous expressions, was signed by Cortes, the officers, and other soldiers, among whom was myself. With this letter father Olmedo, accompanied by one of our men, named Bartolome de Usagre, who had a brother serving in Narvaez's artillery, went off to the latter's headquarters. What kind of reception they met with will be found in the chapter following.

CHAPTER 117

Father Olmedo at Sempoalla

As soon as father Olmedo had arrived at Narvaez's headquarters, he began to fulfil the orders which Cortes had given him. He made secret disclosures in Cortes' name to a number of cavaliers in Narvaez's corps, also to the artillerymen Rodrigo, Mino, and Usagre; and gave them the bars of gold which our general had destined for them. He likewise proposed to Andreas de Duero to pay a visit to our camp, and then called upon Narvaez himself.

Although Olmedo comported himself particularly humble in presence of Narvaez, yet the latter's confidants had their suspicions, and advised their general to throw the father into prison, which was just about being carried into effect, when Duero, private secretary to Velasquez, was secretly apprized of it.

Duero was a native of Tudela, on the Duero, and Narvaez came from the neighbourhood of Valladolid, or from the town itself, and they were not only countrymen, but also related to each other. This Duero had vast influence, stood high in the estimation of the men, and durst take more upon himself than others; he therefore called upon Narvaez, and told him he had been informed of his intention to imprison father Olmedo; and he considered himself called upon to observe, that no good could flow from such a step; for though there might be sufficient grounds for supposing he was intriguing for Cortes, yet, as a messenger from him, he ought not to be ill treated; the more so, because Cortes had honourably received all those whom Narvaez had despatched to him, and dismissed them with presents. Ever since father Olmedo had been here, he had himself frequently discoursed with him; but from all he had uttered could only conclude that Cortes, with the whole of his officers, was desirous of being on friendly terms with Narvaez. He ought likewise to remember that Cortes took every opportunity of speaking in his praise; indeed Cortes, as well as all his men, never pronounced the name of Narvaez but with profound respect, and it would be a small piece of heroism to seize upon the person of a priest; and the other man, who had come with him, was brother to the artilleryman Usagre; it would be therefore better in every respect if they received polite treatment; and he would advise him to ask the father to dinner, when he could himself fish out from him what the views of Cortes were.

With these and such like kind-words, Duero succeeded in softening down Narvaez's anger; upon which the former immediately communicated to father Olmedo all that had transpired. Narvaez then sent for the father to dine with him, and received him most courteously.

Father Olmedo, who was a remarkably judicious and shrewd man, requested Narvaez, with a pleasing smile, to grant him a private interview; and they walked up and down together in the courtyard, when Olmedo addressed him to the following effect: "I am well aware that your excellency had the intention to take me prisoner; though I can assure you there is not a person belonging to your staff more devoted to you than I am. I am likewise convinced that several cavaliers and officers in Cortes' troops would gladly see the latter in your power; indeed I am altogether convinced that we shall all soon stand under your commands. In order to make the necessary preparations for such a step, they have written you a letter full of extravagant expressions, and got it signed by several of our men. This letter I was ordered to hand over to your excellency; but, on account of its contents, I could not make up my mind to do so, but felt more inclined to throw it into the river."

Narvaez then expressed a desire to see this letter, and father Olmedo told him he had left it in his room, but would go for it, and left Narvaez for that purpose. In the meantime Salvatierra, the *braggadocio*, had come up to the latter; while Olmedo hastened to Duero, requesting him to be present when he handed over the letter to Narvaez, and bring with him as many other soldiers as possible, that its contents might be made known to all. Olmedo now returned to Narvaez, and presented him Cortes' letter, with these words: "Your excellency must not feel astonished if in this letter you find Cortes speaking out a little at random; however, notwithstanding all this, I can assure you, if you express yourself in kind terms to him, he will submit to you, with the whole of his troops."

All the bystanders now pressed Narvaez to read the letter; some were greatly annoyed, but Narvaez and Salvatierra merely laughed, and made game of the contents. Duero, however, said: "Really I am unable to make anything out of all this! The reverend father has assured me, that Cortes and the whole of his men are ready to join our standard, and yet they presume to write such nonsense to our general." Augustin Bermudez, who was a captain and *alguacil*-major of Narvaez's camp, followed in the same strain and said: "Father Olmedo has likewise assured me privately, that it merely required some little mediation between them, and Cortes would himself wait upon our general and join his standard with the whole of his men. As he is encamped not far from here, we could certainly do no better than despatch Señor Salvatierra and Señor Duero thither, and I will accompany them myself." This Bermudez merely said to see what Salvatierra would say, who immediately declared that he felt no inclination to visit a traitor.

Do not speak quite so rashly, Señor Salvatierra, said father Olmedo; for by showing a little more moderation you will be able, in a few days, to have him in your power.

However it was resolved that Duero should be despatched to Cortes, and Narvaez held a private conference with him and three other officers, desiring them to try and persuade Cortes to meet him at an Indian village on the road between the two encampments, where they might come to an understanding with each other respecting the division of the country and the boundaries of their respective territories. Narvaez was quite earnest in this matter, and had expressed himself to that effect to about twenty of his men, who were particularly devoted to him. This circumstance soon came to the ears of father Olmedo and Duero, who immediately apprized Cortes of it.

We must now, for a time, leave father Olmedo in Narvaez's camp, where he soon became very intimate with Salvatierra, as the latter was a native of Burgos and he himself of Olmedo, and he dined with him every day. In the meantime we will likewise allow Duero to make preparations for his journey, on which he was accompanied by Usagre, that Narvaez might not fish anything out of him. We must now see what took place in our own camp during this interval.

Chapter 118

Cortes Reviews His Troops

As soon as Cortes was apprized of Narvaez's arrival in New Spain, and had received every information respecting the magnitude of his armament, he despatched a soldier who had served in the Italian campaigns, and who possessed an extensive knowledge of weapons and of the best method of fixing points to lances, into the province of the Tchinantecs,[1] where some of our men had gone in search of gold mines. The Tchinantecs were deadly enemies to the Mexicans, and had only a few days previously made an alliance with us. This people used a species of lance, which was much longer than our Spanish lances, and furnished with a sharp double-edged point made of flint.[2]

Cortes had heard of this weapon, and sent word to the Tchinantecs to forward him three hundred of such lances, from which however he desired they would take off the flint points and substitute a double one of metal, as they had abundance of copper in their country. The soldier who was despatched with these orders took a pattern of the point required with him. Cortes' wishes were readily complied with, and as the inhabitants of every township of that province set diligently to work, the lances were soon finished and they turned out most satisfactory. Besides this, Cortes desired the soldier Tovilla to ask the Tchinantecs to send 2000 of their warriors, all armed with similar lances, on Easter day, into the district of Panguenequita,[3] and there

1. The real name of this province was Chinantla, but our author calls the inhabitants Tchichinatecs.

2. *Hierro* is the Spanish word for iron, and Bernal Diaz always uses Hierro for the point of a lance; otherwise one would suppose,—when he says of the Chinantecs, *"Hizíeron los hierros muy mas perfetamente,"* etc., i.e. "they made the irons (points) much more perfect;"—that the working of iron was known in the country long before the arrival of the Spaniards; but it is evident, from what he says four lines below, that these points were made of copper.

3. Panguenequita, probably another name for Tapanigueta.

make inquiries for our camp. The *caziques* willingly complied with our request, and they also gave Tovilla above 200 of their warriors, all armed with the same lances, to accompany him now on his return to our camp. The rest were to follow with another of our men, called Barrientos, who had been despatched into their country in search of mines, and he may have been from forty to forty-eight miles further inland. The lances which Tovilla brought with him proved most excellent, and he immediately taught us how to use them, particularly against the cavalry.

Upon this Cortes reviewed the whole of his troops, and we found, including all the officers, drummers and pipers, without father Olmedo, our numbers amounted to 260 men, among whom were five cavalrymen, a few crossbow-men, less musketeers, and two artillerymen. Considering the smallness of our numbers we reposed our greatest hopes in the use we intended making of our lances, in which fortunately we were not disappointed, as will afterwards be seen.

Chapter 119

Duero Arrives in Our Camp

I must now trouble the reader to turn back to the first part of this history where I explained how Cortes obtained the appointment of commander-in-chief through the instrumentality of Duero and Amador de Lares: both of whom were on the most confidential terms with Diego Velasquez; the former as his private secretary, the second as royal treasurer. They had by their joint exertions procured Cortes the appointment, who, on his part, again promised to divide with them all the gold, silver, and jewels which should fall to his share. When Duero arrived in our camp he was convinced, from what he saw, of the vast riches and power of Cortes, and he came not merely to bring about a good understanding between both generals, but also to take possession of his share of the acquired riches; as Amador de Lares had died.

Cortes, who was a cunning and far-sighted man, promised Duero not only vast treasures but a command, which would give him the same importance with himself, and he would bestow a vast extent of territory upon him. In consideration of which the latter was to engage to gain Augustin Bermudez, and other chief officers, whose names I will not mention; who were to swear upon their life and honour to oppose Narvaez in every way, and thwart him in all his designs upon us. If Narvaez was killed or taken prisoner, and his army defeated, all the gold and the townships of New Spain were to be divided among the three. To this Bermudez was to be bound down by affixing his signature to these conditions. In order, however, to strengthen the number of their party, Duero took along with him as much gold as two men could carry, besides a quantity of other valuable things, for Bermudez, the two priests, Guevara and Juan de Leon, and other chief personages who were to be let into the secret. Cortes and Duero then carefully talked over how the matter was to be carried out.

Duero arrived in our quarters on the eve of Easter day, and stayed until the evening following. During this time he had several private conversations with Cortes, and before mounting his horse he again called upon the latter, who was heard to say on taking leave of him: "Well, Señor Duero, may God bless you. Remember to abide by all you have promised! Before three days have passed I shall be with my troops in your headquarters; if, however, I find you have not remained true to your word, upon my conscience, (an oath he often used,) you will be the first my lance shall pierce."

To which Duero answered smilingly: "You need be under no apprehension, I assure you. Nothing shall be omitted on my part to further your ends."

Duero then mounted his horse and returned to Narvaez with the most satisfactory accounts, and assured him that Cortes and all of us desired nothing more ardently than to stand under his command. As soon as Duero had left, Cortes sent for Juan Velasquez de Leon, one of his chief officers, a man who had great authority, and although a near relative to the governor of Cuba, was entirely devoted to Cortes. Cortes had also gained him over to his interest by valuable presents and promises of an important command in New Spain, even to raise him as high in command as himself; and, indeed, Velasquez always evinced the most honest attachment to our general, and was unremitting in his services to him, as will sufficiently be seen hereafter.

When Velasquez de Leon came into Cortes' presence, and inquired his commands, the latter said to him with a pleasing smile on his countenance, "I have sent for you, Velasquez, because Duero had assured me it is rumoured among Narvaez's officers that you and I have quarrelled, and that you intend siding with their party. I am, therefore, resolved that you shall ride on your powerful gray mare to Narvaez's headquarters, taking with you all your gold, besides your *fanfarrona*, (so Velasquez termed a heavy gold chain he possessed,) and other valuable matters I shall give you, among which there will be a *fanfarrona* double the weight of yours. When there, you must try to fish out what Narvaez's intentions are. After you, Ordas shall likewise repair thither, as if he came to pay his respects to Narvaez in his capacity of house-steward to the governor of Cuba."

To this Juan Velasquez answered, that he would gladly fulfil his commands, but must refuse either to take his gold or his chain with him. If he were desirous of furnishing him with any valuable trinkets for some other persons, he would promise to deliver them safely;

where he went himself, he thought, he would be better able to serve him by his proper wits than with all the gold and jewels put together. "Of this," replied Cortes, "I am also fully convinced, which is the reason I made choice of you; but if you refuse to take all your gold and valuables with you, you had much better remain here."

Juan Velasquez still refused to comply for some time, when Cortes took him aside, and spoke a few words to him in private; Velasquez then yielded to his request, and set out on his journey, accompanied by Juan del Rio, one of Cortes' servants.

As soon as Velasquez, whom Cortes had merely despatched to Narvaez to annoy the latter, had departed, he issued orders to the drummer Canillas, and our piper Benito, to sound their instruments, and desired Sandoval to draw up the troops in marching order, and we moved briskly forward to Sempoalla. On our road we killed two musk swine, which our soldiers construed into a token of victory. The night following, we encamped on the slope of a hill near to a brook, made, as was our custom, bolsters of large stones, carefully posted our sentinels, and ordered the patrols.

The next morning we marched forward in a straight line, and arrived towards midday at that river on whose banks the town of Vera Cruz at present stands, and goods are landed which arrive from Spain. At that time we found merely a few Indian huts and straggling trees there, under which we rested ourselves for a considerable time, as we found the heat very oppressive. We must now return to Juan Velasquez, and see what befell him in Narvaez's camp.

CHAPTER 120

Juan Velasquez Arrives at Narvaez's Headquarters

Juan Velasquez travelled so fast that he arrived at Sempoalla towards daybreak. He alighted at the house of the fat *cazique*; as the servant whom Cortes had sent with him had no horse, he therefore walked on foot to Narvaez's quarters. The Indians of Sempoalla all recognized him, and were highly pleased to see and converse with him again. When, however, some of Narvaez's men, who were quartered in the *cazique*'s house, heard the Indians say that it was Velasquez de Leon, one of *Malinche*'s officers, they hastened to Narvaez, and told him they brought a piece of news for which they might expect a reward. And before Leon had arrived at the latter's quarters, Narvaez, who was highly delighted to hear of his arrival, hastened out, accompanied by several of his officers, to meet him, and received him with a hearty embrace. After they had entered his abode, he requested Velasquez to take a chair, (for in this expedition they had even furnished themselves with such things,) and reproached him in a friendly tone for not having alighted at his quarters, and immediately sent some of his men for his horse and baggage, as he would not hear of his staying in any house but his own. Velasquez, however, observed, that he could not stay long, as he had merely come to pay his respects to him and his officers, and try if peace and friendship could not be brought about between his excellency and Cortes.

Narvaez's blood rose to his cheeks at this expression, and he asked Velasquez how he could talk of peace and friendship with a man who had, like a traitor, run away with the whole armament of his own cousin, the governor of Cuba?

Juan Velasquez replied, in an equally sharp tone of voice, that Cortes was not a traitor, but a faithful servant to his emperor; that such services as he had rendered to the crown could not be termed the actions of a traitor, and he must beg of him not again to make use of such expressions in his presence.

Upon this Narvaez assumed a different tone, and made Velasquez vast promises if he would remain with him; even promised him, and sealed it with an oath, that he would elevate him to second in command to himself, if he would manage to induce Cortes' troops to join his standard of their own free will. Velasquez, however, assured him he should consider himself the vilest of traitors if he deserted a general to whom he had sworn fidelity, and of whom he was convinced that everything he had done in New Spain was for the emperor's best interest. On the contrary, he was determined to remain as faithful and true to Cortes as to the emperor himself, and he earnestly begged of him not to touch upon that string again.

During this conversation, Narvaez's chief officers had, by degrees, all arrived to pay their respects to Velasquez, which they did with every show of courtesy, as Velasquez was a man of elegant carriage and powerful stature, and had a winning countenance; his beard looked majestic, a heavy gold chain hung from his shoulder in graceful folds, and sat well on this courageous and spirited officer. After this discourse with Narvaez, Velasquez turned to the other officers, and entered into private conversation with father Olmedo, Duero, and Bermudez.

Narvaez's party, however, were of a different opinion with respect to Velasquez, and some of the officers, among whom were Gamarra, Juan Yuste, Juan Bono de Quexo, and the *braggadocio* Salvatierra, pressed Narvaez very hard to throw him into chains, as he was secretly striving to gain over his men in favour of Cortes. This Narvaez was very willing to do, and had already issued orders to that purpose, when Bermudez, Duero, and several others who favoured our general, received intimation thereof, and remonstrated with Narvaez as to the policy of such a step, and the benefit he would derive from it, as Cortes, though he had an additional hundred officers such as Velasquez, would be unable to cope with him. He should also bear in mind how Cortes had received all those who visited his camp; how well he had treated every one, and presented them so plentifully with jewels and other matters, that every one, up to the present moment, had left him laden like bees returning to their hives. It was equally in Cortes' power to have detained Duero, the priest Guevara, and others; this, however, he had not done, but, on the contrary, had shown them every possible respect. It would certainly be more to

Narvaez's advantage to behave courteously to Velasquez in return, and invite him to dinner on the following day.

Narvaez was fully convinced of the truth of these arguments, and requested Velasquez, in the kindest terms, to become mediator between Cortes and himself, and try if he could not succeed to induce the former and his troops to join his standard; and then invited him to dinner on the next day. Velasquez promised to make the attempt, but, at the same time, stated that he entertained few hopes of success, as Cortes was very determined on that head. The best method of settling the matter, in his opinion, was, by a division of the provinces between both generals, and Cortes would gladly leave the choice to him.

Velasquez, however, merely made this observation to make Narvaez a little more tractable. During this discourse, father Olmedo stepped up, and, as one of Narvaez's confidential friends and advisers, (for thus far he had succeeded with him,) proposed, that he should draw out the whole of his troops, with the cavalry and artillery, before Velasquez and his servant Juan, to show them the powerful army he commanded, and that they might relate what they had seen to Cortes, which would certainly produce the desired effect, and convince him he could not do better than submit to him. Narvaez followed this counsel, which Olmedo had merely advised to vex all his cavaliers and soldiers. The alarm was accordingly sounded, and the whole of the troops were thus obliged to march out before Velasquez, his servant Juan, and father Olmedo.

After Velasquez had gazed upon the troops for some time, he said to Narvaez, "Certainly, your excellency's power is considerable, and may God grant you a further increase of it!"

"Well," replied Narvaez, "are you now not fully convinced that it would merely cost me a day's march to overthrow Cortes and the whole of you?"

"I will not say anything about that," said Velasquez; "but you may depend upon it we should not sell our lives cheaply."

The following day Velasquez was to dine with Narvaez. At table he likewise met a nephew of the governor of Cuba, who bore the same name, and had the command of a company. During dinnertime, the conversation turned upon Cortes' obstinacy, and the letter he had written to Narvaez; and, one word leading to another, Diego Velasquez asserted, at length, that Cortes and all those who sided with him were traitors for not submitting to Narvaez.

At this expression, Juan Velasquez rose up from his seat, and said, with much warmth, "General Narvaez, I have once previously begged of you not to allow such language in my presence against Cortes or any man of his troops. It is really scandalous to speak ill of us who have served his majesty so faithfully."

"And I," interrupted Diego Velasquez, in an angry tone, "maintain that I have merely spoken the truth in calling you traitors. You are a traitor, and all the rest of you, and you are unworthy the name of Velasquez which you bear."

Leon now laid hand on his sword, and called Diego a liar; swearing he was a better nobleman than he or his uncle, and that the house of Velasquez to which he belonged was a very different one to Diego's or his uncle's. Of this he would give instant proof if General Narvaez would allow him.

As many of Narvaez's officers and a few of Cortes' were present during this scene, they interfered and prevented any open violence, as Leon was just about to draw his sword against his opponent.

The other officers now advised Narvaez to order Juan Velasquez, his servant, and father Olmedo to quit their camp without any further ceremony, as their stay there would only cause worse blood. Orders to this effect were accordingly issued, and our men delayed not an instant to hasten their departure. Leon was seated on his fine mare, and clad in his coat of mail, which he scarcely ever put off, and had his helmet on, when he once more called upon Narvaez to take leave. Young Diego Velasquez was standing next to the latter at the time, and when Leon inquired of Narvaez if he had any message to Cortes, he replied, in great ill humour, "I beg of you to leave this instant, and it would have been much better if you had stayed away altogether." Young Velasquez then opened his mouth, and threw out most abusive language against him. Leon, in return, assured him his insolence would meet with its due reward, and a few days would show whether the bravery of his arm corresponded with the boldness of his tongue. As they were continually growing more bitter in their expressions, five or six of Cortes' adherents among Narvaez's officers, who intended to escort Leon, came up, and told him, rather harshly, it was time to be moving, and no longer to spend his breath in useless words. They merely assumed this tone to get him as quickly out of the way as possible, for they afterwards told him that Narvaez had already issued orders for seizing his person; indeed, he had every reason to make haste, for a numerous body of cavalry was already hard at his heels when he arrived at the river above mentioned.—We were just taking our midday's nap when our outpost brought information that two or three men on horseback were approaching our camp, and we immediately concluded it must be Leon, his servant Juan, and father Olmedo.

Cortes and all of us were delighted to see them safely returned. Leon then related what the reader has just heard, and how he had secretly distributed the presents as Cortes had desired. We were particularly amused with what father Olmedo related as to the manner in which he had flattered Narvaez, and in mockery advised him to sound an alarm and sally out with his heavy guns; and also with the cunning he had employed to introduce Cortes' letter. But when he came to Salvatierra, and drew a picture of what had taken place between the latter and himself, how he had made out that they were relations, and the intimate friendship which grew up between them, and the bold language Salvatierra had presumed to throw out when he spoke of taking Cortes and all of us prisoners, and how he swore to revenge himself upon the soldiers who had run off with his and another officer's horse, we really laughed and rejoiced as if nothing but mirth and pleasure awaited us, and we no longer gave it a thought we should have to fight a battle next day, and measure our strength with five times our numbers, no other choice being left us but victory or death.

When the heat of the day had somewhat cooled, we continued our march to Sempoalla, and encamped for the night near a brook about four miles from the town, at a spot where, at that time, there was a bridge, and, at present, a farm-house is built.

I must again, however, return to Narvaez's headquarters, and relate what happened there after the departure of Leon and father Olmedo.

Chapter 121
Events at Narvaez's Quarters

The effect of Leon's and father Olmedo's visit to Narvaez's camp soon showed itself. Several of the officers who had got some hints of the valuable presents which Cortes had sent to be distributed among some of them, found that a party was forming in his favour, and advised that the utmost vigilance should be observed; orders were therefore issued that both foot and horse should always hold themselves ready for action.

The fat *cazique* whom I have so often mentioned was in great fear for having delivered up to Narvaez the women, cotton stuffs, and gold of which we had given him charge. For this reason only, therefore, he would have acted as a spy upon our movements had Narvaez even not strictly commanded him to do so.

When his spies brought him intelligence that we were advancing towards Sempoalla, he said to Narvaez, "How can you remain so quiet and careless? Do you imagine that *Malinche* and his *teules* are people like yourselves? I assure you, if you don't keep a sharp look out, he will some time or other fall upon you unawares, and destroy you all."

Narvaez and his partisans, though they could not help laughing at these warnings of the fat *cazique*, nevertheless thought it necessary to adopt some decisive step. He first formally declared open war against us with fire and sword. This we learnt from a soldier named Galleguillo, who had deserted to us from Narvaez during the night, or perhaps had been secretly sent to apprize us of it by Duero.

Narvaez then encamped with the whole of his troops, taking the cannon and all with him, at about a mile from Sempoalla, in order the better to watch our movements and not to allow any of our men to pass without killing or taking them prisoners. But as it rained heavily just about this time, his men soon got tired of standing in the water to await our arrival, and Narvaez's officers, who were neither accustomed to dampness nor the fatigues of war in general, and imagined it would be an easy matter to overcome us, advised him to return with the troops to their former quarters. They likewise pretended it would be a reproach to them if they all marched out against a handful of men as we were, and considered it sufficient if they placed their artillery, which consisted of eighteen heavy guns, in front of their camp. Forty of the cavalry would be sufficient at night to guard the road leading to Sempoalla, along which we should be compelled to advance: besides which, pickets of cavalry and light-armed foot could watch the spot where we should have to pass the river, to give notice of our approach; and another twenty of the cavalry were always to stand in readiness during night-time in the courtyard adjoining Narvaez's quarters.

All this his officers merely advised to return to their former comfortable quarters again. "Do you, then," continued they to Narvaez, "stand in such awe of Cortes as to believe, on the assertion of the fat *cazique*, that he will dare to push forward to our very quarters with his paltry numbers? Only let him come, we will give him the reception he merits."

Narvaez allowed himself to be convinced by these arguments, and returned with the whole of his troops to the former quarters. He then made known that he who brought him Cortes or Sandoval dead or alive, should receive the reward of 2000 *pesos*.

The command of the small detachment at the river he gave to a certain Hurtado and Gonzalo Carrasco, who is now living at Puebla. The watch-word of Narvaez's men, during the battle, was to be Santa Maria! Santa Maria! It was also regulated that a strong body of men should be posted in his quarters during night-time, and like divisions in those of Salvatierra, Gamarra, and Juan Bono.

These were Narvaez's preparations; we must now see what was going on in our camp.

Chapter 122
Our March Against Narvaez

After we had arrived at the above-mentioned brook, about four miles from Sempoalla, we halted in a beautiful meadow by which it was skirted, and posted our sentinels, consisting entirely of men on whom we could place implicit reliance. Cortes, seated on horseback, ordered all the officers and men to assemble around him; he then craved a few moments' silence, and addressed us in a speech replete with flattering expressions and vast promises.

He began with our departure from Cuba, mentioned all the fatigues we had undergone up to that moment, and then continued: "You are perfectly aware, gentlemen, that the governor of Cuba did appoint me captain-general of the armament, though many cavaliers among you were equally deserving of it; you must also remember that you left Cuba with the supposition you were going to found a colony in this country. It was under this pretence that the public were invited to join the expedition, and yet it afterwards appeared that the armament was merely fitted out for commercial speculation. I was preparing to act up to the instructions I had received, and was ready to return to Cuba, in order to render Diego Velasquez a full account of all our proceedings, when you desired me,—yes, you compelled me, to form a settlement here in the name of our emperor, in which we, with God's assistance, have indeed so far succeeded. You then elected me captain-general and chief justice of New Spain, to continue vested with such power until we should know his majesty's pleasure on that head. Once, subsequently, there indeed again arose a dispute respecting the necessity of returning to Cuba; but this I need not mention, as it is still fresh in every one's memory; however, it became afterwards our universal conviction, that the determination we had come to, to remain in this country, had met with grace in the sight of God, and he has blessed all our endeavours in his holy cause, and granted us success in our undertakings in the emperor's service. Above all, however, I must put you in mind of the promise we made the emperor when we forwarded him a full account of our great deeds, with a description of the country. We begged his majesty not to confer the government of this country on any one before our agents had obtained a hearing, as we had all reason to fear that the powerful bishop of Burgos would strive to obtain that appointment for Diego Velasquez, or for one of his friends or relatives. We assured his majesty that this country was of such vast extent as to merit being governed by an *infante* or *grandee* of his empire, and that we were only awaiting his most gracious commands which we should obey with the deepest veneration, and would not acknowledge any appointment unless it came from his majesty himself. With this account we sent our monarch all the gold, silver, jewels, and other valuable things we had collected. These had been, up to that time, our only remuneration for the many fatigues we had undergone; and how often had not death stood before our eyes in the battles we had fought! what various kinds of hardships we have suffered! we have slept on the bare ground both in the rain and snow, and never lay our arms aside. When we reflect on all these hardships, it really sends a thrill through the heart. In the several battles we have fought, we have lost above fifty of our men, and we are all covered with wounds, and many a one still suffers severely from them. First we had to brave all the dangers of the sea; then followed the battles of Tabasco, Almeria, Cingapacinga, with the ambushes which were laid for us in the mountains, defiles, and the villages. How nigh we were being totally worsted in the battles of Tlascalla! We had scarcely time allowed us to take breath, when the affair at Cholulla awaited us, where the pots stood ready in which our flesh was to be cooked for the inhabitants to feast on! None of us can ever forget our march through the mountain passes, where Motecusuma had posted the whole of his troops, and blocked up the road by a heavy fall of trees, intending that none of us should escape death! Notwithstanding all this, we march into Mexico, and quarter ourselves in the very heart of that city; but how oft there again has death not stood before our eyes! Really no human being could have imagined such a series of dangers! And yet there are many among us who have even experienced additional fatigues, those I mean who have twice before visited these coasts, under Cordoba and Grijalva.

In these voyages of discovery they suffered hardships of various natures, lost numbers of their companions, were themselves covered with wounds, and lost everything they possessed. But it would be impossible to enumerate all the miseries that have been suffered; nor have I any time, if I could, for night is fast approaching; and now, after we have undergone all this, Pamfilo Narvaez comes tearing along, like a mad dog, to destroy us all; calls us villains and traitors, and makes disclosures to Motecusuma, not like a prudent general, but with the spirit of a rebel; he has even presumed to throw one of the emperor's auditors into chains—of itself a criminal act; and to sum up, has declared a war of extermination against us, just as if we had been a troop of Moors."

Upon this Cortes launched out in praise of the courage we had shown in every battle: "Up to this moment," he continued, "we have fought to defend our lives, but now we shall have to fight valiantly for our lives and our honour. Our enemies have nothing less in contemplation than to take us all prisoners, and rob us of our property. No one could tell whether Narvaez was commissioned by the emperor himself; all this was merely done at the instigation of our most deadly enemy, the bishop of Burgos. If we were subdued by Narvaez, which God forbid, all the services we had rendered to the Almighty and our emperor would be construed into as many crimes. An investigation would be set on foot against us, and we should be accused of murder, of rapine, and of having revolutionised the country, though the real guilty person would be Narvaez; and the things which would be considered meritorious in him would be construed as criminal in us. As all this must be evident to you," said Cortes, in conclusion, "and we, as honest cavaliers, are bound to defend the honour of his imperial majesty, as well as our own, and all our property, I have marched out from Mexico, reposing my trust in God and your assistance, to bid defiance to such injustice."

Several of our officers and soldiers then answered, in the name of the rest, that he might rely upon our determination either to conquer or to die.

Cortes was excessively rejoiced at our reply, and said he had not expected less. We should find no cause for regret, as wealth and honour would be the reward of our courage and our valour. He then once more begged our attention, and reminded us that, in battle and time of war, prudence and experience accomplished more than the utmost bravery. He was well aware of our great courage, and how every man among us strove who should be the first to dash among the enemy's ranks. At present the first object must be to capture the eighteen pieces of ordnance which Narvaez had arranged in front of his camp. For this purpose he selected sixty of our youngest men, of which number I also was, and placed them under the command of Pizarro, who at that time was a daring young fellow, but in those days as little known to the world as Peru itself. As soon as we should have captured these cannon, we were to storm Narvaez's quarters, which were on the summit of a very high temple. Sandoval, with other sixty men, was ordered to seize Narvaez's person, and his commands were exactly as follow: "Gonzalo de Sandoval, *alguacil*-major of New Spain, I hereby command you to seize the person of Pamfilo Narvaez, and to kill him in case he will not surrender. This we are called upon to do as faithful servants of God and the emperor, and in revenge for the ill-treatment he, the said Narvaez, presumed to exercise against one of his majesty's auditors. Given at our headquarters. Signed, Hernando Cortes; and countersigned, Pedro Hernandez, secretary."

Cortes at the same time promised a reward of 3000 *pesos* to the first man who should lay hands on Narvaez, 2000 to the second, and 1000 to the third.

Leon likewise received the command of sixty men, with instructions to seize the person of Diego Velasquez, with whom he had had such high words. Cortes himself retained twenty men around his person, to render assistance wherever it might be most required; his principal object, however, was to get the persons of Narvaez and Salvatierra into his power.

After Cortes had issued these commands in writing to his principal officers, he said: "I am fully aware that Narvaez has four times the men we have; but most of them are not accustomed to arms. A great number are adverse to their general, many are sick, and we shall fall upon them unawares. All opposition on their part will be fruitless, and I am fully confident the Almighty will grant us the victory. Narvaez's men also know they will lose nothing by the change, and would fare better in every respect by being with us than with him. Thus, gentlemen, after God, our lives and honour entirely depend upon the valour of our arms. The praise of future generations lies in our hands, and it is more honourable to die on the field of battle than to lead a life of dishonour." With this Cortes ended, as it was beginning to rain and getting late.

I have often subsequently, when thinking of this speech of Cortes, wondered that he did not mention a single word of the secret understanding he had with some of Narvaez's officers, but merely impressed upon our minds the necessity of employing our utmost courage. By degrees, however, it became obvious to me that by that very circumstance he had shown the prudence of a great general, for by making us believe that our only hope was in God and our own bravery, he compelled us to exercise the utmost of our power.

The most dangerous part of the work was assigned to us, who were to capture the cannon, under the command of Pizarro: we had to commence the attack and storm up against the cannons' mouths. Pizarro, therefore, gave us very strict commands, and showed us how we were to push forward with our lances lowered, and fight on boldly until we had taken the cannon, when the artillerymen, Mesa and Amenga, were immediately to load the guns with the balls at hand, and fire away at Salvatierra's quarters.

We were altogether in want of defensive armour, and on that night many of us would have given all we possessed for a cuirass, helmet, or steel *gorget*.

Our watch-word was: *Espiritu Santo! Espiritu Santo!* for such words in time of war are given to soldiers in secret, in order that the men may recognize each other. That of Narvaez's men was: *Santa Maria! Santa Maria!*

As I stood in great favour with Sandoval, he begged of me, when we had captured the cannon, should my life be spared, instantly to repair to him and not leave his side; which I promised and fulfilled, as will be seen.

We remained in our camp during the first part of the night, and spent our time in making preparations, and thinking on the arduous task which awaited us; for it was useless to think of any supper, as we had not a morsel of food with us. We sent out the pickets and posted our sentinels, of which I happened to be one. I had not stood long when one of our outposts came up and asked me whether I had not heard a noise? To which I answered no, and immediately after one of our corporals approached and told me that Galleguillo, who had deserted from Narvaez to us, was nowhere to be found, and that he must have been a spy; and as it was certain he had by this time betrayed our approach to the enemy, Cortes had given orders for our immediate advance upon Sempoalla. An instant after I heard the drum and pipe, and we all marched forward. Galleguillo, however, was found a few minutes after fast asleep under some cloaks he had thrown over him, as damp and cold were two things to which the poor devil was wholly unaccustomed.

Cortes now ordered the drum and pipe to be silenced, and we marched steadily forward, until we arrived at the river where, as I have above mentioned, Carrasco and Hurtado were posted with a detachment of the enemy. This, our sudden visit, was the last thing they could have thought of, and we succeeded in capturing the former, but the other escaped and ran to give the alarm.

I shall never forget our crossing this river, how it was swollen by the rain, and the difficulty we experienced in passing over the stones which had become loosened and were very slippery; while, at the same time, we were greatly incommoded by our weapons which we had slung to our backs. I well remember Carrasco, when he was taken prisoner, crying out aloud: "Mind what you are about Señor Cortes, for Narvaez has marched out with all his troops to receive you." As Hurtado had already ran off to give the alarm, it mattered very little whether Carrasco thus strove to inform his general of our approach by his loud cries. Cortes gave him in charge of his secretary Hernandez, and commanded us to the attack. We immediately lowered the points of our lances and made so violent a rush at the cannon, that the artillerymen had scarcely sufficient time to fire off four pieces, every ball of which passed over our heads, excepting one, which killed three of our men. At the same moment our respective officers, with their men, forced their way up under the sound of our drum and pipe. Several of Narvaez's cavalry certainly offered some resistance, but for a short time only, while six or seven of their number lay stretched on the field of battle. We, under Pizarro, had the good fortune to capture all the cannon, but durst not leave them in charge of our artillerymen alone, as Narvaez continued to shower down arrows and musket-balls upon us from the top of the temple. Sandoval now likewise came up with his detachment, and though Narvaez bid a powerful resistance, he nevertheless continued advancing up the steps of the building, and broke through the pikes and lances of his opponents. Seeing this, and that the enemy had given up all attempts to recover the cannon, we gave them in charge of our artillerymen, and flew under the command of Pizarro to Sandoval's assistance. We just arrived at the moment when Narvaez had beaten him back down five or six of the steps; our arrival turned the scale against the enemy, and Sandoval now pushed forward again with renewed vigour. Indeed we had some hard work to do with our long lances before we could clear our way through the enemy's ranks; all at once I heard some one, and it must have been Narvaez, cry out in a loud voice: "Assist me, oh blessed Virgin! I am a dead man! One of my eyes has been thrust out!" At the same moment we all cried out, "*Victory! Victory!* for those of the watchword *Espiritu Santo! Narvaez is fallen!*" Yet we were unable for some time to gain entire possession of the temple, not until Martin Lopez, who built the brigantines, hit upon the thought of setting fire to the straw that lay on the top of the temple, which he immediately set about with his gaunt figure. Narvaez's men now came rolling down the steps one after the other, and he himself was taken prisoner. A certain Pedro Sanchez Farsan was the first to lay hold of him, and I mentioned this to Sandoval and several of Narvaez's officers, who were standing by at the time. In an instant a thousand voices filled the air with cries of: *"Long live the emperor and general Cortes, in his imperial name! Victory, victory! Narvaez is dead!"*

The battle, however, was still continued at various points, as several of Narvaez's officers maintained their positions on the tops of other temples. Cortes, however, with his accustomed forethought, sent round a herald to summons Narvaez's men, under pain of death, immediately to join the imperial standard. This, with the firing of the cannon, our hurrahing, and the belief that Narvaez was dead, had the desired effect, and only the troops of young Diego Velasquez and of Salvatierra, who had taken up a position with the troops under their command, on the summit of a very high temple, where it was difficult to get at them, refused to submit. Sandoval, however, was not to be deterred by their advantageous position. He took the half of his men with him, while the rest remained below, and we attacked them so vigorously with our swords, that at last they surrendered, and we took Salvatierra and Diego Velasquez prisoners.

In the hurry of the moment we had merely fastened fetters around Narvaez's legs; but Sandoval now, ordered him to be better secured. Cortes happened to come up at the time, when Leon, with Ordas, brought in Salvatierra, Diego Velasquez, and other chief officers prisoners; he was still in full armour, and had heated himself to such a degree by riding up and down, the weather besides being very hot, that the perspiration literally dropped from him, and he could scarcely breathe from over-exertion; he twice said to Sandoval, who was unable to catch his words at first, "Where is Narvaez? Where is Narvaez?" "Here he is! here he is!" cried Sandoval, "and quite safe." "That is all right, my son Sandoval," said Cortes in a voice still somewhat feeble; "do not leave this spot for the present, nor suffer any of your men to stir away, and keep a strong guard over the officers you have taken prisoners; I will see now how the battle is going on at the other points."

With these words Cortes rode off, and as he still found Narvaez's men offered resistance, he again sent round a herald to summon them to surrender, and to deliver up their arms to the *alguacil*.

All this took place during night-time, and it rained at intervals. When we first forced our way into the town it was as dark as pitch, and it rained heavily, the moon did not rise until some time after; but even the darkness itself favoured us, for in the midst of darkness numbers of shining beetles[1] kept continually flying about, which Narvaez's men mistook for the lighted matches of our firearms,[2] and this gave them a vast idea of the number of our matchlocks.

Narvaez having lost an eye and being otherwise dangerously wounded, he begged of Sandoval to allow the surgeon he had brought with him to dress his and the other officers' wounds. This the latter unhesitatingly complied with, and while the surgeon was dressing Narvaez's wounds, Cortes stepped up, as he imagined unknown, to see what was going forward. Some one, however, remarked to Narvaez that Cortes was standing near; when the former turned round and said: "Indeed, general, you have reason to be proud of this victory, and of my being taken prisoner!"

"I am," replied Cortes, "every way thankful to God for it, and likewise for the brave companions he has given me; but I can assure you that this victory is the least brilliant we have yet gained in New Spain."

With this Cortes broke off the conversation, and again cautioned Sandoval to guard the prisoners well. As I have above remarked, we had merely thrown fetters about Narvaez's legs, but we now secured him better, and placed a strong guard over him. I was among the latter, and Sandoval gave me secret orders not to allow any of his men to see him until next morning, when Cortes would make further arrangements respecting his person. We did not feel quite safe yet; for the reader will remember that Narvaez had detached forty of his cavalry to oppose our crossing the river. This body was still hovering about, and we feared would fall upon us unawares and release both Narvaez and the other officers again. We therefore kept a sharp look out, while Cortes despatched Oli and Ordas to persuade them, by

1. The *clater nocturnes*.

2. It need scarcely be remarked that the Spanish guns at that time were fired by means of matches, which were made of hempen tow, boiled in the lees of old wine, and when dry and once lighted they burn on until consumed.

enticing promises, to surrender quietly. For this purpose these officers were obliged to take a couple of horses of Narvaez's troops, as ours had been left at the back of a rising ground near Sempoalla.

When Oli and Ordas came up with them, they said so many fine things, and made such vast promises in Cortes' name, that they speedily came to terms, and surrendered themselves.[3]

Daylight in the meantime had broken forth, when this detachment reached our camp again; and the drummers and pipers of Narvaez's corps, without instructions from Cortes or from any one else, suddenly sounded their instruments, and cried out, "Long live these brave Romans, who, though small in numbers, have gained the victory over Narvaez and his troops!" And another merry-making fellow, called Guidela, a negro, cried out at the top of his voice, "Hark ye! the Romans themselves could never boast of so brilliant a victory as this!" Whatever we might say, we were unable to stop their hurrahing or their instruments, until Cortes had ordered one of the drummers, named Tepia, who was half mad, to be seized.

At this moment Oli and Diego de Ordas made their appearance with the detachment of cavalry, accompanied by Duero, Bermudez, and several other friends of our general. These now all came in a body to pay their respects to Cortes, who had taken off his armour, and was seated in an arm-chair, dressed in a wide orange-coloured *surtout*. It was really a most interesting sight to behold the serenity and joy which sat upon his countenance as he welcomed each, and amusing to hear the fine things he told them. He had indeed every reason to be proud of the power and the greatness he had so suddenly acquired!

After these officers had thus paid their respects to him, they repaired to their respective quarters. And now we must look over the list of the dead and wounded on both sides. Among the former was Narvaez's standard-bearer, named Fuentes, of a noble family of Seville; and three of his chief officers, one of whom was named Rojas, a native of Old Castile. One of the three soldiers, named Carretero, who deserted to the enemy, was likewise killed; and the number of their wounded was very great.

On our side we lost four killed, and had several wounded; the fat *cazique* himself being of this number; who, when he heard that we were in the vicinity of Sempoalla, had fled to Narvaez's quarters, and

3. Bernal Diaz has forgotten some circumstances relative to this battle. Three hundred of Narvaez's troops defended themselves bravely for a length of time on one of the temples, nor did they surrender until all their powder was spent.

was wounded there. Cortes ordered his wound to be dressed, then sent him home, and desired that no one should molest him.

Cervantes and Escalona, who had deserted to Narvaez, derived very little benefit from their treachery; the latter had been dangerously wounded, and the other Cortes ordered to be well whipped.

Here I must also not forget the *braggadocio* Salvatierra, whose cowardice his own men declared was beyond all belief. They all swore never in the course of their lives to have witnessed such extreme fear as he evinced when he first heard the clashing of our arms at a distance; and when he heard the cry of *Victory! Victory! Narvaez is fallen!* he became quite ill, and threw down his arms.

Diego Velasquez had almost escaped my memory! He was also wounded, and, as had been previously settled, was taken prisoner by Leon, with whom he had quarrelled at Narvaez's dinner table. The victor, however, acted magnanimously; he took him to his own quarters, had his wounds dressed, and treated him with great respect.

Such is the history of our battle with Narvaez, and now we must see what further took place.

Chapter 123

The 2000 Indians of Chinantla

Late in the evening of the same day on which we had gained the victory over Narvaez, the 2000 Indian troops arrived which Cortes had requested the *caziques* of Chinantla to send us. They came under the command of their *caziques*, and one of our soldiers named Barrientos, and marched into Sempoalla in the best military order possible, two abreast. They were all tall and powerful men, armed with their immense-sized lances and huge shields; every lancer was followed by a bowman. In this manner, under the sound of drums and trumpets, they marched in, with their feathers waving on their head and their colours flying, and continually cried out, *"Long live the emperor! long live Cortes!"* They made such a grand show, that though they were only 2000 in number, one would have thought at first sight there had been 3000. Narvaez's men were not a little astonished when they beheld these men, and remarked to each other that they would have fared worse if they had had to encounter these people, or if they had joined us in the attack.

Cortes received the Chinantlan chiefs most kindly, thanked them for the trouble they had put themselves to, and desired them to return to their homes, after presenting them with various things of Spanish manufacture. Barrientos likewise returned with them, and Cortes particularly admonished him not to allow these Indians to commit any depredations in the townships they passed through.

Chapter 124

Narvaez's Flotilla Captains & Pilots

After the whole of Narvaez's troops had been disarmed, Cortes despatched Francisco de Lugo to the harbour where the flotilla lay, in order to bring all the captains and pilots of the eighteen vessels to Sempoalla. He was likewise to convey on shore all the sails, rudders, and compasses, so as to render it impossible for the governor of Cuba to gain any information respecting the fate of his armament. Whoever refused to submit to Lugo was immediately to be thrown into chains. Cortes likewise ordered the latter to bring along with him a certain Sancho de Barahona, whom Narvaez had imprisoned along with some other soldiers. This Barahona was a man of great wealth, and had settled in Guatimala. He was in very ill health when he arrived in Cortes' quarters, who desired that every attention should be paid him.

When the captains and pilots of the several vessels appeared in Cortes' presence, he made them take a solemn oath to obey his commands in all matters. A certain Pedro Caballero, captain of one of Narvaez's vessels, he appointed admiral of the flotilla. This man, it was rumoured, had been bribed with some bars of gold to favour Cortes' party. Caballero received instructions not to allow any vessel to leave the harbour, and if any others should arrive there from Cuba—for Cortes had received information that there were two other ships fitting out there for this harbour—he was to seize them, send their sails, rudders, compasses on shore, and await further orders. This, as we shall afterwards see, Caballero punctually obeyed.

In our headquarters the following important arrangements were made: Leon was to be sent to subdue the province of Panuco, and to make a settlement there; for which purpose 120 men were placed under his command, of whom 100 were of Narvaez's troops, the rest being made up of our own, who were better acquainted with the mode of warfare in this country. To this detachment were likewise added two vessels, in order more thoroughly to explore the coast and the River Panuco.

A similar commission, with an equal number of troops, composed as the former, and also to be accompanied by two vessels, was given to Diego de Ordas, to form a settlement on the River Guacasualco. He was likewise to despatch some of his men to the island of Jamaica to purchase cows, horses, pigs, goats, sheep, and Spanish fowls, for breeding; the province of Guacasualco being particularly adapted for the breed of cattle.

Cortes now ordered all Narvaez's officers and soldiers to be liberated, with the exception of Salvatierra, who feigned to be taken suddenly ill during the late battle. When their arms were to be returned to them, it occasioned a good deal of ill blood, for many of our men had taken possession of their horses, swords, and other matters, and no one felt inclined to return what he had once taken. When Cortes, therefore, issued orders that every one was to receive his own again, it caused great discontent among our troops; for we maintained we were justified in retaining what we had taken, as Narvaez had declared a war of extermination against us; had literally come with the intention to destroy us, and rob us of all our property; besides that, we, the well-deserving servants of the emperor, had been branded by him with the name of traitors. Cortes, however, was determined upon this point, and as we had elected him our captain-general, we could not do less than obey him. I myself had taken possession of two swords, three daggers, and a target, all of which I had to return.

Alonso de Avila, who was a captain, and one who durst speak out boldly to Cortes, privately reproached him, in conjunction with father Olmedo, for acting thus; and remarked to him, that he was performing the part of Alexander the Macedonian, who, whenever he gained a splendid victory, rewarded and honoured the vanquished instead of the officers and soldiers who had procured him the victory. They had every reason to make this observation, as we had to look quietly on and see Cortes give all the provisions and valuable matters, which the Indians of the surrounding country brought in as presents, to the officers of the vanquished general, and leave us unnoticed. This they maintained was not acting justly, and had every appearance of ingratitude towards them, who by their valour had raised him to the proud position in which he then stood.

Cortes, who was never wanting for an answer, replied, that for all he possessed he was indebted to us; but under existing circumstances he could not act otherwise. It was for the advantage of all to gain the troops of Narvaez by fair words, presents, and promises; their numbers were too great in comparison to ours; and if they were once to rise up in anger, they might easily put us all to the sword.

To this Avila replied in a very haughty manner, which obliged Cortes to exclaim, "Those who do not feel inclined to obey are at liberty to leave my standard; Spanish women bring forth sufficient children into the world, and every son is a soldier in Spain!"

"That is very true," answered Avila, rather disrespectfully; "and among these sons there are also numbers of generals and governors as well as soldiers."

As matters then stood, Cortes was compelled to put on the best countenance he could to this reproof, and to silence this open-hearted man by promises and presents; for the determined and bold character of Avila was too well known to him, and he feared his resentment. He therefore suppressed his injured feelings, and from that moment took every opportunity of sending him to some distance on one or other important commission; so he despatched him some after to St. Domingo, and subsequently to Spain, to present the garderobe and the treasure of Motecusuma to the emperor. This latter voyage, however, terminated very unfortunately, for Avila, with the whole of those treasures, was captured by the redoubted French pirate Jean Florin, as we shall see in the proper place.

But to return to Narvaez. He happened to have a negro servant with him ill with the smallpox, through whom this terrific disease, which, according to the accounts of the inhabitants, was previously unknown in the country, spread itself through New Spain, where it created the greater devastation, from the poor Indians, in their ignorance, solely applying cold water as a remedy, with which they constantly bathed themselves; so that vast numbers were cut off before they had the blessing of being received into the bosom of the Christian church.[1]

1. Of this dreadful disease Gomara says, that it spread from Sempoalla through the whole of New Spain, and that in the greater part of the townships half of the inhabitants were carried off by it. It was a custom among the inhabitants to go immediately from a hot bath into a cold one, so that it was a wonder any escaped death. Those that survived could not help scratching themselves, which naturally left large scars, and rendered them hideous to look at. Torquemada agrees with Gomara, but adds, from the authority of the Indians, that this and other pestilential diseases spread at certain times through the whole of the country; and Bernal Diaz, in describing the person of the younger Xicotencatl, says his face was pitted as if with the smallpox.

It was also about this time that the garrison of Vera Cruz demanded the portion of the gold which fell to their share in the division at Mexico. These men maintained, that, though they had not made the campaign of Mexico with us, they had shown themselves no less deserving in the cause of God and the emperor than ourselves, as they had guarded the coast and built a fortress; and that many of them who had fought at the battle of Almeria were still suffering from their wounds, while others again had been taken prisoners by Narvaez, who had treated them with great severity: they concluded, therefore, they were justly entitled to a share of the treasure found in Mexico.

Cortes acknowledged the justness of their claim, and requested them to despatch two of the principal men from among them to take charge of their respective share, and, if I am not mistaken, he added that it had been deposited for safe keeping in Tlascalla: at least, they immediately after sent two of their numbers there to take possession of it, of whom Juan de Alcantara the elder was one. We shall, however, soon see what became of Alcantara with all the gold; how quickly the wheel of fortune turned against us, and trouble and sorrow followed peace and joy; for we received intelligence that all Mexico had risen up in arms, that Alvarado was besieged in his quarters, and that the Mexicans were attempting to set fire to the new fortifications at every point. Seven of our men had already been killed, many were wounded, and immediate assistance was required.

This information was first brought us by two Tlascallans, and that without any letter from Alvarado. Soon after, however, two other Tlascallans arrived with a letter from him confirmatory of this bad news. God knows how shocked we were at this intelligence! We immediately resolved to hasten to Mexico by forced marches. Narvaez and Salvatierra were sent under escort to Vera Cruz, where Rodrigo Rangel, whom Cortes had just appointed commandant of that place, was made responsible for the safe custody of their persons. Besides these, Rangel took along with him several of Narvaez's men, who were suffering from ill-health.

Just as we were about to commence our march to Mexico, four distinguished personages arrived from that town, who had been sent by Motecusuma to complain to our general of the conduct of Alvarado. They told us, with tears in their eyes, that he had, without any provocation, sallied out with the whole of his troops, and fallen unawares upon their chiefs and *caziques* while they were celebrating a feast in honour of their gods Huitzilopochtli and Tezcatlipuca,

Alvarado himself having previously given his consent to the celebration of that feast. Many of their chief personages had been killed and wounded, so that, at last, they were compelled to defend themselves, and six Spaniards were killed in the affray. To this and other complaints against Alvarado, Cortes told them, with a dark frown on his brow, that he would repair immediately in person to Mexico, and look into the matter. With this message the Indians returned to their monarch, who, it is said, was anything but pleased with it. Cortes, at the same time, wrote word to Alvarado that we were advancing by forced marches upon Mexico, and particularly cautioned him not to let Motecusuma escape out of his hands. He likewise informed him of the victory we had gained over Narvaez, though he had no doubt already been apprized of this, for it was known to Motecusuma.

Chapter 125

We Hasten to Mexico

On receiving the intelligence that Mexico was in rebellion, and Alvarado besieged in his quarters, the plan of forming settlements in Panuco and Guacasualco was for the present abandoned, and Leon and Ordas were again ordered to join the main body.

Cortes soon found that Narvaez's troops were very unwilling to join us in the Mexican campaign; but he desired them, in a most kind manner, to forget the old enmity which had existed between Narvaez and himself, and assured them that their only way to wealth and eminence was to join us in this campaign; by so doing they would enter into a country where they would be able to render services unto God and the emperor; and this, too, was an opportunity which perhaps would not so readily present itself again. In short, he told them so many fine things, that they one and all agreed to accompany us: if, however, they had had any idea of Mexico's vast power, not one of them would have been so ready to join us.

We now broke up our quarters, and marched forward with all expedition. In Tlascalla, we were informed that the Mexicans had continued their hostilities against Alvarado as long as Motecusuma and his generals believed we were at war with Narvaez. They had killed seven of our men and burned down a portion of our quarters there, and had not stayed hostilities until they heard of the recent victory we had gained: they still, however, refused to supply Alvarado with either water or food. This information was received in Tlascalla the moment we arrived there. Cortes now reviewed the whole of his troops, which amounted to 1300 men, 96 horses, 80 crossbow-men, and a like number of musketeers. This body of troops Cortes considered sufficiently strong to venture fearlessly into Mexico with, particularly as the *caziques* of Tlascalla had furnished us with 2000 of their warriors.

We now continued our march with the same briskness until we came to Tezcuco. It was in this large town we began to discover the ill-feeling that was abroad against us. Not the slightest mark of respect was shown us here, nor did any of the chiefs call upon us. It was on St. John's day, in the month of June of the year 1520, we, for the second time, entered the city of Mexico. No *cazique*, none of the principal officers, none of our Mexican friends made their appearance, and the houses were deserted. It was not until we had arrived in front of our quarters that Motecusuma came out into the courtyard to welcome Cortes, and congratulate him on his victory over Narvaez. Our general, however, was flushed with the recent victory, and would not listen to him, so that the monarch returned pensive and sad to his apartments.

We soldiers again took possession of our old quarters, and Narvaez's men were provided with similar ones. Alvarado's men and ours, who had just arrived, now began to relate what had taken place during this interval of separation. The former related how they had been attacked by the Mexicans, and the terrible resistance they had been forced to make. Then we followed, and related how we had defeated Narvaez's troops, and taken him prisoner.

The next thing Cortes did was to inquire into the real cause of the insurrection of the Mexicans. Several soldiers, who were displeased with Alvarado, affirmed that Motecusuma had evinced excessive grief on account of these troubles, and they were quite confident that not a single one of the men under Alvarado would have been spared alive if Motecusuma had been in secret understanding with his subjects; on the contrary, he continually strove to quiet them, and to put down the insurrection. Alvarado, on his part, represented all this to our general in a very different light. According to his assurances, the Mexicans had risen up in arms to liberate their monarch, and to take revenge upon us, by the express command of their god Huitzilopochtli, for our having erected a cross and the image of the holy Virgin on his temple. Several Mexicans, he added, had tried to remove the holy image from the altar on which it is raised, but they had not been able to do so. Even the inhabitants themselves had looked upon this circumstance as a great wonder, and had mentioned it to Motecusuma, who then issued orders that it should not be touched. It was, however, not true, continued Alvarado, that Narvaez had sent word to the monarch he was coming to release him from his confinement, and lead us all away in chains: on the contrary, after Motecusuma found that though we were in possession of a sufficient number of vessels, but made no preparation for embarking, he well foresaw we never intended to leave the country again, but that more of us would continually arrive, and that we should return to Mexico accompanied by Narvaez's troops.

Upon this it was resolved they should put Alvarado with the whole of his men to the sword, and liberate the monarch. The less doubt they had entertained of Narvaez's being able to defeat us, the more sure they made of carrying out their plan successfully. This Alvarado considered sufficient to justify the conduct he had pursued. Cortes then wished to know why he had fallen upon the Mexican chiefs while they were celebrating a feast? Because, replied Alvarado, he had been assured by two of the principal men of the town, by one of the *papas*, and by other of the inhabitants, that the Mexicans intended falling upon him immediately after the feast had ended.

"But the Mexicans," interrupted Cortes, "maintain that they had asked your permission to celebrate the feast, and that you granted their request!"

Alvarado could certainly not deny this, but assured him he had selected that opportunity to punish them that it might come the more unexpectedly, and strike the greater terror among them, and to anticipate them in their premeditated attack upon him.

These statements were by no means satisfactory to Cortes, and he told Alvarado, rather sharply, that he saw very little truth in all this, but a good deal of irregularity hurtful to the Spanish cause: "For it is very certain," added Cortes, "if the Almighty did not allow Motecusuma to regain his liberty, it was because his idols might not construe it into their own merit." Herewith Cortes turned his back upon him, and desired him to say nothing further on the subject.

Besides this, Alvarado related many other things which happened during the interval we had been absent from Mexico; one time, for instance, when he sallied out upon the Mexicans, who were rushing forward in vast numbers to set fire to his quarters, he ordered a cannon, heavily laden with ball and small shot, to be fired against them; this piece, however, did not go off until he had fought his way into the thickest of the enemy, who were forcing him back to his quarters again: it then went off of itself, and committed terrible havoc among the advancing foe. Alvarado assured us, that, without this wonderful assistance, he would certainly have been cut to pieces with all his men; as it was, he lost only two of his soldiers, whom the Mexicans carried off alive. This and many other circumstances were related by Alvarado: the following, however, was told me by several of his men. At one time they were entirely without any water to drink; they dug a well in the yard adjoining their quarters, and behold! they found sweet water, whereas in every other place where wells had been sunk in Mexico, nothing but salt water was to be found. The hand of Providence was certainly often stretched out to our aid; yet I must observe, in behalf of truth, that there was another well in the town, which often, and, indeed, almost always, contained fresh water.

For the rest, there were men who asserted that Alvarado merely made this murderous attack upon the Mexicans from avaricious motives, to possess himself of the splendid garments, the gold, and the jewels which they wore at such festivals. This I do not believe, nor did I ever hear such a thing mentioned at the time, although this and many other circumstances were asserted by the Bishop de las Casas, in which, however, there is not a syllable of truth. For myself, I am convinced that Alvarado merely struck this blow to terrify the Mexicans, and to follow up the old saying, "He who attacks first gains the victory." The consequences were certainly different to what he had expected, and bad became worse.[1]

We have, however, obtained satisfactory proof that no guilt can be imputed to Motecusuma respecting the hostilities which subsequently burst out: on the contrary, he commanded the Mexicans not to attack Alvarado, but they replied that they could no longer endure to see him kept in confinement, and their countrymen murdered in the midst of their festivities. They were determined to set him at liberty, and to kill every *teule* who resisted them.

These and many other facts I learnt from credible persons who were present with Alvarado all the time. I have now, however, to speak of the terrible battles which we fought in this city.

---

1. A formal inquiry was made into this circumstance, by order of Charles the Fifth. The excellent Bartholomew de las Casas gave judgment, and he pronounced the Mexicans entirely innocent of having had any intention to massacre the troops under Alvarado, but that the latter had massacred the Mexicans without any provocation, merely for the purpose of striking terror among them. In pronouncing this judgment, however, Las Casas may have been carried away by his excessive zeal for humanity towards the Indians. Herrera (*Historia de las Indias occidentales*, decade ii, b. x,) says: "The fact, however, is, that the Mexicans intended to have murdered all the Spaniards on this occasion; for which purpose they had concealed their arms in the buildings adjoining the temple. This was told the Spaniards by the women, from whom they always learnt the truth."

Chapter 126

Our Battles With the Mexicans

Cortes, on his march to Mexico, had often bragged to his officers of the great authority and power he then possessed. They should see how the inhabitants would come out from all parts to meet him, and receive him with every splendour; that he was now complete master of Mexico, and Motecusuma and his grandees would not dare to dispute his commands henceforth, but would bring him gold in abundance.

But when Cortes found how the aspect of affairs had changed at Tezcuco, that no one stirred a foot to give the splendid reception he had boasted of, that none of the principal personages showed themselves, that even the worst of provisions were brought him with great reluctance, and found this ill feeling towards us show itself even more strongly in Mexico, and that although he had returned with additional troops, the inhabitants no longer furnished him with provisions, his pride turned into moroseness and anger, so much so that when Motecusuma sent two of his grandees to announce that he was desirous of paying Cortes a visit, as he had something to communicate to him, he said, "He might go to the devil! since he would not allow any weekly markets to be held, nor any provisions to be sent us."

When our other chief officers, Leon, Oli, Avila, and Lugo heard this, they said to him, "Moderate your anger, general, and remember what great honours this monarch has heaped upon us, the kindnesses we have received from him, and how amiable his disposition is: for, had he not existed, the Mexicans would long ago have feasted on our bodies; nor ought you to forget that he has sought your alliance by offering you his daughter in marriage."

These words carried with them the idea of a reproach, and, consequently, only served the more to embitter his feelings, and he burst out as follows: "Why should I stand upon any further ceremony with this dog? Did he not secretly connive with Narvaez, and now refuses us provisions?"

"Our opinion is," returned the other officers, "that he does nothing more than his present situation would prompt him to do, and that he acts most prudently."

Cortes, however, relied upon the strength of his troops, and would not allow his anger to be pacified in any way, but commissioned the two Mexican grandees to tell their master that he must issue immediate orders for the re-opening of the markets, otherwise he should find himself obliged to take other steps. Both these Mexicans had understood the reviling language used by Cortes against their monarch, and also how our other officers had remonstrated with him on that account. They knew these officers well; for they had by turns been captains of the guard which was placed over their monarch's person, and knew they were greatly attached to him. They therefore repaired, either in the bitterness of their hearts, or because the attack upon us had already been determined upon, and related to Motecusuma what they had heard; and scarcely a quarter of an hour had elapsed before one of our men came running up heavily wounded. He had been at Tlacupa, a town near Mexico, to fetch thence some women belonging to Cortes' household, and the daughter of Motecusuma, whom Cortes had given in charge of the king of Tlacupa, her relative, when we marched against Narvaez. This man also related that he had found the town of Tlacupa and the high road filled with warriors. They took the women away and wounded him in two different places. If he had not escaped out of their hands, they would have thrown him into a canoe, and have sacrificed him to their gods. They had also destroyed one of the bridges over the causeway.

When Cortes and some of us soldiers heard this, we began to look very serious, for those among us who had been several times engaged with the Indians knew, from experience, with what vast crowds they always entered the field of battle, and, although our numbers had been greatly augmented, and that there was little doubt but we should defend ourselves courageously, yet we were well aware of our dangerous position. We soldiers also knew that we should run great risk of losing our lives either from hunger or from the advantages which the enemy would have over us in such a strongly fortified city. Cortes, after questioning the man who had come from Tlacupa, despatched Ordas with 400 men, mostly armed with crossbows and muskets, and a few horse, to see what truth there was in his statement. He recommended him, however, to avoid, if possible, all hostilities, and to settle the affair amicably. Ordas had scarcely reached half-way down the causeway when he was met by a vast body of Mexicans, who, with those posted on the tops of the houses, attacked him so furiously that eight of his men were killed at the first onset, and most of them wounded, Ordas himself in three several places. He found it impossible to move on any further, and he therefore gradually retreated to our quarters. On his retreat he lost another excellent soldier named Lezcano, who had done wonders with his broadsword.

If the body of warriors was vast which had fallen upon Ordas, that which at the same instant attacked our quarters was by far more so; and so vigorously did they assail us with lances, arrows, and stones, that, in an instant, forty of our men were wounded, twelve of whom subsequently died. The numbers who attacked us in front, from behind, and from the tops of the houses, were so vast that Ordas was unable, for a length of time, to cut his way through. Our cannon, muskets, crossbows, and lances, did, certainly, great havoc among the enemy's ranks, who, in fact, rushed in upon our weapons; yet they continued the combat with the same fury, and closed their ranks more firmly, nor could we drive them back a single inch. It was only after a good deal of hard fighting that Diego and his men were able to regain our quarters, though with twenty-three soldiers less than when he had left it, and the rest all wounded: add to which, the enemy's numbers were every moment increasing; nor did they spare abusive language, calling us old women, ragged scoundrels, and such like beautiful names. But the loss we sustained at present was nothing to what we subsequently suffered. They even carried their audacity so far as to throw fire into our quarters, while one body attacked us in front and another from behind, so that we should soon have been suffocated by the flames and smoke if we had not succeeded in putting out the fire by throwing quantities of earth on it, and by pulling down the apartments from which the fire was spreading.

The combat continued the whole day until late at night, during which time they continued to throw such quantities of stones and lances into our quarters, that the place was literally covered with them. In the meantime we had to dress our wounds, to repair the damage done to our buildings, and get some rest till the next morning. As soon as day began to dawn, Cortes determined to sally out with the whole of his troops, including those of Narvaez and the cannon, either to beat the enemy out of the field altogether, or at least to give them a greater proof of our power than we had been able to do on the previous day. The Mexicans, it seemed, had also determined to do their utmost, and they not only fought with uncommon bravery but came in overwhelming numbers, so that every instant they poured in fresh men to the attack. Indeed ten thousand Trojan Hectors, and as many Rolands, would in vain have tried to break through the enemy's ranks! At this moment even, that battle is fresh in my memory; but no words can describe the unyielding stubbornness of the foe. All the volleys from our heavy guns and muskets were to no purpose; it was in vain we rushed forward upon them, and killed from thirty to forty of their numbers at a time; their ranks still remained firmly closed, while their courage seemed to increase with every loss. Whenever we did drive them back into the streets to some distance, they had merely retreated in order that we should follow them, and by so doing be drawn further away from our quarters, when they hoped more easily to surround us, and so render our escape impossible. And sure enough by these retrograde movements they invariably made the greatest destruction among our ranks. Neither did it avail us anything whenever we set fire to any of the houses; for, as I have above mentioned, it was only possible to pass from one house to another by means of wooden drawbridges. If the latter were drawn up we had to wade through deep water to gain another house. But our men suffered most from those of the enemy's troops who pelted them with stones and lances from the housetops. Indeed I cannot imagine how I thus coolly relate all that passed. Three or four of our men who had previously served in the Italian wars, swore over and over again that they had never witnessed such furious fighting, neither in the wars with the king of France, nor even in those with the grand Turk himself. Indeed it was no easy matter for us to retreat to our headquarters, so desperately did they assail us under the most horrible sound of drums, pipes and trumpets, accompanied by the most obscene and abusive language. This day we lost ten or twelve men, and none of us escaped without a wound. We passed the night in deliberations and in preparing for another attack. We now resolved that after the lapse of two days as many of us as were healthy should sally out with two moving towers. These we had strongly put together of wood, and were so constructed, that under each of them twenty-five of our men could stand to move them along. These towers contained loopholes, from which our heavy guns could be fired;

besides that there was space enough for a number of musketeers and crossbow-men. At the side of these towers marched a strong body of musketeers and crossbow-men, as also the whole of our horse, who were from time to time to charge the enemy at full gallop. The construction of these towers and the repairing of several small breaches which the enemy had made in our quarters, occupied us the whole of the following day, so that we could not sally out till the next.

The enemy, however, continued their attacks upon our quarters, not merely from ten or twelve, but from twenty different points at once; so that what with the constructing of the towers, repairing the breaches, and beating off our assailants who had fixed ladders to our quarters, we had enough to do. The whole of us, they cried out, were to be sacrificed to their gods, our hearts were to be torn from our bodies, the blood was to be drawn from our veins, and our arms and legs were to be eaten up at their festivals. The remaining parts of our bodies would be thrown to the tigers, lions and serpents, which they kept in cages; these had not been fed for these two days, in order that they might devour our flesh the more greedily. Our gold and other things would be their booty, and they told the Tlascallans they should be locked up in cages where they fattened people for their sacrifices. Only deliver us up our monarch Motecusuma,—added they with great vehemence; while their noise and their attacks continued through the whole night.

As soon as day had fully broken forth, we commended ourselves to the Almighty, and sallied out with our war-towers. This time again we killed a great number of the enemy; but with all our fighting we could not force them to yield ground, and if they had fought courageously the two previous days, they stood the more firm this time, and fought desperately. We however determined, if it were even to cost us all our lives, to push forward to the great temple of Huitzilopochtli. I will not detail the severe struggle we had against one house in particular, which was very strongly fortified, nor the critical position our horse were placed in. For whenever our cavalry galloped in upon the enemy's ranks, our horses were assailed by so many arrows, stones and lances, that they were immediately covered with wounds; while their riders, however courageously they fought, could make but little impression upon the foe. If they pushed further on, the Mexicans either jumped into the canals or into the lake, where the cavalry could not follow them, and where a whole forest of lances stared them in the face: equally fruitless were all our attempts to set fire to their houses, or pull them down, as they stood, in the midst of the water, and were connected to each other by drawbridges only. If at times we did succeed in firing a house, it took a whole day in burning down, nor did the fire spread, from the buildings being at too great distance from each other, and their being surrounded by water, so that all our efforts that way completely failed. At last we succeeded in fighting our way up to the foot of the great temple, but at that instant a body of above four thousand of the enemy rushed up the steps for its defence; besides that, other troops were already stationed on the top of this building, armed with long lances, stones and arrows. For a length of time the guns of our towers and the attacks of our cavalry could make no impression on the enemy, while our horses were scarcely able to step firmly on the smooth pavement of the court yards, but every moment slipped out and fell down. Though our cannon mowed down ten or fifteen of the enemy at a time, and a great many others were cut down by our sabres, yet their numbers were so vast that we could not beat them back, we therefore now determined to quit our towers, which were almost broken into pieces; and leaving them at the foot of the temple, we began fighting our way up the steps of the building.

Here Cortes displayed astonishing courage, though this, I may say, was never wanting in him. What a bloody and terrific conflict was this! The reader should have seen how we were covered with blood and wounds! Above forty of our men lay dead at our feet; but at last, with the aid of Providence, we succeeded in reaching the point where we had erected the image of the holy Virgin. It was, however, no longer there; for Motecusuma, as we subsequently learnt, had either, out of veneration or fear, taken it away, and put it carefully by. We now set fire to the Mexican idols, and part of the chapel was on this occasion burnt down, with Huitzilopochtli and Tetzcatlipuca. While we were occupied with this work, the battle on the platform continued without intermission; for here stood a number of priests, and more than three or four thousand of the principal Mexicans, who fell upon us with great fury, and even beat us back again down the steps of the temple. Nor was it these alone who here set upon us; but numbers of warriors also annoyed us from the landings and battlements of this building, so that we scarcely knew which way to turn our arms.

We had now made every possible exertion, and undergone the greatest perils. Our towers were smashed to pieces, the whole of us were covered with wounds, and forty-six of our men had been killed. We therefore determined to retreat to our quarters in the best way we could. But our position for the moment was not bettered by this step; for the Mexicans now fell upon us in terrific crowds both in our rear and in our flanks: it is impossible to imagine the sight unless one had seen it. Neither have I at all mentioned the numbers who attacked our quarters after we had sallied out, and the difficulty our men had who were left behind to prevent the enemy from setting fire to them. In this battle we took two chief *papas* prisoners, whom Cortes ordered to be kept in close custody.

I have seen many pictures among the Mexicans and Tlascallans which represented our storming this great temple. In their eye it was considered a piece of astonishing heroism. In these pictures they had not omitted to depict our killed, and how great numbers of us were wounded, with the blood streaming from our bodies. And indeed it was no trifling matter, after our towers had been destroyed, to storm this great building, and set fire to the idols, considering that it was defended so vigorously by large bodies of the enemy, both from the platform and from the landings, and by those who were stationed in the open space below.

The retreat to our quarters was no less perilous; and if the multitude through which we had to cut our way was vast, that in front of our quarters was no less so. We just arrived in time, for the enemy had already made breaches in the walls, and a good many had forced their way through them into the rooms. Our arrival certainly put a stop to their dangerous progress, but they did not discontinue, during the rest of the day and all night, to annoy us with their lances, stones, and arrows, under the most terrible yells. Notwithstanding all this, we had during the night to assist our wounded, to bury our dead, repair the breaches, and take repose for the next day's battle. We also held a council of war, to deliberate what mode of attack we should next adopt, that we might not sustain so great a loss of men; but every plan that was proposed seemed insufficient. To all our calamities was added the bad disposition of Narvaez's soldiers, who cursed Cortes, and even the governor of Cuba in every possible manner, who they said had torn them away from the delightful repose and security which they enjoyed on their respective farms, to be harassed to death in this country. These fellows seemed altogether to have lost their senses, and they lent a deaf ear to everything that was said to them.

After lengthened deliberations, we came to the determination of suing the Mexicans for peace, and asking their permission to quit the city. But daylight had scarcely broken forth when our quarters were again attacked at all points by innumerable bodies of the enemy. Their excessive fury in attack, their stubborn firmness, their desperate thrusts and yells, were all more terrific than on the previous days; while our cannon and other firearms seemed to make no impression on them.

In this moment of danger Cortes determined that Motecusuma should address the infuriated multitude from the top of the building, and desire them to stay hostilities, as we had determined to leave the city. When this offer was made known to Motecusuma in the name of Cortes, he is said to have exclaimed, in the height of grief, "Why does *Malinche* now turn to me?—to me, who am tired of life, and who could wish never again to hear his name mentioned, for it is he who has plunged me into all this misery!" Motecusuma obstinately refused to comply with Cortes' request, and is said to have further exclaimed, "I will neither see nor hear anything more of this man. I put no longer any faith in his deceitful words, his promises, and his specious lies."

Upon this father Olmedo and Oli went and spoke to him in the most affectionate terms, to persuade him to alter his determination. "Alas!" replied the monarch, "for all this, it is now too late. I am convinced that the Mexicans, whatever my wishes might be, will not grant any cessation of arms. They have already raised another *cazique* to the throne, and are fully determined that none of you shall leave this place alive. For myself, I am convinced you will every one of you meet with your death in this city."

In the end, however, Motecusuma was prevailed upon to accompany them. Under cover of a strong division of our troops he advanced to the battlements of our quarters, and began to address the Mexicans in the most affectionate manner, desiring them to put a stop to their hostilities, for the *teules* were going to leave the city. The instant the Mexican generals recognized their king they ordered their men to cease firing. Four of them advanced to a spot where they could easily discourse with the monarch; and thus, with tears in their eyes, they addressed him: "Alas! great king, your own misfortune, and that of your children and your relatives, afflicts us sorely. But we dare not hide from you that we have raised one of your cousins to the throne of this country."

Here they named the new monarch. It was the king of Iztapalapan, Cuitlahuatzin, and not Quauhtemoctzin, for he did not ascend the throne until two months after. "They were forced," continued they, "to prosecute the war, for they had promised their gods to do so, and had sworn to them not to desist until every one of the *teules* was killed. They had daily in vain prayed to their gods Huitzilopochtli and Tetzcatlipuca to deliver him out of the enemy's power, and they would hold him in greater veneration than before; and they hoped he would pardon their present conduct."

Several of our men had covered Motecusuma with their shields while he was addressing the enemy; but as the attack was now momentarily suspended, they were not so very particular in shielding his person. Unfortunately, the hostilities immediately again commenced, and before it could be prevented he was struck by an arrow, and three stones from a sling, by which he was wounded in the arm, leg, and in his head; so that the unhappy monarch was forced to be carried back to his apartment. We were immediately going to bandage up his wounds, and begged of him to take something strengthening; but he refused everything, and, contrary to all expectation, we soon heard that he had expired. Cortes, his officers, and all of us, shed tears for this unfortunate monarch; indeed many of our men, who had been in constant attendance on him, mourned for him as if they had lost a parent. Even father Olmedo himself, who never for a moment left his side, and who, notwithstanding all his efforts, had not been able to convert him to Christianity, could not refrain from shedding tears. And no one will feel surprised at this who knew what a very kind-hearted person Motecusuma was.

He was said to have reigned seventeen years up to the day of his death. Mexico never had a better monarch; and, with regard to his personal courage, he had fought three several duels respecting some disputed territory, and had each time come off victorious.

Chapter 127
Motecusuma's Death

After various deliberations on our present critical position, Cortes determined that one of the distinguished Mexicans and one of the *papas* whom we had taken prisoners should be despatched to the *cazique* of Cuitlahuatzin, whom the Mexicans had raised to the throne, to announce to him and his officers the death of Motecusuma, and explain to them the manner in which it had taken place; they were to assure them that they themselves had not only witnessed his death, but that his own subjects were guilty of it, and that we were deeply distressed at the melancholy circumstance. We also desired they would take charge of his body, to pay it the last honours, and to place the crown on the head of that cousin of Motecusuma who was staying with us, and who was entitled to it by right of inheritance; or to elect one of his sons, as the prince they had raised to the throne had no real claim to it. For the rest, we were ready to make a treaty of peace with them, and quit Mexico; they should not allow this opportunity of concluding peace with us to pass by, for, up to the present moment, we had refrained from destroying the city merely from our love and respect of the deceased monarch. If, however, they compelled us to the combat, we would burn down all their houses and cause no end of destruction. Upon this we handed over the corpse of Motecusuma to six other Mexican chiefs and a large body of *papas* whom we had taken prisoners. All these men had been present when the monarch expired, and they informed Cuitlahuatzin faithfully of every circumstance connected with it; how the Mexicans themselves had caused his death by the shot of an arrow and three stones from a sling.

As soon as the Mexicans espied the dead body of their monarch, they broke out into loud lamentations, and moaned bitterly; but still continued the attack upon us, and that with increased fury. "Now," they hollowed out, "we will make you pay dearly for the death of our monarch, and the insult you have offered to our gods! Is it now you beg peace of us? Only come out, and we will show you what terms we mean to make with you!" Many such like insulting speeches they threw out against us, and added, that they had now selected a monarch whose heart was placed in the right spot, and whom we should not so easily deceive with our lies as we had the good-natured Motecusuma. "Don't trouble yourselves," continued they, "about his burial, but think of your own graves, for, in a couple of days, not a single one of you will be left alive!"

Under such like threats, and vehement yells, they attempted to fire our quarters at various points. As it was very evident to us that we could not hold out much longer, it was determined, in a council of war, that we should abandon the metropolis, and continue the war outside on the main land, where we could destroy the plantations.

In this our proposed retreat, the cavalry was to form the vanguard, and at all stakes to break through the enemy's ranks, or drive them into the lake, even if we were to sacrifice all our horses in the attempt. Previous to taking this step, we determined on making such dreadful havoc among the Mexican troops, that they might allow us to depart in peace from the fear of still greater losses. This resolve was carried out the day following with unshaken bravery. We mowed down great numbers of the enemy, set fire to about twenty houses, and had fought our way almost up to the main land; but though we suffered much, and purchased this partial success with above twenty killed, it availed us nothing, for we could not gain possession of any of the bridges, which, besides being half burnt down, were defended by strong bodies of the enemy. Even those places where the horse might have found a way through the water, the enemy had now rendered impassable by sharp stakes which they had driven in. Thus we were beset on all sides by perils of various natures. In this last sally of our cavalry, which happened on a Thursday, there were, besides Sandoval, Lares, Dominiguez, Leon, Morla, and other brave cavalry officers, many of Narvaez's horse, who, however, showed the utmost fear, as they had not yet experienced, as we old soldiers of Cortes had, what it was to fight against Indians.

Chapter 128

We Decide to Leave Mexico

In this way our strength daily diminished, while that of the enemy increased. Several of our men had been killed, and most of us were wounded. Our courage was of no avail against such vast crowds, who kept up a constant attack upon us both during day and night time. Our powder was fast diminishing,[1] and provisions and water were beginning to fail. Motecusuma was gone, and the peace we solicited was refused. All the bridges on the causeways, along which we had to make good our retreat, had been destroyed by the enemy; in short death was staring at us on every hand. It was, therefore, at last determined, in a council of war, that we should leave the city, and choose the night-time to effect our purpose, when the enemy was generally less vigilant. To make more sure, we resolved to despatch one of the chief *papas* we had taken with many other prisoners, to the Mexicans on the evening preceding the night we contemplated making our retreat, to request of them to allow us to march quietly out of the city within the space of eight days, as we intended to leave them all the gold we possessed.

On this our determination one of the soldiers named Botello had had great influence. This man was an Italian by birth, and was remarkable for his honesty and great intelligence. He had been at Rome, and many believed he could conjure up the dead; some said he had a *spiritus familiaris*, and many of us commonly called him the astrologer.

Botello had, four days previously, announced, that, by means of his secret art, he had discovered that every one of us would be killed if we did not leave Mexico on a certain night. He had likewise prophesied of Cortes that great misfortunes awaited him; he would lose his property and honour, but again rise to eminence and riches. Similar horoscopes drawn by him were frequently mentioned by our men.

1. The daily allowance of a soldier during this time was only fifty grains of maize!

As we shall again have to mention this Botello, we must now see what preparations were going on for our retreat; the first and most important of which was, the construction of a moveable bridge, out of strong beams, which was to serve in passing the canals where the former bridges had been burnt down by the enemy. Four hundred Tlascallans, assisted by 150 of our men, were to take charge of this bridge; were to fix it in the proper place each time it was required, then remove it again, and so on, until the whole of us with our baggage and cannon had passed the several openings. The transport of our heavy guns was entrusted to 250 Tlascallans and fifty of our men. Sandoval, Lugo, Ordas, and Tapia, formed the vanguard; these were to clear the streets of the enemy, and for that purpose were reinforced by eight or ten of Narvaez's officers, whose names I will not mention, and 100 of our strongest and most nimble young soldiers. Cortes himself was to take his station, supported by Oli, Avila, Bernardino de Tapia, besides other officers and fifty soldiers, between the baggage, our Indian female servants and the prisoners, in order to render assistance wherever it was most required. The rear-guard was to be commanded by Leon and Alvarado, consisting of the main body of the cavalry, 100 foot, and the greater part of Narvaez's troops. Doña Marina and Doña Luisa, with the prisoners, were to be guarded by 300 Tlascallans and thirty Spaniards.

After these arrangements had been made, and night was fast approaching, Cortes ordered his chamberlain Christobal de Guzman to see that all the gold, silver, and other valuable matters were brought together in one apartment. The royal treasurers, Alonso Avila and Gonzalo Mexia, were then desired to deduct the emperor's portion, and load eight of our wounded horses and eighty Tlascallans with it. The greater part of the treasure consisted of broad bars of gold, with which the horses and men were as heavily laden as possible.

Cortes then called his private secretary Pedro Hernandez, and the other royal secretaries, and spoke to them as follows: "Put down in writing and bear witness that I have done all which lay in my power to save this treasure, which is valued at 700,000 *pesos*. You see it is impossible to load any more of it on the Indian porters and the eight horses; I will, therefore, allow the soldiers to take as much away with them as they can conveniently carry, that this treasure may not fall into the hands of these Mexican dogs."

As soon as Narvaez's men and many of our old soldiers heard this, they stowed away as much as they could. For myself, whose failing had never been to covet gold, I took four *chalchihuis* stones out of a small box, and secreted them between my cuirass. Cortes soon after gave this box in safe keeping to his steward, and I do think he would have demanded the said four *chalchihuis* stones back again of me if I had not quickly secreted them. This small treasure proved afterwards of the greatest value to me towards the curing of my wounds, and in procuring myself food.

All matters being now properly ordered, and the mode of our retreat settled, we began to move forward. It was about the hour of midnight, and rather dark, a thin mist hung over the town, and a gentle rain was falling.

The moment we began to move forward in the above-mentioned order, the rear-guard being already in motion, and our moveable bridge fixed, and Sandoval, with his body of horse, and Cortes, with those under his command, and many other soldiers, had passed across, the wild war music and loud yells of the Mexicans suddenly burst forth. "Up, up, Tlatelulco!" they cried; "out with your canoes! The *teules* are running away: cut off their retreat over the bridges!"

And before we had time to look about us, we were attacked by vast bodies of the enemy, and the whole lake was instantly covered with canoes, so that we were unable to move on any further, although many of our men had already passed the moveable bridge. Now the most obstinate conflict ensued for the possession of this, and, as misfortunes never come singly, it happened that two of our horses should slide out on the wet planks, become unmanageable, and roll over into the lake. This caused the bridge itself to overbalance and fall down. A number of Mexicans that instant fell furiously on us, and, though we exerted ourselves to the utmost, and cut down numbers of the enemy, we were unable to recover the bridge. As, however, those behind, kept continually pushing on those in front, the opening in the canal was speedily filled up with dead horses and their riders, who were inevitably lost if they were unable to swim. The unmerciful enemy now attacked us from all sides. A number of Tlascallans and our Indian female servants were carried off, with the baggage and cannon; numbers of our men were drowned, and no less a number, who were trying to save themselves by swimming, were taken prisoners by those in the canoes. It was heart-rending to behold this scene of misery, and to hear the moans and pitiful cries for assistance. "Help! help! I am drowning," cried one here: "help me, they are killing me!" cried another there. Here one called upon the name of the Virgin Mary for assistance; and there another upon Santiago de Compostella! Here another, who had managed to get to the water's edge, implored us to lift him out; yonder, again, was another clambering over the dead bodies. Many, when they had reached the high road, imagined themselves safe, but here they only met with denser crowds of the foe. Does any believe that there was a man amongst us who still observed the order of retreat as it was first regulated? That man would, indeed, have been a fool who had thought of anything else but of his own safety! Cortes, with the officers and soldiers who were with him, acted similarly, and dashed away, unmindful of the men, at full gallop, over the bridge, and strove to gain the main land: besides which, it must be acknowledged that our cavalry was quite useless here. Exposed on every side to the enemy's arrows and lances, pelted with stones from the housetops, they had also to encounter a forest of our own swords, which the enemy had captured and fixed to their long lances, so that it was a wonder each time a horse with its rider escaped. Neither could we defend ourselves in the water, as the wet had rendered our muskets and crossbows totally useless, while the darkness of the night made every movement uncertain. All our attempts to keep together were fruitless. What did it avail us if, at times, thirty or forty of us managed to make a stand, and boldly faced about? By this means we certainly advanced forward a little, yet none of us would have escaped alive, if, in the end, every one had not strove to save his own life. Thus sadly did we fare in that night, and had it been day we should have fared much worse. Indeed, if the Almighty had not lent us extraordinary powers, every man of us would have been killed! It was really terrific to see the immense crowds which fell upon us from all sides, and the number of canoes which were merely waiting for the moment to carry off the prisoners, all of whom were destined to be sacrificed to their gods! It was a fearful sight indeed!

I shall never forget how at one time about fifty of us had got together, and the Mexicans, while they fell upon us, constantly cried out, *"O, O, Luilones!"* meaning thereby, You wish to live, do you, you varlets? It was only by dint of heavy blows and hard fighting we were able to cut our way through.

At last, as we were approaching the main land near Tlacupa, where the vanguard, under Sandoval, with a large body of the cavalry and of our foot had arrived, we recognized the voices of Oli, Morla, and Sandoval, who were thus addressing Cortes: "Only consider for a moment, general, we are here indeed on safe ground, but there are still such numbers of our men in the streets behind the bridges, who will be inevitably lost unless we hurry back to their assistance. Up to this moment but few have been able to cut their way through, and these are all covered with wounds."

To which Cortes gave the sorrowful answer, "That it was a real wonder every time one of us escaped; if, however, they turned back to the bridges, they would certainly be lost with horses and all."

Nevertheless Cortes, Oli, Avila, Sandoval, Morla, and Dominiguez, turned back and took with them six or seven of the cavalry and a few of the foot who had escaped without a wound. They had not advanced far before they came up with Alvarado. He had lost his brown mare and was coming on limping with one foot, heavily wounded, with lance in hand, having only seven of his Spanish soldiers and eight Tlascallans left, all dripping with blood.

Cortes and those who had accompanied him now returned, and we took up a position close to Tlacupa. But even here the Mexicans had by this time arrived, and were stirring up the inhabitants of this town, of Escapuzalco, and of Tenayuacan against us.

Here again the Mexicans, who had fastened on our swords to their long pikes, set hard upon us, and we had enough to do to maintain our ground.

When Cortes came up with Alvarado and his few followers, and learnt the fate of those left behind, tears flowed from his eyes; for Alvarado and Leon had had above twenty horse and more than one hundred foot with them in the rear-guard. All these, with nearly the whole of the cavalry, and above one hundred and fifty other men of the old and new troops, had perished with Leon. Alvarado related, that after he and his men had all lost their horses, he managed to get together about eighty men, and with these he succeeded in passing over the first opening by clambering over the baggage, dead men and horses. Although I am not sure whether he said that he passed the opening by stepping over the dead bodies, I know that at this bridge more than 200 men, with Leon at their head, were cut to pieces by the enemy, notwithstanding all their courageous fighting. At the second bridge again, it was merely through God's mercy that Alvarado had saved himself, as all the canals and streets were crowded by the enemy.

It was also at this bridge of sorrows that the well-known leap of Alvarado was said to have taken place. At that time, indeed, none of us took notice whether he leaped well or not; for every one had enough to do to escape from the hands of the merciless enemy. I am, however, inclined to believe that this leap was nothing more than what Alvarado told Cortes himself, how he had made his bridge over the canal by clambering over the baggage, dead bodies, and drowned horses; for the water was too deep in that place for him to have swung across the opening by means of his lance, and the width of the canal too great, however nimble Alvarado may have been, for him to have leaped across. It would have been an impossibility I am sure to have crossed it by means of his lance or by leaping. I myself can speak from eyewitness; for the following year when we marched against Mexico, and surrounded the town on all sides, I often came in contact with the enemy at that bridge which now bears the name of Alvarado's leap. At that time the Mexicans had blocked up the passage with palisade and breastwork, and I very frequently spoke with my fellow-soldiers about the circumstance, but none of them ever thought such a leap possible. What people thought of it at the time itself the reader will see from the following anecdote.

Among Garay's troops there was a certain Ocampo who came to Mexico: this man possessed much wit and was always writing *pasquils*, or libelling some one or other. Among other things he wrote a good deal of scandal and falsehood respecting our officers, and accused Alvarado, that he had left Leon with upwards of 200 men and the whole of our cavalry which composed the rear-guard, in the lurch, and that in order to save his own life he had taken the Alvarado's leap indeed, in accordance with the old proverb: Leap and save your life![2]

As I have above mentioned, we had certainly reached Tlacupa, but had not escaped all danger there, for here again great numbers of Mexicans, with the troops of Tlacupa, Escapuzalco, Tenayuacan, and of the surrounding districts, continually assailed us; but it was from the maize plantations they did us most injury, and here we lost three more of our men, who had been previously wounded. The best thing we could therefore do was to quit this terrible neighbourhood as soon as possible. Some few of the Tlascallans knew a bye-road to Tlascalla, and they safely conducted us to a row of houses which stood on a rising ground, and here we quartered ourselves in a temple, which had also the appearance of a fortress. During the whole of this march

2. According to other accounts, it certainly appears that Alvarado made this astonishing leap. (*Monarchia* In., iv, c. 71.) We find that Alvarado was distinguished from his brother by the surname of Alvarado of the leap. Humboldt, in his interesting work on New Spain, has thought it worth his while to rescue the honour of this brave officer with regard to this leap. Even to the present day there is a small bridge near Bonavista, called Salto de Alvarado.

the Mexicans continually harassed our troops, and greatly annoyed us with their arrows, slings, and lances. The reader must not be displeased if I am forced to depict the same miserable scenes over again.

It was not until we had reached this temple that we were able to defend ourselves successfully. Here we lighted several fires, and dressed our wounds.

After the conquest of Mexico, we turned this building into a church, and dedicated it to our dear lady *de los remedios*. This church in course of time became very celebrated, and to this day numerous people make pilgrimages to that place, particularly females, from Mexico.

We found, however, nothing to eat here, and it was grievous indeed to see with what miserable rags we were obliged to dress our wounds, which had become chilled by the cold, and this increased their severity. But what grieved us most was the great loss of horses, and of so many of our brave companions. Of our old troops there were missing Leon, Salcedo, Morla, the brave lancer Lares, and several others. And yet I merely mention these few; for if I wished to mention the names of all those whom we had to mourn, I should not finish so easily. Most of Narvaez's men met with their death at the bridges, from the weight of the gold with which they had overburdened themselves. The Tlascallans, who had charge of the crown treasures, shared a similar fate. The astrologer Botello[3] found no protection in all his art, and perished with many others. Even Motecusuma's sons,[4] and other princes we had taken prisoners, met with their deaths in that dreadful night.[5]

Before coming to any determination as to what our next step should be, we proceeded to consider our present condition. The whole of us were wounded, and only twenty-three horses had escaped alive; our cannon were all lost, and we had not a grain of powder left; there were

---

3. According to other accounts Cortes put great faith in the secret art of this man. It was upon Botello's advice that he also attacked Narvaez in the night time. He had likewise advised the retreat from Mexico in the night time, although he knew, he said, that neither himself, his brother, nor several others of his company would escape alive.

4. During this retreat three of Motecusuma's sons lost their lives; but there were two other sons of this monarch who survived the fall of their house and became the founders of the distinguished *grandee* families of Spain, the earls of Montezuma and Tula; one was called Cano and the other Andrada Montezuma.

5. One circumstance Bernal Diaz has omitted to mention. After the enemy had taken possession of the bridges there were one hundred Spaniards, who, seeing no further chance of making good their retreat, fortified themselves on a *teocalli* or temple. Here these brave men maintained their position against the whole armed force of the town for three days, but hunger at length compelled them to surrender, and the whole of them were sacrificed to the idols.

but few crossbows remaining, though these, with the arrows, might speedily be replaced. Besides all this, the enemy were day and night at our heels, and we no longer knew on what footing we stood with our friends of Tlascalla. Nevertheless, we resolved to continue our march towards that country, and we set out at midnight. Our guides, with the Tlascallans, marched in advance; those who were more severely wounded, and obliged to use the support of a stick, were placed in the centre; and those who were not capable of moving at all were bound fast to the horses of those who were unable to fight. All who could bear arms were stationed in the flanks, and had some of the cavalry to support them; while the rear-guard was composed of the remaining horse. The Tlascallans who were wounded likewise marched in the centre, and those who were still capable of defending themselves joined our ranks, that we might be ready to receive an attack at any point, as the Mexicans were still close at our heels, yelling most hideously, and crying out from time to time, "Go on! go on! not one of you will escape alive!" At that moment we did not exactly understand what they meant, but soon after we discovered it, as we shall presently see.

I must not, however, forget to mention how greatly rejoiced we were to find that Doña Marina and Doña Luisa, who had left Mexico with the vanguard, were quite safe; but the greater part of our other Indian females, who had been presented to us by the Mexicans and Tlascallans, had not been so fortunate; almost the whole of these perished at the bridges. On this day's march we arrived at a considerable township, named Quauhtitlan, once the property of Alonso de Avila; there likewise we were received with reviling language, stones, and arrows, all of which we patiently endured. We fared no better in the numerous other small villages we passed through, while the pursuing Mexicans were continually increasing in numbers. They strove to lock us in on all sides, and sent forth so many stones, arrows, and lances upon us, while we were passing through a narrow defile, that two more of our men were killed who had been dangerously wounded in the last conflict, and also one of our horses; besides that, numbers of us were wounded. We certainly destroyed some of the enemy in return, but the number was small.

This night we quartered ourselves in a few straggling houses, and supped off the horse which had been killed.[6] The next morning early

6. The hunger which the Spaniards suffered during these days must have been excessive; for Torquemada states it as a fact, that one of the soldiers had cut out the liver from the body of another and devoured it; for which Cortes was nearly going to hang the man.

we continued our route, and marched in closer order than on the day previous, the half of our cavalry being always in advance. We had marched to the distance of about four miles along an open plain, where we considered ourselves in safety, when three of our horse came galloping up to inform us that the fields were covered with Mexicans, who were lying in wait for us. We were not a little dismayed at this intelligence; however, our courage did not flag so far as to prevent us from making immediate preparations for battle, and we determined to defend ourselves to the last. We halted for a few moments, and Cortes gave instructions for the cavalry to dash in a body full gallop upon the enemy, to aim at the face, and break their line. Our infantry were to direct their blows and thrusts at the enemy's lower quarters. In this way it was said we should be certain to revenge our dead and wounded, if it pleased the Almighty to spare our lives in the approaching battle.

We then commended ourselves to God and the holy Virgin, and boldly rushed forth upon the enemy, under the cry of *Santiago! Santiago!* Our cavalry charged the enemy's line five abreast, and broke it, we rushing in after them close at their heels. What a terrific battle and remarkable victory was this! How we fought man to man! and those dogs like the very furies themselves! and many of our men did they kill and wound with their pikes and huge broad swords.[7]

The level ground, however, was uncommonly favourable for the manoeuvres of our horse, which every now and then galloped at full speed in upon the enemy, and then retired, to watch another favourable opportunity. Although both horse and rider were severely wounded, yet they continued to fight most valiantly. It seemed as if we who formed the cavalry had double our usual strength; for, though we were covered with wounds, and each moment received fresh ones, yet we never gave them thought, but kept dashing in upon the foe without intermission. Cortes, Oli, Alvarado (who had borrowed a horse from one of Narvaez's men), and Sandoval, though all covered with wounds, were always present where the danger was greatest. Neither did Cortes omit to cheer us on by the most animating words, and to bring under our notice what a fine booty we should make of the enemy's rich apparel and ornamental weapons. But it was above all glorious to hear

7. Torquemada says, "That the Spaniards stood like a small island in the midst of the ocean, against which the rolling billows beat on every side." When Cortes decided the fate of the day by his courageous attack upon the Mexican commander, the battle had lasted five hours.

the brave and spirited Sandoval cry out, "On, my fellow-soldiers? this day the victory must be ours! Our trust is in God! We shall not lose our lives here, for God has destined us for better things!"

In this way we continued fighting courageously, for God and the blessed Virgin strengthened us, and St. Santiago de Compostella certainly came to our assistance; and one of Quauhtemoctzin's chief officers, who was present at the battle, beheld him with his own eyes, as he afterwards affirmed. At this moment it pleased the Almighty that Cortes' attention should be drawn to that part of the enemy's troops where the Mexican general-in-chief was stationed with the flying standard, clothed in the richest armour, shining with gold, and a *penache* of large white feathers on his head. As soon as Cortes espied him among his glittering retinue, he cried out to Alvarado, Sandoval, Oli, Avila, and many other officers, "Follow me, my brave companions; these are the men we must attack!" The words were scarcely out of his mouth, when they commended themselves to God, and galloped among the enemy; Cortes poised his lance, and made a rush at the Mexican commander-in-chief, who dropped the standard; our other officers at the same moment cutting down the other chiefs, by whom he was immediately surrounded.[8]

The Mexican generalissimo was about to snatch up the standard again and flee; but Juan de Salamanca, a native of Ontiveras, galloped after him on his splendid horse, and brought him to the ground, wrested the standard from his hand, and the rich bunch of feathers from his head, and presented both to Cortes, who had made the first run at the chief. Salamanca was subsequently rewarded for this piece of heroism; for a few years afterwards the emperor allowed him to assume a bunch of feathers in his coat of arms, which his descendants bear to this day.

After the Mexican chief had fallen and the royal standard was lost, and numbers of the enemy killed, they began to give way, and then fled. Our cavalry, however, kept close at their heels, and punished them severely. Now, indeed, we no longer felt our wounds, nor hunger, nor thirst, and it appeared to us all as if we were beginning the attack with renewed vigour! Our friends of Tlascalla had likewise changed into real lions, and hacked in furiously among the enemy with, the broad swords they had captured.

---

8. The Mexican general's name was Cihuacatzin; he was the Matlaxopilli, commander-in-chief, and carried the imperial standard, called Tlahuizmatlaxopilli, being a golden net ten palms in length.

After our cavalry had returned from the pursuit, we offered up thanks unto the Almighty for this victory, and our escape from the hands of so numerous an enemy; for the Spaniards had never before in India encountered so vast an army as on this occasion. It was composed of the flower of the joint armies of Mexico, Tezcuco, and of Xaltocan; while every Indian had entered the battle with the determination that not a soul of us should escape alive. It was also evident, from the richness of their arms and apparel, that a greater portion were officers and men of distinction.

Near to the place where this terrible and bloody battle was fought lay the township of Otumpan, by which name this battle will be known through all times to come. The Mexicans and Tlascallans have given a faithful representation of it in their numerous paintings of the battles we fought up to the conquest of Mexico.

For memory's sake, I must here note down that we marched into Mexico on the 24th of June, 1520, to Alvarado's assistance, with an army of nearly 1400 men, among which there were seventy-nine horse, eighty crossbow-men, and a like number of musketeers, with above 2000 Tlascallan troops, and a fine park of artillery. On the 10th[9] of July following we commenced our retreat, and on the 14th we fought the battle of Otumpan.

I must now likewise recount the loss we sustained in that time. In five days, including the battle of Otumpan, we lost in killed, and those who were taken prisoners, above 870 of our troops, and above 1200 Tlascallans; to which must be added 72 men and five Spanish females, all of Narvaez's division, whom the Mexicans put to death in Tustepec. About the same time the Mexicans likewise murdered old Juan de Alcantara, and three others, who were on their road from Vera Cruz to Mexico to receive their share of the gold. Thus these persons not only lost their gold, but their lives also. Indeed, if it be well considered, it will be found that none of us derived any blessings from the gold the Indians gave us. The reason why Narvaez's troops suffered more at the bridges than those of Cortes', was from their having overloaded themselves with gold, the weight of which prevented them from swimming, and otherwise encumbered their movements.

9. Bernal Diaz errs here with respect to dates, for the disastrous retreat from Mexico, according to Cortes' despatches and other accounts, took place on the 1st of July, and thus *la noche triste* (the night of sorrows) was on the night between the 1st and 2nd of July, and the battle of Otumpan took place on the 7th. There must either have been some mistake in the original manuscript or in the printing, for the years are also dated erroneously.

After this splendid victory, we dined off some gourds which grew in the fields, and joyfully continued our march to Tlascalla. We carefully avoided passing through any villages, as our enemies still continued at a distance to fly their arrows at us, and to pour out abusive language. It was not until the approach of evening that we resolved to enter a Mexican township, because it contained a temple and a large building, in which we could fortify ourselves. Here we quartered our troops for the night, dressed our wounds, and enjoyed a little repose. The Mexicans had certainly followed us, but without venturing too nigh, and it was visible in their countenances what they would say: "A good journey to you, you will now quickly have passed our boundaries!" Soon after we had left this place, the range of hills near Tlascalla came into view, and we felt equal joy at beholding these as if our native country had been there; yet we could not tell what the present feeling of that people towards us might be, or whether they had remained faithful! And we were also quite ignorant as to how matters stood at Vera Cruz, where the enemy might also have cut the garrison to pieces.

Our whole strength now merely consisted in 440 men, twenty horses, twelve crossbows, and seven muskets; besides that, we were all excessively weak, and covered with wounds; our cannon, with our store of powder lost; we were at present, therefore, doubly vigilant, and returned fervent thanks to God for having so miraculously rescued us out of the enemy's hand. Our troops, Cortes said, were now dwindled down again to the same number of men with which we had first set sail from Cuba, and entered the city of Mexico. We should therefore be particularly cautious not to give the Tlascallans any reason of complaint. This was especially intended for Narvaez's men, who were not so accustomed to subordination as we were. For the rest, continued Cortes, he hoped to God we should find the Tlascallans as faithful and true to us as before. If, however, they should have turned against us, we were not therefore to lose courage, but to trust in our strong arm, which had the power to overcome any foe.

We now continued our march with every military precaution, and arrived at a fountain on the slope of a hill, near to which were standing the walls and enclosures of ancient temples. These the Tlascallans said formed the boundaries between their territory and the Mexican empire. Here therefore we felt in greater safety, washed ourselves, and ate some little food. After we had sufficiently rested from our fatigues, we again marched forward, and arrived at a township called Gualiopar,[10] situated in the Tlascallan territory, where the inhabitants allowed us to quarter, and furnished us with food; but we were obliged to give them small pieces of gold or *chalchihuis* in exchange. In this spot we remained a whole day, to dress our wounds and those of our horses.

When the news of our arrival was received in the metropolis of Tlascalla, Maxixcatzin, the old Xicotencatl, and Chichimeclatecl, accompanied by the principal inhabitants of that town, and those of Huexotzinco, immediately set out to welcome us. They gave us the most hearty reception, and several of the chiefs wept aloud. "Alas! *Malinche, Malinche*," cried they, "how deeply we take your misfortune to heart, and lament the death of so many of your brothers, and of our countrymen, who have perished with them! How oft have we not warned you not to trust to the Mexicans, and told you they would certainly, one time or other, fall suddenly upon you; but you would not believe us. However, what has happened cannot be recalled; the only thing you must think of at present is, to cure your wounds and strengthen yourselves with good food. Do, therefore, just as if you were at home in your own country. Rest yourselves a little and then proceed to our town, where we will find you quarters. For the rest, *Malinche*, you may look upon it as no small piece of heroism that you fought your way out of that strong city after the bridges had been destroyed; and if we previously looked upon you as men of extraordinary courage, we do so now in a much wider sense. We are well aware that numbers of men and women of this country have to mourn the loss of their sons, their husbands and their brothers, but let not this be matter of too much grief to you. You have likewise great reason to be thankful to your gods who have conducted you here in safety, and who gave you power to gain the victory over that vast army, which we were well aware had been lying four days in wait for you at Otumpan. It was our intention to have come to your assistance with 30,000 men, but we were unable to collect such a body of troops in sufficient time."

Cortes, with the whole of the officers and soldiers embraced these excellent men in the most affectionate manner, and we made them a present in gold and jewels, to which every man among us was glad to contribute his mite. They were also extremely rejoiced to find that Doña Marina and Doña Luisa had escaped the carnage; but their joy

10. This is certainly a corrupted name, for it is dissimilar in sound to all others, and terminates differently.

soon turned into lamentations when they discovered what numbers of their countrymen were missing; and Maxixcatzin evinced excessive grief at the loss of Doña Elvira his daughter, and of Leon, to whom he had presented her.

We now, in company of all the *caziques* marched into the metropolis of Tlascalla. Cortes was quartered in the house of Maxixcatzin, and Alvarado in that of Xicotencatl. We dressed our wounds with great care, and patiently awaited their cure; four of our men, however, soon after died, and many others suffered for a length of time before they were completely restored.

Chapter 129
In Tlascalla

I have already mentioned that we rested a day at Gualiopar, where we were visited by the *caziques* of Tlascalla, who kindly offered us every assistance, which was the more praiseworthy in them when we take the time and circumstances into consideration.[1]

As soon as we had arrived in the Tlascallan metropolis, Cortes made inquiries respecting the 40,000 *pesos* worth of gold which he had forwarded to the latter place for the garrison of Vera Cruz; when Maxixcatzin, Xicotencatl, and one of our soldiers who had remained behind in Tlascalla on account of ill health, informed him that a certain Juan de Alcantara, with two others of the garrison lying in Vera Cruz had arrived there and taken all the gold with them, as they had produced a written permission to that effect signed by Cortes, which he, Maxixcatzin, had carefully saved. Upon being questioned as to the time they had left with the gold, we found it must have been during the days we had the severe engagements with the Mexicans. Subsequently we learnt that Alcantara and his companions had been murdered and robbed of their treasure on their road to Vera Cruz. Cortes was sorely grieved at this loss, and was most anxious to know how matters stood in the latter place. He therefore despatched three Tlascallans to that town with a letter, in which he gave a full account of all that had transpired at Mexico, but very wisely omitted to mention the number of men we had lost there. He likewise admonished the garrison to observe the utmost vigilance, and to keep Salvatierra and Narvaez close prisoners. They were desired to send their sick to

1. According to Torquemada, Cortes had left one of his officers, named Juan Perez, with eighty Spaniards in Tlascalla, when he first marched to Mexico. On learning from this officer that Maxixcatzin had offered to march at the head of 100,000 men to his assistance, he grew excessively angry with him, and reproached him in the severest terms for not having accepted of the offer.

Tlascalla with all their store of powder and crossbows. He at the same time wrote to Caballero, and particularly cautioned him not to allow any vessel to depart for Cuba, and to see that Narvaez did not escape. If he considered the two vessels of Narvaez which lay in the harbour there unfit for use, he was to run them on shore, and immediately send him the sailors and as many arms as he could spare.

These three messengers made all haste and soon returned with an answer from Vera Cruz, which gave us the good news that they had enjoyed the profoundest peace there, but had been apprized of our misfortune at Mexico by the fat *cazique* of Sempoalla. They also informed us that Juan de Alcantara and his companions had been murdered on their return.

Pedro Caballero sent word that all Cortes' commands should be attended to. One of the two vessels was still in good condition, but with the other he would act as he had been ordered and send the men to us, though he had not over-sufficient hands, as many of the sailors were sick and several had died.

All the reinforcement we received, on this occasion, consisted in seven men, of whom three were sailors. They arrived in Tlascalla under the command of a certain Lencero, to whom the tavern belonged, known to this day by the name of Venta de Lencero. Every one of these men were in bad health; five of them were covered with sore swellings, and the two others limped helplessly about with their bellies enormously swollen, so that the succours brought by Lencero became quite a byword among us.

I must now, however, relate something of a more serious nature. The reader cannot have forgotten the younger Xicotencatl, who commanded the whole armed power of Tlascalla against us, and who had always shown his hatred of us. This feeling was again aroused in him when the news of our flight from Mexico, and of the number of troops we had lost arrived in Tlascalla; and how we were marching towards the latter place to seek protection and assistance. Xicotencatl now, therefore, assembled his relations and friends, with all those whom he thought would enter into his views, and proposed that they should select some favourable opportunity, either in the day or night-time to fall upon us unawares and destroy us all. "He would," he said, "form a friendly alliance with the Mexican monarch, for which the present moment was particularly favourable, as the Mexicans had just elected a new monarch in the person of Cuitlahuatzin. We had," he continued, "left quantities of cotton stuffs and gold behind us in Tlascalla, and had brought an additional quantity with us, and they would all become wealthy personages by such a booty."

When the elder Xicotencatl received information of this rebellious movement, he grew excessively angry, and commanded his son to banish all such thoughts from his mind. Such a step as that, he said, would be altogether unjustifiable, and he might be sure, if Maxixcatzin and Chichimeclatecl got intelligence of it, they would certainly order him to be put to death, to which he himself would give his consent. Old Xicotencatl, however, might say what he liked, his son remained firm to his purpose, and set earnestly about to make the necessary preparations, when Chichimeclatecl, who was at enmity with the younger Xicotencatl, got secret information of his intentions, which he instantly communicated to Maxixcatzin, and both determined to call a meeting of the chief personages of the town, with the elder Xicotencatl and the *caziques* of Huexotzinco, and commanded the younger Xicotencatl to appear before them.

After all had been assembled, Maxixcatzin addressed the meeting as follows: "I ask you, do you yourselves think, or have you ever heard others say that such riches or so much prosperity was ever known for the last hundred years in the land of Tlascalla as since the time these *teules* have appeared among us? Were we ever so much respected by all our neighbours? It is only since their arrival we possess abundance of gold and cotton stuffs; it is since that time only we eat salt again, of which we had been deprived for such a length of time. Wherever our troops have shown themselves with these *teules*, they have been treated with the utmost respect; and if many of our countrymen have lately perished in Mexico, they certainly fared no worse than the *teules* themselves. All of you must likewise bear in mind the ancient tradition handed down to us by our forefathers, that, at some period or other, a people would come from where the sun rises, to whom the dominion of these countries was destined. How dare Xicotencatl, taking all this into consideration, contemplate this horrible treachery, from which nothing can flow but war and our destruction? Is this not a crime which ought not to be pardoned? Is it not exactly in accordance with the evil designs with which this man's head always runs full? Now that misfortune has led these *teules* to us for protection, and that we may assist them with our troops to renew the war with Mexico, are we to act treacherously to these our friends?"

To these reproaches, in which his own blind father joined, the younger Xicotencatl replied, that he persevered in his opinion that, under the present circumstances, it would be most politic to form an alliance with the Mexicans; and allowed himself many other impudent expressions, which so enraged the old chiefs that Maxixcatzin, Chichimeclatecl, and the elder Xicotencatl, notwithstanding his blindness, rose up from their seats, then fell upon the young man, and pushed him down the steps of the building, under the most abusive language. He would certainly have been killed on the spot, if respect for his aged father had not withheld them. In the meantime they imprisoned all those who had sided with him. To punish Xicotencatl himself, this was not exactly the time, and Cortes refused in any way to meddle in the matter. I have mentioned this circumstance to convince the reader how loyal and honest the Tlascallans were towards us, and how much we were indebted to them, particularly to the elder Xicotencatl, who, it is even said, had given orders for his son to be put to death, as soon as he had been informed of all his intrigues and treacherous designs.[2]

We had now rested twenty-two days, and had patiently awaited the cure of our wounds; and Cortes now determined upon making an incursion into the neighbouring province of Tepeaca, where several of Narvaez's men and some of ours had been killed on their march to Mexico. He accordingly told our officers what his plan was; but when Narvaez's men heard of a new campaign, they became quite low-spirited. The latter were not accustomed to war, and had had a sufficient taste of it in our overthrow at Mexico, the carnage at the bridges, and in the battle of Otumpan; and were very clamorous in their requests to our general to return to their commendaries and their gold mines in Cuba. They peremptorily refused to obey him any longer, and declared they would take no further part in his conquests; and Duero, who, from the very beginning, had been in secret understanding with Cortes, protested most loudly against this contemplated invasion of Tepeaca. They cursed the gold Cortes had given them, which had all been lost again in their flight from Mexico,

2. Torquemada throws more light on the reason of the younger Xicotencatl's wishing to form an alliance with Mexico. The Mexicans being aware that the Spaniards would derive great advantages by their alliance with Tlascalla, sent an embassy of six distinguished personages to draw this republic into an alliance with them. The matter was formally discussed by the Tlascallan chiefs in council, and though the Mexican ambassadors tried their utmost to persuade them into an alliance, the majority decided against it. At the head of the minority stood the younger Xicotencatl, and the debate was carried on with such asperity that the young hero, who had more penetration than the rest, was at length forcibly expelled the meeting.

and assured him they were glad enough to have escaped with their lives from that terrific battle. They were unanimously determined to return to Cuba, and said they were not desirous of suffering any further losses than they already had in this expedition.

Cortes, however, did not so soon give up all hopes of persuading them to join him in this campaign. He spoke to them in a very quiet and kind manner, and made many very excellent remarks, but all to no purpose; and when they found that Cortes persevered in his determination, they desired one of the royal secretaries to draw up a formal protest, in which they gave a circumstantial account of our present position, how we were in want of horses, muskets, crossbows, and even cords for the latter; in short, of everything necessary to carry on a war. They further went on to say, that the whole of us were covered with wounds, and that only 440 men remained of the united troops of Narvaez and Cortes; the Mexicans occupied every pass and every mountain, and the vessels would rot away with the worm if they lay any longer in the harbour; and so on.

After they had presented this protest in form to our general, he altogether objected to it, and we others of his old troops begged of him most earnestly not to allow any of Narvaez's men to return to Cuba, as it would every way prove injurious to the cause of God and the interest of our emperor.

When they found that all the steps they had taken were fruitless, and that we maintained they were imperatively called upon to remain, both for the service of God and of our emperor, they at last consented to stay, and declared their willingness to join us in the contemplated campaign; but Cortes was obliged to promise that he would allow them to depart for Cuba as soon as ever circumstances would permit. This, however, did not put an end to their murmurs. We heard nothing but complaints against Cortes and his conquests,—how dearly they had paid for all this, left comfortable homes, and peace and security, to serve in a country where they lived in constant danger of losing their lives. They likewise considered it would be unpardonable in us to commence a second war with the Mexicans, with whom we should never be able to cope in the open field for any length of time, after what we had seen of their vast power both in Mexico and at Otumpan. Cortes, they continued, would not relinquish his purpose as long as his ambition to command was satisfied, and we others merely stuck to him because we had nothing to lose but our lives. Many similar reproaches did they throw out against Cortes, who, under the present circumstances, thought it was best to leave them unnoticed; and he was glad, a few months after, to send them home, as will be related in the proper place.

Here again I am bound to notice a number of errors in Gomara's history; in order, however, not to go too much into detail, I will confine myself to the following remarks.

Respecting the above-mentioned protest against the projected campaign of Tepeaca, Gomara does not exactly state with which party it originated, whether from Cortes' old troops or those of Narvaez. Everything he relates concerning this matter merely goes to raise Cortes to the skies and to cast the rest of us in the shade. We, the true Conquistadores, on reading his work, soon discovered that Gomara had been bribed by presents to relate the circumstances in that way. Were we not the very men who supported Cortes in all the battles, and in every other matter? and yet Gomara has the impudence to consider this as nothing, and affirms that we protested against the further conquest of New Spain. Gomara likewise commits a terrible blunder when he makes Cortes say, in answer to this protest, in order to inspire us with courage, that he would recall Leon and Ordas, of whom one, he says, was engaged forming a settlement with 300 men in Panuco, and that the other, with a like detachment, had been sent for a similar purpose to the River Guacasualco. Every word of this is false; for, when we marched to Alvarado's assistance in Mexico, those projected settlements were relinquished, as I have above mentioned, and both these officers went along with us to Mexico. Leon even met with his death at one of the bridges, as we saw, and Ordas was severely wounded in three several places. What a great pity it is that Gomara does not write with equal veracity as he does beauty!

I was likewise amazed to read what he says of the battle of Otumpan. He boldly asserts that we should have been defeated if Cortes had not been present, for he alone decided the fate of the day by his attack upon the Mexican commander-in-chief, who carried the royal standard. I should indeed be loth to do Cortes an injustice, and, as an excellent and brave general, I have the highest esteem for him; but certainly we have, above all, to thank the Almighty, who mercifully protected us in all the dangers we encountered, and who put under Cortes' commands such courageous officers and soldiers. The second praise is certainly due to us, whose valiant arms overcame every obstacle. We it were who firmly withstood the enemy's attack, who broke their line, and who punctually obeyed the commands of our general and his officers. And yet Cortes is said to have done all himself at the battle of Otumpan! Why does this Gomara not mention as well the heroic deeds of the officers and soldiers in that battle? But it is quite evident that all he relates in his book is intended for the praise of Cortes only, otherwise he could not have passed by all the rest of us in silence. He should have asked how often the brave Christobal de Olea had saved Cortes' life, until he met with his death in a similar attempt during the subsequent siege of Mexico?

I had nearly forgotten to mention the battle near Sochimilco, where Olea again saved Cortes' life, but which had nearly cost him his own, for he was severely wounded.

In order not to confound names, I must observe that we had among our troops a Christobal de Olea and a Christobal de Oli.

Gomara is right when he says that Cortes made a run at the Mexican commander-in-chief, which caused the latter to drop the standard from his hands; but then it is also a fact that Juan Salamanca, of Ontiveras, who became *alcalde* mayor of Guacasualco after the fall of Mexico, killed that chief with a thrust of his lance, tore away the splendid crest of plumes which adorned his head, and presented it to Cortes; for which reason he was subsequently permitted to add a bunch of feathers to his armorial bearings.

I do not mention these things to diminish Cortes' glory, for the praise and merit of all the victories we gained, and of the battles we fought, down to the total conquest of New Spain, are due to him, and he has deserved those honours with which the Castillians were wont to crown their generals after some splendid victories, and the triumphs which the Romans decreed to Pompey, Julius Caesar, and the Scipios. Cortes, indeed, has merited greater honours than all these Romans!

Gomara further relates that Cortes ordered the younger Xicotencatl to be secretly executed in Tlascalla as punishment for his treacherous designs against us; but this likewise is an untruth, for Cortes ordered him to be hung in a village near Tezcuco, as will be seen hereafter.

In the same way Gomara sends so many thousands of Indians with us into the field of battle, that there is neither sense nor meaning in what he says; and he likewise gives a very exaggerated account of the numbers of cities, towns, and villages, of which not one fifth part ever existed; and if we sum up what he says of the population, we shall find there are more millions than there are villages in Spain. Wherever he speaks of 80,000, we must really write down 1000. Everything certainly sounds very fine in his work, because he never at any time relates all that happened. When, therefore, the reader compares his account with mine, he must not allow himself to be blinded by the ornaments of his beautiful style, for mine is plain and rude, but truth supplies the place of art and eloquence. How much it is to be regretted that Dr. Illescas and Paul Jovio should have copied him so closely!

I must, however, return to my history on the campaign of Tepeaca.

Chapter 130

March into Tepeaca Province

Cortes had desired the *caziques* of Tlascalla to furnish him with 5000 men to join him on his march into the province of Tepeaca, whose inhabitants he was going to punish for the murder of several Spaniards. It was the township of Tepeaca, Quauhquechola, and Tecalco, which lay from twenty-four to twenty-eight miles from Tlascalla, against which our arms were particularly bent. If our desire to be revenged upon them was great, that of Maxixcatzin and the elder Xicotencatl was more so, as the inhabitants of those places had done great damage to their plantations; four thousand Tlascallan warriors, therefore, stood ready equipped to join us. All the provinces, however, which we intended to invade were quite prepared to receive us; for when the inhabitants there learnt that we had met with a kind reception in Tlascalla after our overthrow in Mexico, they did not doubt for an instant that, after we had recruited our strength a little, we should invade their territories in conjunction with the armed force of the former republic. Mexican troops were therefore stationed everywhere on the confines, and Tepeaca itself was strongly garrisoned. Maxixcatzin and the elder Xicotencatl were well aware of this, and, consequently, not without their fears. Notwithstanding all this, we commenced our march thither, but without either cannon or matchlocks, for we had lost all these in our flight from Mexico: though we had saved a few of the latter, we could make no use of them as we had not a grain of powder left.

Our small army now consisted of seventeen horse, six crossbowmen, and 420 Spaniards, most of whom were only armed with swords and shields, and 4000 Tlascallans. We merely took a single day's provision with us, as the provinces we were going to invade were very populous, and contained quantities of maize, fowls, and musk swine.

We observed our usual good custom of sending out a few scouts in advance, and we quartered ourselves for the first night about twelve miles from Tepeaca. The inhabitants, upon the news of our approach, had everywhere fled away, and carried off everything they could with them, so that we only found six men and four women in a small settlement near Tepeaca. Cortes, who always observed the strictest justice and order in all matters, questioned these prisoners respecting the eighteen Spaniards who had been murdered without any cause, and for what reason such vast numbers of Mexican troops had arrived, and why the property of our friends the Tlascallans had been destroyed?

He desired these prisoners whom he sent to Tepeaca to ask the inhabitants there these same questions, and they were to signify to them that they should send away the Mexicans who were there, and conclude a treaty with us, otherwise we should look upon them as rebels, murderers, and robbers, desolate their country with fire and sword, and carry off all the inhabitants into slavery.

These prisoners fulfilled their commission faithfully, and returned with two Mexicans. If we had sent a haughty message to our enemies, they returned answer in a still haughtier tone. The two Mexicans came with perfect confidence, as they well knew it was our custom to treat all ambassadors with great courtesy, and even make them presents. In this they had certainly not deceived themselves; and, still puffed up with the recent victory, they spoke with terrible assurance. Cortes, after they had done speaking, presented each with a mantle, and sent them back with offers of peace, adding, at the same time, he was well aware they could not return him his Spaniards alive; but if they would sue for peace, he would pardon the past. With this message he likewise sent a letter containing the same offers, though we very well knew they could not read it, yet by this time they had learnt so much as to know it contained some command, and Cortes desired the ambassadors to return with an answer. This they speedily brought, and was to the following effect: "We were to return to where we had come from; and if we refused to do so immediately, they would fall upon us the next day, and procure themselves a more abundant repast from the flesh of our bodies than they had done at the bridges of Mexico and in the battle of Otumpan."

On receiving this declaration Cortes called a council of war, in which the whole of these circumstances were taken down in writing by a royal secretary, and it was further resolved that whichsoever of the allies of the Mexicans had been found guilty of murdering Spaniards should be turned into slaves, since, after swearing allegiance to his majesty, they had rebelled, and caused us so great a loss of men and horses. This determination was likewise made known to the enemy, and they were again admonished to make peace with us; but we met with nothing but defiance in return; and if we did not quit the province they would march against us and put us all to death. Both sides thus made preparations for war, and a severe battle ensued the day after; but as the level ground, which consisted entirely of maize and *maguey* plantations, was particularly favourable for our manoeuvres, the bravery of our enemies availed them very little, and our few horse soon put them to the route. The rest of us likewise fell vigorously upon them, and our friends of Tlascalla behaved most valiantly, and pursued the enemy with great loss. Considerable numbers of Tepeacans and Mexicans were killed, while on our side we lost only three Tlascallans. Twelve Spaniards were slightly wounded, and one of our horses so severely that it died soon after. The consequence of this victory was, that numbers of women and children were brought in prisoners to us,—for the men we turned over to the Tlascallans, who made slaves of them all.

The Tepeacans, seeing that the Mexican garrison was no protection to them, and that they would only become the victims of any further opposition, without so much as consulting the Mexicans, now sent messengers of peace to us, who were very kindly received by Cortes; these Tepeacans then, for the second time, took the oath of allegiance to our emperor, and sent off the Mexicans.

We now, therefore, entered Tepeaca, and founded a town there, to which we gave the name of Villa de Segura de la Frontera, from its lying on the road to Vera Cruz, in a populous district, very productive of maize, and because it was covered by the close neighbourhood of Tlascalla. *alcalde*s and *regidors* were appointed, and a regular government introduced.

We likewise visited all the districts where Spaniards had been murdered, and we cast an iron mark, with the letter G, meaning *guerra*, (war,) with which those were to be branded whom we turned into slaves. In this way we severally visited the townships Quauhquechola, Tecalco, Las Guayavas, and others whose names I have forgotten. In the former place alone, fifteen Spaniards had been murdered in their quarters; we therefore spared this township least of all, and turned a vast number of its inhabitants into slaves.

About this time another king had been raised to the throne of

Mexico, as the former, who beat us out of the town, had died of the smallpox. The new monarch was a nephew, or, at least, a very near relative of Motecusuma, and was called Quauhtemoctzin. He was about twenty-five years of age, and a very well-bred man for an Indian. He was likewise a person of great courage, and soon made himself so greatly feared among his people that they trembled in his presence. His wife was one of Motecusuma's daughters, and passed for a great beauty among her countrywomen.

When this new king received intelligence of the overthrow of his troops at Tepeaca, and of the consequent submission of that province to the emperor Charles the Fifth, he began to fear for his other provinces. He therefore despatched messengers to every township, commanding the inhabitants to hold themselves ready for action; and in order that he might make sure of their obedience to his commands, he sent one *cazique* a present, and another he freed from paying tribute. His most able generals were despatched with troops to protect the boundaries, and he admonished them to behave better than they had done at Tepeaca.

That the reader may not confound the two names, I must take the opportunity to acquaint him that there was a Cachula and Guacachula. I must, however, defer for the present what I have to say about the last-mentioned place, to relate the news we received from Vera Cruz.[1]

---

1. According to Torquemada, these two townships were called Quauhquechulla and Quauhquechola.

Chapter 131

A Ship Arrives at Vera Cruz

We had scarcely punished these Tepeacans for the murder of our eighteen companions, and restored peace to the country, when letters arrived from Vera Cruz with the information that a vessel had run in there, commanded by a good friend of Cortes named Pedro Barba, who had been sub-governor of the Havannah under Velasquez. He had brought along with him thirteen soldiers and two horses, besides letters for Pamfilo Narvaez, whom Velasquez thought had by this time taken possession of New Spain in his name. In these letters, Velasquez desired Narvaez, if Cortes were yet alive, to transport him, with the whole of his principal officers, to Cuba, whence he would send them to Spain, for such were the commands of Don Juan Rodriguez de Fonseca, bishop of Burgos, and archbishop of Rosano, and president of the council of India.

As soon as Barba had entered the harbour and cast anchor, Caballero went on board to pay his respects to him. The boat he went in was well manned with sailors, and the arms they carried were carefully hidden from view.

After both parties had welcomed each other, Caballero inquired after the health of the governor of Cuba, and Barba, on his side, asked after Narvaez, and what had become of Cortes. Caballero gave him the most favourable account of Narvaez, spoke about his power, wealth, and his vast authority in these countries; as for Cortes, he had escaped with twenty men, and was wandering about from place to place.

Upon this, Caballero proposed to Barba that he should disembark at the next township, where he would meet with excellent quarters. This he readily agreed to, and stepped into Caballero's boat, which, by this time, had been joined by those of the other vessels, and so all went on shore; but he had scarcely set foot on land when Caballero exclaimed, "Sir, you are my prisoner, in the name of the captain-general Cortes!" One can easily imagine the astonishment of Barba and his men; however, they could do no better than patiently submit. The sails, compass, and rudder were immediately taken out of the vessel, and were all sent to Cortes' headquarters at Tepeaca.

Our joy was excessive when these succours arrived, and certainly they could not have come more opportunely, for we had not yet recovered from our wounds, or regained our usual strength. Every one of us suffered more or less from ill health, and as blood and dust had coagulated in our entrails, we consequently emitted nothing else. Add to all this, we were obliged to be under arms both night and day, and thus it may be imagined our condition was truly pitiable; and five of our men had died within the last fortnight of pleurisy.

There likewise arrived with Barba a certain Francisco Lopez, who settled at Guatimala, and became *regidor* of that place.

Cortes received Pedro Barba with every mark of distinction, and immediately gave him a company of crossbow-men. He likewise learnt from him that there was another smaller vessel at Cuba, which was taking in a cargo of provisions, and was also destined by the governor for New Spain. This vessel actually arrived at Vera Cruz eight days after, and was commanded by a cavalier, named Rodrigo Morejon. She had on board eight soldiers, a mare, six crossbows, and other kinds of ammunition. Morejon, with his vessel, was captured by Caballero in the same manner, and sent to Segura de la Frontera. Our joy at the arrival of these new guests was, if possible, greater than on the previous occasion. Cortes received them most kindly, gave each an appointment, and we thanked God most heartily for this reinforcement of men, arms, and horses.

We must now, however, return to the Mexican troops, which lay on the confines of Quauhquechola.

Chapter 132

The Quauhquechollans Ask Cortes For Liberation

The new king of Mexico had thrown strong garrisons into all the townships which lay on the boundaries, particularly into Quauhquechola and Ozucar,[1] which lay about twelve miles from each other, as he was sure we should enter his territories at those points. These garrisons allowed themselves excessive liberties under their new master, and committed so many atrocities against the inhabitants, that these were determined to bear it no longer. They not only complained of being robbed of their garments, their maize, their fowls, and their gold, but that the Mexicans likewise forcibly carried off their daughters and wives, if they were pretty, and violated them in the presence of their parents and their husbands.

When the Quauhquechollans saw how peaceably and quiet the Chollulans lived ever since they had been without a Mexican garrison, and that the same happiness and security might be enjoyed in Tepeaca, Tecalco, and in Quauhquechola, they secretly despatched four distinguished personages to Cortes, begging of him to send them his *teules*, with their horses, to rid them of their oppressors. They themselves, with the inhabitants of the whole district, would assist us, and both together could easily overcome the Mexican troops. Cortes, on this representation, resolved to send thither, under Oli, a strong detachment, consisting of 300 men, with the greater part of our cavalry and crossbow-men, besides a numerous body of Tlascallans, who had greatly increased in numbers since the rich booty they had made in Tepeaca.

Among the 300 of our own troops there were many of Narvaez's men who became quite terrified when they understood they

1. Most probably Iztucan.

were going to march against Indians; besides which, they had been informed that all the fields and houses were filled with Mexican troops, and that their numbers were even greater than at the battle of Otumpan, and that Quauhtemoctzin commanded in person. They had, indeed, from the beginning showed great unwillingness to join us in this new campaign, and all their thoughts were bent upon their return to Cuba. Now again all their late misfortunes, and the perils they had undergone, came forcibly to their minds: the lamentable flight out of Mexico, the terrible struggle at the bridges, and the battle of Otumpan. Such dangers, they said, they would not run the risk of encountering again, and they most earnestly begged of Oli to return to headquarters, as this expedition could not fail to end more seriously than all the foregoing, and every man of them would perish. It was in vain that Oli expostulated with them, and told them they were bound to march forward, and were in every way a match for the Mexicans; that a retreat would inspire the enemy with fresh courage, and that the level country was remarkably favourable for the manoeuvres of the cavalry; they absolutely refused to advance another step. Cortes' old soldiers, however, were determined to march forward, saying they had braved greater dangers than this; that a merciful Providence had everywhere protected them, and brought them forth victorious. But all these arguments were fruitless, and at last they succeeded in persuading Oli, by their prayers and lamentations, to turn back; and he took the road to Cholulla, from whence he wrote Cortes word of the state of things.

When the latter received this information he was greatly vexed, and he immediately despatched two crossbow-men with a letter to Oli, in which he expressed great surprise at his indetermination and weakness of mind; as on former occasions no arguments had ever been able to dissuade him from fulfilling the commands he had once received.

When Oli had read this letter he became furious with chagrin, and bitterly reproached those who had advised the retreat, and thereby induced him to disobey his general's commands. He immediately issued orders for every one to join his standard, and those who refused should be sent back to our headquarters, there to be punished by Cortes as cowards and deserters.

The vexation which this matter occasioned Oli had converted him into a very lion, and in this mood he marched his men onwards to Quauhquechola. He had scarcely arrived to within four miles of this place, when he was met by the *caziques*, who pointed out to him the best mode of attacking the Mexicans, and assured him he would be assisted by the inhabitants. They had hardly done speaking, when the Mexicans, who had received intelligence of Oli's approach, marched boldly against him. The battle now soon commenced, and the Mexicans certainly fought courageously for a considerable time, wounded several Spaniards, killed two horses, and wounded eight others from out a species of fortification which they had constructed here; but after an hour's fighting they were completely beaten out of the field. The Tlascallans behaved with uncommon bravery, and killed many of the enemy, besides taking a great number of prisoners; and as they were joined by the inhabitants of the surrounding country, the carnage among the Mexican troops was very great. The latter now retreated, and fortified themselves in a township named Ozucar,[2] which had been garrisoned by another body of Mexicans. This place was even rendered strong by nature, and the enemy had burnt down a bridge, to prevent our cavalry from entering the town. But, as I have before stated, vexation had turned Oli into a very lion, and he was determined that nothing should obstruct his progress. He therefore marched, with all those who would follow him, immediately upon Ozucar, passed the river with his new allies of Quauhquechola, and fell so furiously upon the Mexicans, that they soon gave way, and fled in disorder. Here again two horses were killed, Oli himself wounded in two places, and his horse very severely.

He remained two days at Ozucar, during which time the *caziques* of the whole surrounding country came to sue for peace, and declared themselves vassals of our emperor. After he had thus restored tranquillity to the whole country he returned to Villa Segura.

I myself was not present at this battle, and I therefore merely relate what I learnt from others respecting it. Cortes and the whole of us marched out to meet the returning conquerors, and the rejoicings, as may be imagined, were very great on this occasion. The retreat to Cholulla was now turned into matter of ridicule. Oli himself could not help laughing at it, and observed, that many of his troops thought more of their mines in Cuba than of their arms, and he swore that he would never again command any of those rich followers of Narvaez on such occasions, but only take with him a few of the poor soldiers of Cortes.

On this occasion Gomara relates, that Oli turned back in conse-

2. Cortes, in his despatches, calls this place Izzucan; the same, no doubt, as Iztucan.

quence of a mistake between the interpreters, and had feared there was some treachery on hand. This, however, is incorrect; for his return to Cholulla was entirely owing to the fear and anxiety of Narvaez's men, whom the Indians had crammed with all manner of fearful tales.

Gomara likewise says, that Cortes commanded in person on this occasion, but this is an untruth, for it was Oli. It is equally erroneous when he says that it were the Huexotzincans who had alarmed Narvaez's men with the exaggerated account respecting the Mexicans, when the former passed through their town. This is a shocking blunder, for it would be equally absurd for any one who wished to go from Tepeaca to Quauhquechola, to turn back to Huexotzinco, as it would be in going from Medina del Campo to Salamanca, to take the road over Valladolid. In the meantime other news had arrived from Vera Cruz, which will be found in the following chapter.

CHAPTER 133

Francisco de Garay's Ship

While we were lying at Villa Segura, Cortes was informed by letter that one of the vessels which Garay had fitted out for the object of forming settlements on the River Panuco had arrived at Vera Cruz. This vessel was commanded by a certain Comargo, and had on board above sixty soldiers, but who were all in very bad health, with their stomachs largely swelled.

This Comargo related how unfortunately Garay's expedition to the River Panuco had terminated. The Indians had massacred the commander-in-chief Alvarez Pinedo, with the whole of his troops and horses, and then set fire to his vessels. Comargo alone had been fortunate enough to escape with his men on board one of the vessels, and had steered for Vera Cruz, where they arrived half famished, for they had not been able to procure any provisions from the enemy. This Comargo, it was said, had taken the vows of the order of the Dominicans.

Comargo and his men, by degrees, all arrived at Villa Segura; which indeed took a considerable time, for they were so weakened that they could scarcely move along. When Cortes saw in what a terrible condition they were, he recommended them to our care, and showed Comargo and all his men every possible kindness. If I remember rightly, Comargo died soon after, and also several of his men. We used to call them, jokingly, *verdigris bellies*, from the immense size to which the latter were swollen, and the death-like appearance of the men.

In order not to break the thread of my history too frequently, I will take this opportunity of enumerating the different vessels of Garay's expedition which arrived by degrees in Vera Cruz.

The first which came after Comargo was commanded by a native of Aragon, named Miguel Diaz, whom Garay had sent with succours to Alvarez Pinedo, who, he imagined, had run up the River Panuco. Diaz, however, meeting nowhere with any traces of him, had soon got into a conflict with the natives, by whom he was informed of the unfortunate termination of that expedition; he then again hoisted sail and made for Vera Cruz, where he disembarked his troops, consisting of upwards of fifty men and seven horses, with which he immediately repaired to Cortes' headquarters. These were the most valuable succours we ever received, and certainly they could not have come more opportunely.

This Miguel Diaz subsequently rendered our emperor the most signal services in the conquest of New Spain. He was for some time engaged in a lawsuit respecting the possession of half Mistitan, with a brother-in-law of Cortes, named Andreas de Barrios, of Seville, whom he commonly termed the dancer. This lawsuit terminated in his favour in this way, that he was to receive the whole of the yearly rents of that estate, amounting annually to above 2500 *pesos*; but he himself was prohibited from setting foot in that district for the space of two years, for having there, as well as in other townships belonging to him, put several Indians to death.

A few days after this vessel another arrived in Vera Cruz, which Garay had likewise despatched for the protection of his armament in the River Panuco, where he thought all was going on prosperously. This vessel brought above forty men, ten horses, and various kinds of ammunition, and was commanded by an elderly man named Ramirez, whom we called the elder to distinguish him from another Ramirez, who served in our troops. In this way Garay lost one ship after another, and no one derived any advantage from them excepting Cortes and ourselves. All these troops arrived by degrees in Tepeaca, and respectively obtained some by-name or other from our men. Those of Diaz, who were all stout, fat fellows; were called the *stiff-backs*, and those of Ramirez, *pack-saddles*, because they all wore heavy cotton cuirasses, which no arrow could pierce. The officers, as the reader may imagine, received most distinguished treatment from Cortes.

I have now, however, to speak of another expedition, of which Cortes gave the command to Sandoval, and was directed against the tribes of Xalatzinco and Zacatemi.

Chapter 134

Sandoval and 200 Men

After we had received these reinforcements, first the twenty-five men and three horses, which arrived in the two small vessels sent by Diego Velasquez, and then the 120 men, with the seventeen horses which arrived in Garay's vessels, we learnt that many of Narvaez's men on their retreat from Mexico had been murdered in the townships of Zacatemi and Xalatzinco; likewise that the inhabitants of these places had plundered and killed Juan de Alcantara and his two companions who were returning from Tlascalla with the gold above mentioned. Cortes, therefore, ordered Sandoval, a remarkably bold and clever officer, to march against them with 200 men, composed for the greater part of Cortes' old soldiers, among which there were twenty horse and twelve crossbow-men, to which was added a strong body of Tlascallans.

Sandoval, on his march thither, received intelligence that the inhabitants were all under arms, and had put these towns in a good state of defence; and were, moreover, assisted by a powerful body of Mexicans. They well foresaw that we should equally chastise them for the Spaniards they had murdered, as we had the Tepeacans, Quauhquechollans, and Tecalcans.

Sandoval placed his troops in the most advantageous manner, and explained to the cavalry how they were to break through the enemy's line. But previous to entering on the enemy's territory he sent messengers with offers of peace to them, and to demand the gold they had stolen, with promises that he would pardon the murder of the Spaniards. These messengers went several times to the enemy with these offers, but each time returned with the same answer, namely, that they would serve Sandoval and his soldiers in the same manner as they had those *teules*, respecting whom he now came to make inquiries. Sandoval then sent them word that he would treat them as traitors and highwaymen, and turn them all into slaves; they might therefore prepare for a struggle for life or death. He then fell upon them from two several points at the same time, and though the Mexicans, as well as the inhabitants, defended themselves with great bravery, he nevertheless soon put them to flight, and captured numbers of the commoner people, whom, however, he set at liberty again, for want of men to guard them. In one of the temples he found a quantity of clothes, arms, and horse-trappings, among which were two saddles; all of which the Indians had brought as offerings to their idols.

In this place Sandoval stayed three days, during which time the *caziques* of the country came to beg pardon of him, and to take the oath of allegiance to his majesty; but he informed them they must return the stolen gold before he could think of granting their request. To which the *caziques* answered, that the Mexicans had taken away all the gold, and presented it to their new king. Upon this Sandoval referred them to Cortes himself, and he marched back to our head-quarters, with a great number of women and young men, whom he had taken prisoners, and marked with the iron.

Cortes was highly delighted at beholding these troops return in so good a condition, though they had three horses killed and eight men heavily wounded, among whom was Sandoval himself, who had been struck by an arrow. For myself, I was not present in this expedition, for I was suffering severely at the time from fever and spitting of blood; but thank God I recovered, after frequent bleeding.

The *caziques* of Xalatzinco and Zacatemi, besides several other chiefs of the neighbouring districts, now came to Cortes; they begged for peace, took the oath of allegiance to our emperor, and furnished us with provisions.

This expedition was attended by many beneficial results; for the whole country was thereby tranquillized, while it spread a vast idea of Cortes' justice and bravery throughout the whole of New Spain; so that every one feared him, and particularly Quauhtemoctzin, the new king of Mexico. Indeed Cortes' authority rose at once to so great a height, that the inhabitants came from the most distant parts to lay their disputes before him, particularly respecting the election of *caziques*, right of tenure, and division of property and subjects. About this time thousands of people were carried off by the smallpox, and among them numbers of *caziques*; and Cortes, as though he had been lord of the whole country, appointed the new *caziques*, but made a point of nominating those who had the best claim.

Such a case happened with a near relative of Motecusuma, who was married to the sovereign of Iztucan, by whom she had a son, who was acknowledged as nephew to Motecusuma; the point in dispute being who the heir was to that principality, this nephew, or some other *grandee* of the country. Cortes decided in favour of Motecusuma's nephew, and they adhered to his decision. Numerous similar disputes were brought for Cortes' arbitration, even from the most distant districts.

About this time we also learnt that nine of our countrymen had been put to death in the township Cocotlan, called by us Castel Blanco, being about twenty-four miles from our headquarters. Sandoval therefore was ordered thither, with thirty horse, one hundred foot, eight crossbow-men, five musketeers, and a strong body of Tlascallans, who always proved themselves faithful friends and brave warriors. Here again Sandoval sent five distinguished personages of Tepeaca to the Cocotlans with the usual offers of peace, accompanied by threats; but as there was a strong garrison of Mexicans lying in the town, they returned for answer that they had already a king in Quauhtemoctzin, and wanted no other; nor did they see any reason why they should send us ambassadors. They would meet us on the field of battle; their strength was as great now as it was in Mexico, at the bridges, and the canals; and how much our valour had availed us there they had sufficiently experienced.

On receiving this answer, Sandoval regulated the order of attack, in which the instructions he gave the Tlascallans were remarkable, namely, that they should not rush in upon the enemy at the same moment with the Spaniards, for fear of shying our horses, and lest they should expose themselves to the fire of our muskets, as had often been the case on previous occasions. They were commanded to remain stationary until the enemy was routed, and then follow in pursuit.

Having made these regulations, Sandoval marched towards the township. He had not advanced far before he came up with two bodies of the enemy, who had taken up a position in a hollow at the back of a barricade, which had been constructed of trees cut for the purpose. For a time the enemy's troops fought with desperate courage; but Sandoval kept up so sharp a fire upon them with the crossbows and muskets, that he soon was enabled to force a passage with the horse. In this attack four of his men and nine horses were wounded, one of which died soon after. Though the number of loose stones here were great obstacles to the cavalry, yet he succeeded in breaking through the enemy's ranks, and he advanced up to the town itself, in front of which stood a large building and fortification, besides several temples, in which other detachments of the enemy were stationed. Here Sandoval encountered a momentary and desperate resistance, but the Indians were again beaten, with seven killed. The Tlascallans now no longer waited the signal for pursuit, but rushed forward the more bravely, as this district lay near to their own territory. Numbers of females and people of the lower classes were taken prisoners.

After this victory, Sandoval remained there two days, and despatched one of the Tepeacan chiefs to the *caziques* of the district to summon them into his presence. They were not long before they made their appearance, and begged forgiveness for the murder of the Spaniards. He told them this would be granted on condition they delivered up all the property they had found on those they had put to death. They answered, however, that this was out of their power, since everything had been burnt, but owned that the greater part of the Spaniards had been eaten up by themselves, and that five had been sent alive to Quauhtemoctzin in Mexico. They had now, they thought, received sufficient chastisement for those they had murdered by the losses they had sustained in this battle; they hoped, therefore, he would pardon them, and they would, in return, furnish us with excellent provisions, and also forward a large supply to *Malinche*'s headquarters. Sandoval, finding that nothing further was to be got out of them, granted their request, for which they appeared very grateful, and offered to do him all manner of good services. Sandoval now returned with his troops to Tepeaca, and met with a most hearty reception from us all.

Chapter 135
Branding Slaves

After peace had thus been restored to the whole province, and the inhabitants had submitted to the sceptre of his majesty, Cortes, finding there was nothing further to be done at present, determined, with the crown officers, to mark all the slaves with the iron, and set apart the fifth of them for his majesty. Notice was, therefore, given that every person was to come with his slaves to a certain house appointed for the purpose, that they might be marked with the red-hot iron. Every man, accordingly, brought the females and young men he had taken prisoners; for grown-up men were of no use to us, as they were so difficult to watch, and we cared not to admit them into our service, as we were well satisfied with the Tlascallans. After all the slaves had been brought together and severally marked with the letter G, the emperor's fifths and then Cortes' were deducted before we were aware of it; and, besides this, on the night preceding, the finest of the Indian females had been secretly set apart, so that when it came to a division among us soldiers, we found none left but old and ugly women. This occasioned excessive murmuring against Cortes and all those who had thus picked and chosen before us; and some of Narvaez's men told Cortes to his face that they were not aware, up to the present moment, there were two kings in the Spanish dominions, and that two royal fifths could be demanded. A certain Juan Bono, who was also loud in his complaints, added, that such proceedings should not be permitted in New Spain, and that he would send information of it to his majesty and the council of India. Another soldier asked Cortes if the division he had made of the gold in Mexico was not a sufficient imposition? for, at first, he had merely spoken of 300,000 *pesos*, but when we were obliged to retreat from the city, it was estimated at 700,000 *pesos*. And now he was going to deprive the poor soldier, who had undergone so many hardships, and suffered from innumerable wounds, of this small remuneration, and not even allow him a pretty Indian female for a companion! When notice was given, continued he, that each person was to produce his prisoners, in order that they might be marked, it was thought they would have been valued, and that the emperor's fifths would have been deducted therefrom in money, and that no mention would have been made of fifths for Cortes.

Similar and even severer speeches were in every one's mouth respecting Cortes' fifths, until the latter began to consider it high time to pacify these daring spirits. He stated, therefore, and swore upon his conscience, (for this was his usual oath,) that it should not happen in future, but that all the prisoners should be valued, and sold at their valuation, which would put a stop to all further discontent on that head. This resolution was subsequently adhered to, particularly after the conquest of Tezcuco, where we took a vast number of prisoners.

If this circumstance had occasioned ill blood, another of a different nature occasioned worse. The reader will remember that, on the night of sorrows, after as much of the gold had been stowed away as could be, Cortes had given what remained as prize-money to the soldiers. Many of Narvaez's men and several of ours had dived deep into the gold, and most of those who had overloaded themselves with it lost their lives in the retreat. Several, however, had had the good fortune to escape with their treasures, but had paid dearly for it with severe wounds and the risk of their lives.

When Cortes learnt that there were still a great many bars of gold among the men, and heavy gambling in consequence, (for, according to the old saying, gold and love cannot lie long concealed,) he made known, under threats of severe punishment, that every one should produce the gold he had obtained on the night of our retreat from Mexico, of which one third was to be returned to him; but that any one who refused to pay this, should have the whole taken from him. Many of our men refused downright to comply with this; yet Cortes managed to extort a good deal of it under the pretence of a loan: but, as most of the officers and crown officials had also well stocked themselves with gold on that occasion, Cortes suddenly dropped the question, and nothing further was heard of it. It is certain, however, that this circumstance injured him vastly in every one's opinion.

Chapter 136

Narvaez's Officers Return to Cuba

The officers of Narvaez's troops and those who had come from Jamaica in Garay's expedition, seeing that the whole province of Tepeaca was now tranquillized, begged Cortes would fulfil his promise, and allow them to depart for Cuba; who not only granted them their request, but promised them, and particularly Duero and Bermudez, that he would give them much more gold after the total conquest of New Spain and Mexico, than they had previously received. In the meantime he furnished them with provisions of the kinds we had, consisting in maize, salted dog's flesh, and fowls. He likewise gave them one of our best vessels, and sent by them letters to his wife Catalina Suarez de Mercayda, and to his brother-in-law Juan Suarez, who was then staying at Cuba. These letters were accompanied by a few bars of gold and some jewels, and contained, among other things, an account of our overthrow at Mexico.

All those who left New Spain on that occasion had accumulated great riches, and I will give their names, as far as my memory permits. Duero, Bermudez, Bono, Bernardino Quesada, Francisco Velasquez, with the hunchback, a relation of the governor of Cuba; Carrasco, who afterwards returned to New Spain, and now lives at Puebla; Melchior de Velasco, of Guatimala; a certain Ximenes, who lives at Quaxaca, and was obliged to go to Cuba on account of his son; the accountant Leon de Cervantes, who made the same excuse to see his daughter there, for whom he concluded a most excellent match after the conquest of Mexico; Maldonado de Medellin was forced to leave on account of ill health; the other of that name, who was surnamed the proud, and was married to a lady named Maria Arias, likewise left us; further, a certain Vargas, of Trinidad, who, at Cuba, was commonly called the gallant; lastly, one of Cortes' old warriors, the pilot Cardenas, who said to one of his companions, "We soldiers may now take our repose, since New Spain has two kings." Cortes had presented him with 300 *pesos*, to induce him to return with his wife and family. Besides these men, there were many others whose names I have forgotten, which, indeed, is a good thing, for it prevents me from going too much into detail.

As soon as Cortes had given them permission to leave, we asked him why he had allowed them to depart, as he knew there would be so few of us remaining? Cortes said he had done so to rid himself of their eternal complaints and solicitations. We likewise knew that many of them were not fit for service, and it was better to be alone than in bad company.

Pedro de Alvarado was commissioned to see them safe on board, with orders to return immediately to headquarters after they had left.

About this time Cortes also despatched Ordas and Alonso de Mendoza on business to Spain, but for what particular purpose he never told us. We only heard that the bishop of Burgos told Ordas to his face that we were all villains and traitors, and that Ordas had boldly defended us. The latter, on this occasion, was made *comptoir* of Santiago, and received permission from the emperor to assume a burning mountain in his coat of arms. What he further did in Spain I will relate hereafter.

Alonso de Avila, who was treasurer of New Spain, and Alvarez Chico, another thorough man of business, were despatched in another vessel to St. Domingo to render an account of all we had done to the royal court of audience there, and to the Hieronymite brothers, who were appointed viceroys over the whole of the islands, to gain their approbation of our proceedings against Narvaez, and their sanction of the manner in which we had enslaved and punished the inhabitants who had murdered the Spaniards and rebelled against his majesty: and their opinion as to whether Cortes should not similarly punish all those tribes who, as allies of the Mexicans, had been guilty of like offences. Lastly, Cortes begged of them to inform his majesty of all this, and of the great services we had rendered and still daily rendered to the crown; and requested them to favour our just cause against the bishop of Burgos, who was striving to work out our ruin.

A third vessel was despatched by Cortes to Jamaica, to purchase horses there, the command of which was given to Solis, who was the son-in-law of the bachelor Ortega. Here the reader might be induced to ask whence Cortes obtained the money to do all this? In reply to which, I can only say that of the gold stowed away by Narvaez's and our own troops, particularly by the horse, a great quantity was certainly saved. Besides that, many of the eighty Tlascallans, who were loaded with the gold, and retreated from Mexico in the vanguard, got safely over the bridges. We poor soldiers, who had not to command but to obey, cared very little at that time whether there was plenty of gold or not, but were happy if we escaped alive and were able to cure our wounds. However, of the gold that was saved, Cortes received as much back as he could possibly lay his hands on; our men likewise suspected that he had put into his own pocket again the 40,000 *pesos*, being the share of the Mexican treasure belonging to the garrison ofVera Cruz. With this money he sent persons to Spain and St. Domingo on his own private business, and others to Jamaica to purchase horses.

Perfect tranquillity being now again restored to the province of Tepeaca, Cortes marched back with his troops to Tlascalla, and left Francisco de Orozco behind, with twenty invalid soldiers, as commandant ofVilla Segura.

Cortes then ordered the necessary quantity of wood to be felled for building thirteen brigantines, with which another attack was to be made upon Mexico; for we were convinced we should not be able to make any impression upon that town without a small fleet, nor ever again be able to enter it by the causeways. Martin Lopez was appointed by Cortes to superintend the important business of constructing these brigantines, for he was not only a good soldier, but, upon the whole, rendered his majesty the greatest services in all our warlike operations. On this occasion again, he set to work with his usual assiduity, and it was very fortunate that this man had been with us from the beginning; for, if we had been forced to send for a ship-builder from Spain, we should have lost much valuable time, and we might not have found a man who suited so well.

On our arrival in Tlascalla, we found that our old friend Maxixcatzin, one of his majesty's most faithful vassals, was no more, he having died of the smallpox. We were all sorely grieved at this loss, and Cortes himself, as he assured us, felt it as much as if he had lost his own father. We put on black cloaks in mourning for him, and paid the last honours to the remains of our departed friend, in conjunction with his sons and relations.

A dispute having arisen in Tlascalla respecting the heir to the *caziquedom*, Cortes pronounced in favour of the deceased's son, in accordance with the last wishes of his late father. Maxixcatzin, on his death-bed, strongly advised his whole family to remain faithful to *Malinche* and his brothers; for they, he said, were certainly those people for whom the dominion of these countries had been predestined.

However, let us leave the dead in peace, and turn to the living. The elder Xicotencatl, Chichimeclatecl, and the other *caziques* of Tlascalla, one and all gladly offered their assistance to Cortes in cutting wood for the building of the brigantines, and generally to aid in prosecuting the war against Mexico.

Cortes gave them all a hearty embrace, and thanked them for their great kindness, especially Chichimeclatecl and Xicotencatl, the latter of whom eventually became a convert to Christianity, and was baptized by father Olmedo with every solemnity, and received the name of Don Lorenzo de Vargas.

In the meantime the preparations for the building of our brigantines were going on very fast; the wood being soon felled and prepared for use with the assistance of the Indians; an excellent soldier named Andreas Nuñez, and Ramirez the elder, an old carpenter who had been lamed by a wound, rendering most efficient services. Matters being thus far advanced, Cortes sent for a quantity of ironwork, anchors, sails, and ropes, from the vessels which had been destroyed at Vera Cruz, and ordered all the smiths of that town to repair to Tlascalla. Above 1000 Indians were despatched thither to transport these things. The cauldrons for boiling and preparing the tar were likewise brought from Vera Cruz, and we were now only in want of the materials for making it, the preparation of which was wholly unknown to the Indians; but here again Cortes was not at a loss, for he picked out four men from among the sailors who understood its preparation, and for that purpose sent them off to a forest of pine trees near Huexotzinco.

Though it may, perhaps, be rather out of place here, I must answer a question which has been put to me by several cavaliers respecting Alonso de Avila, with whom they were well acquainted. They knew that this man, though treasurer of New Spain, was, at the same time, an excellent soldier, and felt more inclination for the life of a warrior than for business; they could not, therefore, imagine why Cortes should exactly have selected him to confer with the Hieronymite brothers at St. Domingo, and that he had not rather chosen some person of more business-like habits; as, for instance, Alonso de Grado, or Juan de Cacares, called the wealthy, or others whose names they mentioned to me. Cortes had no other motive than to get Avila out of the way, because he spoke his mind too freely, and took every occasion to side with us soldiers if he saw we were unjustly dealt with. To this was added, that the latter had fallen out with several of our officers, from a frankness of disposition displeasing to them. And, lastly, Cortes was desirous of conferring the command of a company on Andreas de Tapia, and of appointing Alonso de Grado treasurer, both of which were only possible by removing Avila.

Cortes now determined to march, with the whole of his men, to Tezcuco, as the wood for constructing the brigantines was ready prepared, and we had got rid of Narvaez's men, who made difficulties in all our expeditions, and always argued against any attempt to besiege Mexico, maintaining we were not sufficiently numerous for that purpose; by which means they infected others with their cowardice. Previous to our leaving for Tezcuco, however, various deliberations took place as to which would be the most eligible spot for launching our brigantines. Some of our men maintained that Ayotzinco, near to Chalco, on account of its canals and harbour, was better adapted for this purpose; others, again, preferred Tezcuco, and were of opinion that, once having taken possession of that town, standing as it did in the midst of so many other populous townships, we should be better able to plan our operations against Mexico.

We had scarcely decided in favour of the latter place, when three men arrived with the news from Vera Cruz that a large Spanish vessel had run in there from the Canaries, having on board a quantity of crossbows, muskets, powder, and other ammunition, besides three horses and thirteen soldiers. The owner of the cargo was a certain Juan de Burgos, and the captain of the vessel was named Francisco Medel.

The reader may easily imagine our joy at this news; and if we had previously felt in good spirits for our intended expedition, we now felt the more so on hearing of the arrival of these timely succours. Cortes immediately bargained with Burgos for the whole of the ammunition and cargo, who himself, with Medel and all the passengers, came to our headquarters, where they met with the kindest reception. Among the passengers there was a certain rich man, named Juan del Espinar, who once lived in Guatimala; further, a certain Sagredo, from Medellin; a Biscayan, named Monjaraz, uncle of the other two of that name serving among us. This Monjaraz had a very beautiful daughter, who subsequently came to Mexico, and was commonly called Monjaraza. But this Monjaraz did not accompany us in any of our expeditions, as he was always suffering from ill health. It was not until we had laid regular siege to Mexico that he came to us in good health, and told us he was desirous of seeing how we carried on this war, and our mode of attacking the Mexicans, of whose bravery he entertained a very mean opinion. On this occasion he mounted to the top of an Indian temple, which was shaped like a tower; from that moment, however, we never saw him again, nor did we ever learn how the Mexicans got at him, or what became of him. Many persons who had known him on the island of St. Domingo saw the hand of God in his sudden death: for they related that he had put his own wife, a most virtuous, excellent, and beautiful woman, to death, without any cause or provocation; and that he had escaped punishment for his crime by proving, through false witnesses, she had attempted to poison him. I must, however, leave these old tales, and begin earnestly to think of our march to Tezcuco.

Bernal Diaz's story continues in Volume 2

ALSO FROM LEONAUR

AVAILABLE IN SOFTCOVER OR HARDCOVER WITH DUST JACKET

A HISTORY OF THE FRENCH & INDIAN WAR *by Arthur G. Bradley*—The Seven Years War as it was fought in the New World has always fascinated students of military history—here is the story of that confrontation.

WASHINGTON'S EARLY CAMPAIGNS *by James Hadden*—The French Post Expedition, Great Meadows and Braddock's Defeat—including Braddock's Orderly Books.

BOUQUET & THE OHIO INDIAN WAR *by Cyrus Cort & William Smith*—Two Accounts of the Campaigns of 1763-1764: Bouquet's Campaigns by Cyrus Cort & The History of Bouquet's Expeditions by William Smith.

NARRATIVES OF THE FRENCH & INDIAN WAR: 2 *by David Holden, Samuel Jenks, Lemuel Lyon, Mary Cochrane Rogers & Henry T. Blake*—Contains The Diary of Sergeant David Holden, Captain Samuel Jenks' Journal, The Journal of Lemuel Lyon, Journal of a French Officer at the Siege of Quebec, A Battle Fought on Snowshoes & The Battle of Lake George.

NARRATIVES OF THE FRENCH & INDIAN WAR *by Brown, Eastburn, Hawks & Putnam*—Ranger Brown's Narrative, The Adventures of Robert Eastburn, The Journal of Rufus Putnam—Provincial Infantry & Orderly Book and Journal of Major John Hawks on the Ticonderoga-Crown Point Campaign.

THE 7TH (QUEEN'S OWN) HUSSARS: Volume 1—1688-1792 *by C. R. B. Barrett*—As Dragoons During the Flanders Campaign, War of the Austrian Succession and the Seven Years War.

INDIA'S FREE LANCES *by H. G. Keene*—European Mercenary Commanders in Hindustan 1770-1820.

THE BENGAL EUROPEAN REGIMENT *by P. R. Innes*—An Elite Regiment of the Honourable East India Company 1756-1858.

MUSKET & TOMAHAWK *by Francis Parkman*—A Military History of the French & Indian War, 1753-1760.

THE BLACK WATCH AT TICONDEROGA *by Frederick B. Richards*—Campaigns in the French & Indian War.

QUEEN'S RANGERS *by Frederick B. Richards*—John Simcoe and his Rangers During the Revolutionary War for America.

AVAILABLE ONLINE AT **www.leonaur.com**
AND FROM ALL GOOD BOOK STORES

07/09

ALSO FROM LEONAUR

AVAILABLE IN SOFTCOVER OR HARDCOVER WITH DUST JACKET

JOURNALS OF ROBERT ROGERS OF THE RANGERS *by Robert Rogers*—The exploits of Rogers & the Rangers in his own words during 1755-1761 in the French & Indian War.

GALLOPING GUNS *by James Young*—The Experiences of an Officer of the Bengal Horse Artillery During the Second Maratha War 1804-1805.

GORDON *by Demetrius Charles Boulger*—The Career of Gordon of Khartoum.

THE BATTLE OF NEW ORLEANS *by Zachary F. Smith*—The final major engagement of the War of 1812.

THE TWO WARS OF MRS DUBERLY *by Frances Isabella Duberly*—An Intrepid Victorian Lady's Experience of the Crimea and Indian Mutiny.

WITH THE GUARDS' BRIGADE DURING THE BOER WAR *by Edward P. Lowry*—On Campaign from Bloemfontein to Koomati Poort and Back.

THE REBELLIOUS DUCHESS *by Paul F. S. Dermoncourt*—The Adventures of the Duchess of Berri and Her Attempt to Overthrow French Monarchy.

MEN OF THE MUTINY *by John Tulloch Nash & Henry Metcalfe*—Two Accounts of the Great Indian Mutiny of 1857: Fighting with the Bengal Yeomanry Cavalry & Private Metcalfe at Lucknow.

CAMPAIGN IN THE CRIMEA *by George Shuldham Peard*—The Recollections of an Officer of the 20th Regiment of Foot.

WITHIN SEBASTOPOL *by K. Hodasevich*—A Narrative of the Campaign in the Crimea, and of the Events of the Siege.

WITH THE CAVALRY TO AFGHANISTAN *by William Taylor*—The Experiences of a Trooper of H. M. 4th Light Dragoons During the First Afghan War.

THE CAWNPORE MAN *by Mowbray Thompson*—A First Hand Account of the Siege and Massacre During the Indian Mutiny By One of Four Survivors.

BRIGADE COMMANDER: AFGHANISTAN *by Henry Brooke*—The Journal of the Commander of the 2nd Infantry Brigade, Kandahar Field Force During the Second Afghan War.

BANCROFT OF THE BENGAL HORSE ARTILLERY *by N. W. Bancroft*—An Account of the First Sikh War 1845-1846.

ALSO FROM LEONAUR

AVAILABLE IN SOFTCOVER OR HARDCOVER WITH DUST JACKET

AFGHANISTAN: THE BELEAGUERED BRIGADE *by G. R. Gleig*—An Account of Sale's Brigade During the First Afghan War.

IN THE RANKS OF THE C. I. V *by Erskine Childers*—With the City Imperial Volunteer Battery (Honourable Artillery Company) in the Second Boer War.

THE BENGAL NATIVE ARMY *by F. G. Cardew*—An Invaluable Reference Resource.

THE 7TH (QUEEN'S OWN) HUSSARS: Volume 4—1688-1914 *by C. R. B. Barrett*—Uniforms, Equipment, Weapons, Traditions, the Services of Notable Officers and Men & the Appendices to All Volumes—Volume 4: 1688-1914.

THE SWORD OF THE CROWN *by Eric W. Sheppard*—A History of the British Army to 1914.

THE 7TH (QUEEN'S OWN) HUSSARS: Volume 3—1818-1914 *by C. R. B. Barrett*—On Campaign During the Canadian Rebellion, the Indian Mutiny, the Sudan, Matabeleland, Mashonaland and the Boer War Volume 3: 1818-1914.

THE KHARTOUM CAMPAIGN *by Bennet Burleigh*—A Special Correspondent's View of the Reconquest of the Sudan by British and Egyptian Forces under Kitchener—1898.

EL PUCHERO *by Richard McSherry*—The Letters of a Surgeon of Volunteers During Scott's Campaign of the American-Mexican War 1847-1848.

RIFLEMAN SAHIB *by E. Maude*—The Recollections of an Officer of the Bombay Rifles During the Southern Mahratta Campaign, Second Sikh War, Persian Campaign and Indian Mutiny.

THE KING'S HUSSAR *by Edwin Mole*—The Recollections of a 14th (King's) Hussar During the Victorian Era.

JOHN COMPANY'S CAVALRYMAN *by William Johnson*—The Experiences of a British Soldier in the Crimea, the Persian Campaign and the Indian Mutiny.

COLENSO & DURNFORD'S ZULU WAR *by Frances E. Colenso & Edward Durnford*—The first and possibly the most important history of the Zulu War.

U. S. DRAGOON *by Samuel E. Chamberlain*—Experiences in the Mexican War 1846-48 and on the South Western Frontier.

ALSO FROM LEONAUR

AVAILABLE IN SOFTCOVER OR HARDCOVER WITH DUST JACKET

THE 2ND MAORI WAR: 1860-1861 *by Robert Carey*—The Second Maori War, or First Taranaki War, one more bloody instalment of the conflicts between European settlers and the indigenous Maori people.

A JOURNAL OF THE SECOND SIKH WAR *by Daniel A. Sandford*—The Experiences of an Ensign of the 2nd Bengal European Regiment During the Campaign in the Punjab, India, 1848-49.

THE LIGHT INFANTRY OFFICER *by John H. Cooke*—The Experiences of an Officer of the 43rd Light Infantry in America During the War of 1812.

BUSHVELDT CARBINEERS *by George Witton*—The War Against the Boers in South Africa and the 'Breaker' Morant Incident.

LAKE'S CAMPAIGNS IN INDIA *by Hugh Pearse*—The Second Anglo Maratha War, 1803-1807.

BRITAIN IN AFGHANISTAN 1: THE FIRST AFGHAN WAR 1839-42 *by Archibald Forbes*—From invasion to destruction-a British military disaster.

BRITAIN IN AFGHANISTAN 2: THE SECOND AFGHAN WAR 1878-80 *by Archibald Forbes*—This is the history of the Second Afghan War-another episode of British military history typified by savagery, massacre, siege and battles.

UP AMONG THE PANDIES *by Vivian Dering Majendie*—Experiences of a British Officer on Campaign During the Indian Mutiny, 1857-1858.

MUTINY: 1857 *by James Humphries*—Authentic Voices from the Indian Mutiny-First Hand Accounts of Battles, Sieges and Personal Hardships.

BLOW THE BUGLE, DRAW THE SWORD *by W. H. G. Kingston*—The Wars, Campaigns, Regiments and Soldiers of the British & Indian Armies During the Victorian Era, 1839-1898.

WAR BEYOND THE DRAGON PAGODA *by Major J. J. Snodgrass*—A Personal Narrative of the First Anglo-Burmese War 1824 - 1826.

THE HERO OF ALIWAL *by James Humphries*—The Campaigns of Sir Harry Smith in India, 1843-1846, During the Gwalior War & the First Sikh War.

ALL FOR A SHILLING A DAY *by Donald F. Featherstone*—The story of H.M. 16th, the Queen's Lancers During the first Sikh War 1845-1846.

ALSO FROM LEONAUR

AVAILABLE IN SOFTCOVER OR HARDCOVER WITH DUST JACKET

AT THEM WITH THE BAYONET *by Donald F. Featherstone*—The first Anglo-Sikh War 1845-1846.

STEPHEN CRANE'S BATTLES *by Stephen Crane*—Nine Decisive Battles Recounted by the Author of 'The Red Badge of Courage'.

THE GURKHA WAR *by H. T. Prinsep*—The Anglo-Nepalese Conflict in North East India 1814-1816.

FIRE & BLOOD *by G. R. Gleig*—The burning of Washington & the battle of New Orleans, 1814, through the eyes of a young British soldier.

SOUND ADVANCE! *by Joseph Anderson*—Experiences of an officer of HM 50th regiment in Australia, Burma & the Gwalior war.

THE CAMPAIGN OF THE INDUS *by Thomas Holdsworth*—Experiences of a British Officer of the 2nd (Queen's Royal) Regiment in the Campaign to Place Shah Shuja on the Throne of Afghanistan 1838 - 1840.

WITH THE MADRAS EUROPEAN REGIMENT IN BURMA *by John Butler*—The Experiences of an Officer of the Honourable East India Company's Army During the First Anglo-Burmese War 1824 - 1826.

IN ZULULAND WITH THE BRITISH ARMY *by Charles L. Norris-Newman*—The Anglo-Zulu war of 1879 through the first-hand experiences of a special correspondent.

BESIEGED IN LUCKNOW *by Martin Richard Gubbins*—The first Anglo-Sikh War 1845-1846.

A TIGER ON HORSEBACK *by L. March Phillips*—The Experiences of a Trooper & Officer of Rimington's Guides - The Tigers - during the Anglo-Boer war 1899 - 1902.

SEPOYS, SIEGE & STORM *by Charles John Griffiths*—The Experiences of a young officer of H.M.'s 61st Regiment at Ferozepore, Delhi ridge and at the fall of Delhi during the Indian mutiny 1857.

CAMPAIGNING IN ZULULAND *by W. E. Montague*—Experiences on campaign during the Zulu war of 1879 with the 94th Regiment.

THE STORY OF THE GUIDES *by G.J. Younghusband*—The Exploits of the Soldiers of the famous Indian Army Regiment from the northwest frontier 1847 - 1900.

ALSO FROM LEONAUR

AVAILABLE IN SOFTCOVER OR HARDCOVER WITH DUST JACKET

ZULU:1879 *by D.C.F. Moodie & the Leonaur Editors*—The Anglo-Zulu War of 1879 from contemporary sources: First Hand Accounts, Interviews, Dispatches, Official Documents & Newspaper Reports.

THE RED DRAGOON *by W.J. Adams*—With the 7th Dragoon Guards in the Cape of Good Hope against the Boers & the Kaffir tribes during the 'war of the axe' 1843-48'.

THE RECOLLECTIONS OF SKINNER OF SKINNER'S HORSE *by James Skinner*—James Skinner and his 'Yellow Boys' Irregular cavalry in the wars of India between the British, Mahratta, Rajput, Mogul, Sikh & Pindarree Forces.

A CAVALRY OFFICER DURING THE SEPOY REVOLT *by A. R. D. Mackenzie*—Experiences with the 3rd Bengal Light Cavalry, the Guides and Sikh Irregular Cavalry from the outbreak to Delhi and Lucknow.

A NORFOLK SOLDIER IN THE FIRST SIKH WAR *by J W Baldwin*—Experiences of a private of H.M. 9th Regiment of Foot in the battles for the Punjab, India 1845-6.

TOMMY ATKINS' WAR STORIES: 14 FIRST HAND ACCOUNTS—Fourteen first hand accounts from the ranks of the British Army during Queen Victoria's Empire.

THE WATERLOO LETTERS *by H. T. Siborne*—Accounts of the Battle by British Officers for its Foremost Historian.

NEY: GENERAL OF CAVALRY VOLUME 1—1769-1799 *by Antoine Bulos*—The Early Career of a Marshal of the First Empire.

NEY: MARSHAL OF FRANCE VOLUME 2—1799-1805 *by Antoine Bulos*—The Early Career of a Marshal of the First Empire.

AIDE-DE-CAMP TO NAPOLEON *by Philippe-Paul de Ségur*—For anyone interested in the Napoleonic Wars this book, written by one who was intimate with the strategies and machinations of the Emperor, will be essential reading.

TWILIGHT OF EMPIRE *by Sir Thomas Ussher & Sir George Cockburn*—Two accounts of Napoleon's Journeys in Exile to Elba and St. Helena: Narrative of Events by Sir Thomas Ussher & Napoleon's Last Voyage: Extract of a diary by Sir George Cockburn.

PRIVATE WHEELER *by William Wheeler*—The letters of a soldier of the 51st Light Infantry during the Peninsular War & at Waterloo.

LEONAUR

LEONAUR

ALSO FROM LEONAUR

AVAILABLE IN SOFTCOVER OR HARDCOVER WITH DUST JACKET

OMPTEDA OF THE KING'S GERMAN LEGION *by Christian von Ompteda*—A Hanoverian Officer on Campaign Against Napoleon.

LIEUTENANT SIMMONS OF THE 95TH (RIFLES) *by George Simmons*—Recollections of the Peninsula, South of France & Waterloo Campaigns of the Napoleonic Wars.

A HORSEMAN FOR THE EMPEROR *by Jean Baptiste Gazzola*—A Cavalryman of Napoleon's Army on Campaign Throughout the Napoleonic Wars.

SERGEANT LAWRENCE *by William Lawrence*—With the 40th Regt. of Foot in South America, the Peninsular War & at Waterloo.

CAMPAIGNS WITH THE FIELD TRAIN *by Richard D. Henegan*—Experiences of a British Officer During the Peninsula and Waterloo Campaigns of the Napoleonic Wars.

CAVALRY SURGEON *by S. D. Broughton*—On Campaign Against Napoleon in the Peninsula & South of France During the Napoleonic Wars 1812-1814.

MEN OF THE RIFLES *by Thomas Knight, Henry Curling & Jonathan Leach*—The Reminiscences ofThomas Knight of the 95th (Rifles) by Thomas Knight, Henry Curling's Anecdotes by Henry Curling & The Field Services of the Rifle Brigade from its Formation to Waterloo by Jonathan Leach.

THE ULM CAMPAIGN 1805 *by F. N. Maude*—Napoleon and the Defeat of the Austrian Army During the 'War of the Third Coalition'.

SOLDIERING WITH THE 'DIVISION' *by Thomas Garrety*—The Military Experiences of an Infantryman of the 43rd Regiment During the Napoleonic Wars.

SERGEANT MORRIS OF THE 73RD FOOT *by Thomas Morris*—The Experiences of a British Infantryman During the Napoleonic Wars-Including Campaigns in Germany and at Waterloo.

A VOICE FROM WATERLOO *by Edward Cotton*—The Personal Experiences of a British Cavalryman Who Became a Battlefield Guide and Authority on the Campaign of 1815.

NAPOLEON AND HIS MARSHALS *by J. T. Headley*—The Men of the First Empire.

ALSO FROM LEONAUR

AVAILABLE IN SOFTCOVER OR HARDCOVER WITH DUST JACKET

COLBORNE: A SINGULAR TALENT FOR WAR *by John Colborne*—The Napoleonic Wars Career of One of Wellington's Most Highly Valued Officers in Egypt, Holland, Italy, the Peninsula and at Waterloo.

NAPOLEON'S RUSSIAN CAMPAIGN *by Philippe Henri de Segur*—The Invasion, Battles and Retreat by an Aide-de-Camp on the Emperor's Staff.

WITH THE LIGHT DIVISION *by John H. Cooke*—The Experiences of an Officer of the 43rd Light Infantry in the Peninsula and South of France During the Napoleonic Wars.

WELLINGTON AND THE PYRENEES CAMPAIGN VOLUME I: FROM VITORIA TO THE BIDASSOA *by F. C. Beatson*—The final phase of the campaign in the Iberian Peninsula.

WELLINGTON AND THE INVASION OF FRANCE VOLUME II: THE BIDASSOA TO THE BATTLE OF THE NIVELLE *by F. C. Beatson*—The final phase of the campaign in the Iberian Peninsula.

WELLINGTON AND THE FALL OF FRANCE VOLUME III: THE GAVES AND THE BATTLE OF ORTHEZ *by F. C. Beatson*—The final phase of the campaign in the Iberian Peninsula.

NAPOLEON'S IMPERIAL GUARD: FROM MARENGO TO WATERLOO *by J. T. Headley*—The story of Napoleon's Imperial Guard and the men who commanded them.

BATTLES & SIEGES OF THE PENINSULAR WAR *by W. H. Fitchett*—Corunna, Busaco, Albuera, Ciudad Rodrigo, Badajos, Salamanca, San Sebastian & Others.

SERGEANT GUILLEMARD: THE MAN WHO SHOT NELSON? *by Robert Guillemard*—A Soldier of the Infantry of the French Army of Napoleon on Campaign Throughout Europe.

WITH THE GUARDS ACROSS THE PYRENEES *by Robert Batty*—The Experiences of a British Officer of Wellington's Army During the Battles for the Fall of Napoleonic France, 1813 .

A STAFF OFFICER IN THE PENINSULA *by E. W. Buckham*—An Officer of the British Staff Corps Cavalry During the Peninsula Campaign of the Napoleonic Wars.

THE LEIPZIG CAMPAIGN: 1813—NAPOLEON AND THE "BATTLE OF THE NATIONS" *by F. N. Maude*—Colonel Maude's analysis of Napoleon's campaign of 1813 around Leipzig.

ALSO FROM LEONAUR

AVAILABLE IN SOFTCOVER OR HARDCOVER WITH DUST JACKET

BUGEAUD: A PACK WITH A BATON *by Thomas Robert Bugeaud*—The Early Campaigns of a Soldier of Napoleon's Army Who Would Become a Marshal of France.

WATERLOO RECOLLECTIONS *by Frederick Llewellyn*—Rare First Hand Accounts, Letters, Reports and Retellings from the Campaign of 1815.

SERGEANT NICOL *by Daniel Nicol*—The Experiences of a Gordon Highlander During the Napoleonic Wars in Egypt, the Peninsula and France.

THE JENA CAMPAIGN: 1806 *by F. N. Maude*—The Twin Battles of Jena & Auerstadt Between Napoleon's French and the Prussian Army.

PRIVATE O'NEIL *by Charles O'Neil*—The recollections of an Irish Rogue of H. M. 28th Regt.—The Slashers—during the Peninsula & Waterloo campaigns of the Napoleonic war.

ROYAL HIGHLANDER *by James Anton*—A soldier of H.M 42nd (Royal) Highlanders during the Peninsular, South of France & Waterloo Campaigns of the Napoleonic Wars.

CAPTAIN BLAZE *by Elzéar Blaze*—Life in Napoleons Army.

LEJEUNE VOLUME 1 *by Louis-François Lejeune*—The Napoleonic Wars through the Experiences of an Officer on Berthier's Staff.

LEJEUNE VOLUME 2 *by Louis-François Lejeune*—The Napoleonic Wars through the Experiences of an Officer on Berthier's Staff.

CAPTAIN COIGNET *by Jean-Roch Coignet*—A Soldier of Napoleon's Imperial Guard from the Italian Campaign to Russia and Waterloo.

FUSILIER COOPER *by John S. Cooper*—Experiences in the 7th (Royal) Fusiliers During the Peninsular Campaign of the Napoleonic Wars and the American Campaign to New Orleans.

FIGHTING NAPOLEON'S EMPIRE *by Joseph Anderson*—The Campaigns of a British Infantryman in Italy, Egypt, the Peninsular & the West Indies During the Napoleonic Wars.

CHASSEUR BARRES *by Jean-Baptiste Barres*—The experiences of a French Infantryman of the Imperial Guard at Austerlitz, Jena, Eylau, Friedland, in the Peninsular, Lutzen, Bautzen, Zinnwald and Hanau during the Napoleonic Wars.

ALSO FROM LEONAUR

AVAILABLE IN SOFTCOVER OR HARDCOVER WITH DUST JACKET

CAPTAIN COIGNET *by Jean-Roch Coignet*—A Soldier of Napoleon's Imperial Guard from the Italian Campaign to Russia and Waterloo.

HUSSAR ROCCA *by Albert Jean Michel de Rocca*—A French cavalry officer's experiences of the Napoleonic Wars and his views on the Peninsular Campaigns against the Spanish, British And Guerilla Armies.

MARINES TO 95TH (RIFLES) *by Thomas Fernyhough*—The military experiences of Robert Fernyhough during the Napoleonic Wars.

LIGHT BOB *by Robert Blakeney*—The experiences of a young officer in H.M 28th & 36th regiments of the British Infantry during the Peninsular Campaign of the Napoleonic Wars 1804 - 1814.

WITH WELLINGTON'S LIGHT CAVALRY *by William Tomkinson*—The Experiences of an officer of the 16th Light Dragoons in the Peninsular and Waterloo campaigns of the Napoleonic Wars.

SERGEANT BOURGOGNE *by Adrien Bourgogne*—With Napoleon's Imperial Guard in the Russian Campaign and on the Retreat from Moscow 1812 - 13.

SURTEES OF THE 95TH (RIFLES) *by William Surtees*—A Soldier of the 95th (Rifles) in the Peninsular campaign of the Napoleonic Wars.

SWORDS OF HONOUR *by Henry Newbolt & Stanley L. Wood*—The Careers of Six Outstanding Officers from the Napoleonic Wars, the Wars for India and the American Civil War.

ENSIGN BELL IN THE PENINSULAR WAR *by George Bell*—The Experiences of a young British Soldier of the 34th Regiment 'The Cumberland Gentlemen' in the Napoleonic wars.

HUSSAR IN WINTER *by Alexander Gordon*—A British Cavalry Officer during the retreat to Corunna in the Peninsular campaign of the Napoleonic Wars.

THE COMPLEAT RIFLEMAN HARRIS *by Benjamin Harris as told to and transcribed by Captain Henry Curling, 52nd Regt. of Foot*—The adventures of a soldier of the 95th (Rifles) during the Peninsular Campaign of the Napoleonic Wars.

THE ADVENTURES OF A LIGHT DRAGOON *by George Farmer & G.R. Gleig*—A cavalryman during the Peninsular & Waterloo Campaigns, in captivity & at the siege of Bhurtpore, India.

AVAILABLE ONLINE AT **www.leonaur.com**
AND FROM ALL GOOD BOOK STORES

07/09

ALSO FROM LEONAUR

AVAILABLE IN SOFTCOVER OR HARDCOVER WITH DUST JACKET

THE LIFE OF THE REAL BRIGADIER GERARD VOLUME 1—THE YOUNG HUSSAR 1782-1807 *by Jean-Baptiste De Marbot*—A French Cavalryman Of the Napoleonic Wars at Marengo, Austerlitz, Jena, Eylau & Friedland.

THE LIFE OF THE REAL BRIGADIER GERARD VOLUME 2—IMPERIAL AIDE-DE-CAMP 1807-1811 *by Jean-Baptiste De Marbot*—A French Cavalryman of the Napoleonic Wars at Saragossa, Landshut, Eckmuhl, Ratisbon, Aspern-Essling, Wagram, Busaco & Torres Vedras.

THE LIFE OF THE REAL BRIGADIER GERARD VOLUME 3—COLONEL OF CHASSEURS 1811-1815 *by Jean-Baptiste De Marbot*—A French Cavalryman in the retreat from Moscow, Lutzen, Bautzen, Katzbach, Leipzig, Hanau & Waterloo.

THE INDIAN WAR OF 1864 *by Eugene Ware*—The Experiences of a Young Officer of the 7th Iowa Cavalry on the Western Frontier During the Civil War.

THE MARCH OF DESTINY *by Charles E. Young & V. Devinny*—Dangers of the Trail in 1865 by Charles E. Young & The Story of a Pioneer by V. Devinny, two Accounts of Early Emigrants to Colorado.

CROSSING THE PLAINS *by William Audley Maxwell*—A First Hand Narrative of the Early Pioneer Trail to California in 1857.

CHIEF OF SCOUTS *by William F. Drannan*—A Pilot to Emigrant and Government Trains, Across the Plains of the Western Frontier.

THIRTY-ONE YEARS ON THE PLAINS AND IN THE MOUNTAINS *by William F. Drannan*—William Drannan was born to be a pioneer, hunter, trapper and wagon train guide during the momentous days of the Great American West.

THE INDIAN WARS VOLUNTEER *by William Thompson*—Recollections of the Conflict Against the Snakes, Shoshone, Bannocks, Modocs and Other Native Tribes of the American North West.

THE 4TH TENNESSEE CAVALRY *by George B. Guild*—The Services of Smith's Regiment of Confederate Cavalry by One of its Officers.

COLONEL WORTHINGTON'S SHILOH *by T. Worthington*—The Tennessee Campaign, 1862, by an Officer of the Ohio Volunteers.

FOUR YEARS IN THE SADDLE *by W. L. Curry*—The History of the First Regiment Ohio Volunteer Cavalry in the American Civil War.

ALSO FROM LEONAUR

AVAILABLE IN SOFTCOVER OR HARDCOVER WITH DUST JACKET

IRON TIMES WITH THE GUARDS *by An O. E. (G. P. A. Fildes)*—The Experiences of an Officer of the Coldstream Guards on the Western Front During the First World War.

THE GREAT WAR IN THE MIDDLE EAST: 1 *by W. T. Massey*—The Desert Campaigns & How Jerusalem Was Won---two classic accounts in one volume.

THE GREAT WAR IN THE MIDDLE EAST: 2 *by W. T. Massey*—Allenby's Final Triumph.

SMITH-DORRIEN *by Horace Smith-Dorrien*—Isandlwhana to the Great War.

1914 *by Sir John French*—The Early Campaigns of the Great War by the British Commander.

GRENADIER *by E. R. M. Fryer*—The Recollections of an Officer of the Grenadier Guards throughout the Great War on the Western Front.

BATTLE, CAPTURE & ESCAPE *by George Pearson*—The Experiences of a Canadian Light Infantryman During the Great War.

DIGGERS AT WAR *by R. Hugh Knyvett & G. P. Cuttriss*—"Over There" With the Australians by R. Hugh Knyvett and Over the Top With the Third Australian Division by G. P. Cuttriss. Accounts of Australians During the Great War in the Middle East, at Gallipoli and on the Western Front.

HEAVY FIGHTING BEFORE US *by George Brenton Laurie*—The Letters of an Officer of the Royal Irish Rifles on the Western Front During the Great War.

THE CAMELIERS *by Oliver Hogue*—A Classic Account of the Australians of the Imperial Camel Corps During the First World War in the Middle East.

RED DUST *by Donald Black*—A Classic Account of Australian Light Horsemen in Palestine During the First World War.

THE LEAN, BROWN MEN *by Angus Buchanan*—Experiences in East Africa During the Great War with the 25th Royal Fusiliers—the Legion of Frontiersmen.

THE NIGERIAN REGIMENT IN EAST AFRICA *by W. D. Downes*—On Campaign During the Great War 1916-1918.

THE 'DIE-HARDS' IN SIBERIA *by John Ward*—With the Middlesex Regiment Against the Bolsheviks 1918-19.

AVAILABLE ONLINE AT **www.leonaur.com**
AND FROM ALL GOOD BOOK STORES

07/09

www.ingramcontent.com/pod-product-compliance
Lightning Source LLC
LaVergne TN
LVHW050911080826
845145LV00001B/50

* 9 7 8 0 8 5 7 0 6 2 9 1 8 *